LITURGIES OF THE WESTERN CHURCH

LITURGIES OF THE WESTERN CHURCH

BARD THOMPSON

A FONTANA BOOK

COLLINS WORLD

Cleveland and New York

BARD THOMPSON

Bard Thompson was born on June 18, 1925, in Waynesboro,
Pennsylvania. He has degrees from Haverford College, Union
Theological Seminary, and Columbia University, where he
took his Ph.D. in 1953. Mr. Thompson has taught church
history at Emory University, at Vanderbilt University, Lancaster Theological Seminary, and Drew University.

Published by The William Collins + World Publishing Company, Inc.
First printing February 1962
Seventh Printing 1975
Copyright © 1961 by The World Publishing Company.
Library of Congress Catalog Card Number: 61-15750
Typography and design by Elaine Lustig.
Printed in the United States of America.

ISBN #0-529-02077-7

To
Charles Herbert Thompson
Frances Beard Thompson

CONTENTS

CONTENTS

INTRODUCTION

We live in an era of liturgical revival.

In the past fifty years, Catholic scholars have devoted prodigious research to the sources and history of the Roman rite. In the first quarter of the century, the Benedictines contributed the monumental *Dictionnaire d'archéologie chrétienne et de Liturgie* (1903 *seq.*). From the start of that project to the present time, the lively output of books has continued steadily, and with it our debt to such scholars as Cabrol, Duchesne, Baumstark, and Jungmann. Their work, augmented by that of countless others, has already brought certain changes in Catholic practice and has penetrated to parish life itself.

The liturgical renaissance in Protestantism (and especially in America) has not enjoyed such an orderly course, for it has been stimulated by a variety of forces. Certainly the scholars have had their share in it. Maxwell has aroused considerable interest in the origins of the Reformed rite, while Davies offered virtually the first insight into the worship of the English Puritans. Lutherans, here and abroad, have devoted themselves to Luther's liturgical ideas and to the relationship between theology and worship. Brilioth and Dix have contributed books of the highest order concerning the history of the Eucharist. But perhaps the scholars were not the main contributors. In the American churches there began an amorphous revival of "liturgy," which left almost no group untouched, not even the Dunkers. In part it may have been inspired by aesthetic considerations, in part by reaction to stale theology or to the prevailing intellectualism of some American traditions—the bases of it are hard to decipher. With it came both sound practices and bric-a-brac; and its signs are to be seen in the "divided chancel" and reinstatement of the altar, in acceptance of the Church Year, in vestments and choir robes, in new books of worship and hymnals unloaded of Gospel songs. At the same time, the question of worship became a significant topic of conversation in the ecumenical movement, provoking widespread interest in the liturgy and in intercommunion. In America, where denominational unions have proceeded apace, the churches have often had to face the ecumenical issues in the immediacy of preparing new liturgical books. Revisions have been made, or are soon to be made, in at least five of the major denominations.

Considering the wealth of books on worship, one may be undecided whether to herald this extra volume or not. This much may be said for it, that it gathers up the liturgies themselves and tries to make them plain to a fairly broad segment of readers. The more we learn about liturgies, the less likely we will be to stumble into the pitfalls of the liturgical renaissance, notably, the idolatry of liturgical antiques and the importation of usages that are irrelevant, if not utterly contradictory, to doctrine and to the contemporary scene.

This book makes available in a single volume the principal liturgies of Western Christianity, some of which are not readily accessible. Each text is supplied with an introduction that is meant to elucidate both the liturgy and the tradition in which it stands. Bibliographies are appended to each chapter. Thus, I hope that the introductions will point first to the liturgies and then away from the volume entirely to additional reading.

Some limitations have been necessary to fashion a book of this sort. Of necessity it pertains only to the Western church; and its scope is further circumscribed by the liturgies of the Word and the Lord's Supper. The American services will have to await another volume.

The reader will have no great difficulty in finding those chapters about which I know a little bit and those about which I know even less. Care has been taken, at least, to produce accurate texts, some of which are fresh translations, while others have been drawn from the best available translations or from microfilm copies of the originals.

The following publishers deserve my thanks for permission to make copyright citations:

The Society for Promoting Christian Knowledge, for the selections from *The Apostolic Tradition of St. Hippolytus,* copyright 1937;

The Newman Press, for the Ordinary of Low Mass from *The Missal in Latin and English,* copyright 1959;

Sheed & Ward, Inc., for the scripture translations in the Mass: from the *Old Testament in English,* Vol. II, in the translation of Monsignor Ronald A. Knox, copyright 1950; and from the *New Testament in English,* in the translation of Monsignor Ronald A. Knox, copyright 1944;

Muhlenberg Press, for *Formula Missae* and *Deutsche Messe* from *Works of Martin Luther,* Vol. VI, copyright 1932.

I express my appreciation to Frank Grisham, the good and generous librarian of Vanderbilt Divinity School; to Bertha, my wife, who labored long at proofreading; to Professors Paul S. Sanders and Kendrick Grobel, esteemed colleagues at Vanderbilt; to Professor Cyril C. Richardson of Union Seminary who taught me whatever it is that I know about the liturgy; to Milos Strupl and Margaret Koehnke, who repaired my translations; and to John Batsel, Freeman Sleeper, Jean McMahon, and Virginia Mills, who served the cause by mind and typewriter. I am particularly grateful to Professors Robert Duke and George Bricker of the Lancaster Theological Seminary, who read and criticized the manuscript.

SELECTED BOOKS ON WORSHIP

This is a general bibliography, complementary to the specific list of books at the end of each introduction.

1. THE LITURGICAL REVIVAL

J.-D. Benoit, *Liturgical Renewal; Studies in Catholic and Protestant Developments on the Continent.* London, 1958.

E. B. Koenker, *The Liturgical Renaissance in the Roman Catholic Church.* Chicago, 1954.

Massey H. Shepherd (ed.), *The Liturgical Renewal of the Church.* New York, 1960.

Massey H. Shepherd, *The Reform of Liturgical Worship.* New York, 1961.

2. THE HISTORY OF CHRISTIAN WORSHIP

Yngve Brilioth, *Eucharistic Faith & Practice.* London, 1956.

W. K. Lowther Clarke and Charles Harris (eds.), *Liturgy and Worship.* London, 1947.

Horton Davies, *Christian Worship; Its History and Meaning.* New York, 1957.

Gregory Dix, *The Shape of the Liturgy.* Westminster, 1944.

A. A. McArthur, *The Evolution of the Christian Year.* London, 1953.

W. D. Maxwell, *An Outline of Christian Worship.* London, 1945.

Nathaniel Micklem (ed.), *Christian Worship; Studies in Its*

History and Meaning by Members of Mansfield College.
London, 1936.
Darwell Stone, *A History of the Doctrine of the Holy Eucharist.* 2 vols. London, 1909.

3. THE NATURE OF CHRISTIAN WORSHIP

Raymond Abba, *Principles of Christian Worship.* New York, 1957.
S. F. Brenner, *The Way of Worship.* New York, 1944.
Henry S. Coffin, *The Public Worship of God.* Philadelphia, 1946.
A. G. Hebert, *Liturgy and Society.* London, 1935.
Friedrich Heiler, *The Spirit of Worship.* London, 1926.
D. H. Hislop, *Our Heritage in Public Worship.* Edinburgh, 1935.
W. Nicholls, *Jacob's Ladder; the Meaning of Worship. Ecumenical Studies in Worship,* No. 4. London, 1958.
J. E. Rattenbury, *Vital Elements of Public Worship.* London, 1936.
Clarence Seidenspinner, *Form and Freedom in Worship.* Chicago, 1941.
Evelyn Underhill, *Worship.* New York, 1937.
Ways of Worship; the report of a theological commission of Faith and Order, edited by Pehr Edwall, Eric Hayman, and W. D. Maxwell. New York, 1951.
Robert Will, *Le Culte; étude d'histoire et de philosophie religieuses.* 3 vols. Paris, 1925-35.

I
THE FIRST APOLOGY
OF JUSTIN MARTYR

Ca. 155

JUSTIN MARTYR

Born in Samaria at the opening of the second century, Justin lived for a time at Ephesus, and presently went to Rome, where he offered instruction in Christianity until his martyrdom, about A.D. 165. In his *Dialogue with Trypho* he spoke the part of an earnest seeker who had searched the philosophical schools one by one, without satisfaction, and had at last found truth at the hands of Christian teachers. And when he beheld the heroism of the faithful under bitter persecution, he was incited to become one of them. On his advent to Christianity, he did not throw off the philosopher's mantle, but elected to be a lay professor of the *divine* philosophy. As such we see him in Rome.

Justin was one of the foremost Apologists of the Ante-Nicene church. His writings were designed to communicate the Gospel to outsiders in such fashion as to evoke their understanding and to dispel their prejudice. In the *I Apology*, which he composed at Rome around 155, he ventured to reveal the faith and practice of the church for the inspection of inquirers, devoting the last seven chapters (61-7) to a description of Christian worship. He had no intention of leading his readers through the labyrinth of liturgics but took patience to explain that "we call this food the Eucharist" and to define the bishop as "the president of the brethren." His purpose was rather to disclose the general nature of the divine service and to offset persistent rumors that the Christian

3

cultus was a dark assembly of seditious and fanatical men who engaged in orgies and cannibalistic feasts. He described the Eucharist twice.• In the first instance (Ch. 65) it was preceded by the sacrament of Baptism; in the second (Ch. 67), by the liturgy of the Word. These two accounts, supplemented by incidental references in the *Dialogue*, provide a useful summary of worship at Rome in the middle of the second century.

On the Lord's day, Christians of town and countryside gathered "in one place"—which was almost certainly a spacious house belonging to one of the wealthier members of the church. Yet the sense of the expression, "in one place," was not comprehended by the four walls of a Roman dwelling, any more than the word, "church" (*ecclesia*) referred to a building. In both cases the intended meaning was the corporate assembly of Christians for divine worship, distinguished from all other meetings by the official presence of the bishop and the deacons.•• We should note in passing that the church at Rome employed the *Greek* language, Latin being "the vernacular" of Justin's day.

The liturgy of the Word had already claimed its place before the Eucharist in the regular Sunday service (although Justin's description made it clear that the two were not yet inseparable). "The ministry of the Word," which came to be known as "the Mass of the Catechumens," passed into Christian use from the Jewish synagogue, where it consisted of lessons from the Law and the prophets, a sermon, and prayers; but whether the prayers were first or last is uncertain. In the experience of Justin, Sunday worship commenced as the "lector" read indefinitely from "the memoirs of the apostles or the writings of the prophets." Whether this extended reading was relieved by the singing of psalms, we are not told; but in the synagogue psalms were likely sung before and after the lessons. As the teacher of the faith in apostolic succession, the bishop proceeded to deliver his "discourse," namely, the sermon, in which he impressed the meaning of the lessons upon the hearts of the people. No doubt he sat in the *kathedra*, the teacher's chair, which was the pose of the preacher in both synagogue and church. When the bishop finished the sermon,

---

• The name the early church applied to the sacrament of Holy Communion.
•• On this point, cf. Ignatius of Antioch, *Trallians* 3; *Smyrnaeans* 8; *Magnesians* 7.

4

all arose for the common prayers. There was, as yet, no sign that the unbaptized were turned out of the assembly after the sermon, in preparation for the church-prayer, which was the prerogative of those alone who belonged to the Body of Christ; but Justin intimated something of the same in Chapter 65, when he observed that the neophyte, having been baptized, was taken directly into "the assembly of those who are called brethren" to exercise his Christian ministry by joining the faithful in making Intercessions.

The Eucharist commenced with the Kiss of Peace, which meant, quite simply, that the men of the church kissed one another in Christian love, and the women did likewise. While Justin may have been the first writer to fix its position in the liturgy, the Kiss of Peace was an ancient symbol, residing in the experience of both Jews and early Christians, for whom it sealed peace and reconciliation among men—the *wholeness* of human relationships. In the liturgy it stood at the threshold of the Eucharist, protecting and exalting one of the central meanings of the sacrament, namely, the love and unity among those who are members of the Body of Christ.

Then, said Justin, "bread and a cup of water mingled with wine are presented to the president of the brethren." By that, he referred to the Offertory, which was, on the practical level, merely a way of getting the elements to the table for the Eucharist. But utility may not have been the only purpose of this ceremony. The bread and wine were brought to the assembly by the people, to be given over to the bishop at this time, perhaps by the hands of the deacons. In giving these things, the people gave *of themselves* to God: even as God, *by the same signs*, would presently give of Himself to them in holy communion. Hence, this corporate "offering" anticipated the Consecration and Communion and was the commencement of the whole Eucharistic action. While such an idea may not have been within the purview of Justin—Dix believes it was, but Jungmann doubts it—the Offertory certainly attained this meaning by the end of the second century.

Then the president offered the Eucharistic prayer "according to his ability"—which could only mean that he prayed in extempore fashion. Nevertheless, Justin was sufficiently accustomed to the normal content of this prayer that he could comment upon it. In the *I Apology* (65) he wrote:

> He [the bishop] sends up praise and glory to the Father
> of all, through the name of the Son and Holy Spirit, and
> offers thanksgiving at some length that we have been
> deemed worthy to receive these things at His hand.

And in the *Dialogue* (41), he observed further:

> We give thanks to God for having created the world, with
> all things therein, for the sake of man; and for delivering
> us from the evil in which we live; and for utterly over-
> throwing the principalities and powers, through Him who
> suffered according to His will.

From these accounts we judge that the prayer commenced
with praise and thanks for our creation, preservation, and
redemption. In view of Justin's comment in Chapter 66, we
may also assume that it included the recital of Christ's Institution of the Eucharist according to "the Gospels":

> that Jesus took bread, and having given thanks, He said,
> Do this for my *anamnesis,* this is my body; and likewise
> taking the cup and giving thanks, He said, This is my
> blood.

By this means the commands and promises of the Lord were
published, according to which the church fulfilled His
ordinance. Finally, Justin stated that the bread and wine
were consecrated δι' εὐχῆς λόγου τοῦ παρ' αὐτοῦ. Some scholars
have understood this to mean, "by the prayer of the Word
[Logos] which comes from him [=God]," in which case the
elements were hallowed by the operative power of the Logos.
But other scholars have taken it to say, "by the word
[formula] of prayer which comes from Him [=Jesus]," in
which case the elements were blessed after the example of
the Lord, who took bread, *gave thanks,* and said, Do this for
my *anamnesis.* . . . It seems most likely that Justin intended the latter, for he conceived the Eucharistic prayer
to be essentially "thanksgiving," and he referred to the consecrated elements as having been "eucharistized"—"thanked
upon." Indeed, Gavin suggests that for this technical circumstance, chiefly, the sacrament itself came to be called "the
Eucharist."

At the close of the prayer, the congregation added its assent, saying, "Amen." Hence, the thanksgiving, which had
been made by the president of the brethren, came from the

heart of the whole assembly, and was so confirmed by the people's Amen. Thereupon the deacons administered the "eucharistized" bread and cup to each one, and carried them to those who were absent.

How did Justin conceive of this sacrament? (1) It was an *anamnesis*, a re-calling of Christ's passion, indeed of the whole Incarnation; the bread and wine were eaten in remembrance that Christ, "being incarnate by God's Word, took flesh and blood for our salvation" and suffered on our behalf (*Dialogue*, 70; *1 Apology*, 66). (2) It was a "sacrifice" unto God, fulfilling Malachi's prophecy of the pure offering of the Gentiles (*Dialogue*, 41)—a theme that nevertheless remained tentative in Justin. (3) It was a Communion-fellowship that united all of the baptized, even those who were absent, through the common participation in the "flesh and blood of that incarnate Jesus." (4) It was a "thanksgiving" for creation and providence, and most especially for the Incarnation and Passion of Jesus Christ.

FOR FURTHER READING

Yngve Brilioth, *Eucharistic Faith & Practice*. London, 1956.

F. Cabrol (ed.), *Dictionnaire d'archéologie chrétienne et de Liturgie*. 12 vols. Paris, 1907 *seq.*

Gregory Dix, *The Shape of the Liturgy*. Westminster, 1947.

L. Duchesne, *Christian Worship: Its Origin and Evolution*. London, 1949.

F. Gavin, *The Jewish Antecedents of the Christian Sacraments*. London, 1933.

Joseph A. Jungmann, *The Mass of the Roman Rite*. Vol. I. New York, 1951.

H. Lietzmann, *Messe und Herrenmahl*. Bonn, 1926.

W. O. E. Oesterley, *The Jewish Background of the Christian Liturgy*. Oxford, 1925.

J. H. Srawley, *The Early History of the Liturgy*. Cambridge, 1947.

THE FIRST APOLOGY
OF JUSTIN MARTYR [1]

65. Having thus baptized the one who has been convinced and has given his assent, we escort him into the assembly of those who are called brethren. Then they earnestly offer common prayers for themselves, for the one who has been enlightened, and for all men everywhere: that having learned the truth, we may be deemed worthy, according to our works, to be esteemed good citizens and keepers of the commandments, so that we may be saved with an everlasting salvation. Our prayers being ended, we greet one another with a kiss. Then bread and a cup of water mingled with wine are presented to the president of the brethen.[2] Taking them, he sends up praise and glory to the Father of all, through the name of the Son and Holy Spirit, and offers thanksgiving at some length that we have been deemed worthy to receive these things at His hand. When he has finished the prayers and the thanksgiving, all the people present shout their assent, saying, "Amen." ("Amen" in the Hebrew tongue means "so be it.") When the president has given thanks, and all the people have assented, those whom we call deacons give to each one present a portion of the "eucharistized"[3] bread and wine-with-water; and they carry it also to those who are absent.

66. We call this food the Eucharist, of which no one is allowed to partake except he is convinced of the truth of our teaching and has received the washing for the forgiveness of his sins and for his regeneration, and so lives as Christ has taught us. For we do not receive these things as common bread or common drink; but as Jesus Christ our Saviour, being incarnate by the Word of God, took flesh and blood for our salvation, so also have we been taught that the food, "eucharistized" by the formula of prayer which comes from Him,[4] and from which our flesh and blood are nourished by transformation,[5] is the flesh and blood of that incarnate Jesus. The apostles in the memoirs composed by them (which are called "Gospels") have handed down what was commanded of them: that Jesus took bread, and having given thanks, He said, Do this for my *anamnesis*, this is my body; and likewise taking the cup and giving thanks, He said, This is my blood; and to them alone did He give it. The

8

evil demons, in imitation of this, ordered the same thing to
be done in the mysteries of Mithra; for as you know or may
learn, bread and a cup of water are brought out with certain
incantations in their secret rites of initiation.

67. Thereafter we continually remind one another of these
things. The rich among us come to the aid of the poor, and
we always stay together. Over all that we receive, we make
a blessing to the Creator of all things, through his Son Jesus
Christ and through the Holy Spirit. On the day which is
called Sunday, all who live in the cities or in the countryside
gather together in one place.[6] And the memoirs of the apostles or the writings of the prophets are read as long as there
is time. Then, when the reader[7] has finished, the president,[8]
in a discourse, admonishes and invites the people to practice
these examples of virtue. Then we all stand up together and
offer prayers. And, as we mentioned before, when we have
finished the prayer, bread is presented, and wine with water;
the president likewise offers up prayers and thanksgivings
according to his ability,[9] and the people assent by saying,
Amen. The elements which have been "eucharistized" are
distributed and received by each one; and they are sent to
the absent by the deacons. Those who are prosperous, if they
wish, contribute what each one deems appropriate; and the
collection is deposited with the president; and he takes care
of the orphans and widows, and those who are needy because
of sickness or other cause, and the captives, and the strangers
who sojourn amongst us—in brief, he is the curate of all who
are in need. Sunday, indeed, is the day on which we all hold
our common assembly, inasmuch as it is the first day on
which God, transforming the darkness and matter, created the
universe; and on the same day our Saviour Jesus Christ rose
from the dead. For they crucified Him on the day before
Saturday;[10] and on the day after, which is Sunday, He appeared to His apostles and disciples, and taught them these
things which we have transmitted to you also for your earnest
consideration.

NOTES

1. This translation is based on the critical text of P. Maran, re-
printed in Migne, *Patrologiae Graeca,* VI (Paris, 1857), 427-
32.

2. τῷ προεστῶτι τῶν ἀδελφῶν which could be translated, "to the one presiding over the brethren."
3. εὐχαριστηθέντος ἄρτου that is, bread over which thanks has been offered.
4. δι᾽ εὐχῆς λόγου τοῦ παρ᾽ αὐτοῦ. On this point, see the introduction, and J. H. Srawley, *The Early History of the Liturgy* (Cambridge, 1947), p. 32.
5. μεταβολήν.
6. αὐτό. This expression refers not merely to the appointed place of the meeting; it has almost the technical sense of "common assembly." Cf. Gregory Dix, *The Shape of the Liturgy* (Westminster, 1947), pp. 19-27.
7. ὁ ἀναγινώσκων. On the "reader," cf. A. J. Maclean, *The Ancient Church Orders* (Cambridge, 1910), pp. 85f.
8. προεστώς.
9. ὅση δύναμις αὐτῷ that is, in extempore fashion.
10. By this device Justin skillfully dissociates Christian worship from the Jewish Sabbath (carefully unnamed) and from the pagan Friday (day of Aphrodite), Saturday (day of Saturn), and Sunday (day of the sun).

II
THE APOSTOLIC TRADITION
OF HIPPOLYTUS

Rome: Ca. 200

HIPPOLYTUS

Of angular personality and conservative temper, Hippolytus came to prominence as a theologian at Rome during the pontificate of Bishop Victor (189-97), by whom he was ordained to the presbyterate. His teaching was related to the Greek manner of thought, reflecting the Logos Christology that Justin Martyr had published at Rome some fifty years before; but he professed a special indebtedness to Irenaeus, who had sojourned in the Eternal City on one known occasion, and perhaps on others.

The death of Victor was attended by the accession of Bishop Zephyrinus (197-217), whom Hippolytus assailed as "an ignorant and illiterate individual, unskilled in ecclesiastical definitions." Of all his errors, none was so grievous as the elevation of one Callistus to be his archdeacon and confidant. Rivalry and hatred supplied gall to Hippolytus' pen when he described Callistus—"a man cunning in wickedness and subtle where deceit is concerned, impelled by ruthless ambition to mount the episcopal throne."

Throughout the tenure of Zephyrinus, the church at Rome was wracked by doctrinal controversy. Montanism was first to occasion trouble. Having arisen out of Phrygia upon the utterances of Montanus, who purported to be the mouthpiece of the Paraclete foretold in John, this prophetic enthusiasm swept westward, flouting the apostolic tradition and threatening the order and unity of the church. It arrived in

• *Refutation of All Heresies,* IX. 2; IX. 6.

Rome during the pontificate of Bishop Eleutherus (175-89), who was promptly warned of its peril by Irenaeus, an ambassador sent down from the church in Gaul. We hear no more of it until the accession of Zephyrinus. Then Praxeas appeared at Rome—the first to propagate Monarchianism (Sabellianism) in the West. Discovering that "the bishop of Rome had acknowledged the prophetic gifts of Montanus," Praxeas swiftly brought Zephyrinus to renounce that error by citing "the authority of the bishop's predecessors in the See"; and in the same instant, he prevailed upon Zephyrinus to allow Monarchianism to be taught at Rome. Tertullian, who wrote these things after he himself had become enamored of the Montanist charisms, complained that Praxeas thus "did a two-fold service for the devil in Rome: he drove out prophecy and brought in heresy; he put to flight the Paraclete and crucified the Father." •

Monarchianism was a well-intended heresy. Reacting to polytheistic tendencies of every sort—including the Montanist tendency to separate and exalt the Paraclete—its proponents insisted upon the uniqueness, oneness, and perfection of the divine nature—hence, upon the *monarchia* of God. But this led them to efface the distinctions of persons in the Godhead. It was the one undifferentiated God who created as "Father," redeemed as "Son," and abided in the church as "Spirit"— these names being merely the *modes* of God's manifestations as they *seem to men,* rather than real relationships within the Godhead. Thus, Noetus of Smyrna, father of Monarchianism, is reported to have said: "Christ is the Father himself, and it was the Father himself who was born, suffered, and died."

Hippolytus, who was unaware of the activities of Praxeas, blamed Cleomenes for establishing this "heresy" at Rome, and assailed Zephyrinus and Callistus for giving him leave to open a school. The school flourished and produced a stout protagonist in Sabellius of Libya, by whose prominence the whole movement came to be called Sabellianism. Presently the battle was joined between the Sabellians and the defenders of the Logos Christology, of whom Hippolytus was the chief. When the bishop and his archdeacon sought to embrace both parties to the quarrel—a latitude that was typical of

• *Against Praxeas,* i. The evidence is difficult to decipher. This interpretation follows that of P. de Labiolle, *La crise montaniste* (Paris, 1913). In his *Dogmengeschichte,* I, 742, Harnack assigns these events to the episcopate of Eleutherus.

the Roman See when it faced speculative disputes—Hippolytus accused them of conniving with both sides by giving out contradictory statements. Seeing that Hippolytus remained obstinate, Callistus proceeded to expose the fatal weakness of the Logos Christology, namely, its tendency toward subordinationism. "Ye," said Callistus, "are worshipers of two gods."

Smarting under this charge, Hippolytus yet remained within the community. But at the elevation of Callistus to the episcopal throne (217), his patience gave out; he established himself as the legitimate bishop, obtaining consecration in some irregular manner, and proceeded to damn the sect of "Callistines." Not even the excommunication of Sabellius allayed his suspicions of Callistus, whose further efforts at a theology of compromise he judged to be "some sort of heresy." And when his rival issued the notable decrees on Penance and Marriage, he blustered that Callistus "inculcated adultery and murder at the same time." • Aside from the indeterminate number who adhered to Hippolytus, the Catholic world rejected his claims; but he persisted in schism through the succeeding pontificates of Urban and Pontian. In the persecution of Maximin in 235, both Pontian and Hippolytus were deported to Sardinia, where together they suffered and died. Hippolytus may have been reconciled before the end; but at least his martyrdom was received in Rome as the expiation for his schism, and he was duly honored as presbyter and martyr.

His *Apostolic Tradition* was a manual of church order and worship, written, according to many scholars, *after* the schism of 217, either as an attack upon Callistus or as the service-book of the new sect. The date is important: it means that the tractate, which sheds so much light on the interior life of the early church and contains (in Lietzmann's view) "the model of all liturgies known to us," was written by a schismatic bishop who may not have been a trustworthy custodian of tradition at all. Dix ventured "four indications" that the treatise was written *before* 217, in the last years of Zephyrinus; but he left the purpose of the manual still entangled with the expectant elevation of Callistus. Surely Richardson was more nearly correct in ascribing the work to the year 197, when the "ignorant" and "unskilled" Zephyrinus was about to mount the episcopal throne. Hippolytus

On this point, cf. *Refutation*, IX. 7.

15

intimated as much in the prologue to the tractate, where he expressed the intention to set forth "the tradition which is proper for the churches," observing that:

This is now the more necessary because of that apostasy or error which was recently invented out of ignorance and because of certain ignorant men.

And in the epilogue he returned to the same theme:

Many heresies increased because those who were at the head would not learn the purpose of the Apostles, but according to their own pleasure do what they choose and not what is fitting.

Richardson supposed that the tractate was prepared *immediately* after the election of Zephyrinus, and that the crisis at hand was Montanism, which threatened "the orderly course of Catholic life" by its charismatic emphasis. Perhaps the year 200 would be a more accurate date,• when the bishop's ineptitude had fully manifested itself, first by his inclination toward Montanism, and then by his sufferance of the Monarchian heresy. At any event there appears to be little doubt that Hippolytus wrote the tractate as an avowed reactionary, still within the Roman community, and that we have in this text a record of rites and customs that were already a part of the tradition.

Hippolytus described the Eucharist in two settings. In the first instance (Ch. iv) it was preceded by the consecration of a bishop; in the second (Ch. xxiii), by Baptism and Confirmation.

After his Consecration, the bishop was given the Kiss of Peace by all of the faithful.•• Then the deacons carried up the oblation (*prosphora*) of bread and wine, which the people had brought as symbols of the inward offering of themselves.

• Richardson assumes that the *Ap. Trad.* was written immediately prior to Zephyrinus' Consecration, in anticipation of trouble; but Hippolytus everywhere makes it clear that trouble had already come over the church, and lays the blame upon those who were "at the head." Moreover, it was Zephyrinus, as bishop, who brought Callistus from Antium and made him archdeacon, with care over the cemetery. Thus Richardson is at a loss to explain Hippolytus' subtle attack upon Callistus as deacon (ix. 2) and as administrator of the cemetery (xxxiv).

•• This and other usages in the liturgy have been discussed in the previous chapter.

These were presented to the bishop; and he, "with all the presbyters," laid his hands upon them as a gesture of blessing. Then the bishop engaged in the Eucharistic dialogue with the people, according to the same simple forms that have prevailed in the Roman and Egyptian rites. As there was no Sanctus, the dialogue led directly into the Eucharistic prayer. While the presbyters appeared as "con-celebrants" at the time of the Offering, the bishop himself, as "high priest," made the Eucharistic prayer, which was a part of his special "liturgy." The time had not yet come, however, when a fixed formulary was required. Hippolytus stated specifically (x. 3) that the bishop was not bound to the published text of the Canon, but could "pray according to his own ability."

Taking its departure from the dialogue, the prayer commenced: "We give thanks unto thee, O God . . ." and then it proceeded to offer thanksgiving for creation by the Word, for the Incarnation of the Word, and for redemption through the passion of the Word—in all of which we cannot fail to find traces of Hippolytus' Christology.[*] The rehearsal of Christ's passion led ingeniously into the simple narrative of the Institution. And after that came the Lord's command, "When ye do this, ye do my *anamnesis*," in obedience to which the church then offered up the bread and cup, making the *anamnesis* of Christ's death and passion. This strange Greek word, which we have already encountered in Justin, has nowhere been more expounded and extruded than in Dom Dix's *The Shape of the Liturgy*. Certainly he is correct in saying that the term is not comprehended by our words "memorial" and "remembrance." Having been shaped by modern patterns of thought, those words connote a bygone event, now quite remote, with which we have a historical sort of communion by our willful acts of memory and devotion. By *anamnesis*, however, the early church meant nothing less than the "re-calling" or "re-presentation" of the passion of Christ so that (in the view of Dix) *"it becomes here and now operative by its effects in the communicants."*

Then followed what appears to be the epiclesis or Invocation of the Holy Spirit. Dix consigned the phrase to brackets as a fourth-century interpolation; but most scholars, taking it to be genuine, have read it with the rest of verse 12. In

[*] Cf. Elfers, pp. 50-4; cf. R. H. Connolly, "The Eucharistic Prayer of Hippolytus," *Journal of Theological Studies*, XXXIX, 350-69.

17

such a context, it is difficult to interpret, partially because the reconstruction of the text is also uncertain. Unlike the *epiclesis* in the later Greek rite,· it did not make reference to the conversion of the elements; rather it asked that the Holy Spirit, descending "upon the oblation of Holy Church," would work effectively in the hearts of the communicants.··

Additional details are to be found in the Easter Eucharist (Ch. xxiii) at which the newly baptized received their first Communion. This action really commenced in the preceding chapter (xxii). There we learn that the neophytes, having received Baptism and Confirmation, were led directly into the company of the faithful to participate for the first time in the ministry of Intercession. After these prayers of the faithful, the people greeted one another with the Kiss of Peace. Then occurred the Offertory and Consecration, as they are described at the opening of Chapter xxiii. Besides the bread, *three* cups were "eucharistized" in this special celebration: (1) wine and water, as the "antitype" of the blood that was shed by Christ; (2) milk and honey, as the food of the newborn children of God and as tokens of their admission to the Promised Land; and (3) water, as a sign of the laver of Baptism, which, being consumed, would benefit the "inner man." All of these things were to be explained to the neophytes by the bishop.

The bishop himself administered the bread. Having made the Fraction, he delivered a morsel to each one, saying, "The Bread of Heaven in Christ Jesus." Then the presbyters, assisted by the deacons when necessary, administered the cups, the wine being given last. To the Words of Delivery, with which the food and drink were distributed, each communicant responded, "Amen," making the proclamation of his faith at the moment of Communion.

At the close of the Eucharist the bishop occasionally received other kinds of offerings from the people—oil, which

---

· In the Divine Liturgy of S. John Chrysostom, the *epiclesis* reads: "Send down thy Holy Spirit upon us and upon the gifts here set forth, and make this bread indeed the precious body of our Lord and God and Saviour Jesus Christ. . . ." Later on, the action of the Holy Spirit is described as "having wrought the change."

·· For Dix's opinion, cf. his *Ap. Trad.*, pp. 75-9. There has been much discussion of this passage. Cf. Lietzmann, pp. 80-1; R. H. Connolly, *Journal of Theological Studies*, XXXIX, 367; Connolly and J. W. Turner, *Journal of Theological Studies*, XXV, 139-50, 337-64.

was used in healing, and cheese and olives. These were blessed in a little ceremony (Chs. v, vi) consisting of prayer and the doxology.

Alarmed that the true Catholic life would be overturned by capricious contemporaries, Hippolytus consigned to writing "the tradition which befits the churches"; and by doing that, he brought the history of the liturgy out of obscurity into full vision. Yet this curator of apostolic customs was himself the victim of the caprice of history. His writings, done entirely in Greek, were shortly forgotten when Latin prevailed over the Christian West. But inasmuch as he wrote in the name of tradition, his canons and his liturgy were honorably received in the East, and claimed a place in the churches of Egypt and Syria.

FOR FURTHER READING

R. H. Connolly, *The So-called Egyptian Church Order.* Cambridge, 1916. To Dom Connolly, chiefly, belongs the credit for the recovery of the *Apostolic Tradition.*

Gregory Dix, *The Shape of the Liturgy.* Westminster, 1947.

Gregory Dix (ed.), *The Treatise on the Apostolic Tradition of St. Hippolytus of Rome.* London, 1937. The best available text.

H. Elfers, *Die Kirchenordnung Hippolyts von Rom.* Paderborn, 1938.

Joseph A. Jungmann, *The Mass of the Roman Rite,* Vol. I. New York, 1951.

H. Lietzmann, *Messe und Herrenmahl.* Bonn, 1926.

C. C. Richardson, "The Date and Setting of the Apostolic Tradition of Hippolytus," *Anglican Theological Review,* XXX (1948), 38-44.

J. H. Srawley, *The Early History of the Liturgy.* Cambridge, 1947.

THE APOSTOLIC TRADITION
OF HIPPOLYTUS [1]

iv. ⟨*The Liturgy*⟩

Kiss of Peace

1 And when he has been made bishop let every one offer him the kiss of peace saluting him, for he has been made worthy ⟨*of this*⟩.

Offertory

2 To him then let the deacons bring the oblation and he with all the presbyters[2] laying his hand on the oblation shall say giving thanks:
3 The Lord be with you. And the people shall say: And with thy spirit. [*And the bishop shall say:*] Lift up your hearts. [*And the people shall say:*] We have them with the Lord. [*And the bishop shall say:*] Let us give thanks unto the Lord. [*And the people shall say:*] ⟨*It is*⟩ meet and right. And forthwith he shall continue thus:

Canon

4 We render thanks unto thee, O God, through Thy Beloved Child Jesus Christ, Whom in the last times Thou didst send to us ⟨*to be*⟩ a Saviour and Redeemer and the Messenger of Thy counsel;
5 Who is Thy Word inseparable ⟨*from Thee*⟩, through Whom Thou madest all things and in Whom Thou wast well-pleased;
6 ⟨*Whom*⟩ Thou didst send from heaven into ⟨*the*⟩ Virgin's womb and Who conceived within her was made flesh and demonstrated to be Thy Son being born of Holy Spirit and a Virgin;
7 Who fulfilling Thy will and preparing for Thee a holy people stretched forth His hands for suffering that He might release from sufferings them who have believed in Thee;
8 Who when He was betrayed to voluntary suffering that He might abolish death and rend the bonds of the devil and tread down hell and enlighten the righteous and establish the ordinance and demonstrate the resurrection:
9 Taking bread ⟨*and*⟩ making eucharist [i.e., giving thanks]

20

to Thee said: Take eat: this is My Body which is broken for
you [*for the remission of sins*]. Likewise also the cup, saying:
This is My Blood which is shed for you.

10   When ye do this [ye] do My "anamnesis."

11   Doing therefore the "anamnesis" of His death and resurrection we offer to Thee the bread and the cup making
eucharist to Thee because Thou hast bidden us [or, *found
us worthy*] to stand before Thee and minister as priests to
Thee.

12   And we pray Thee that [*Thou wouldest send Thy Holy
Spirit upon the oblation of Thy holy Church*] Thou wouldest
grant to all [*Thy Saints*] who partake to be united [*to Thee*]
that they may be fulfilled with the Holy Spirit for the confirmation of ⟨*their*⟩ faith in truth,

13   that [we] may praise and glorify Thee through Thy
[*Beloved*] Child Jesus Christ through whom glory and honour
⟨*be*⟩ unto Thee with ⟨*the*⟩ Holy Spirit in Thy holy Church
now [and for ever] and world without end. Amen.

v. ⟨*Blessing of Oil*⟩

1   If any one offers oil, he [*i.e., the bishop*] shall make
eucharist [or, *render thanks*] as at the oblation of bread and
wine. But he shall not say word for word ⟨*the same prayer*⟩
but with similar effect, saying:

2   [O God] who sanctifiest [this] oil, as Thou dost grant
unto all who are [anointed] and receive of it [the hallowing]
wherewith Thou didst anoint kings ⟨*and*⟩ priests and prophets,
so ⟨*grant that*⟩ it may give strength to all that taste of it
and health to all that use it.

vi. ⟨*Blessing of Cheese and Olives*⟩

1   Likewise if any one offers cheese and olives he shall say
thus:

2   Sanctify this solidified milk, solidifying us also unto Thy
charity.

3   Grant also that this fruit of the olive depart not from Thy
sweetness, ⟨*this fruit*⟩ which is the type of thy fatness which
Thou hast caused to flow from the Tree[3] for the life of them
that hope in Thee.

4   But in every blessing shall be said: To Thee be glory,
to the Father and to the Son with ⟨*the*⟩ Holy Spirit in the
holy Church now and for ever and world without end. Amen.

xxiii. ⟨The Paschal Mass⟩

Offertory and Consecration

1 And then let the oblation [at once] be brought by the deacons to the bishop, and he shall eucharistize [first] the bread into the representation [*which the Greek calls the antitype*] of the Flesh of Christ; [and] the cup mixed with wine for the antitype, [*which the Greek calls the likeness*] of the Blood which was shed for all who have believed in Him;

Milk and Honey

2 and milk and honey mingled together in fulfillment of the promise which was ⟨made⟩ to the Fathers, wherein He said I will give you a land flowing with milk and honey; which Christ indeed gave, ⟨even⟩ His Flesh, whereby they who believe are nourished like little children, making the bitterness of the ⟨human⟩ heart sweet by the sweetness of His word;

Water

3 water also for an oblation for a sign of the laver, that the inner man also, which is psychic, may receive the same ⟨rites⟩ as the body.
4 And the bishop shall give an explanation concerning all these things to them who receive.

Communion

5 And when he breaks the Bread in distributing to each a fragment he shall say:

The Bread of Heaven in Christ Jesus.

6 And he who receives shall answer: Amen.
7 And the presbyters—but if there are not enough ⟨of them⟩ the deacons also—shall hold the cups and stand by in good order and with reverence: first he that holdeth the water, second he who holds the milk, third he who holds the wine.
8 And they who partake shall taste of each ⟨cup⟩ thrice, he who gives ⟨it⟩ saying:

22

In God the Father Almighty;

and he who receives shall say: Amen.
9   And in the Lord Jesus Christ;

⟨*and he shall say: Amen.*⟩

10   And in ⟨*the*⟩ Holy Spirit [*and*] in the Holy Church;
and he shall say: Amen.
11   So shall it be done to each one.
12   And when these things have been accomplished, let
each one be zealous to perform good works and to please
God, living righteously, devoting himself to the Church,
performing the things which he has learnt, advancing in the
service of God.
13   And we have delivered to you briefly these things concerning Baptism and the Oblation because [*you have already
been instructed*] concerning the resurrection of the flesh and
the rest according to the Scriptures.
14   But if there is any other matter which ought to be told,
let the bishop impart it secretly to those who are communicated. He shall not tell this to any but the faithful and only
after they have first been communicated. This is the white
stone of which John said that there is a new name written
upon it which no man knows except him who receives [*the
stone*].

NOTES

1. Gregory Dix ⟨ed.⟩, *The Treatise on The Apostolic Tradition of
   St. Hippolytus of Rome* (London: Society for Promoting Chris-
   tian Knowledge, 1937), pp. 6-11, 40-3. The following symbols
   are used in the text:
   ⟨   ⟩ = Words or phrases having no authority from any version,
        but introduced into the English translation to assist the
        sense.
   [   ] = Words or phrases having authority from one or more
        versions, but probably forming no part of the original
        Greek.
   [   ] = Words or phrases having authority from one or more
        versions, but not all, yet probably forming part of the
        original Greek. Italicized words in such brackets are
        more doubtful.

23

2. On the practice of "concelebration," in which the presbyters were associated with the bishop in the celebration of the Eucharist, see Gregory Dix, *The Shape of the Liturgy* (Westminster, 1947), p. 126.
3. "Tree" here seems to mean the Cross, not the olive tree.

III

THE MASS
IN LATIN AND ENGLISH

THE ROMAN RITE

Latin Christianity arose in North Africa at the close of the second century and gradually attained pre-eminence over the West, informing the liturgy, the Vulgate, the speech of popes, and the writings of the Fathers. By the end of the fourth century, local Latin rites had begun to appear. Compared to the great Eastern liturgies, they had several distinguishing features. While the East was inclined toward a type of worship that was timeless and changeless, transfixed in holiness, and celebrated at the threshold of heaven, the West, being greatly taken up with the history of salvation, employed many variable elements in the liturgy to keep pace with the movement of the Church Year. And while the East was given to resplendent ceremonial and embellished speech, the Roman genius lay rather in a high sense of brevity, sobriety, and order. Finally, the West retained Latin as the one, normal language of worship.

We should not suppose, however, that the Western rite was everywhere the same. There were, in fact, two basic traditions: (1) the Roman type, which was used in the Eternal City and perhaps in North Africa;[*] and (2) the Gallic type, which prevailed at Milan and beyond the Alps.

To be exact, the Gallic type included four principal forms. The *Ambrosian* (Milanese) liturgy[**] evolved in the archdiocese of Milan, where it is still employed. From earliest times,

[*] Cf. F. Cabrol, "Afrique (Liturgie)," *DACL*, I, 591-657.
[**] Cf. P. Lejay, "Ambrosienne (Liturgie)," *DACL*, I, 1373-1442.

owing to the immediacy of Rome, it took on Roman features, including the Canon—a circumstance that has obscured its identity with the Gallic type, prompting some recent scholars to suppose that it belonged rather to the primitive Roman tradition. The *Mozarabic* liturgy—the ancient Visigothic rite —was used by those "arabized" · Christians who persisted in Spain after the invasion of the Moors (711). Given authority and regulation by the powerful See of Toledo, it prevailed against the encroachments of the Roman liturgy until the eleventh century. Cardinal Ximenes (d. 1517), who was resolved to perpetuate its use, founded a chapel at Toledo, where it has continued to be celebrated to this day. The *Celtic* rites·· were Latin formularies used in Scotland and Ireland through the eleventh century. They were the peculiar custody of Celtic missionaries who roamed the continent at the opening of the Middle Ages and, being ardent lovers of the liturgy, collected ceremonies and forms from many sources, not the least of which were Eastern. Although this tradition was therefore ecclectic and variable, it produced a number of liturgical books, notably the Stowe Missal,··· which offers an example of Celtic worship during the eighth to tenth centuries. The *Gallican* liturgy···· was employed in the Frankish kingdom until the era of Charlemagne, when it was deliberately suppressed in deference to the Roman rite. It was rather fully delineated in the notations of Gregory of Tours (d. 594) and in several liturgical texts of the seventh century.·····

The origin of the Gallic type remains obscure. Some scholars, Fortescue for example, assume that it was originally the common liturgy of the West, which was carried about by the first missionaries and underwent local development in the "Gallic" provenance. Other scholars, notably Benedictines Dom Cagin and Dom Cabrol, declare that it was none other than the old Roman rite, which was exported throughout

---

· The word Mozarabic has been variously interpreted; cf. Fortescue, p. 105n.
·· Cf. L. Gougaud, "Celtiques (Liturgies)," *DACL*, II, 2969-3032.
··· Edited by the Henry Bradshaw Society, 1906-15. Cf. W. D. Maxwell, *Outline of Christian Worship* (London, 1945), pp. 51-4.
···· Cf. L. Leclercq, "Gallicane (Liturgie)," *DACL*, VI, 473-593.
····· Notably the Alsatian sacramentary, *Missale Gothicum* (*PL*, LXXII, 225-318), and an *Expositio* of the Gallican Mass (*PL*, LXXII, 89-98), which bears the name of St. Germain of Paris (d. 576) but probably belongs to the seventh century.

the West, the assumption being that subsequently the Roman rite itself suffered modification. Others, chiefly Anglican, defend the older view that the Gallic type derived from the East, specifically from the liturgy of Ephesus which was brought to Lyons by none other than the disciples of St. John, and spread thence over Gaul, Spain, and Britain. Duchesne protests, however, that the Gallic rites were not merely complicated, but quite *formal* in their complication, and could scarcely have been earlier than the late fourth century. But the solution that he proposes, and which Jungmann repeats with apparent satisfaction, is plainly conjectural. He suggests that the Gallic type arose at Milan, which rivaled the hegemony of Rome in the fourth century. By virtue of its stature as the imperial residence, that city presumed to be the center of ecclesiastical affairs in the West, engaging itself with Constantinople and Asia Minor, and exerting influence over the churches of Spain and Gaul. For twenty years (355-74) the See of Milan was ruled by an Eastern bishop, Auxentius of Cappadocia. Granting that he inaugurated there the Gallic type, we are able to explain its similarities to Eastern usage, for example, the peculiar position of the Kiss of Peace and the appearance of an epiclesis in the Canon. Brilioth vociferously denies this view. Taking his departure from the Benedictines, he contends that the Gallic rites were faithful to "a common early tradition," from which *Rome* was guilty of deviation. The so-called Roman simplicity and terseness, having been carefully contrived and stylized, was actually less primitive than the Gallic exuberance, while the Roman Canon was a "clumsy" effort to replace the ancient and noble Eucharistic prayer of the Gallic type. Such, then, are the major opinions that have been given to this highly controverted problem.

The Gallic type could not withstand the tide of history. It tended to dissociate its churches from the papacy at the very moment when the great missionaries labored to bring the entire West into closer communion with Rome. In the Frankish kingdom its demise was most pronounced. There it had no regulating center and, consequently, no controlled development; but it spun out diverse forms that suffered by comparison to the sober and orderly character of Roman worship. In fact, elaboration was the chief temptation of the Gallic type everywhere. The liturgies were more symbolic, dramatic, and diffuse than the Roman rite—copious in music, rich in ceremonial, overflowing with words. Moreover they abounded in variable elements to such an extent that virtually every feast day was fitted out with its own distinctive formulary. Incited by the "apostle" Boniface and by Chrodegang, bishop of Metz, both Pepin the Short and Charlemagne were resolved to bring uniformity to the Frankish church on the basis of Roman usage. Service-books were procured from the papacy. But those scholars in Charlemagne's entourage who were charged to copy out the Roman formularies saw no harm in furnishing them with sundry good features of the Gallican Mass. In this manner a composite liturgy was gradually fashioned, which spread throughout the Frankish kingdom and, reaching Rome at last, overcame the ancient Roman rite. We shall have more to say of this later.

The Gallic type of the late seventh century had approximately this form:

The liturgy commenced with an antiphon, called the *Ingressa* at Milan, the *Officium* in Toledo. Like the Roman Introit, it accompanied the entrance of the clergy. Presently the bishop greeted the people: *Dominus sit semper vobiscum.* And they replied: *Et cum spiritu tuo.* Three canticles followed: the Trisagion of the Byzantine rite (in some instances), the Kyrie eleison, and the Benedictus (Lk. 1: 68-79). Thereupon the bishop made a prayer that alluded to the Benedictus or to the festival of the day.

Three lessons were read: the first from the Old Testament, the second from the Epistles (or Acts), the third from the Gospels. Either before or after the second lesson —the order varies according to the several texts—the *Benedictus es* was interposed, with a responsorial chant. Prior to the third lesson, the Gospel book was brought forth in a solemn procession, led by seven torch-bearers, while (in some instances) the Trisagion was chanted. At the announcement of the Gospel, the people exclaimed: *Gloria tibi Domine.* After the Gospel, the Trisagion was chanted again, and a homily was delivered by the bishop or a priest. There followed the church-prayer, cast in the form of a litany, each petition being made by the deacon, to which the people responded by "Lord, have mercy" or some other expression. According to the examples available, this litany appears to have been taken over entirely from Eastern usage. The bishop summed up the prayer by saying the collect; and thereupon the catechumens were dismissed at the bidding of the deacon.

The Mass itself commenced with a solemn procession in which the Eucharistic gifts—having been offered by the people and prepared by the clergy before the Mass—were brought to the altar and veiled. Even at this time the gifts were afforded the honor that would accrue to them at the Consecration. During the procession, the choir chanted the *Sonus,* which corresponded to the *Cherubicon* in the Byzantine rite. At the close of the procession, another sacred song was chanted. Then came an opening address, called *praefatio missae,* in which the meaning of the holy action was rehearsed; it was followed by a collect. The diptychs were then read, giving the names of those who were offering the sacrifice, as well as the names of those for whom the sacrifice was being offered. This was concluded by the collect "after the names" (*post nomina*). Then the Kiss of Peace was given, accompanied by the collect "at the peace" (*ad pacem*).

After his customary dialogue with the people, the celebrant began the Preface, which exceeded the Roman Preface in length and dwelt upon thanksgiving for the life and work of the Saviour; it led to the Sanctus. The collect "after the Sanctus" (*post Sanctus*) served as the transition to the Words of Institution. The Words themselves were followed by a prayer (variously called *post secreta, post pridie, post mysterium*), which apparently embraced both the anamnesis and the epiclesis; by means of the latter, the Consecration was completed. There followed the Fraction, or breaking of the bread, which was concluded by an elaborate arrangement of the particles of bread upon the altar, usually in cruciform, illustrating the Gallic tendency toward symbolic action. This ceremony was accompanied by an antiphonal chant. Then the whole congregation recited the *Pater Noster,* which was set off by a brief preface and conclusion. The high moment of the Mass occurred as the deacon invited the people to bow their heads for the Benediction, which was then given to them by the bishop or, in his absence, by the priest. Although this blessing changed with the feasts, the following example may be accounted a typical formula, appointed for the use of priests: "Peace, faith, and love, and the communication of the Body and Blood of Christ be with you always." The Communion itself was accompanied by an antiphon, which was often based on Psalm 33. Finally, after a brief prayer of thanksgiving, the people were dismissed by such words as: *Missa acta est—in pace.*

Turning back to the Roman rite, we are at some disadvantage of having no text of the Mass after the time of Hippolytus until the appearance of the sacramentaries in the seventh century. Only a few ideas can be entertained with confidence. There is reason to believe that the Roman rite evolved at Rome itself, although influences from abroad may have affected it. Its appearance coincided with the gradual transition of that community from Greek to Latin, which was underway by the pontificate of Cornelius (251-3) and was completed more than a century later. The liturgy could scarcely have remained unaffected by the terse and austere quality of the new language; and some scholars believe that the advent of Latin was the motivation for remodeling the Canon. The core of the Roman Mass must have been fixed at the beginning of the fifth century, and certainly no later than the end of that century. And when it appeared, the liturgy no longer countenanced the primitive freedom of extempore prayer and unfixed forms, but presented a very definite shape and text, within which, of course, provision was made for variable elements to accommodate the Church Year.

Aside from these considerations, however, much uncertainty remains. The questions are: How did the Roman type develop? How are we to understand its peculiarities with reference to the Eastern and Gallic liturgies? And, above all, how are we to account for the apparent dislocation of the prayers of the Canon? To answer these questions, one has to deal, not with two or three theories, but with eight or ten.[*] And inasmuch as these theories have often succeeded in demolishing one another, recent scholars tend to stare at the ruins and circumvent the issues. We shall do no more than note the salient historical evidence that remains to us.

1. In *De Sacramentis*—the authenticity of which is now generally conceded[**]—Ambrose of Milan (d. 397) rehearsed the prayers of the Canon as they were known to him (IV. 5),

[*] Cf. F. Cabrol, "Canon Romain," *DACL*, II, 1847-1905; Fortescue, pp. 138-71.
[**] On this problem, cf. King, pp. 16ff., and Srawley, p. 155.

making it clear that it was the *Roman* use he honored and meant to follow (III. 1). His text included some striking peculiarities, compared to the Gelasian sacramentary; nevertheless there were sufficient parallels to conclude that the core of the Canon—from *Quam oblationem* to *Unde et memores,* and perhaps even to *Supplices te*—had already been established. In another passage (IV. 14), Ambrose discussed the Consecration, which he attributed, not to an epiclesis, but to "the words of Christ" ("This is my Body" and "This is my Blood"); and he concluded: "Thus the word of Christ consecrates (*conficit*) this sacrament." Aside from certain references by Pope Gelasius, the record is silent concerning the epiclesis in the Roman rite. Some authorities believe that its removal, for dogmatic reasons, was the primary occasion for the rearrangement of the Canon.·

2. The references of Jerome·· (d. 420), while they tend to be random and tentative, cannot be dismissed. We learn from him that the names of those who "offered" the Eucharistic gifts were read (from the diptychs?) by the deacon at the altar;··· that the Sanctus and the Lord's Prayer···· had been given places in the liturgy; that the Kiss of Peace had likely been removed to its present position after the Canon; and that each communicant said "Amen" at the administration.

3. In 416, Innocent I addressed a response to the Umbrian bishop Decentius,····· in which he alluded to the inroads of Gallic influence and declared that the church in all the West ought to conform to the liturgical use of the Apostolic See. In reply to specific questions, he informed Decentius that the Kiss of Peace should *follow* the Canon and should signify the people's "consent" and "seal" upon the "mysteries" that had been performed. Pope Innocent also advised Decentius— in a passage that has been subjected to a variety of interpretations······—that the names of those who had "offered" should not be recited until the gifts had been commended to God. From this it may be inferred that the Mass already contained the Offertory prayer (corresponding to the present *Secreta*) by which the gifts were commended, and that the names

· Cf. Fortescue, pp. 402-7.
·· For documentation and details, cf. Srawley, pp. 168-70.
··· This practice was discussed in canons 28, 29 of the Spanish Council of Elvira, *ca.* 305.
···· Its position was fixed before the Fraction by Gregory the Great.
····· *PL,* XX, 551ff.
······ Cf. Fortescue, pp. 133, 170f.

were recited at some point within the Canon, perhaps immediately after a prayer corresponding to the present *Te igitur.*

4. Pope Felix II (483-92) was the last to refer to the church-prayer, with its twofold division: for the catechumens and for the faithful. But in this era the collect appeared before the lessons; and Jungmann takes this to mean that the introductory part of the Mass was being developed. He is inclined to think that it was Gelasius I (492-96)— a pope celebrated for his liturgical contributions—who filled out the introductory action, importing the Kyrie eleison from the East, and who removed the general prayer, since it assumed the separation of the catechumens from the faithful, which was no longer actually practiced.

5. By the time of Pope Leo the Great· (440-61), the name "Mass" was applied to the Eucharist. There is little doubt about the origin of this term: mass = *missa* = *missio* = *dismissio.* It meant the "dismissal" of the church as we find it in the formula at the conclusion of the liturgy: *Ite missa est.* How odd that the service should be named according to its dismissal. And yet, as Jungmann has said, the dismissal involved a blessing, not merely the benediction with which the people were sent away, but that blessing that was the Mass itself.

Taking these considerations together, we may conceive of the Mass at the close of the fifth century. It commenced with the Introit psalm, which was sung at the entrance of the clergy. Following the Kyries, the celebrant said the collect; and readings were given from the Scriptures, interposed by a psalm. At the Offertory, the gifts of the people in bread and wine were presented at the altar, while the choir sang another psalm; and presently the celebrant commended them to God by the collect, now called the Secret. And then, having engaged the people in the ancient Eucharistic dialogue, the celebrant said the Preface, which terminated in the singing of the Sanctus. Thereupon he commenced the Canon, which embodied the Consecration and the sacrifice. When the Kiss of Peace had been given, the people received the Communion under the forms of bread and wine, saying "Amen" as they received. At length, having offered the collect of thanksgiving, the celebrant dismissed the congregation. Edmund Bishop was impressed by the simple dignity

· *PL,* LIV, 627.

of this service, by its care for order, gravity, and sobriety.
In a frequently quoted phrase he described the chief characteristics of the Roman rite as "soberness and sense" and
protested that those sensuous qualities, popularly conceived
to be "Romanism," did not accrue from Rome at all. While
this correction is well taken, it does not seem to account for
the manifestations we shall see in the Stational Mass of the
seventh century, namely, that the same concern for order
would produce a magnificence of detail, and that the same
sense of solemnity would express itself in unfolding splendor.

The oldest Mass-books were drawn up according to the
exclusive functions of those who performed the liturgy. The
sacramentarium supplied the celebrant with the collects and
prefaces, which varied according to the Church Year, the
"Ordinary" of the Mass (i.e., its fixed parts) being committed
to a tablet and generally recited from memory. The reader
who gave the Epistle used the *apostolus,* while the deacon
who read the Gospel employed the *evangelium.* The singers
found their parts in the *schola cantorum.* And the priest
whose function it was to oversee the performance of the
liturgy consulted the books of rubrics, called *ordines.*

Three of the sacramentaries have come down to us. The
Leonine is extant in a single manuscript of the seventh
century.· When and by whom it was compiled are questions
outside our purview; but perhaps it would be fair to say that
most authorities assign substantial parts of the sacramentary
to the period from Gelasius (d. 496) to Vigilius (d. 555).
There are many indications that it was a Roman book; but
whether it was an *official* book is doubtful. The compiler
seems rather to have been a private collector who drew
upon all manner of sources, and saw fit to include no less
than twenty-eight Masses for the feast of SS. Peter and Paul.
But that fact did not diminish the authority of the Leonine
sacramentary, which supplied some 174 texts to the modern
Missal, including three prayers in the Ordinary of the Mass.

The *Gelasian* sacramentary·· presents no less of a puzzle. In
the first half of the ninth century, Walafrid Strabo declared
that it had been arranged by Gelasius himself; and he
observed that it had been used in the Frankish churches, but
that Gregory the Great, seeing its imperfections, had remodeled it to make the Gregorian sacramentary. Fifty years later,

· *PL,* LV, 21-156.
·· Edited by H. A. Wilson. (Oxford, 1894.)

Gregory's biographer, John the Deacon, rehearsed the same information: "He [Gregory] collected the book of Gelasius for the solemnities of the Mass into one volume, leaving out much, changing little, adding something for the exposition of the lessons of the Gospel." Thus, two Roman sacramentaries were current across the Alps in the ninth century. One was deemed to be the compilation of Gelasius, the other a revision of it by Gregory. The ascription of this text to Gelasius was apparently due to a reference in the highly esteemed *Liber Pontificalis,*· which described that pope as the author of a sacramentary. There is no evidence, however, to confirm the designation, although it is conceivable that the basic content of the sacramentary may have taken shape in the era of Gelasius (492-6). The earliest extant manuscript, however, is a text of the eighth century, which was based upon Roman materials imported into France, as whole books or in parts, at an earlier time. Internal evidence suggests that the Roman sources of this manuscript belonged to the era from Gregory I to Gregory II, namely, 604-731. The Gelasian sacramentary, unlike the Leonine, was in all respects a proper Mass-book, which presented in three main divisions the Masses for the Church Year, for the feasts of the saints, and for all sorts of special purposes. While it may not have been "Gelasian" nor even purely Roman, it contributed substantially to the modern Missal.

Fifty years ago Duchesne pronounced it a "grave error" to suppose that the *Gregorian* sacramentary was the work of Gregory the Great (590-604). Today it is a grave mistake not to suppose it. Archdale King has ventured to say that the Gregorian reforms, which were undertaken to abridge the Roman sacramentary and make it more practical, were authorized in the precise year of 595. Leaving these considerations to wiser writers,·· we turn to the central importance of this document. At the close of the eighth century, Pope Hadrian I dispatched to Charlemagne, at the latter's request, a copy of the Gregorian sacramentary to be used as the basis of liturgical reform in the Frankish kingdom. That text, called the *Hadrianum,* was a papal feast day and Stational Missal, and was therefore deficient in parochial services: It did not even furnish Masses for Sundays. For this reason a supplement was

· A history of the popes, which was probably begun in the 6th century. Edited by L. Duchesne in 2 vols. (Paris, 1886-92.)
·· Cf. King, pp. 24-9.

added to the sacramentary, quite likely by Alcuin or some other scholar in Charlemagne's employ, in which Gallican materials were mixed with the Roman. While at first these additions were marked off as such, they gradually became fused into the sacramentary itself, and, being taken back to Rome, became one of the bases of the Romano-Gallican liturgy, out of which the modern Missal was finally derived.

Of all the *ordines* the most important was *Ordo I* (*Ordo Romanus Primus*),• which in its oldest form can be dated at least as early as the seventh century. It included a careful description of the papal stational service as it was performed in the era of Gregory the Great. Besides the Mass, which was celebrated on Sundays and feast days in the churches of Rome, there arose a civic service, which was conducted by the pope in a church designated as the *statio* of the day, and which was attended by people from all parts and parishes of the Eternal City. Here we see the Mass in a moment of stability, when all of its parts had found their place in a fixed arrangement, and before the liturgical initiative passed from Rome to the Carolingian empire. And here is revealed the transcendence of the Roman "soberness and sense" in a pattern of magnificent detail and solemn splendor.

The pope came on horseback in a stately procession from the Lateran to the appointed stational church. The nave was already filled by the worshipers who had arrived in seven processions, from the seven regions of Rome. In the middle of the apse was the table-altar (*mensa*). Behind it, against the far wall of the apse, was the pope's cathedra, or throne. Most of the clergy were already seated in a semicircle around the altar, the suburbicarian bishops to the right of the cathedra, presbyters to the left of it. Meanwhile in the sacristy (*secretarium*), near the entrance to the basilica, the pope and his ministers were vested. Presently the Gospel book was opened and borne to the altar by one of the acolytes, accompanied by a subdeacon. The pope signaled with his maniple, whereupon the singers at the front of the sanctuary (*presbyterium*) were alerted to begin the Introit; and thus the procession commenced. Seven acolytes preceded with torches and censers; and two deacons assisted the pope in walking. Presently two other acolytes approached the dignitaries with an open

• Edited by E. G. C. F. Atchley. (London, 1905.)

casket containing a portion of the bread consecrated at the previous Mass. The pope bowed low before it. Reaching the altar he gave the Kiss of Peace to one of the bishops, one of the presbyters, and to the assembled deacons. At his signal the choir (*schola*) brought the Introit to an end. Having prostrated himself momentarily on a carpet in submission to God, the pope arose and kissed both the Gospel book and the altar. While the choir sang the Kyrie eleison, he proceeded to his cathedra and there he stood, facing East in the attitude of prayer. Having signaled the choir to terminate the Kyrie, he intoned the Gloria in excelsis, if it were appointed for that day. Then he greeted the people, saying, *Pax vobis,* and sang the collect, to which the people responded "Amen."

After that splendid introduction came the office of the lessons. A subdeacon went into the pulpit (*ambo*) and read the Epistle. When he descended, a singer mounted the *ambo* and, chanting alternately with the choir, sang the Gradual and (on occasion) the Alleluia or the Tract. There followed the ceremonies at the Gospel. The deacon went first to the cathedra and, kissing the foot of the pope, begged his blessing. Then he took up the Gospel book from the altar, kissed it, and carried it to the *ambo,* being preceded by two subdeacons—one carrying a censer—and two acolytes with torches. After the Gospel had been read, a subdeacon carried round the book to be kissed by all the clergy. Then it was taken back to the Lateran by one of the acolytes. There was apparently no sermon. Nor was there any longer a dismissal of the catechumens.

Again the pope greeted the people: *Dominus vobiscum.* He added, *Oremus* ("Let us pray") even though there was no prayer forthcoming. Instead, preparations were undertaken for the action of the Mass. An acolyte and a deacon proceeded to cover the altar with the corporal, after which the Offertory commenced. The pope himself received the bread offered by the nobility, while the archdeacon accepted their offerings of wine; other members of the clergy continued to receive the gifts of the people as the pope returned to his cathedra. Presently the loaves to be consecrated were arranged on the altar; and the chalice was filled with wine, to which water was added. That done, the pope received the offerings of the clergy and, at last, placed his own oblation of two small loaves upon the altar. Meanwhile the choir sang the Offertory psalm. At length the singers stopped, so that a single Offertory prayer (now called the Secret) could be said.

Then it was time for the Eucharistic prayer. Each one took his place in a configuration of the holy community at worship, with the pope standing behind the altar, facing the people, and the other clergy ranged variously around him. Now the pope began to speak with a loud voice. He commenced with the ancient dialogue, to which the sub-deacons responded. After the Sanctus had been sung, the pope entered upon the familiar prayers of the Canon, saying each one audibly and without ornament or display. The Elevation had not yet become associated with the act of Consecration; but when the pope recited the final doxology, he lifted up the host, while the archdeacon elevated the chalice, indicating thereby the conclusion of the Canon. This part of the Mass was called *Canon actionis,* "the rule of action," because of its solemn nature and almost invariable character.

The preparation for Communion began with the recitation of the *Pater Noster* and its appended embolism (i.e., a brief prayer based on the last petition of the Lord's Prayer, *libera nos a malo*). Presently the church exchanged the Kiss of Peace, that ancient sign of Christian unity and charity. Considerable time was then devoted to the Fraction, for ordinary loaves had been consecrated and remained to be broken. The pope initiated the Fraction and returned to his cathedra, leaving the rest of the preparations to the archdeacon. He committed the precious Blood of the chalice to the care of a subdeacon, and placed the loaves into linen bags, held by the acolytes, to be delivered over to the bishops and presbyters who continued the Fraction. In Gregory's day, all this was done in silence. According to the *Liber Pontificalis,* it was Pope Sergius I (687-701) who assigned the Agnus Dei to be sung at the Fraction.

The Holy Communion was accompanied by the singing of a psalm. The paten was carried first to the pope, who communicated of the consecrated bread, but saved aside a small particle, which he put into the chalice, saying the words of commingling. Then he communicated of the chalice. After that, Communion was administered to the clergy and to the people, who stood to receive the ele-

39

ments. The Communion under the form of bread was delivered into their hands. The Communion of the Blood of Christ was given in cups of ordinary wine, each of which contained a few drops from the consecrated chalice. Yet the Faithful were not permitted to drink directly from the cups, but by means of a tube (*pugillaris* or *fistula*). When everyone had communicated, the pope returned to the altar to make the prayer of thanksgiving. Then, at his signal, a deacon dismissed the people by singing *Ite missa est*, to which came the response, *Deo gratias*. The pope returned to the sacristy in solemn procession, blessing all as he retired.

The detail and the constrained pomp of this liturgy are extraordinary. But its communal character is perhaps even more impressive. Here we see the people of Rome, drawn around their bishop, in a corporate act of praise and sacrifice, participating by sight, hearing, and physical motion, sharing in the action of the Mass by the offering of their gifts and by their actual reception of the Body and Blood of the Redeemer.

The gift of the Gregorian sacramentary by Pope Hadrian to Charlemagne in 788 proved to be the gift of liturgical initiative by the Apostolic See to the Carolingian Empire—an initiative that Rome did not fully retrieve until the sixteenth century. Although Charlemagne received the Roman books in fidelity and gave them authority throughout his dominions, he was not disposed to preserve them inviolate. When they crossed the Alps, they entered a realm that did not altogether appreciate "soberness and sense" but possessed a religious temperament all its own, which had been given expression in the Gallican rites. Thus the Franks did not scruple to make alterations—sometimes profound alterations—to the Roman liturgy over the years. And, as we have seen, this process was begun at the very outset by Charlemagne and the members of his Palace School.•

• Being eager to establish preaching in his domain, Charlemagne enjoined that a sermon must be delivered in all churches every Sunday (cf. the capitulary of March 23, 789; and the canons of the councils of Arles, Mainz, and Rheims in the year 813). Moreover, the Carolingian reforms obliged every Christian to know the *Credo* and *Pater Noster*. In these injunctions, some scholars see the beginning of Prone, a vernacular pulpit service that was inserted into the Mass on Sundays and holy days in Medieval

The Gallic delight in drama produced what Jungmann called "the dramatic build-up of the Mass-liturgy." Copious use was now made of incense. The ceremonies at the Gospel were remodeled to suggest Christ's triumphal entrance, at which the church now exclaimed: *Gloria tibi domine.* Moreover, the prayers of the liturgy were multiplied, so that the clean structure of the Roman rite became overlaid with a profusion of items. Prayers were introduced for the commencement of Mass, during the Offertory, prior to Communion and after it, while extra collects were appointed before the Epistle. Not a few of these were cast into the singular, designed to be said inaudibly by the priest. Indeed, they were directly related to a peculiar Gallican prayer-form called *apologia sacerdotis*—a long and intensely personal avowal of sin and unworthiness on the part of the celebrant, reflecting the Frankish tendency toward introspection. While most of these *apologiae* disappeared after the eleventh century, some remnants still survive in the modern liturgy, notably in the Confiteor. The most respected authorities on the Mass judge that the silent recital of such prayers was alien to the Roman spirit. Jungmann detects the manifestation of this new influence even in the priest's deportment at prayer. No longer did he pray with outstreched arms, but with hands folded in the Teutonic gesture of homage and submissiveness.

Another Gallican peculiarity derived from earlier struggles against Arianism, when orthodoxy was riveted into the liturgy by prayers addressed to the Holy Trinity (*Suscipe sancta Trinitas* being a case in point) and by carefully contrived endings to the collects, which labored the equality of the three Persons. Both of these devices now appeared in the Romano-Frankish rite, the latter being obvious alongside the crisp Roman conclusion, "through Christ our Lord."

Aside from these alterations, which are readily identifiable

France and Germany. In connection with the sermon, the service included a Bidding Prayer, the Lord's Prayer, the Creed, the General Confession of sins, as well as church announcements. Traces of Prone are found in documents of the ninth century, and its full development may be dated no later than the era of Honorius of Autun (d. *ca.* 1150). Cf. "Prone" in *DACL*, XIV/2, 1898-1902. The sources are given in F. E. Brightman, *The English Rite,* II, 1020-45. Brightman tried to make the case that Prone underlay the Sunday Morning Service of the Reformed churches. With reference to Zwingli, he was correct (cf. Ch. V); otherwise his claims are exaggerated.

as the marks of Gallic piety, the Mass underwent a profound transformation, which had its beginnings in the transalpine provenance and arose from a constellation of factors. Perhaps the language of the liturgy was itself a factor. As·Latin became ever more remote to the people, the Mass took on more accoutrements of a mystery, and presented itself as something performed exclusively by the clergy on behalf of the people. The latter idea was reinforced by the increased emphasis upon the juridical conception of the church as a divine institution governed by the hierarchy, rather than as a community of the redeemed. In addition to these matters, there occurred a major shift in Eucharistic doctrine. When creativity was revived in theology after the Teutonic invasions, one of the first issues to be discussed was the Eucharist. The problem was to frame a doctrine that would more nearly express the elemental religious experience of the Carolingian milieu, permeated, as it was, with the miraculous and the mysterious. In the Mass, men sought a manifestation of the hidden God, who was otherwise inscrutable in his omnipotence, and a concrete realization of the mysteries of the Incarnation and Passion of Christ. Thus, about 831, Paschasius Radbertus proposed as doctrine that the body of Jesus Christ was present in the Mass by virtue of a miraculous transformation of the elements that left only their sensuous appearance unchanged. To call this transubstantiation, however, would be premature; for while the reality of Christ's body was miraculously created prior to all faith, it was neither apprehended nor eaten apart from faith. Nevertheless, the line of development had now been laid out; and the formal doctrine of transubstantiation received authority in the Berengarian controversey of the eleventh century,· becoming dogmatic at the IV Lateran Council, in 1215.

By virtue of this doctrine, the idea gained precedence that the Mass was no longer *a corporate action of the church* in making Eucharist unto God, but rather *the action of God*, who manifests himself among men at the climactic moment of the liturgy, namely, the Consecration. Thus, as Catholic

· In 1059, Berengar of Tours was forced to confess: "The bread and wine . . . after consecration are the real Body and Blood of our Lord Jesus Christ . . . and that Body is sensibly, not merely sacramentally, but in reality handled by the priest's hands and crushed by the teeth of the faithful." Cf. A. Harnack, *History of Dogma*, VI, 47n.

scholars are wont to say, the *eucharistia* became an *epiphania.*
The Canon of the Mass, in the course of which this "epiphany" occurred, was now spoken by the priest in muted
tones, as if he alone could afford to enter upon this innermost
sanctuary. Moreover, the reality of Christ's presence provided a proper basis for the idea of his ever-renewed sacrifice
in the Mass, which had been inherited from Gregory the
Great and was now firmly fixed as a salient feature of sacramental theology, overshadowing the act of Communion. Already in the ninth century, Walafrid Strabo expressly justified
the celebration of Mass without communicants.•

Under the influence of these new conceptions, the arrangement of the churches also underwent change, beginning, it
appears, in the ninth century. It was deemed appropriate to
move the altar back to the rear wall of the apse in solemn
isolation. This required a general shift in furniture. The
bishop's cathedra was brought out to one side, and the seats
for the clergy were extended in two rows along the sanctuary
wall, facing each other. As a result, the sanctuary became
elongated, the altar being farther removed from the people.
According to this new arrangement the priest found it convenient to celebrate with his back to the congregation. It is in-
teresting to see how these ninth-century vogues are catching
on in Protestantism.

In the era of Ivo of Chartres (d. 1117), the Gospel came
to be read at the right side, the Epistle at the left—these
positions being reckoned not from the standpoint of the congregation, but from the ancient position of the bishop's
cathedra, which governed all decisions of honor. This separation of the Gospel side from the Epistle side may account for
the extension of the altar lengthwise; and being built up with
reliquaries and altar pieces, the once simple *mensa* was transformed into a veritable shrine.

Conceived as the extraordinary mystery of God's manifestation, the Mass lost some of its association with ordinary life.
This is seen in the tendency of the people to adore the Crucified Redeemer concealed under the appearance of bread and
wine, rather than to communicate in his Body and Blood. It
is also seen in the introduction of unleavened bread in the
first half of the ninth century, which presently appeared in
the form of a pure white wafer. This change brought an end

• *PL,* CXIV, 943ff.

to the rich symbolism that once centered in the loaf. The primitive offertory of bread and wine gradually became an offering of money, while the procession of the gifts was abandoned, except at the greater feasts. The meaning of the Fraction was necessarily diminished. The small particles of the host could not be given conveniently into the hands of the communicants, but were now laid upon the tongue. And, for the sake of reverence, the people eventually knelt to receive the elements, whereupon the Communion rail was introduced.

As part and parcel of this whole development, but augmented especially by the silent recital of prayers and the strangeness of Latin, came the allegorical interpretation of the Mass, which was already under way by the time of Alcuin (d. 804) and was brought into special prominence by his pupil Amalarius (d. *ca.* 850). The intention was not to interpret the Mass as a liturgy, but as a sacred drama of the life and passion of the Lord, which was perceptible to the eye and could thereby claim the participation of everyman. Each vestment, utensil, motion, and "actor" was given an allegorical signification. For example, the extension of the celebrant's hands after the Consecration became a vivid imitation of the outstretched arms of the Crucified.

Toward the middle of the tenth century, the Romano-Frankish rite was carried back to Rome in numerous liturgical books, and eventually displaced the older sacramentaries. The acquiescence of the Apostolic See to the Carolingian Mass was due, in no small measure, to the influence of the Holy Roman Emperors over papal affairs, beginning in the time of Otto the Great (d. 973). We note that it was Henry II, upon his coronation (1014), who presumed to say that the Creed should be sung in the Mass.

The thirteenth century was especially important in the history of the Latin rite. According to the new conception of liturgical uniformity, in which the head of the church conformed rather to its members, there was a prolific growth of diocesan and monastic usages. While these did not presume upon the fixed character of the Mass, they did admit a bewildering variety in ceremonial and in the silent devotions of the priest. The religious communities were the first to curb this tendency by prescribing careful regulations of the liturgy. The Franciscans, however, performed a singular service. They adopted the *Missale Romanum*·—-a much simplified Mass-book prepared by the papal curia in the age of Innocent III —and transmitted it to every quarter of the church. Given the further assistance of printing (in 1474), that book acquired public favor everywhere, and prepared the way for the liturgical reforms of the Counter Reformation.

In the same century the *Missale Plenum,* or complete missal, finally replaced the sacramentary, illustrating the prevalence of private Mass, out of which Low Mass rose to great prominence. Until the eleventh century, the Eucharist remained basically a community service of worship, its corporate character being secured by the fact that it was *sung* in some communal setting by the celebrant, the assisting ministers, and the choir. But in view of the special graces that accrued from the sacrifice of the Mass and the devotion that attended its celebration, there was every inducement to offer it frequently and in private, for the benefit of the living and the dead. Already by the ninth century, the multiplicity of Masses was under way. Leo III (795-816) set the example by offering the sacrifice seven and nine times a day. Endowments were established for that purpose; and side altars were erected in the great churches in burgeoning numbers. This development was manifest in the *Missale Plenum;* for, according to the new arrangement of liturgical materials, the priest now had at hand the texts of the lessons and chants, and could thereby celebrate without the choir and sacred ministers necessary for High Mass. What happened in the later Middle Ages was that private Mass gained public recognition as the *normal* way of celebrating *public* worship: it became *the* Mass. Thus, the Roman Missal that was developed in the Counter Reformation represented Low Mass as the basic form of the Eucharist, consigning the celebration of High Mass to special and solemn occasions.

Finally, the pontificate of Innocent III·· (1198-1216) included two events that illustrated the contemporary character of Eucharistic devotion. The people, having been nursed

---

· *Missale secundum consuetudinem Romanae curiae.*
·· Innocent gave precise definition to the liturgical colors. White was the festive color, being reminiscent of the clouds at Ascension. Red honored the blood of martyrs and the holy fire of Pentecost. Black was appointed for seasons of penance and Masses for the dead. Green was used on occasions that were without special significance.

on allegory and taught that the Mass was an epiphany of God in their midst, contemplated the unfolding drama and gazed with adoration at the Crucified Redeemer under the appearance of bread and wine. Thus, in 1210, the bishop of Paris required the Elevation of the host and chalice to be performed directly after the Consecration, in order to correct certain improprieties associated with reverencing the host. In that way, the Mass acquired its focal point and highest moment. But the centrality of the Elevation was also the sign that the actual communication of the people had, over the years, been seriously diminished. To stay this tendency, the IV Lateran Council, at which Innocent presided, decreed in 1215 (even as it confirmed the doctrine of transubstantiation) that each of the faithful should receive "the sacrament of the Eucharist at least at Paschal time." The new character of Eucharistic devotion brought with it an increased reverence toward the sacred elements. In the course of the twelfth and thirteenth centuries, communion under the form of wine was discontinued to the people, lest it be spilled or irreverently used. This was no deprivation to the laity, however, for it was understood that "by concomitance" (*per concomitantiam*) the entire Christ is present under both species.

The multiplicity of Masses, especially of Votive Masses, and the exaggerated claims of their efficacy; the bewildering variety of rites; and the appearance of doubtful formularies—these, chiefly, were the factors that provoked demands for reform and uniformity. Already in the 1450's Nicholas of Cusa called in all the Mass-books of the diocese of Brixen and corrected them according to an exemplar. In the following century, the demand for a reformed Missal was intensified. The German Parliament, meeting at Speier in 1526, called for urgent attention to this matter. Presently, in 1549, the provincial synod of Trier prescribed a single Missal for all the dioceses of the province, while in Mainz a similar policy was pursued. These efforts of the German church were augmented by appeals of the same sort from all quarters of the West. Meanwhile, the Reformers had commenced to assail the Mass itself, in criticisms which were ordinarily harsh and sometimes reckless. This we shall see in the subsequent chapters.

Therefore, the Council of Trent, despite the magnitude of its labors, took up the matter of the liturgy. In Session XIII it dealt with the Eucharist and reiterated the doctrine of transubstantiation, while in Session XXII it confirmed the objective character of the sacrifice of the Mass. At this time (1562), a special committee was assigned to prepare a list of desirable reforms. The investigators pursued their responsibility zealously and raised all manner of issues, great and narrow, for consideration. Having weighed their report, the Council published the *Decretum de observandis et evitandis in celebratione missae* (September 17, 1562),· by which most of the glaring abuses were put down. At last, by a decree of Session XXV, it turned over the reform of the Missal and Breviary to Pope Pius IV.··

The liturgical commission appointed by Pius IV (d. 1565) completed its work under his successor. By the Bull, *Quo primum tempore* of July 14, 1570, the *Missale Romanum* of Pius V was imposed upon all priests and congregations of the Latin rite. It was prefaced by two texts of authorized directions, the *Rubricae Generales Missalis* and the *Ritus servandus in celebratione Missae*. According to the several documents, we are able to ascertain the principles of reform. It is clear that the papal commission embraced the policy of strict uniformity; for the new Missal was meant to prevail over the entire church, admitting neither concessions nor alterations. Only those communities that had kept to their liturgy continuously for two hundred years were permitted to retain a divergent use.··· Moreover, the uniform Missal was designedly Roman: its basis lay in the *Missale Romanum* which had been prepared by the papal curia in the age of Innocent III. Indeed, there are many indications that the commission meant to recover the ancient rite, disengaging it from all accretions of Franco-German origin that distorted its primitive shape. In the introductory Bull, Pius V declared that the revision had been pursued "according to the pristine norm and rite of the holy Fathers." It is apparent that the new Missal fell short of the mark; but Jungmann is quite fair in his judgment that a few men, given a few years, could scarcely be expected to amass the vast liturgical knowledge necessary to arrive at the *pristinam normam*. Nevertheless the

---

· Carl Mirbt (ed.), *Quellen zur Geschichte des Papsttums and des Römischen Katholizismus* (Tübingen, 1924), pp. 325-6.
·· *Ibid.*, p. 337.
··· Some of the religious Orders and some of the dioceses (Trier, Cologne, Liege, Braga, and Lyons) took advantage of this stipulation. Braga, Lyons, Milan, and the Mozarabic chapel at Toledo are the only places that still observe their traditional rites.

amount of purification was appreciable. Unfit accessories were eliminated without regard for their association with popular piety. Words and phrases were refined according to the literary artistry of humanism. The Church Year was reduced to those feasts that were observed in Rome prior to the eleventh century. And the people were commended to receive Communion each time they attended Mass.

To preside over the new-found uniformity, Sixtus V established the Congregation of Rites on January 22, 1588. It was not designed to be an agency of liturgical development, but rather the guardian of the Missal of Pius V, charged with the responsibility of making interpretations on doubtful points, giving out dispensations, and generally conserving the proper celebration of the Roman rite. The only prominent changes that have occurred since the sixteenth century have been handed down by the popes themselves; and even those have in no way affected the basic character of the Mass. In the reform of worship undertaken by the Counter Reformation, Catholic scholars see both advantages and disadvantages: if it halted the pious tampering of the Middle Ages and arrested the luxuriant growth of prayers and ceremonies, interpretations and promises that had accrued to the Mass, it also conceived of uniformity too narrowly and left insufficient provision for the development of new forms of liturgical expression.•

What is the Mass? In the Middle Ages, as we have seen, three conceptions attained prominence: (1) the Mass as an "epiphany" of God amongst men, which focused attention upon the reality of the Eucharistic Presence, upon the Consecration at which it occurred, and upon the priest by whose action it was effected; (2) the Mass as a sacrifice offered unto God for the benefit of the living and the dead; and (3) the Mass as an allegorical drama of the whole economy of redemption. How do these ideas fit together in an orderly pattern?

The Mass is, among other things, the *memorial of the passion* and redeeming death of Jesus, according to his own commandment: "Do this *in mei memoriam*." By "memorial," however, Catholic doctrine does not intend a mere historical recollection of a bygone event. Rather, the Lord's passion is continually being made present and actual in the liturgy.

• On this point, cf. O'Shea, pp. 134f.

Calvary is "arrested" and "held fast" (said Jungmann, in words reminiscent of the Council of Trent) so that all the generations after Jesus might be witnesses of that redemptive event. Moreover, this representation of the passion is indissolubly connected with the presence of the Crucified Redeemer, under the appearance of bread and wine, in whose Body and Blood the faithful are fed. And according to the *de tempore* principle of Western worship, it is constantly being invigorated by the movement of the Church Year, which itself unfolds the history of redemption and leaves the church in anticipation of the climactic events of Holy Week and Easter. The *memoria passionis* captured the piety of Medieval man, inspiring the allegorical interpretation of the entire liturgy.

The Mass is also a *holy meal,* in which the faithful gather at the table of the Lord to enjoy the communion of his Body and Blood, and to experience their communion with one another as his members. But, historically, this expression of the sacrament has been difficult to realize in practice. Through the greater part of the Middle Ages, the Communion of the people was regarded as an incidental, indeed an exceptional, feature in the performance of the liturgy. The descent of Christ to meet man was not summed up in the act of Communion, but rather in the act of sacrifice and in the adoration of the sacred elements. Thus, the motif of the holy meal verged on being overwhelmed by the collateral idea that the Mass was distinguished as a *sacrificial meal.* In the later Middle Ages, the utmost importance was laid upon the Mass-oblation, and upon the benefits to the living and the faithful departed which could be got by such a propitiation. It was this conception, above all, that the Reformers saw fit to condemn. But the Council of Trent overruled them (Session XXII, canons 1, 3):

> If anyone says that a true and real sacrifice is not offered to God in the Mass . . . let him be anathema.
>
> If anyone says that the sacrifice of the Mass is only one of praise and thanksgiving; or that it is a mere commemoration of the sacrifice consummated on the Cross, but not one of propitiation; or that it is of profit to him alone who receives; or that it ought not to be offered for the living and the dead, for sins, punishments, satisfactions, and other necessities: let him be anathema.

The Mass is therefore a sacrifice that has its own immediate power of atonement. It is the sacrifice of Christ. It is the sacrifice of the Church. Let us consider these ideas in turn.

The sacrifice of Christ in the Mass was thrust into the forefront of Catholic discussion because the Reformers condemned this entire notion as a flagrant contradiction of Scriptural teaching that Christ made on Calvary a full, perfect, and sufficient sacrifice, which admits no manner of repetition. To that objection, the Council of Trent responded as follows (Session XXII, Ch. 2):

> In this divine sacrifice which is celebrated in the Mass, that same Christ is contained and immolated in an unbloody manner, who on the altar of the Cross "once offered Himself" in a bloody manner [Heb. 9:27]. . . . For it is one and the same Victim, and the same Person who now makes the oblation by the ministry of priests, as He who once offered Himself on the Cross. Only the manner of offering is different. The fruits of that oblation (bloody, that is) are received most abundantly through this unbloody one, so far is the latter from being derogatory in any way to Him.

Theologians do not interpret this passage in precisely the same way. Jungmann understands it to mean: •

> By means of the consecration, the Body immolated on the Cross and the Blood shed thereon are presented to the Father once again at this point of time and space. [Hence, the "different" manner of offering refers to the act of Consecration.] In this re-presentation which Christ fulfills through the priest . . . we have the oblation in which, according to the testimony of Christian tradition, the great high-priest offers himself at every Mass. *This new offering is necessarily also a sacrifice in its own right, but not one that has independent redemptive value, since it is nothing else than a sacramental extension of the one and only redemptive sacrifice on Calvary which the Epistle to the Hebrews had in view.*

In the Mass, then, Christ re-presents to God his one sacrifice through a "different" manner of offering (as Trent phrased it), namely, through the act of Consecration that is performed by his own priests, according to the commission and power

• Vol. I, p. 184; italics mine.

derived from him. It is therefore *his* work, which is offered to God *in this moment*.

But the Mass is also the sacrifice of the Church. Indeed, that thought is far more prominent in the prayers of the Canon than is the sacrifice of Christ. The Fathers and the Scholastics never failed to dwell upon it. Even the Council of Trent, preoccupied as it was with the Reformation attack on the sacrifice of Christ in the Mass, did not allow this point to pass without notice. It declared (Session XXII, Ch. 1) that by his Supper the Lord meant to leave the Church "a visible sacrifice" in order to satisfy the *fundamental requirement of human nature to honor God by sacrificial means.* The oblation of the Church is accomplished by the fact that she participates in the oblation of Christ, which is made present in her midst. Thus, the offering that the Church makes to the glory of God—and which is intrinsically human to make —is the offering of the Saviour's Body and Blood. But note: these sacrificial gifts that are offered up to God arise out of the very gifts of bread and wine that the people have brought as the tokens of their life and self-giving. That fact brings us back to the Consecration; for the action by which this powerful symbol is realized, by which the bread and wine cease to be what they naturally are, by which the offering of the Church is bound up with that of Christ—is again the Consecration. And here we must see that the priest performs a twofold ministry. What he does by the power of Christ, he does also at the bidding of the Church.

FOR FURTHER READING

DACL = *Dictionnaire d'archéologie chrétienne et de Liturgie.* 12 vols, Paris, 1907 *seq.*

PL = *Patrologiae Latina,* edited by J. P. Migne. Paris, 1844-64.

Anton Baumstark, *Missale Romanum.* Eindhoven-Nimwegen o.J., 1929.

Edmund Bishop, *Liturgica Historica.* Oxford, 1918.

Yngve Brilioth, *Eucharistic Faith & Practice.* London, 1956.

F. Cabrol, *The Books of the Latin Liturgy.* London, n.d.

Gregory Dix, *The Shape of the Liturgy.* Westminster, 1947.

L. Duchesne, *Christian Worship: Its Origin and Evolution.* London, 1949.

Adrian Fortescue, *The Mass: A Study of the Roman Liturgy.* London, 1950.

Joseph A. Jungmann, *The Mass of the Roman Rite*. 2 vols. New York, 1951-5.

A. A. King, *The Liturgy of the Roman Church*. Milwaukee, 1957.

Theodor Klausner, *The Western Liturgy*. London, 1932.

William O'Shea, *The Worship of the Church*. Westminster, Maryland, 1957.

J. H. Srawley, *The Early History of the Liturgy*. Cambridge, 1947.

When the priest enters, those present rise and remain standing until he descends to the foot of the altar to begin Mass. They then kneel throughout the Mass except during the two Gospels, when they stand; but usage permits them to sit from the Offertory to the beginning of the Preface, and after the giving of Holy Communion until the reciting of the Communion antiphon.

The priest crosses himself and says aloud:
IN NOMINE PATRIS, ET FILII, ET SPIRITUS SANCTI. Amen.

Introibo ad altare Dei.

The server responds:
℞. Ad Deum qui laetificat juventutem meam.

Then, except in the Masses of Passiontide and of the Dead, the celebrant and server say alternately Psalm 42: 1-5:
Judica me, Deus, et discerne causam meam de gente non sancta: ab homine iniquo et doloso erue me.

℞. Quia tu es, Deus, fortitudo mea: quare me repulisti, et quare tristis incedo, dum affligit me inimicus?

Celebrant: Emitte lucem tuam et veritatem tuam: ipsa me deduxerunt, et adduxerunt in montem sanctum tuum, et in tabernacula tua.

℞. Et introibo ad altare Dei: ad Deum qui laetificat juventutem meam.

C. Confitebor tibi in cithara, Deus, Deus meus: quare tristis es, anima mea, et quare conturbas me?

℞. Spera in Deo, quoniam adhuc confitebor illi: salutare vultus mei, et Deus meus.

C. Gloria Patri, et Filio, et Spiritui Sancto.

℞. Sicut erat in principio, et nunc, et semper: et in saecula saeculorum. Amen.

C. Introibo ad altare Dei.

ORDER OF LOW MASS

When the priest enters, those present rise and remain standing until he descends to the foot of the altar to begin Mass. They then kneel throughout the Mass except during the two Gospels, when they stand; but usage permits them to sit from the Offertory to the beginning of the Preface, and after the giving of Holy Communion until the reciting of the Communion antiphon.

The priest crosses himself and says aloud:
IN THE NAME OF THE FATHER, AND OF THE SON, AND OF THE HOLY GHOST. Amen.

I will go up to the altar of God.

The server responds:
℞. To God, the giver of youth and happiness.

Then, except in the Masses of Passiontide and of the Dead, the celebrant and server say alternately Psalm 42: 1-5:
O God, sustain my cause; give me redress against a race that knows no piety; save me from a treacherous foe and cruel.

℞. Thou, O God, art all my strength, why hast thou cast me off? Why do I go mourning, with enemies pressing me hard?

Celebrant: The light of thy presence, the fulfilment of thy promise, let these be my escort, bringing me safe to thy holy mountain, to the tabernacle where thou dwellest.

℞. There I will go up to the altar of God, the giver of youth and happiness.

C. Thou art my own God, with the harp I hymn thy praise. Soul, why art thou downcast, why art thou all lament?

℞. Wait for God's help; I will not cease to cry out in thankfulness: My champion and my God!

C. Glory be to the Father, and to the Son, and to the Holy Ghost.

℞. As it was in the beginning, is now, and ever shall be, world without end. Amen.

C. I will go up to the altar of God.

℟. Ad Deum qui laetificat juventutem meam.

The priest crosses himself, saying:
C. Adjutorium nostrum in nomine Domini.

℟. Qui fecit caelum et terram.

Then he bows low and says:
Confiteor Deo omnipotenti, beatae Mariae semper Virgini, beato Michaeli Archangelo, beato Joanni Baptistae, sanctis Apostolis Petro et Paulo, omnibus sanctis, et vobis, fratres: quia peccavi nimis cogitatione, verbo, et opere: *He strikes his breast three times, saying:* mea culpa, mea culpa, mea maxima culpa. Ideo precor beatam Mariam semper Virginem, beatum Michaelem Archangelum, beatum Joannem Baptistam, sanctos Apostolos Petrum et Paulum, omnes sanctos, et vos, fratres, orare pro me ad Dominum Deum nostrum.

℟. Misereatur tui omnipotens Deus, et, dimissis peccatis tuis, perducat te ad vitam aeternam.

C. Amen.

The server repeats the Confession:
Confiteor Deo omnipotenti, beatae Mariae semper Virgini, beato Michaeli Archangelo, beato Joanni Baptistae, sanctis Apostolis Petro et Paulo, omnibus sanctis, et tibi, pater: quia peccavi nimis cogitatione, verbo, et opere: *He strikes his breast three times, saying:* mea culpa, mea culpa, mea maxima culpa. Ideo precor beatam Mariam semper Virginem, beatum Michaelem Archangelum, beatum Joannem Baptistam, sanctos Apostolos Petrum et Paulum, omnes sanctos, et te, pater, orare pro me ad Dominum Deum nostrum.

C. Misereatur vestri omnipotens Deus, et, dimissis peccatis vestris, perducat vos ad vitam aeternam.

℟. Amen.

All cross themselves as the priest says:
Indulgentiam, absolutionem, et remissionem peccatorum nostrorum tribuat nobis omnipotens et misericors Dominus.

℟. Amen.

℟. To God, the giver of youth and happiness.

The priest crosses himself, saying:
C. Our help is in the name of the Lord.

℟. Who made heaven and earth.

Then he bows low and says:
I confess to almighty God, to blessed Mary, ever-virgin, to blessed Michael the archangel, to blessed John the Baptist, to the holy apostles Peter and Paul, to all the saints, and to you, brethren, that I have sinned exceedingly in thought, word, and deed; *He strikes his breast three times, saying:* through my fault, through my own fault, through my own most grievous fault. Therefore I beseech the blessed Mary, ever-virgin, blessed Michael the archangel, blessed John the Baptist, the holy apostles Peter and Paul, all the saints, and you, brethren, to pray to the Lord our God for me.

℟. May almighty God have mercy upon you, pardon your sins, and bring you to everlasting life.

C. Amen.

The server repeats the Confession:
I confess to almighty God, to blessed Mary, ever-virgin, to blessed Michael the archangel, to blessed John the Baptist, to the holy apostles Peter and Paul, to all the saints, and to you, father, that I have sinned exceedingly in thought, word, and deed; *He strikes his breast three times, saying:* through my fault, through my own fault, through my own most grievous fault. Therefore I beseech the blessed Mary, ever-virgin, blessed Michael the archangel, blessed John the Baptist, the holy apostles Peter and Paul, all the saints, and you, father, to pray to the Lord our God for me.

C. May almighty God have mercy upon you, pardon your sins, and bring you to everlasting life.

℟. Amen.

All cross themselves as the priest says:
May the almighty and merciful Lord grant us pardon, absolution, and remission of our sins.

℟. Amen.

He bows his head and continues:

C. Deus, tu conversus vivificabis nos.

℟. Et plebs tua laetabitur in te.

C. Ostende nobis, Domine, misericordiam tuam.

℟. Et salutare tuum da nobis.

C. Domine, exaudi orationem meam.

℟. Et clamor meus ad te veniat.

C. Dominus vobiscum.

℟. Et cum spiritu tuo.

C. Oremus.

Then, as he goes up to the altar, he says silently:

Aufer a nobis, quaesumus, Domine, iniquitates nostras: ut ad Sancta sanctorum puris mereamur mentibus introire. Per Christum Dominum nostrum. Amen.

Bowing down, he says:

Oramus te, Domine, per merita sanctorum tuorum, quorum reliquiae hic sunt *He kisses the altar in the middle,* et omnium sanctorum: ut indulgere digneris omnia peccata mea. Amen.

The priest now makes the sign of the cross, and, standing at the Epistle corner, begins the Introit, which will be found in the Mass proper to the day.

When the Introit is finished he returns to the middle of the altar and recites the Kyrie *in alternation with the server.*

C. Kyrie, eleison.

℟. Kyrie, eleison.

C. Kyrie, eleison.

℟. Christe, eleison.

C. Christe, eleison.

℟. Christe, eleison.

C. Kyrie, eleison.

58

The Mass

He bows his head and continues:

C. Thou wilt relent, O God, and bring us to life.

℟. And thy people will rejoice in thee.

C. Show us thy mercy, Lord.

℟. And grant us thy salvation.

C. Lord, heed my prayer.

℟. And let my cry be heard by thee.

C. The Lord be with you.

℟. And with you.

C. Let us pray.

Then, as he goes up to the altar, he says silently:

Take away from us our iniquities, we entreat thee, Lord, so that, with souls made clean, we may be counted worthy to enter the Holy of holies: through Christ our Lord. Amen.

Bowing down, he says:

We pray thee, Lord, by the merits of thy saints whose relics are here *He kisses the altar in the middle,* and of all the saints, that thou wilt deign to pardon all my sins. Amen.

The priest now makes the sign of the cross, and, standing at the Epistle corner, begins the Introit, which will be found in the Mass proper to the day.

When the Introit is finished he returns to the middle of the altar and recites the Kyrie *in alternation with the server.*

C. Lord, have mercy.

℟. Lord, have mercy.

C. Lord, have mercy.

℟. Christ, have mercy.

C. Christ, have mercy.

℟. Christ, have mercy.

C. Lord, have mercy.

℟. Kyrie, eleison.

C. Kyrie, eleison.

The Gloria, which follows, is omitted when the vestments are black or violet; in votive Masses (other than the votive Masses of Angels, and of our Lady when said on a Saturday); and in certain other Masses where its omission is directed in the rubrics.

Gloria in excelsis Deo, et in terra pax hominibus bonae voluntatis. Laudamus te, benedicimus te, adoramus te, glorificamus te, gratias agimus tibi propter magnam gloriam tuam: Domine Deus, Rex caelestis, Deus Pater omnipotens. Domine Fili unigenite, Jesu Christe: Domine Deus, Agnus Dei, Filius Patris: Qui tollis peccata mundi, miserere nobis; qui tollis peccata mundi, suscipe deprecationem nostram; qui sedes ad dexteram Patris, miserere nobis. Quoniam tu solus Sanctus, tu solus Dominus, tu solus Altissimus: Jesu Christe, cum Sancto Spiritu: in gloria Dei Patris. Amen.

The priest turns to the people and says:
C. Dominus vobiscum.

℟. Et cum spiritu tuo.

He then moves to the Epistle side and says: Oremus. *After this he recites one or more Collects, to the first and last of which the server responds:* Amen.

The Epistle is now read, and at its close the server responds:
℟. Deo gratias.

The priest then recites the Gradual (or during Eastertide the Alleluja), and the Tract when one is prescribed. These, the Collect, and the Epistle are to be found in the Mass proper to the day.

The missal is now moved to the Gospel side, while the priest, bowing at the middle of the altar, says silently:

Munda cor meum ac labia mea, omnipotens Deus, qui labia Isaiae prophetae calculo mundasti ignito: ita me tua grata miseratione dignare mundare, ut sanctum Evangelium tuum digne valeam nuntiare. Per Christum Dominium nostrum. Amen.

℟. Lord, have mercy.

C. Lord, have mercy.

The Gloria, which follows, is omitted when the vestments are black or violet; in votive Masses (other than the votive Masses of Angels, and of our Lady when said on a Saturday); and in certain other Masses where its omission is directed in the rubrics.

Glory be to God on high, and on earth peace to men who are God's friends. We praise thee, we bless thee, we adore thee, we glorify thee, we give thee thanks for thy great glory: Lord God, heavenly King, God the almighty Father. Lord Jesus Christ, only-begotten Son; Lord God, Lamb of God, Son of the Father, who takest away the sins of the world, have mercy upon us; thou who takest away the sins of the world, receive our prayer; thou who sittest at the right hand of the Father, have mercy upon us. For thou alone art the Holy One, thou alone art Lord, thou alone art the Most High: Jesus Christ, with the Holy Spirit: in the glory of God the Father. Amen.

The priest turns to the people and says:
C. The Lord be with you.

℟. And with you.

He then moves to the Epistle side and says: Oremus. *After this he recites one or more Collects, to the first and last of which the server responds:* Amen.

The Epistle is now read, and at its close the server responds:
℟. Thanks be to God.

The priest then recites the Gradual (or during Eastertide the Alleluja), *and the Tract when one is prescribed. These, the Collect, and the Epistle are to be found in the Mass proper to the day.*

The missal is now moved to the Gospel side, while the priest, bowing at the middle of the altar, says silently:
Cleanse my heart and my lips, almighty God, who didst cleanse the lips of the prophet Isaias with a live coal. In thy gracious mercy deign so to cleanse me that I may be able to proclaim fitly thy holy Gospel: through Christ our Lord. Amen.

Jube, Domine, benedicere.

Dominus sit in corde meo et in labiis meis: ut digne et competenter annuntiem Evangelium suum. Amen.

Then, facing the book, he says:
C. Dominus vobiscum.

℟. Et cum spiritu tuo.

He now makes the sign of the cross upon the book, and all cross themselves on forehead, lips, and breast, while he says:
Sequentia (*or* Initium) sancti Evangelii secundum N.

℟. Gloria tibi, Domine.

The priest then reads the Gospel, which will be found in the Mass proper to the day; after which the server answers:
℟. Laus tibi, Christe.

The celebrant kisses the book and says:
C. Per evangelica dicta deleantur nostra delicta.

If there is to be a sermon, it is delivered after the reading of the Gospel.

The priest then returns to the middle of the altar and says the Creed, if so directed in the Mass proper to the day.

Credo in unum Deum, Patrem omnipotentem, factorem caeli et terrae, visibilium omnium et invisibilium. Et in unum Dominum Jesum Christum, Filium Dei unigenitum. Et ex Patre natum ante omnia saecula. Deum de Deo, lumen de lumine, Deum verum de Deo vero. Genitum, non factum, consubstantialem Patri: per quem omnia facta sunt. Qui propter nos homines et propter nostram salutem descendit de caelis. *Here he genuflects.* Et incarnatus est de Spiritu Sancto ex Maria Virgine: et homo factus est. Crucifixus etiam pro nobis: sub Pontio Pilato passus, et sepultus est. Et resurrexit tertia die, secundum Scripturas. Et ascendit in caelum: sedet ad dexteram Patris. Et iterum venturus est cum gloria judicare vivos et mortuos: cujus regni non erit finis. Et in Spiritum Sanctum, Dominum et vivificantem: qui ex Patre, Filioque procedit. Qui cum Patre et Filio simul adoratur, et

Lord, grant a blessing.

The Lord be in my heart and on my lips, so that I may fitly and worthily proclaim his Gospel. Amen.

Then, facing the book, he says:
C. The Lord be with you.

℞. And with you.

He now makes the sign of the cross upon the book, and all cross themselves on forehead, lips, and breast while he says:
A passage from *(or* The beginning of*)* the holy Gospel according to *N*.

℞. Glory to thee, Lord.

The priest then reads the Gospel, which will be found in the Mass proper to the day; after which the server answers:
℞. Praise to thee, Christ.

The celebrant kisses the book and says:
C. Through the Gospel words may our sins be wiped away.

If there is to be a sermon, it is delivered after the reading of the Gospel.

The priest then returns to the middle of the altar and says the Creed, if so directed in the Mass proper to the day.
I believe in one God, the almighty Father, maker of heaven and earth, maker of all things visible and invisible. I believe in one Lord Jesus Christ, only-begotten Son of God, born of the Father before time began; God from God, light from light, true God from true God; begotten, not made, one in essence with the Father, and through whom all things were made. For us men, and for our salvation *(here all genuflect)*, he came down from heaven, took flesh of the Virgin Mary by the action of the Holy Spirit, and was made man. For our sake too, under Pontius Pilate, he was crucified, suffered death, and was buried. And the third day he rose from the dead, as the scriptures had foretold. And he ascended to heaven where he sits at the right hand of the Father. He will come again in glory to judge the living and the dead; and his reign will have no end. I believe too in the Holy Spirit, Lord and life-giver, who proceeds from the Father and the Son; who together with the Father and the Son is adored and glorified;

conglorificatur: qui locutus est per Prophetas. Et unam sanctam catholicam et apostolicam Ecclesiam. Confiteor unum baptisma in remissionem peccatorum. Et exspecto ressurectionem mortuorum. Et vitam venturi saeculi. Amen.

The priest turns to the people and says:
C. Dominus vobiscum.

R̸. Et cum spiritu tuo.

C. Oremus.

He then recites the Offertory, which is to be found in the Mass proper to the day.

He now takes the paten with the host, which he offers up, saying:

Suscipe, sancte Pater, omnipotens aeterne Deus, hanc immaculatam hostiam, quam ego indignus famulus tuus offero tibi Deo meo vivo et vero, pro innumerabilibus peccatis, et offensionibus, et negligentiis meis, et pro omnibus circumstantibus, sed et pro omnibus fidelibus christianis vivis atque defunctis: ut mihi et illis proficiat ad salutem in vitam aeternam. Amen.

Moving to the Epistle side, the priest now pours wine and water into the chalice. He blesses the water, saying:

Deus, qui humanae substantiae dignitatem mirabiliter condidisti, et mirabilius reformasti: da nobis per hujus aquae et vini mysterium ejus divinitatis esse consortes, qui humanitatis nostrae fieri dignatus est particeps, Jesus Christus, Filius tuus, Dominus noster: Qui tecum vivit et regnat in unitate Spiritus Sancti Deus: per omnia saecula saeculorum. Amen.

He returns to the middle of the altar and offers up the chalice, saying:

Offerimus tibi, Domine, calicem salutaris, tuam deprecantes clementiam: ut in conspectu divinae majestatis tuae pro nostra et totius mundi salute cum odore suavitatis ascendat. Amen.

Bowing slightly, he continues:

In spiritu humilitatis et in animo contrito suscipiamur a te, Domine: et sic fiat sacrificium nostrum in conspectu tuo hodie, ut placeat tibi, Domine Deus.

who spoke through the prophets. And I believe in one holy, catholic, and apostolic Church. I acknowledge one baptism for the remission of sins. And I look forward to the resurrection of the dead, and the life of the world to come. Amen.

The priest turns to the people and says:

C. The Lord be with you.

℞. And with you.

C. Let us pray.

He then recites the Offertory, which is to be found in the Mass proper to the day.

He now takes the paten with the host, which he offers up, saying:

Holy Father, almighty, everlasting God, accept this unblemished sacrificial offering, which I, thy unworthy servant, make to thee, my living and true God, for my countless sins, offences, and neglects, and on behalf of all who are present here; likewise for all believing Christians, living and dead. Accept it for their good and mine, so that it may save us and bring us to everlasting life. Amen.

Moving to the Epistle side, the priest now pours wine and water into the chalice. He blesses the water, saying:

O God, by whom the dignity of human nature was wondrously established and yet more wondrously restored, grant that through the sacramental use of this water and wine we may have fellowship in the Godhead of him who deigned to share our manhood, Jesus Christ, thy Son, our Lord, who is God, living and reigning with thee in the unity of the Holy Spirit, for ever and ever. Amen.

He returns to the middle of the altar and offers up the chalice, saying:

We offer thee, Lord, the chalice of salvation, entreating thy mercy that our offering may ascend with a sweet fragrance in the presence of thy divine majesty for our salvation and for that of all the world. Amen.

Bowing slightly, he continues:

Humbled in spirit and contrite of heart, may we find favour with thee, Lord, and may our sacrifice be so offered in thy sight this day that it may please thee, Lord our God.

He then stands erect and invokes the Holy Spirit, making the sign of the cross over the bread and wine:

Veni, sanctificator, omnipotens aeterne Deus: et benedic hoc sacrificium, tuo sancto nomini praeparatum.

The priest now goes to the Epistle side, where he washes his hands, reciting Psalm 25: 6-12:

Lavabo inter innocentes manus meas et circumdabo altare tuum, Domine, ut audiam vocem laudis, et enarrem universa mirabilia tua. Domine, dilexi decorem domus tuae, et locum habitationis gloriae tuae. Ne perdas cum impiis, Deus, animam meam, et cum viris sanguinum vitam meam; in quorum manibus iniquitates sunt, dextera eorum repleta est muneribus. Ego autem in innocentia mea ingressus sum; redime me, et miserere mei. Pes meus stetit in directo in ecclesiis benedicam te, Domine.

The Gloria Patri *is omitted in the Masses of Passiontide and of the Dead.*

Gloria Patri, et Filio, et Spiritui Sancto.
Sicut erat in principio, et nunc, et semper, et in saecula, saeculorum. Amen.

Then, returning to the middle of the altar, the priest says:

Suscipe, sancta Trinitas, hanc oblationem, quam tibi offerimus ob memoriam passionis, resurrectionis, et ascensionis Jesu Christi, Domini nostri: et in honorem beatae Mariae semper Virginis, et beati Joannis Baptistae, et sanctorum Apostolorum Petri et Pauli, et istorum, et omnium sanctorum: ut illis proficiat ad honorem, nobis autem ad salutem: et illi pro nobis intercedere dignentur in caelis, quorum memoriam agimus in terris. Per eundem Christum Dominum nostrum. Amen.

The priest then asks the prayers of the people, turning towards them as he says the first two words aloud, then facing the altar:

Orate, fratres: ut meum ac vestrum sacrificium acceptabile fiat apud Deum Patrem omnipotentem.

℟. Suscipiat Dominus sacrificium de manibus tuis ad laudem et gloriam nominis sui, ad utilitatem quoque nostram, totiusque Ecclesiae suae sanctae.

He then stands erect and invokes the Holy Spirit, making the sign of the cross over the bread and wine:

Come, thou sanctifier, almighty, everlasting God, and bless these sacrificial gifts, prepared for the glory of thy holy name.

The priest now goes to the Epistle side, where he washes his hands, reciting Psalm 25: 6-12:

With the pure in heart I will wash my hands clean, and take my place among them at thy altar, Lord, listening there to the sound of thy praises, telling the story of all thy wonderful deeds. How well, Lord, I love thy house in its beauty, the place where thy own glory dwells! Lord, never count this soul for lost with the wicked, this life among the bloodthirsty: hands ever stained with guilt, palms ever itching for a bribe! Be it mine to guide my steps clear of wrong: deliver me in thy mercy. My feet are set on firm ground; where thy people gather, Lord, I will join in blessing thy name.

The Gloria Patri *is omitted in the Masses of Passiontide and of the Dead.*

Glory be to the Father, and to the Son, and to the Holy Ghost. As it was in the beginning, is now, and ever shall be, world without end. Amen.

Then, returning to the middle of the altar, the priest says:

Holy Trinity, accept the offering we here make to thee in memory of the passion, resurrection, and ascension of our Lord Jesus Christ; in honour, too, of blessed Mary, ever-virgin, of blessed John the Baptist, of the holy apostles Peter and Paul, of the Martyrs whose relics are here, and of all the saints. To them let it bring honour, to us salvation; and may they whom we are commemorating on earth graciously plead for us in heaven: through the same Christ our Lord. Amen.

The priest then asks the prayers of the people, turning towards them as he says the first two words aloud, then facing the altar:

Pray, brethren, that my sacrifice and yours may find acceptance with God the almighty Father.

℞. May the Lord accept the sacrifice at your hands, to the praise and glory of his name, for our welfare also, and that of all his holy Church.

C. Amen.

He now says one or more Secret prayers. Their number and order are those of the Collects. At the end of the last he says aloud:

C. Per omnia saecula saeculorum.

℟. Amen.

He then begins the Preface.

The Preface to the Canon

The celebrant, with hands laid upon the altar, says or chants:
C. Dominus vobiscum.

℟. Et cum spiritu tuo.

C. Sursum corda.

℟. Habemus ad Dominum.

C. Gratias agamus Domino Deo nostro.

℟. Dignum et justum est.

Any special Preface prescribed in the Mass proper to the day will be found in the section of special Prefaces, pp. 733-50 [The Missal in Latin and English, Westminster: Newman Press, 1959]. On Sundays which have no special Preface that of the Holy Trinity is said, and on weekdays, unless otherwise directed, the Common Preface.

PREFACE OF THE HOLY TRINITY

Vere dignum et justum est, aequum et salutare, nos tibi semper et ubique gratias agere: Domine, sancte Pater, omnipotens aeterne Deus. Qui cum unigenito Filio tuo, et Spiritu Sancto, unus es Deus, unus es Dominus: non in unius singularitate personae, sed in unius Trinitate substantiae. Quod enim de tua gloria, revelante te, credimus, hoc de Filio tuo, hoc de Spiritu Sancto, sine differentia discretionis sentimus. Ut in confessione verae sempiternaeque Deitatis, et in personis proprietas, et in essentia unitas, et in majestate adoretur aequalitas. Quam laudant Angeli, atque Archangeli, Cherubim

C. Amen.

He now says one or more Secret prayers. Their number and order are those of the Collects. At the end of the last he says aloud:

C. For ever and ever.

℟. Amen.

He then begins the Preface.

The Preface to the Canon

The celebrant, with hands laid upon the altar, says or chants:
C. The Lord be with you.

℟. And with you.

C. Let us lift up our hearts.

℟. We lift them up to the Lord.

C. Let us give thanks to the Lord our God.

℟. That is just and fitting.

Any special Preface prescribed in the Mass proper to the day will be found in the section of special Prefaces, pp. 733-50 [The Missal in Latin and English, Westminster: Newman Press, 1959]. On Sundays which have no special Preface that of the Holy Trinity is said, and on weekdays, unless otherwise directed, the Common Preface.

PREFACE OF THE HOLY TRINITY

Just it is indeed and fitting, right, and for our lasting good, that we should always and everywhere give thanks to thee, Lord, holy Father, almighty and eternal God; who with thy only-begotten Son and the Holy Ghost art one God, one Lord, not one as being a single person, but three Persons in one essence. Whatsoever by thy revelation we believe touching thy glory, that too we hold, without difference or distinction, of thy Son, and also of the Holy Spirit, so that in acknowledging the true, eternal Godhead, we adore in it each several Person, and yet a unity of essence, and a co-equal majesty; in praise of which the Angels and Archangels,

quoque ac Seraphim: qui non cessant clamare quotidie, una voce dicentes:

•

THE COMMON PREFACE

Vere dignum et justum est, aequum et salutare, nos tibi semper et ubique gratias agere: Domine, sancte Pater, omnipotens aeterne Deus: per Christum Dominum nostrum. Per quem majestatem tuam laudant Angeli, adorant Dominationes, tremunt Potestates. Caeli caelorumque Virtutes ac beata Seraphim socia exsultatione concelebrant. Cum quibus et nostras voces ut admitti jubeas, deprecamur, supplici confessione dicentes:

•

Here the bell is rung thrice.

Sanctus, Sanctus Sanctus Dominus Deus Sabaoth. Pleni sunt caeli et terra gloria tua. Hosanna in excelsis.
Benedictus qui venit in nomine Domini.
Hosanna in excelsis.

the Cherubim too and the Seraphim, lift up their endless
hymn, day by day with one voice singing:

•

THE COMMON PREFACE

Just it is indeed and fitting, right, and for our lasting good,
that we should always and everywhere give thanks to thee,
Lord, holy Father, almighty and eternal God, through Christ
our Lord. It is through him that thy majesty is praised by
Angels, adored by Dominations, feared by Powers; through
him that the heavens and the celestial Virtues join with the
blessed Seraphim in one glad hymn of praise. We pray thee
let our voices blend with theirs as we humbly praise thee,
singing:

•

Here the bell is rung thrice.

Holy, holy, holy art thou, Lord God of hosts. Thy glory fills
all heaven and earth. Hosanna in high heaven! Blessed be he
who is coming in the name of the Lord. Hosanna in high
heaven!

CANON OF THE MASS

The celebrant, bowing low over the altar, says silently:

Te igitur, clementissime Pater, per Jesum Christum, Filium tuum, Dominum nostrum, supplices rogamus ac petimus uti accepta habeas, et benedicas, haec dona, haec munera, haec sancta sacrificia illibata, in primis, quae tibi offerimus pro Ecclesia tua sancta catholica: quam pacificare, custodire, adunare, et regere digneris toto orbe terrarum: una cum famulo tuo Papa nostro N. et Antistite nostro N. et omnibus orthodoxis atque catholicae et apostolicae fidei cultoribus.

Memento, Domine, famulorum famularumque tuarum N. et N. (*here the celebrant makes silent mention of those for whom he wishes to pray*), et omnium circumstantium, quorum tibi fides cognita est et nota devotio, pro quibus tibi offerimus: vel qui tibi offerunt hoc sacrificium laudis, pro se suisque omnibus: pro redemptione animarum suarum, pro spe salutis et incolumitatis suae: tibique reddunt vota sua aeterno Deo, vivo et vero.

Communicantes, et memoriam venerantes, in primis gloriosae semper Virginis Mariae, Genitricis Dei et Domini nostri Jesu Christi: sed et beatorum Apostolorum ac Martyrum tuorum, Petri et Pauli, Andreae, Jacobi, Joannis, Thomae, Jacobi, Philippi, Bartholomaei, Matthaei, Simonis, et Thaddaei: Lini, Cleti, Clementis, Xysti, Cornelii, Cypriani, Laurentii, Chrysogoni, Joannis et Pauli, Cosmae et Damiani: et omnium Sanctorum tuorum; quorum meritis precibusque concedas, ut in omnibus protectionis tuae muniamur auxilio. Per eundem Christum Dominum nostrum. Amen.

The bell is rung once as the celebrant spreads his hands over the bread and wine. He continues:

Hanc igitur oblationem servitutis nostrae, sed et cunctae familiae tuae, quaesumus, Domine, ut placatus accipias: diesque nostros in tua pace disponas, atque ab aeterna damnatione nos eripi, et in electorum tuorum jubeas grege numerari. Per Christum Dominum nostrum. Amen.

Quam oblationem tu, Deus, in omnibus, quaesumus, benedictam, adscriptam, ratam, rationabilem, acceptabilemque facere

CANON OF THE MASS

The celebrant, bowing low over the altar, says silently:

And so, through Jesus Christ, thy Son, our Lord, we humbly pray and beseech thee, most gracious Father, to accept and bless these offerings, these oblations, these holy, unblemished sacrificial gifts. We offer them to thee in the first place for thy holy Catholic Church, praying that thou wilt be pleased to keep and guide her in peace and unity throughout the world; together with thy servant our Pope N., and N. our Bishop, and all who believe and foster the true Catholic and Apostolic faith.

Remember, Lord, thy servants N. and N. (*here the celebrant makes silent mention of those for whom he wishes to pray*), and all here present. Their faith and devotion are known to thee. On their behalf we offer, and they too offer, this sacrifice in praise of thee, for themselves and for all who are theirs, for the redemption of their souls, for the hope of safety and salvation, paying homage to thee, their living, true, eternal God.

United in the same holy fellowship we reverence the memory, first, of the glorious ever-virgin Mary, Mother of our God and Lord Jesus Christ, and likewise that of thy blessed apostles and martyrs Peter and Paul, Andrew, James, John, Thomas, James, Philip, Bartholomew, Matthew, Simon, and Jude: of Linus, Cletus, Clement, Sixtus, Cornelius, Cyprian, Laurence, Chrysogonus, John and Paul, Cosmas and Damian; and of all thy saints. Grant for the sake of their merits and prayers that in all things we may be guarded and helped by thy protection: through the same Christ our Lord. Amen.

The bell is rung once as the celebrant spreads his hands over the bread and wine. He continues:

And so, Lord, we thy servants, and with us thy whole household, make this peace-offering which we entreat thee to accept. Order our days in thy peace, and command that we be rescued from eternal damnation and numbered with the flock of thy elect: through Christ our Lord. Amen.

We pray thee, God, be pleased to make this offering wholly blessed, a thing consecrated and approved, worthy of the human spirit and of thy acceptance, so that it may become

digneris: ut nobis Corpus et Sanguis fiat dilectissimi Filii tui, Domini nostri Jesu Christi.

He takes the host in his hands and consecrates it, saying:

Qui pridie quam pateretur, accepit panem in sanctas ac venerabiles manus suas, et elevatis oculis in caelum ad te Deum, Patrem suum omnipotentem, tibi gratias agens, benedixit, fregit, deditque discipulis suis, dicens: Accipite, et manducate ex hoc omnes:

HOC EST ENIM CORPUS MEUM.

The bell is rung thrice as he genuflects, shows the Sacred Host to the people, and genuflects again.

He now consecrates the wine, saying:

Simili modo postquam coenatum est, accipiens et hunc praeclarum Calicem in sanctas ac venerabiles manus suas: item tibi gratias agens, benedixit, deditque discipulis suis, dicens: Accipite, et bibite ex eo omnes.

HIC EST ENIM CALIX SANGUINIS MEI,
NOVI ET AETERNI TESTAMENTI
:MYSTERIUM FIDEI:
QUI PRO VOBIS ET PRO MULTIS EFFUNDETUR
IN REMISSIONEM PECCATORUM.

He genuflects, saying:

Haec quotiescumque feceritis, in mei memoriam facietis.

He then shows the chalice to the people, genuflecting after doing so. The bell is again rung thrice. He continues:

Unde et memores, Domine, nos servi tui, sed et plebs tua sancta, ejusdem Christi Filii tui, Domini nostri, tam beatae passionis, necnon et ab inferis resurrectionis, sed et in caelos gloriosae ascensionis: offerimus praeclarae majestati tuae de tuis donis ac datis, hostiam puram, hostiam sanctam, hostiam immaculatam, Panem sanctum vitae aeternae, et Calicem salutis perpetuae.

Supra quae propitio ac sereno vultu respicere digneris: et accepta habere, sicuti accepta habere dignatus es munera pueri tui justi Abel, et sacrificium Patriarchae nostri Abrahae: et quod tibi obtulit summus sacerdos tuus Melchisedech, sanctum sacrificium, immaculatam hostiam.

for us the Body and Blood of thy dearly beloved Son, our Lord Jesus Christ.

He takes the host in his hands and consecrates it, saying:

He, on the day before he suffered death, took bread into his holy and worshipful hands, and lifting up his eyes to thee, God, his almighty Father in heaven, and giving thanks to thee, he blessed it, broke it, and gave it to his disciples, saying: Take, all of you, and eat of this,

FOR THIS IS MY BODY.

The bell is rung thrice as he genuflects, shows the Sacred Host to the people, and genuflects again.

He now consecrates the wine, saying:

In like manner, when he had supped, taking also this goodly cup into his holy and worshipful hands, and again giving thanks to thee, he blessed it, and gave it to his disciples, saying: Take, all of you, and drink of this,

FOR THIS IS THE CHALICE OF MY BLOOD,
OF THE NEW AND EVERLASTING COVENANT,
A MYSTERY OF FAITH.
IT SHALL BE SHED FOR YOU AND MANY OTHERS,
SO THAT SINS MAY BE FORGIVEN.

He genuflects, saying:

Whenever you shall do these things, you shall do them in memory of me.

He then shows the chalice to the people, genuflecting after doing so. The bell is again rung thrice. He continues:

Calling therefore to mind the blessed Passion of this same Christ, thy Son, our Lord, and also his resurrection from the grave, and glorious ascension into heaven, we thy servants, Lord, and with us all thy holy people, offer to thy sovereign majesty, out of the gifts thou hast bestowed upon us, a sacrifice that is pure, holy, and unblemished, the sacred Bread of everlasting life, and the Cup of eternal salvation.

Deign to regard them with a favourable and gracious countenance, and to accept them as it pleased thee to accept the offerings of thy servant Abel the Just, and the sacrifice of our father Abraham, and that which thy great priest Melchisedech sacrificed to thee, a holy offering, a victim without blemish.

Bowing low over the altar, he says:

Supplices te rogamus, omnipotens Deus: jube haec perferri per manus sancti Angeli tui in sublime altare tuum, in conspectu divinae majestatis tuae: ut quotquot ex hac altaris participatione sacrosanctum Filii tui Corpus et Sanguinem sumpserimus, omni benedictione caelesti et gratia repleamur. Per eundem Christum Dominum nostrum. Amen.

Memento etiam, Domine, famulorum famularumque tuarum *N*. et *N*. qui nos praecesserunt cum signo fidei, et dormiunt in somno pacis. *Here the celebrant makes silent mention of those dead for whom he wishes to pray.* Ipsis, Domine, et omnibus in Christo quiescentibus, locum refrigerii, lucis, et pacis, ut indulgeas, deprecamur. Per eundem Christum Dominum nostrum. Amen.

Striking his breast, and raising his voice as he says the first three words, he continues:

Nobis quoque peccatoribus famulis tuis, de multitudine miserationum tuarum sperantibus, partem aliquam et societatem donare digneris, cum tuis sanctis Apostolis et Martyribus: cum Joanne, Stephano, Matthia, Barnaba, Ignatio, Alexandro, Marcellino, Petro, Felicitate, Perpetua, Agatha, Lucia, Agnete, Caecilia, Anastasia, et omnibus Sanctis tuis: intra quorum nos consortium, non aestimator meriti, sed veniae, quaesumus, largitor admitte. Per Christum Dominum nostrum.

Per quem haec omnia, Domine, semper bona creas, sanctificas, vivificas, benedicis, et praestas nobis.

The celebrant makes the sign of the cross thrice over the chalice, with the Sacred Host, and twice between the chalice and himself, then raises the Host and chalice slightly, saying meanwhile:

Per ipsum, et cum ipso, et in ipso, est tibi Deo Patri omnipotenti, in unitate Spiritus Sancti, omnis honor et gloria.

Replacing the Host and chalice upon the altar, he then chants or says aloud:

C. Per omnia saecula saeculorum. ℟. Amen.

Oremus. Praeceptis salutaribus moniti, et divina institutione formati, audemus dicere:

Bowing low over the altar, he says:

Humbly we ask it of thee, God almighty: bid these things be carried by the hands of thy holy angel up to thy altar on high, into the presence of thy divine majesty. And may those of us who by taking part in the sacrifice of this altar shall have received the sacred Body and Blood of thy Son, be filled with every grace and heavenly blessing: through the same Christ our Lord. Amen.

Remember also, Lord, thy servants N. and N., who have gone before us with the sign of faith and sleep the sleep of peace. *Here the celebrant makes silent mention of those dead for whom he wishes to pray.* To them, Lord, and to all who rest in Christ, grant, we entreat thee, a place of cool repose, of light and peace: through the same Christ our Lord. Amen.

Striking his breast, and raising his voice as he says the first three words, he continues:

To us also, thy sinful servants, who put our trust in thy countless acts of mercy, deign to grant some share and fellowship with thy holy apostles and martyrs: with John, Stephen, Matthias, Barnabas, Ignatius, Alexander, Marcellinus, Peter, Felicity, Perpetua, Agatha, Lucy, Agnes, Cecily, Anastasia, and all thy saints. Into their company we pray thee to admit us, not weighing our deserts, but freely granting us forgiveness: through Christ our Lord.

It is ever through him that all these good gifts, created so by thee, Lord, are by thee sanctified, endowed with life, blessed, and bestowed upon us.

The celebrant makes the sign of the cross thrice over the chalice with the Sacred Host, and twice between the chalice and himself, then raises the Host and chalice slightly, saying meanwhile:

Through him, and with him, and in him, thou, God, almighty Father, in the unity of the Holy Spirit, hast all honour and glory,

Replacing the Host and chalice upon the altar, he then chants or says aloud:

C. World without end. ℟. Amen.

Let us pray. Urged by our Saviour's bidding, and schooled by his divine ordinance, we make bold to say:

Pater noster, qui es in caelis, sanctificetur nomen tuum. Adveniat regnum tuum. Fiat voluntas tua, sicut in caelo, et in terra. Panem nostrum quotidianum da nobis hodie. Et dimitte nobis debita nostra, sicut et nos dimittimus debitoribus nostris. Et ne nos inducas in tentationem:

℞. Sed libera nos a malo.

C. silently: Amen.

Taking the paten in his right hand, he continues silently:
Libera nos, quaesumus, Domine, ab omnibus malis, praeteritis, praesentibus, et futuris: et intercedente beata et gloriosa semper Virgine Dei Genitrice Maria, cum beatis Apostolis tuis Petro et Paulo, atque Andrea, et omnibus Sanctis (*he crosses himself with the paten and kisses it*), da propitius pacem in diebus nostris: ut ope misericordiae tuae adjuti, et a peccato simus semper liberi, et ab omni perturbatione securi.

He then breaks the Sacred Host over the chalice, saying:
Per eundem Dominum nostrum Jesum Christum, Filium tuum, qui tecum vivit et regnat in unitate Spiritus Sancti Deus.

He concludes the prayer aloud:
C. Per omnia saecula saeculorum.

℞. Amen.

He makes the sign of the Cross thrice with a particle of the Sacred Host over the chalice, chanting or saying aloud:
C. Pax Domini sit semper vobiscum.

℞. Et cum spiritu tuo.

Then he drops the particle into the chalice and continues silently:

Haec commixtio, et consecratio Corporis et Sanguinis Domini nostri Jesu Christi, fiat accipientibus nobis in vitam aeternam. Amen.

He strikes his breast three times as he says aloud:
Agnus Dei, qui tollis peccata mundi:
miserere nobis.

78

Our Father, who art in heaven, hallowed be thy name. Thy kingdom come. Thy will be done, on earth as it is in heaven. Give us this day our daily bread. And forgive us our trespasses, as we forgive those who trespass against us. And lead us not into temptation:

℟. But deliver us from evil.

C. silently: Amen.

Taking the paten in his right hand, he continues silently:
Deliver us, we pray thee, Lord, from every evil, past, present, and to come, and at the intercession of the blessed and glorious ever-virgin Mary, Mother of God, of thy blessed apostles Peter and Paul, of Andrew, and of all the saints (*he crosses himself with the paten and kisses it*), be pleased to grant peace in our time, so that with the help of thy compassion we may be ever free from sin and safe from all disquiet.

He then breaks the Sacred Host over the chalice, saying:
Through the same Jesus Christ, thy Son, our Lord, who is God, living and reigning with thee in the unity of the Holy Spirit:

He concludes the prayer aloud:
C. World without end.

℟. Amen.

He makes the sign of the Cross thrice with a particle of the Sacred Host over the chalice, chanting or saying aloud:
C. The peace of the Lord be always with you.

℟. And with you.

Then he drops the particle into the chalice and continues silently:

May this sacramental mingling of the Body and Blood of our Lord Jesus Christ be for us who receive it a source of eternal life. Amen.

He strikes his breast three times as he says aloud:
Lamb of God, who takest away the sins of the world, have mercy on us.

Agnus Dei, qui tollis peccata mundi:
miserere nobis.
Agnus Dei, qui tollis peccata mundi:
dona nobis pacem.

After this he says silently:
Domine Jesu Christe, qui dixisti Apostolis tuis: Pacem re-
linquo vobis, pacem meam do vobis: ne respicias peccata mea,
sed fidem Ecclesiae tuae: eamque secundum voluntatem
tuam pacificare et coadunare digneris: Qui vivis et regnas
Deus per omnia saecula saeculorum. Amen.

•

*At Solemn Mass the kiss of peace is given here. The celebrant
gives the kiss to the deacon and says:*
Pax tecum.

The deacon responds:
℟. Et cum spiritu tuo.

*Next the deacon gives the kiss, with the same salutation and
response, to the subdeacon, who passes it on to the clergy
in choir, who in turn give it to one another.*

•

The celebrant now says:
Domine Jesu Christe, Fili Dei vivi, qui ex voluntate Patris,
cooperante Spiritu Sancto, per mortem tuam mundum vivi-
ficasti: libera me per hoc sacrosanctum Corpus et Sanguinem
tuum ab omnibus iniquitatibus meis, et universis malis: et fac
me tuis semper inhaerere mandatis, et a te nunquam separari
permittas: Qui cum eodem Deo Patre et Spiritu Sancto vivis
et regnas Deus in saecula saeculorum. Amen.

Perceptio Corporis tui, Domine Jesu Christe, quod ego
indignus sumere praesumo, non mihi proveniat in judicium
et condemnationem: sed pro tua pietate prosit mihi ad tuta-
mentum mentis et corporis, et ad medelam percipiendam:
Qui vivis et regnas cum Deo Patre in unitate Spiritus Sancti
Deus, per omnia saecula saeculorum. Amen.

Panem caelestem accipiam, et nomen Domini invocabo.

Lamb of God, who takest away the sins of the world, have mercy on us.

Lamb of God, who takest away the sins of the world, give us peace.

After this he says silently:

Lord Jesus Christ, who didst say to thy apostles: I leave peace with you; it is my own peace that I give you: look not upon my sins but upon thy Church's faith, and graciously give her peace and unity in accordance with thy will: thou who art God, living and reigning for ever and ever. Amen.

•

At Solemn Mass the kiss of peace is given here. The celebrant gives the kiss to the deacon and says:

Peace be with you.

The deacon responds:

℟. And with you.

Next the deacon gives the kiss, with the same salutation and response, to the subdeacon, who passes it on to the clergy in choir, who in turn give it to one another.

•

The celebrant now says:

Lord Jesus Christ, Son of the living God, who, by the Father's will and the co-operation of the Holy Spirit, didst by thy death bring life to the world, deliver me by this most holy Body and Blood of thine from all my sins and from every evil. Make me always cling to thy commandments, and never allow me to be parted from thee: who with the selfsame God the Father and the Holy Spirit art God, living and reigning for ever and ever. Amen.

Let not the partaking of thy Body, Lord Jesus Christ, which I, unworthy as I am, make bold to receive, turn against me into judgement and damnation, but through thy loving-kindness let it safeguard me, body and soul, and bring me healing: thou who art God, living and reigning with God the Father in the unity of the Holy Spirit, world without end. Amen.

I will take the Bread of Heaven, and will call upon the name of the Lord.

He takes the two pieces of the Sacred Host in his left hand. Then, saying the opening words audibly each time, and striking his breast with his right hand as he does so, he says thrice:

Domine, non sum dignus ut intres sub tectum meum: sed tantum dic verbo, et sanabitur anima mea.

The bell is rung as he says these words, and those of the congregation who are to communicate go to the altar rails.

The celebrant crosses himself with the Sacred Host, saying:

Corpus Domini nostri Jesu Christi custodiat animam meam in vitam aeternam. Amen.

He then receives the Host.

After a short pause the celebrant collects any fragments of the Host that may be on the corporal, and puts them into the chalice, saying:

Quid retribuam Domino pro omnibus quae retribuit mihi? Calicem salutaris accipiam, et nomen Domini invocabo. Laudans invocabo Dominum, et ab inimicis meis salvus ero.

Crossing himself with the chalice, he says:

Sanguis Domini nostri Jesu Christi custodiat animam meam in vitam aeternam. Amen.

He drinks the contents of the chalice.

•

If any wish to communicate, the Confession is now repeated by deacon or server:

Confiteor Deo omnipotenti, beatae Mariae semper Virgini, beato Michaeli Archangelo, beato Joanni Baptistae, sanctis Apostolis Petro et Paulo, omnibus Sanctis, et tibi, pater: quia peccavi nimis cogitatione, verbo, et opere: *He strikes his breast three times, saying:* mea culpa, mea culpa, mea maxima culpa. Ideo precor beatam Mariam semper Virginem, beatum Michaelem Archangelum, beatum Joannem Baptistam, sanctos Apostolos Petrum et Paulum, omnes Sanctos, et te, pater, orare pro me ad Dominum Deum nostrum.

The celebrant turns to the people and says aloud:

He takes the two pieces of the Sacred Host in his left hand. Then, saying the opening words audibly each time, and striking his breast with his right hand as he does so, he says thrice:

Lord, I am not worthy that thou shouldst enter beneath my roof, but say only the word, and my soul will be healed.

The bell is rung as he says these words, and those of the congregation who are to communicate go to the altar rails.

The celebrant crosses himself with the Sacred Host, saying:
The Body of our Lord Jesus Christ preserve my soul for everlasting life. Amen.

He then receives the Host.

After a short pause the celebrant collects any fragments of the Host that may be on the corporal, and puts them into the chalice, saying:
What return shall I make to the Lord for all that he has given me? I will take the chalice of salvation and invoke the name of the Lord. Praised be the Lord! When I invoke his name I shall be secure from my enemies.

Crossing himself with the chalice, he says:
The Blood of our Lord Jesus Christ preserve my soul for everlasting life. Amen.

He drinks the contents of the chalice.

•

If any wish to communicate, the Confession is now repeated by the deacon or server:
I confess to almighty God, to blessed Mary, ever-virgin, to blessed Michael the archangel, to blessed John the Baptist, to the holy apostles Peter and Paul, to all the saints, and to you, father, that I have sinned exceedingly in thought, word, and deed: *He strikes his breast three times, saying:* through my fault, through my own fault, through my own most grievous fault. Therefore I beseech the blessed Mary, ever-virgin, blessed Michael the archangel, blessed John the Baptist, the holy apostles Peter and Paul, all the saints, and you, father, to pray to the Lord our God for me.

The celebrant turns to the people and says aloud:

Misereatur vestri omnipotens Deus, et, dimissis peccatis vestris, perducat vos ad vitam aeternam.

℞. Amen.

All cross themselves as he says:
Indulgentiam, absolutionem, et remissionem peccatorum vestrorum tribuat vobis omnipotens et misericors Dominus.

℞. Amen.

The celebrant, taking the ciborium from the altar, holds up a consecrated Host, and says:
Ecce Agnus Dei, ecce qui tollit peccata mundi.

Then he says three times:
Domine, non sum dignus, ut intres sub tectum meum: sed tantum dic verbo, et sanabitur anima mea.

He then goes to the altar rails and gives Holy Communion, saying to each communicant:
Corpus Domini nostri Jesu Christi custodiat animam tuam in vitam aeternam. Amen.

When all have communicated he returns to the altar and replaces the ciborium in the tabernacle.

•

The congregation may now sit. Wine is poured into the chalice; the celebrant drinks it, and says:
Quod ore sumpsimus, Domine, pura mente capiamus: et de munere temporali fiat nobis remedium sempiternum.

Wine and water are poured into the chalice over the fingers of the celebrant, who dries them with the purificator, saying silently:
Corpus tuum, Domine, quod sumpsi, et Sanguis, quem potavi, adhaereat visceribus meis: et praesta; ut in me non remaneat scelerum macula, quem pura et sancta refecerunt sacramenta: Qui vivis et regnas in saecula saeculorum. Amen.

He then drinks the wine and water, after which, at High Mass, the subdeacon dries the inside of the chalice with the

May almighty God have mercy upon you, pardon your sins, and bring you to everlasting life.

℟. Amen.

All cross themselves as he says:
May the almighty and merciful Lord grant you pardon, absolution, and remission of your sins.

℟. Amen.

The celebrant, taking the ciborium from the altar, holds up a consecrated Host, and says:
Behold the Lamb of God, behold him who takes away the sins of the world.

Then he says three times:
Lord, I am not worthy that thou shouldst enter beneath my roof, but say only the word, and my soul will be healed.

He then goes to the altar rails and gives Holy Communion, saying to each communicant:
The Body of our Lord Jesus Christ preserve your soul for everlasting life. Amen.

When all have communicated he returns to the altar and replaces the ciborium in the tabernacle.

•

The congregation may now sit. Wine is poured into the chalice; the celebrant drinks it, and says:
That which our mouths have taken, Lord, may we possess in purity of heart; and may the gift of the moment become for us an everlasting remedy.

Wine and water are poured into the chalice over the fingers of the celebrant, who dries them with the purificator, saying silently:
May thy Body, Lord, which I have taken, and thy Blood which I have drunk, cleave to every fibre of my being. Grant that no stain of sin may be left in me, now that I am renewed by this pure and holy sacrament; who livest and reignest world without end. Amen.

He then drinks the wine and water, after which, at High Mass, the subdeacon dries the inside of the chalice with the

*purificator. He then lays it across the chalice and places on it
the paten and pall. Then he veils the chalice and takes it
to the credence. If there is no subdeacon the celebrant dries
and veils the chalice and leaves it in the middle of the altar.
The celebrant now goes to the Epistle side and says the Communion antiphon, which will be found in the Mass proper to
the day. Then he goes to the middle of the altar, and, turning
to the people (who at High Mass stand, but at Low Mass
kneel) says or chants:*
C. Dominus vobiscum.

Rℐ. Et cum spiritu tuo.

*After which he reads one or more Postcommunion prayers.
Their number and order are those of the Collects. Before the
first and second of these prayers he says or chants: Oremus;
and at the end of the first and last the server or choir responds: Amen.*

*Coming back to the middle of the altar, the celebrant turns
to the people, and says or chants:*
C. Dominus vobiscum.

Rℐ. Et cum spiritu tuo.

Then, if it is a day upon which the Gloria *has been said, the
deacon turns to the people and chants, or at Low Mass the
celebrant says aloud:*
Ite, missa est.

Rℐ. Deo gratias.

•

In the Masses of Holy Saturday and Easter week the words
alleluja, alleluja, *are added, thus:*
Ite, missa est; alleluja, alleluja.

Rℐ. Deo gratias, alleluja, alleluja.

If the Gloria *has not been said, the deacon or celebrant chants
or says instead:*
Benedicamus Domino.

Rℐ. Deo gratias.

purificator. He then lays it across the chalice and places on it the paten and pall. Then he veils the chalice and takes it to the credence. If there is no subdeacon the celebrant dries and veils the chalice and leaves it in the middle of the altar. The celebrant now goes to the Epistle side and says the Communion antiphon, which will be found in the Mass proper to the day. Then he goes to the middle of the altar, and, turning to the people (who at High Mass stand, but at Low Mass kneel), says or chants:

C. The Lord be with you.

℞. And with you.

After which he reads one or more Postcommunion prayers. Their number and order are those of the Collects. Before the first and second of these prayers he says or chants: Oremus; *and at the end of the first and last the server or choir responds:* Amen.

Coming back to the middle of the altar, the celebrant turns to the people, and says or chants:
C. The Lord be with you.

℞. And with you.

Then, if it is a day upon which the Gloria *has been said, the deacon turns to the people and chants, or at Low Mass the celebrant says aloud:*
Go, this is the dismissal.

℞. Thanks be to God.

•

In the Masses of Holy Saturday and Easter week, the words alleluia, alleluia, *are added, thus:*
Go, this is the dismissal; alleluia, alleluia.

℞. Thanks be to God, alleluia, alleluia.

If the Gloria *has not been said, the deacon or celebrant chants or says instead:*
Let us bless the Lord.

℞. Thanks be to God.

Bowing before the altar, the celebrant says silently:

Placeat tibi, sancta Trinitas, obsequium servitutis meae: et praesta; ut sacrificium, quod oculis tuae majestatis indignus obtuli, tibi sit acceptabile, mihique, et omnibus pro quibus illud obtuli, sit, te miserante, propitiabile: Per Christum Dominum nostrum. Amen.

He kisses the altar, and all kneel as he gives the blessing, saying:

Benedicat vos omnipotens Deus, Pater, et Filius, et Spiritus Sanctus.

℟. Amen.

The congregation rises when, at the Gospel side, he says:
C. Dominus vobiscum.

℟. Et cum spiritu tuo.

He then makes the sign of the cross upon the altar, and all cross themselves on forehead, lips, and breast, as he says:
Initium sancti Evangelii secundum Joannem

or, if the second Gospel is that of a commemoration:
Sequentia sancti Evangelii secundum N.

℟. Gloria tibi, Domine.

He then reads the Gospel, John 1. 1-14:

In principio erat Verbum, et Verbum erat apud Deum, et Deus erat Verbum. Hoc erat in principio apud Deum. Omnia per ipsum facta sunt: et sine ipso factum est nihil, quod factum est: in ipso vita erat, et vita erat lux hominum: et lux in tenebris lucet, et tenebrae eam non comprehenderunt. Fuit homo missus a Deo, cui nomen erat Joannes. Hic venit in testimonium, ut testimonium perhiberet de lumine, ut omnes crederent per illum. Non erat ille lux, sed ut testimonium perhiberet de lumine. Erat lux vera, quae illuminat omnem hominem venientem in hunc mundum. In mundo erat, et mundus per ipsum factus est, et mundus eum non cognovit. In propria venit, et sui eum non receperunt. Quotquot autem receperunt eum, dedit eis potestatem filios Dei fieri, his qui credunt in nomine ejus: qui non ex sanguinibus, neque ex voluntate carnis, neque ex voluntate viri, sed

The Mass

Bowing before the altar, the celebrant says silently:

May the tribute of my humble ministry be pleasing to thee, Holy Trinity. Grant that the sacrifice which I, unworthy as I am, have offered in the presence of thy majesty may be acceptable to thee. Through thy mercy may it bring forgiveness to me and to all for whom I have offered it: through Christ our Lord. Amen.

He kisses the altar, and all kneel as he gives the blessing, saying:

Almighty God bless you: the Father, the Son, and the Holy Ghost.

℟. Amen.

The congregation rises when, at the Gospel side, he says:

C. The Lord be with you.

℟. And with you.

He then makes the sign of the cross upon the altar, and all cross themselves on forehead, lips, and breast, as he says:

The beginning of the holy Gospel according to John

or, if the second Gospel is that of a commemoration:

A passage from the holy Gospel according to N.

℟. Glory to thee, Lord.

He then reads the Gospel, John 1. 1-14:

At the beginning of time the Word already was; and God had the Word abiding with him, and the Word was God. He abode, at the beginning of time, with God. It was through him that all things came into being, and without him came nothing that has come to be. In him there was life, and that life was the light of men. And the light shines in darkness, a darkness which was not able to master it. A man appeared, sent from God, whose name was John. He came for a witness, to bear witness to the light, so that through him all men might learn to believe. He was not the Light; he was sent to bear witness to the light. There is one who enlightens every soul born into the world; he was the true Light. He, through whom the world was made, was in the world, and the world treated him as a stranger. He came to what was his own, and they who were his own gave him no welcome. But

ex Deo nati sunt. *Here all genuflect.* Et Verbum caro factum est, et habitavit in nobis; et vidimus gloriam ejus, gloriam quasi Unigeniti a Patre, plenum gratiae et veritatis.

℟. Deo gratias.

all those who did welcome him he empowered to become the children of God, all those who believe in his name; their birth came, not from human stock, not from nature's will or man's, but from God. *Here all genuflect.* And the Word was made flesh, and came to dwell among us; and we had sight of his glory, glory such as belongs to the Father's only-begotten Son, full of grace and truth.

℟. Thanks be to God.

NOTES

1. Transcribed from *The Missal in Latin and English,* being the text of the *Missale Romanum* with English rubrics and a new translation (Westminster: Newman Press, 1959), pp. 676-720.

IV
MARTIN LUTHER

Formula Missae, 1523
Deutsche Messe, 1526

LUTHER

With Luther in seclusion at the Wartburg, Carlstadt, emboldened by popular excitement, took it upon himself to repair the liturgy at Wittenberg. On Christmas Day, 1521, he appeared in the Castle Church without vestments; and, having explained to the people that faith, rather than confession, was the sole prerequisite to the sacrament, he proceeded to perform a purified Mass, from which the Canon and Elevation had been expunged. Following the Words of Institution, which were read in German, he invited all comers to communicate in both bread and wine, receiving the same by hand. These innovations, which were attended by unseemly demonstrations against the Mass, he repeated on New Year's and the Sunday following, and again on Epiphany. They invited a bolder iconoclasm against the other "idols" that remained in the churches.

Some regulation was brought to these proceedings by the *Ordnung der Stadt Wittenberg·* (January 22, 1522), which was devised by the city fathers and the theologians. The document proposed to remodel the life of Wittenberg along evangelical lines, but in an orderly fashion. Henceforth the Mass was to be celebrated according to Christ's institution; yet the framers of the *Ordnung* did not scruple at any of the features of the fore-Mass—up to the Canon itself, which was specifically proscribed. To administer "the evangelical meal," the priest was directed to proceed immediately with the Consecration and deliver Communion in both kinds into the hands

· Sehling, I, 697-8.

or the mouths of the people, as they wished. To curtail idolatry, only three altars were permitted to remain in each church.

Although Burgomaster Beyer intended to carry out the last provision with decorum, he was anticipated by excited people who presently burst into the Town Church and did away with the "graven images," against which Carlstadt had been preaching. Such tumult, coupled with other untoward circumstances, brought the return of Luther on March 6. Taking to the pulpit on the following Sunday, he commenced a series of eight sermons on behalf of moderation. First of all, he required to know what had happened to the love of these innovators who had pursued rash and impatient actions without regard for the conscience of their weaker brethren. He reminded them that the true way of reformation—a reform that reaches to the heart of man—is not pursued by force, but by the proclamation of the Word, which accomplishes everything. He feared that Scripture was being turned into a new law, whereas one must distinguish in Scripture between that which is commanded and that which is left free; and he himself would place in the latter category images, pictures, and fasting. Not even Communion in both kinds could be made a matter of compulsion.• Moreover, he detected a foolish biblicism in the assertion (Carlstadt's?) that the words, "take, eat," required men to seize the sacrament in their hands; and, while he conceded that the people had done no wrong in touching the consecrated elements, he reminded them of the "universal custom" of receiving the same directly from the hands of the priest.

Luther's conservatism was plain in these sermons. And, according to Brilioth, that conservatism underlay "the fact that he was never really interested in liturgical forms; to him they were indifferent things wherein a man might be content to conform to established usage." Brilioth also chided Luther for scolding the Wittenbergers when they only meant to execute the reforms that he himself had laid down. Had he not proposed a German Mass in 1519;•• had he not assailed Rome, in the *Babylonian Captivity*, for withdrawing the cup from the laity, for the doctrine of transubstantiation, and for the sacrifice of the Mass; and had he not lately rehearsed

• Cf. *Receiving Both Kinds in the Sacrament,* 1522; *Luther's Works,* 36: 231ff.
•• *A Treatise on the New Testament; Luther's Works,* 35: 90.

these same complaints in a treatise on *The Misuse of the Mass?*

Pelikan has taken another view of the matter: If Luther regarded liturgical forms as indifferent things (*adiaphora*), he was by no means indifferent to liturgical forms. Neither the psychological nature of man, nor the spiritual immaturity of Christians, nor the manner of God's own self-disclosure in the Incarnate One permitted such indifference. Pelikan has shown that Luther's conservatism pertained to the "Catholic substance" of his liturgical thought. If he looked askance at the innovators, it was because he understood that the liturgy provided order and stability, within which worship and teaching were possible.• Nor did he find much virtue in rash changes that wrenched away the staves of the weaker brethren. Such innovations were an abuse of Christian liberty, to say nothing of love. Indeed, those symbolic actions that properly reinforced the spoken and visible Word—the Elevation being a case in point—were not to be despised nor idly thrown away. Luther also prized the historical dimension of the liturgy that preserved the continuity with the faithful of all ages. He commended the *de tempore* principle of worship, which saved the church from mere subjectivity but grounded its life upon those objective events in the history of redemption that the Church Year unfolds. Finally, he resisted the notion that, tradition having been cast down, a liturgy could be evolved out of the Bible. Scripture was the norm of worship, but no rubric-book, no new Leviticus. In *Deutsche Messe* he did not hesitate to paraphrase the very prayer of the Lord.

Luther's first encounter with the improvisers momentarily stayed his own initiative in the work of revision. Meanwhile, certain impatient ministers tried their hand at a German liturgy. The first was Kaspar Kantz, prior of the Carmelite brothers at Nördlingen, who published an "Evangelical Mass" in 1522. The following year a German "Mass" appeared at Allstedt. It was the work of the spiritualist and revolutionary reformer, Thomas Müntzer, whom Luther taunted as having "swallowed the Holy Ghost, feathers and all." Yet, Müntzer's enthusiasm was scarcely manifest in the richness and variety of his conservative rite. Although these liturgies•• kept to the

• Cf. *Exhortation to the Christians in Livonia*, 1525; *Works of Martin Luther*, 6: 145-8.
•• The texts are in Smend, pp. 72-8; 94-111.

structure of the Latin Mass, both entertained drastic reductions to the Canon.

In the spring of 1523, Luther himself issued instructions *Concerning the Ordering of Divine Worship in the Congregation.* Beginning with typical conservatism, he declared that the liturgy and the preaching office both had "a high Christian origin"; and although they had been corrupted by "tyrants" and "hypocrites," both deserved to be restored rather than abolished. Presently his conservatism deferred to the evangelical side of his liturgical thought. In the Latin rite, he detected certain grave abuses, of which the suppression of the Word was the most critical of all. In lieu of the Word, "a host of unchristian fables and lies" were imported into the liturgy. And, as a result of these things, worship had been transformed from a gracious gift of God into a good work of man. To correct such abuses, Luther proposed that Christians should not assemble for worship unless a sermon were preached; and he proceeded to outline the services of the Word that should be conducted each morning and evening, replacing the daily Masses. Luther concluded:

> This is the sum of the matter: that everything shall be done so that the Word prevails. . . . We can spare everything except the Word. We profit by nothing so much as by the Word. For the whole Scripture shows that the Word should have free course among Christians. And in Luke 10, Christ himself says: "One thing is needful"—that Mary sit at the feet of Christ and daily hear his Word. . . .

In his determination to restore the proclamation of the Gospel to Christian worship, Luther made his finest contribution to the liturgy. Rome drew his ire for the "prattling and rattling" that had supplanted good preaching. And the Medieval church stood condemned for ordering its worship irrespective of the Word; but "all the Masses stacked together [were] worthless without the Word of God." · The issue was extremely vital: "Neither you nor I could ever know anything of Christ, or believe in him, or have him for our Lord, except as this is offered to us by the Holy Spirit through the preaching of the Gospel." ·· To hear the Word lay at the center of worship.

The *Formula Missae* was published in December of 1523.

· *Psalm 68; Luther's Works,* 13: 27.
·· Weimar Ausgabe 30¹: 188.

In the preface Luther explained why he had been tardy in making such a liturgy. Previously he had tried to wean men from godless ceremonies by his sermons and writings, taking care not to offend the weaker brethren by introducing "new and untried" forms in place of the "old and accustomed" ways. He had been doubly hesitant in view of the "frivolous" souls who thrive upon novelty. But now the time was ripe for a revision—not that he intended to deal severely with the liturgy, but merely to purge it of its "abominable additions." After all, the Mass had been instituted by Christ himself. The pity of it was, that Christ meant to have his Supper celebrated in high simplicity, without the accretion of ceremonies. Now, alas, nothing remained of it but the name. Luther did not speak idly of simplicity. If he did not accede to the biblicism of the *Schwärmer*, nor doubt the usefulness of external forms, neither did he spare his anger at the "chancel prancers" · of the Medieval church; for he was convinced that real paganism accrued from idolatrous attachment to symbols, and that true worship was always in danger of being overwhelmed by burgeoning ceremonies.

Luther hastened to add that he had no qualms about those additions supplied by the early Fathers. But the Latin Canon was another matter.·· That he assaulted with pure Thuringian invective. By means of the Canon, the Mass had been turned into a sacrifice, and the sacrifice had brought sacerdotalism, ecclesiastical avarice, Votive Masses, proliferating rites, and untold items of pomp. All this was due to be scrapped. Here we encounter Luther's distinction between worship as *sacrificium*—a sacrifice offered by men to God—and as *beneficium* —a gracious gift of God to men. The error of *sacrificium* was manifold. Not the least of its evils was the implication that God was an angry God who demanded to be appeased. Moreover, as an act of propitiation, it presented itself as one of the chief good works, by which righteousness could be got. Nor did it require the presence of communicants to be propitious, but sponsored the private Mass and overcame the very act of Communion. Finally, the sacrifice of Christ in the Mass involved a real denial of Christ's one all-sufficient sacrifice on Calvary. For all of these reasons, Luther deemed the

· So: Pelikan, p. 31.
·· In 1525, Luther made a thorough analysis of the prayers of the Canon in *The Abomination of the Secret Mass; Luther's Works,* 36: 311ff.

Medieval conception of *sacrificium* to be antithetical to the Gospel: it could no longer be tolerated. All of worship, and the Mass in particular, must be viewed as a *beneficium* of God, "who gives, but does not take"—who gives freely, out of pure mercy for the undeserving, asking only to be confessed and glorified.· But Brilioth observed that as this principle worked out in history, it tended to associate the "gift" with the "individual" and sponsored the "individualistic outlook that came to dominate the Lutheran view of the sacrament," diminishing also the sense of the Eucharist as a corporate act of praise and thanks to God.

In the *Formula Missae*, Luther's conservative and evangelical views coalesced. He proposed merely to revise the Missal, retaining the Latin language, but purging the Mass of those things that could not support an evangelical interpretation. Most of the fore-Mass withstood the test and therefore remained. Luther did suggest that when it came time to cast the liturgy into the vernacular, it would be profitable to revise the lectionary (some "friend of works" had obviously arranged the Epistles); but meanwhile vernacular preaching would suffice to teach faith in Christ. He could not make up his mind where the sermon should go. By tradition it belonged after the Creed; but he toyed with the idea of giving it a striking place before the whole Mass, as a "voice calling in the wilderness and bidding believers to faith."

Beyond the fore-Mass, however, the liturgy commenced to "reek of sacrifice." Inasmuch as the Offertory inaugurated the sacrificial action, it was removed; and the bread and wine were now prepared during the Creed or after the sermon. That done, the *Sursum corda* was recited; and it was followed by an abbreviated Preface, which led, not to the Sanctus, but directly into the Words of Institution. Luther hoped that the *Verba* would be sung audibly, for they were the heart of the Mass—indeed, the sum of the Gospel. Directly after the Consecration, the choir took up the Sanctus and the Benedictus, at which point the Elevation occurred. Luther—no liturgical purist was he—removed the Sanctus from its position of a thousand years, so that the Words of Institution could be hitched on to the last phrase of the Preface ("through Christ our Lord"). The Elevation was succeeded by the Pater Noster and subsequently by the Pax

· Cf. Vajta, pp. 27-63.

("The peace of the Lord be with you always"), which Luther reinterpreted to mean "the Gospel voice announcing the remission of sins"; for the gift of the Mass was above all the forgiveness of sins. The priest communicated himself and then gave Communion to the people, using the Roman words of administration.

Luther appended certain exhortations concerning liberty in the conduct of worship. Men should not attempt to absolutize those things that are left free; "only let them keep the Words of Consecration uncorrupted." When this or that form had outlived its usefulness, let it be changed or discarded: no liturgy was worth being idolized. Diversity itself might be wholesome, if it would keep men from making uniformity a fetish. And though external forms were necessary to church life, as food and drink to human life, let no one suppose that they were able somehow to commend us to God. We shall refer later to the sense of these observations.

In the second part of the *Formula,* Luther laid down certain principles "Concerning the Communion of the People." First, as the Mass was now conceived to be a Holy Communion involving all the members of Christ's spiritual Body, it could no longer be celebrated without the presence of the congregation. Second, the people were expected to notify the minister ("bishop") of their intention to communicate, so that he might ascertain "their manner of life" and the status of their religious knowledge. Ignorant saints, no less than obdurate sinners, were deemed unfit to approach the Lord's table. But those who grieved over their faults should be received at the Supper which was instituted for no other purpose than to refresh and strengthen the penitents. While private confession in preparation for Communion could not be counted compulsory, it was nevertheless "useful and not to be despised." Third, out of simple respect to the institution of Jesus Christ, Christians would henceforth receive Communion in both kinds. Finally, a call was made for German poets who would put their talents to pious use in the creation of spiritual songs, so that the voice of the people might once again resound in worship, and, at length, the whole Mass be transformed into the vernacular.• These

• Cf. Paul Nettl, *Luther and Music* (Philadelphia, 1948); Otto Schlisske, *Handbuch der Lutherlieder* (Göttingen, 1948); Friedrich Blume, *Die Evangelische Kirchenmusik* (New York, 1931); H. J. Moser, *Die Evangelische Kirchenmusik in Deutschland* (Ber-

provisions—the "common" character of Communion, the preparatory examination, and the introduction of hymnody—proved of great importance in shaping the life of the Lutheran churches.

The *Formula Missae* did not fulfill the expectation of the times. Already in 1524, Strassburg received a "German Mass," which quickly established itself at the head of a new and important liturgical tradition (Ch. VI). The following year, Zwingli abolished the Mass in Zurich and inaugurated far-reaching reforms of worship (Ch. V). At the same time, Oecolampadius introduced simplified services at Basel, and Farel brought out the first evangelical liturgy in the French language (Ch. VII). Within Germany itself, the production of vernacular rites continued apace, with new forms appearing in Prussia, at Nördlingen, and Nürnberg. Frightened, perhaps, by the dangers inherent in this tendency, Luther summoned Bugenhagen and Jonas to his assistance, and commenced the preparation of *Deutsche Messe*. It was introduced to the Town Church of Wittenberg on October 29, 1525, and fell into regular use at Christmas, Luther seeing that this must be "God's wish."

As the document opened, Luther reaffirmed the principle of Christian liberty. He had no intention of legislating the new liturgy against freedom, but wished merely to offer a German Mass that might be sufficiently acceptable to satisfy the "clamor" for such services, and to arrest the serious growth of diversity. Yet it was a disquieting thought that the Germans might receive the liturgy as having the *imprimatur* of Wittenberg, and therefore make it the symbol of the Reformation, an instrument of some new works-righteousness. But what was his view of a liturgy? In the initial pages of *Deutsche Messe*, he expressed himself on this matter, yet his thoughts were both ironic and unclear. Brilioth concluded: "He regards the value of a liturgy as almost wholly educative." Indeed, the "pedagogical" interpretation of Luther's liturgical ideas has arisen largely from these passages, and has been accepted by a number of authorities. But on the face of it, it seems inconceivable that a monk nurtured in the Divine Office and a priest who served at the altar for nearly twenty years would relegate the liturgy to the status

lin, 1954); and the introduction to Luther's hymns in the Weimar Ausgabe, Vol. XXXV.

of a "teaching workshop." Vilmos Vajta has enabled us to read these passages in a new light. It is apparent that Luther was attempting to deal here with the problem of form and freedom. *In faith*—he seems to say—man is free of all human forms and rites; for faith does not depend on these: it is rather inward trust in the redeeming work of Christ. Therefore faith implies liberty. But *in love,* man is bound to serve his neighbor, and must honor the rites and ceremonies that bring his neighbor into the realm of the Word, where faith is born and nourished. Therefore love pertains to external order. Vajta observed:

> The believer indeed is free of stated forms of worship. He worships in spirit and truth. Yet he submits to them, first because he himself is not a perfect Christian and needs to be trained in the faith, and second, in order to help his neighbor become a Christian and grow in the faith.•

Luther proceeded to describe three kinds of services. The *Formula Missae* ought to be used occasionally, if only to exercise the youth in the Latin language. It was most unprofitable to conduct worship exclusively in the vernacular. Ideally, the liturgy should be celebrated successively in German, Latin, Greek, and Hebrew, lest the Christian religion be imprisoned by provincialism.•• Yet "for the simple layman," the *Deutsche Messe* was unquestionably the more suitable. Aside from these two types of public worship, Luther could conceive of a "truly evangelical" service, which would be observed by select groups of "real Christians." They would meet "by themselves" in one of their homes "to pray, read, baptize, receive the Sacrament, and do other Christian works," their fellowship being guarded and invigorated by discipline. But Luther had no plans for these *ecclesiolae;* they required a special personnel, and he did not see many who were "shaping that way."

According to the new "Sunday Service for the Laity," vestments, altars, and candles would remain for the time being; but someday the altar ought to be moved away from the wall, enabling the priest to take the basilican position, "as doubt-

• Pp. 174-5.
•• These statements should be read alongside Luther's stress upon the importance of languages that incase the Gospel. Cf. *To the Councilmen of All Cities in Germany that They Establish and Maintain Christian Schools; Works of Martin Luther,* 4: 113ff.

less Christ did at the Last Supper." The liturgy commenced with a hymn or German psalm, replacing the Introit; there was no General Confession of sin as had developed at Strassburg. The Kyrie eleison became threefold, instead of ninefold; and the Gloria in excelsis disappeared entirely. The Collect, Epistle, and Gospel were appointed in their traditional places; but the Gradual between the lessons became a German hymn. After the Gospel, the whole congregation sang the Apostles' Creed according to Luther's metrical version. Then the sermon was appointed, Luther having resolved his indecision about its location. But other matters concerned him. Disturbed by the Peasants' Revolt, the appalling ignorance of the parochial clergy, Müntzer's enthusiasm, and Carlstadt's defection, he surmised that it would be better to require a homily, instead of subjecting the church to the pronouncements of some sectarian, or to the whims of a poor preacher who elects to preach about "blue ducks."

The Offertory having been obliterated, the liturgy of the Faithful began with Luther's paraphrase of the Lord's Prayer —a device that had been tried in the Medieval Prone, and of which Calvin was also enamored. This was followed by an Exhortation, replacing the Preface, which led directly into the Words of Institution. According to biblical evidence, Luther preferred to have the administration of the bread immediately after its consecration; that is, before the Cup was consecrated and delivered. German hymns were appointed to be sung during the Communion; and among these were Luther's own version of the Sanctus and Agnus Dei. The Elevation survived because it "went well" with the Sanctus and functioned as a sort of pictorial *anamnesis*. It was finally abandoned by Bugenhagen in 1542.

Luther made a distinction between the Mass and the sacrifice of the Mass. If he loathed the latter, he did not lose sight of the historical character and religious values of the Latin rite. It was, at least, the model from which he would not depart, the liturgy that he chose to purge and reinterpret rather than destroy. Three of his own contributions were of the highest order: the recovery of the sermon, the introduction of German hymns, and the triumphant restoration of the Communion of the people.

FOR FURTHER READING

Yngve Brilioth, *Eucharistic Faith & Practice*. London, 1956.
Leonhard Fendt, *Der Lutherische Gottesdienst des 16. Jahrhunderts*. Munich, 1923.
Paul Nettl, *Luther and Music*. Philadelphia, 1958.
Jaroslav J. Pelikan, *Luther and the Liturgy*, in *More About Luther: Martin Luther Lectures*, Vol. 2. Decorah, Iowa, 1958.
Emil Sehling (ed.), *Die evangelischen Kirchenordnungen des XVI. Jahrhunderts*. 5 vols. Leipzig, 1902-13. This is a voluminous collection of the Lutheran church-orders.
Julius Smend (ed.), *Die evangelischen deutschen Messen bis zu Luthers Deutscher Messe*. Göttingen, 1896. This contains the texts of Communion liturgies—German and Swiss—which appeared prior to Luther's *Deutsche Messe*.
Luther D. Reed, *The Lutheran Liturgy*. Philadelphia, 1947.
Vilmos Vajta, *Luther on Worship*. Philadelphia, 1958.

FORMULA MISSAE ET COMMUNIONIS [1]
PRO ECCLESIA WITTEMBERGENSIS
VENERABILI
IN CHRISTO D. NICOLAO HAUSMAN
EPISCOPO CYGNEAE ECCLESIAE
IN CHRISTO SANCTO
MART. LUTHER

•

FORMULA OF MASS AND COMMUNION
FOR THE CHURCH AT WITTENBERG
By Martin Luther
Wittenberg
MDXXIII *

•

To the Venerable
in Christ D. Nicholas Hausman
Bishop of the Church at Zwickau
in Christ blessed.
Mart. Luther.

Grace and peace in Christ he wishes (him). Thus far I have tried by means of books and sermons among the people to call their hearts away from godless opinions of ceremonies, thinking I would be doing something Christian and salutary if I would be the cause whereby the abomination, which Satan has set up in the holy place through the man of sin, might be removed without violence. Therefore, I have undertaken nothing either by force or command; nor have I changed old things for new, always being hesitant and fearful on account of those souls weak in the faith from whom the old and accustomed is not to be taken away suddenly or among whom a new and untried method of worshiping God is to be introduced; and especially on account of those light and fastidious spirits who, without faith, without reason, like unclean swine, rush wildly about and rejoice only in the novel, and as soon as the novelty has worn off forthwith become disgusted with it. A species of men than whom, as in other things, nothing is more troublesome than their sort; so, too, in sacred things they are most troublesome and intolerable. Nevertheless, even though I am moved with wrath, I am compelled to suffer them unless I would desire to have the Gospel itself taken away from the public.

But now since there is hope that the hearts of many have been enlightened and strengthened by the grace of God, and since the matter itself demands that the scandals be removed from the Kingdom of Christ, something must be dared in the name of Christ. For it is right that we provide for the few, lest while we fear constantly the levity and abuse of some others we provide for none at all, and while we wish to guard against the future scandals of such as these, we strengthen all of their abominations. Therefore, most excellent Nicolas, since you have requested it so frequently, we will busy ourself concerning some pious form of saying Mass (as they say) and of administering Communion. And thus will we do: we will no longer rule hearts by word of doctrine only, but we will put our hand to it also, and make that effective in the public administration; nevertheless, prejudicing no one, nor forbidding any one to embrace or follow some other method. Indeed we beg through Christ, from the heart, if something better shall be revealed to those who are in advance of us in these things, that they command us to be silent so that by common work we may aid the common cause.

In the first place we assert, it is not now, nor has it ever been, in our mind to abolish entirely the whole formal cultus of God, but to cleanse that which is in use, which has been vitiated by most abominable additions, and to point out a pious use. For this cannot be denied, that masses and the communion of bread and wine are a rite divinely instituted by Christ, which was observed, first under Christ Himself, then under the apostles, most simply and piously and without any additions. But so many human inventions have been added to it in course of time, that nothing of the mass and communion has come down to our age except the name.

Now the additions of the early fathers, who are said to have prayed one or two psalms in a subdued voice before blessing the bread and wine, were commendable: such Athanasius and Cyprian were thought to have been. Then they who added *Kyrie Eleison,* these also pleased; for we read that under Basil the Great *Kyrie Eleison* was in public use by the whole people. Now the reading of the *Epistles* and *Gospels* was and is necessary, unless it be a fault to read them in a language which is not understood by the common people. Afterward when chanting began, the psalms were changed into the *Introit:* then the Angelic Hymn was added, the *Gloria in excelsis et in terra pax;* also the *Graduals* and *Alleluia* and *Nicene Creed,* the *Sanctus, Agnus dei* and *Communio.* All these are such as cannot be censured, especially those which are sung as *de tempore* or Lord's Day uses. These days only testify to ancient purity, the Canon excepted.

But when there was license to add and to change as it suited anyone, then because of the tyranny of avarice and sacerdotal ambition, those altars and images of Baal and all gods began to be placed in the temple of the Lord by our impious kings, that is, the bishops and pastors (shepherds). Here impious Ahaz took away the brazen altar and erected another brought from Damascus. But I am speaking about the Canon, that mangled and abominable thing gathered from much filth and scum. Then the Mass began to be a sacrifice; the Offertories and paid-for prayers were added; then Sequences and Proses were inserted in the *Sanctus* and the *Gloria in excelsis.* Then the Mass began to be a priestly monopoly, exhausting the wealth of the whole world, deluging the whole earth like a vast desert with rich, lazy, powerful and lascivious celebates. Then came masses for the dead, for travelers, for riches, and who can name the titles alone for which the Mass was made a sacrifice?

Nor do they cease to add to the Canon today: now it is for these feasts, then for others; now these *actiones,* then other *communicantes* are approved. And I will keep quiet about the *memores,* the commemoration of the living and of the dead, not yet brought to its end. And what shall I say of the external additions, vestments, vessels, candles, palls; then the organ and everything musical; images? There is scarcely one of the handicrafts in all the world, which does not contribute a great part of its activity to, and derive its gain from, the Mass.

Therefore, let these be passed by, and also let them pass—all such abominations being revealed by the Gospel—until they be entirely abolished. In the meanwhile we will test all things; what is good, we will retain. But in this book we omit saying that the Mass is (not)[2] a sacrifice or a good work, because we have taught about it sufficiently at other places.[3] We accept it as Sacrament, or Testament, or Blessing as in Latin, or Eucharist as in Greek, or the Table of the Lord, or the Lord's Supper, or the Lord's Memorial, or Communion, or by whatever pious name you please, so long as it be not polluted by the name of sacrifice or work; and we will set forth the rite according to which, as it seems to us, it should be used.

In the first place, we approve and preserve the introits for the Lord's Day and for the Festivals of Christ, such as Easter, Pentecost, Nativity, although we prefer the Psalms from which they were taken as of old; but now we agree to the received usage. But if any desire to approve the introits for Apostles' Days, for Feasts of the Virgin and of other saints, we do not condemn this, if they have been chosen from Psalms and other Scriptures. We, of Wittenberg, seek to celebrate only on Lord's Days and on Festivals of the Lord, abrogating completely the festivals of all of the saints; or if there is anything worthy in them we think they should be referred to in the Lord's Day preaching. We regard the Festivals of the Purification and of the Annunciation as Festivals of Christ, like the Epiphany and the Circumcision. In place of the Festivals of St. Stephen and of St. John, the Evangelist, it pleases us to use the office of the Nativity. Let the Festivals of the Holy Cross be anathema. Let others act according to their own consciences, or according to the infirmity of others—whatever the Spirit may suggest.

In the second place, we accept *Kyrie Eleison* as it has been used customarily, with the various melodies for the different seasons, together with the Angelic Hymn, *Gloria in excelsis*, which follows; nevertheless its use rests on the judgment of the bishop, or, how often he desires its omission.

In the third place, the *Oratio* (prayer), or Collect which follows, if it is pious (and those appointed for the Lord's Days usually are), should be preserved in its accustomed use; but there should be but one. After this the *Epistle* lesson. Certainly the time has not yet come to attempt revision here, as nothing ungodly is read. But something seems to be needed, since those parts of the Epistles of Paul in which faith is taught are rarely read, but most frequently those parts dealing with morals and exhortations. While the originator of the Epistles seems to have been a singularly unlearned and superstitious friend of works, the office required the rather that, for the greater part, those sections in which faith in

Christ is taught, be appointed. This certainly may be seen more frequently in the Gospels, whoever has been the originator of those lessons. But in the meantime vernacular preaching will supply this lack. If it shall come to pass in the future that Mass shall be celebrated in the vernacular (which may Christ grant!), attention must be given so that Epistles and Gospels, chosen from the best and more weighty parts of these writings, be read in the Mass.

In the fourth place, the *Gradual* of two verses, likewise with the *Alleluia,* or both, should be sung as the bishop decides. But the Quadragesima Graduals and the like, which are longer than two verses, any one who wishes may sing these in his own home. In church, we do not wish to extinguish the spirit of the faithful with tedious things. It is not fitting to distinguish the Quadragesima, or the Greater Week, or the Feria Sexta, with rites other than those customary elsewhere, lest we seem to banter and ridicule Christ further with half a mass and the one part of the Sacrament. For *Alleluia* is the perpetual voice of the Church, just as the memorial of His (Christ's) passion and victory is perpetual.

In the fifth place, we allow no *Sequences* or *Proses,* unless it please the bishop to use the short one for the Nativity of Christ, *Grates nunc omnes.* Nor are there hardly any which are redolent of the Spirit save those of the Holy Spirit: *Sancti Spiritus* and *Veni Sancte Spiritus,* which one may sing after breakfast or at Vespers or at Mass (if the bishop pleases).

In the sixth place, the *Gospel* lection follows, where we prohibit neither candles nor censing. But we do not demand this; let this be free.

In the seventh place, the custom of singing the Nicene Creed is not displeasing. Likewise concerning vernacular preaching, we are of the opinion that it does not matter whether this is done after the *Symbolum* or before the Introit of the Mass, although there is a reason why it might be more aptly done before Mass, because the Gospel is the voice calling in the wilderness and bidding unbelievers to faith.

The Mass indeed should be the use of the Gospel and also the Communion of the Table of the Lord, which certainly belongs to the faithful and is fitting to be celebrated privately; but nevertheless that reason does not bind us who are free, especially because all things which are done in the Mass up to the *Symbolum* are ours and are free, not exacted by God, on which account they do not necessarily pertain to the Mass.

In the eighth place, there follows that complete abomination, into the service of which all that precedes in the Mass has been forced, whence it is called *Offertorium,* and on account of which nearly everything sounds and reeks of oblation. In the midst of these things those words of life and salvation[4] have been placed, just like in times past the ark of the Lord was placed in the temple of idols next to Dagon. And there is no Israelite there who is able either to approach or lead back the ark, until it has made its enemies infamous, smiting them on the back with eternal shame, and has compelled them to send it away, which is a parable for the present time. Therefore repudiating all those things which smack of sacrifice and of the Offertory, together with the entire *Canon,* let us retain those things which are pure and holy, and then we will order our Mass in this fashion.

I. During the Creed or after the Canon,[5] let bread and wine be prepared in the customary way for consecration. Except that I am not yet fixed in my mind as to whether or not water should be mixed with the wine, although I rather incline to the preparation of pure wine, because the indication strikes me as wrong which Isaiah advances in Chapter I, "Your wine," he says, "is mixed with water." For pure wine symbolizes beautifully the purity of the teaching of the Gospel. Then, too, nothing has been poured out for us save the blood of Christ only, unmixed with ours, of which we make commemoration here. Neither can the dream of those stand who say that our union with Christ is here symbolized, the commemoration of which union we do not make here. Nor are we united before the shedding of His blood, otherwise at the same time we would be celebrating the pouring out of our own blood with the blood of Christ for ourselves. Nevertheless in opposition to liberty, I will not introduce a superstitutious law. Christ will not care very much about this, nor are these matters worthy of contention. Enough foolish contention over this has been engaged in by the Roman and Greek Churches as also in many other matters. And because some assert that blood and water flowed from the side of Christ, that does not prove anything. For that water signifies something other than what they wish to be signified by that mixed water. Nor was that mixed with the blood. Moreover the figure proves nothing, and the example does not stand; hence as a human invention it is held to be free.

II. The bread and the wine having been prepared, then let the order be in this manner: The Lord be with you. Response: And with thy spirit. Lift up (your) hearts. Response: Let us lift them to the Lord. Let us give thanks unto our Lord God. Response: It is meet and right. It is truly meet and right, just and salutary for us to give thanks to Thee always and everywhere, Holy Lord, Father Almighty, Eternal God, through Christ our Lord.

III. Then . . . Who the day before He suffered took bread, giving thanks, broke and gave to His disciples, saying, Take, eat. This is my body, which is given for you.

Similarly also the cup, after He supped, saying, This cup is the new testament in my blood which is poured out for you and for many in remission of sins. As often as ye shall do this, do it in memory of me.

I wish these words of Christ, allowing a moderate pause after the Preface, to be recited in the same tone of voice in which the Lord's Prayer is sung at another place in the Canon; so that it will be possible for those standing by to hear, although in all these things liberty is allowed to pious minds to recite these words either silently or audibly.

IV. The Consecration ended, let the choir sing the Sanctus, and when the Benedictus is sung, let the bread and chalice be elevated according to the rite in use up to this time, chiefly on account of the infirm who might be greatly offended by the sudden change in this more noted rite in the Mass, especially where they have been taught through vernacular sermons what is sought by this elevation.

V. After this the Lord's Prayer is read. Thus: Let us pray: Taught by thy saving precepts, etc., omitting the prayer following: Deliver us, we beseech, with all signs, which they were wont to make over the host and with the host over the chalice; nor shall the host be broken or mixed in the chalice. But immediately after the Lord's Prayer shall be said, The Peace of the Lord, etc, which is, so to speak, a public absolution of the sins of the communicants, truly the Gospel voice announcing remission of sins, the one and most worthy preparation for the Lord's Table, if it be apprehended by faith and not otherwise than though it came forth from the mouth of Christ Himself. On account of this I wish it to be announced with face turned to the people, as the bishops were accustomed to do, which is the sole vestige of the ancient bishops left among our bishops.

VI. Then let him communicate himself first, then the people; in the meanwhile let the *Agnus dei* be sung. But if he should desire to pray the prayer, O Lord Jesus Christ, Son of the living God, who according to the will of the Father, etc., before communing, he will not pray wrongly, only change the singular number to the plural, *ours* and *us* for *mine* and *me*. Likewise the prayer, The Body of the Lord, etc., guard *my* soul, or *thy* soul unto life eternal. And the Blood, of *our* Lord, guard *thy* soul unto life eternal.

VII. If he desires to sing the Communion let it be sung. But in place of the *ad complendam* or final collect which so frequently savors of sacrifice, let this prayer be read in the same tone: What we have taken with the mouth, O Lord. This one also may be read: Thy Body, O Lord, which we have received, etc., changing to the plural number. Who livest and reignest, etc. The Lord be with you, etc. In place of the *Ite missa*, let *Benedicamus domino* be said, adding Alleluia according to its own melodies where and when it is desired; or Benedicamus may be borrowed from Vespers.

VIII. Let the customary Benediction be given. Or take that from Numbers 6, which the Lord Himself arranged and ordered: *The Lord bless us and guard us: May He show us His face and be merciful to us; The Lord turn His face to us and give us peace. Or that in Psalm 96, May God, our God, bless us: May God bless us and all the ends of the earth fear Him. Amen.* I believe Christ used something of this kind when, ascending into heaven, He blessed His disciples.

And this, too, should be free to the bishop, namely, by what order he may desire either to receive or to administer both species. For assuredly he may consecrate both bread and wine consecutively before he receives the bread; or between the consecration of the bread and wine he may communicate with the bread both himself and as many as desire it, and thereupon consecrate the wine and at length give to all to drink of it. After which manner Christ seems to have acted, as the words of the Gospel reveal, where He commanded to eat the bread before He blessed the cup. Then is said expressly: Likewise also the cup after He supped. Thus you perceive the cup was blessed only after eating the bread. But this quite new rite will not permit the doing of those things following the Consecration about which we spoke above, unless they should be changed.

This is the way we think about the Mass, but at the same time taking care in all such matters lest we make binding things which are free, or compel those to sin who either would do some other thing or omit certain things; only let them keep the Words of Consecration uncorrupted, and let them do this in faith. For these should be the usages of Christians, that is of children of the free woman, who observe these things voluntarily and from the heart, changing them as often as and in whatever manner they might wish. Wherefore it is not right that one should either require or establish some indispensable form as a law in this matter, by which he might ensnare or vex consciences. Whence also we find no complete example of this use in the ancient fathers and in the primitive Church, save only in the Roman Church. But if they have appointed something as a law in this matter, it should not be observed; because these things neither can nor should be bound by laws. Then, even if different people make use of different rites, let no one either judge or despise the other; but let each one abound in his own opinion, and let them understand and know even if they do differently; and let each one's rite be agreeable to the other, lest diverse opinions and sects yield diverse uses, just as happened in the Roman Church. For external rites, even if we are not able to do without them—just as we cannot do without food and drink—nevertheless, do not commend us to God, just as food does not commend us to God. But faith and love commend us to God. Wherefore let this word of Paul govern here: The kingdom of God is not food and drink, but righteousness, peace and joy in the Holy Spirit. Thus no rite is the Kingdom of God, but faith within you, etc.

We have passed by vestments. But we think about these as we do about other uses; we permit them to be used without restraint, only let pomp and the excess of splendor be absent. For neither are you the more acceptable if you should consecrate in vestments; nor are you the less acceptable if you should consecrate without vestments. For vestments do not commend us to God. But I do not wish them to be consecrated or blessed—as if they were about to be something sacred as compared with other garments—except by that general benediction, by which it is taught that every good

114

creature of God is sanctified through word and prayer; otherwise it would be an utter superstition and impiety, introduced through the abominations of the pontiffs, as also other things.

Concerning the Communion of the People

We have said these foregoing things about the Mass and the office of the minister or bishop; now we will speak about the custom of communicating the people, on account of whom chiefly this Supper of the Lord was instituted and is called by that name. For as it is most absurd for a minister of the Word to act so foolishly as to publish the Word in public ministration where there is no hearer, and to cry aloud to himself alone amid rocks and woods and in the open air, so it is most wrong if ministers make ready and adorn the common Supper of the Lord where there would be no guests who would eat and drink, and they alone, who ought to minister to others, would eat and drink at an empty table and in an empty sanctuary. Wherefore if we wish truly to prize the institution of Christ, no private Mass should be left remaining in the Church, unless in this connection either infirmity or necessity should be tolerated for a time.

Moreover the custom is to be preserved here which is observed in connection with baptism; namely, that notice must first be given to the bishop, by those who are about to commune, that they request to be communicated with the Lord's Supper, so that he may be able to know both their names and manner of life. Then let him not admit those seeking, unless they should give a reason for their faith; and being questioned, should answer, whether they understand what the Supper of the Lord is; what it stands for; and of what they wish to become partakers by its use; to wit, if they are able to recite the Words of Consecration from memory and explain that they come because of the consciousness of sin, or the fear of death, or, troubled by some other evil of the temptation of the flesh, of the world, of the devil, they hunger and thirst for that word and sign of grace and salvation from the Lord Himself through the ministry of the bishop by which they may be consoled and comforted, such as Christ out of priceless love gave and instituted in this Supper when He said: Take and eat, etc.

But I think it will be sufficient if this questioning and investigation of him who seeks to be communicated is done once a year. Indeed it is possible that the one who seeks may be so understanding that he should be questioned either once only in his entire life, or in fact never. For through this custom we desire to guard against this: that the worthy and unworthy do not rush blindly to the Supper of the Lord, as we have seen done in the Roman Church hitherto, where nothing else is sought but to be communicated. Of faith, of comfort, of the whole use and fruits of the Supper absolutely neither mention nor consideration of these has had a place. Indeed they have concealed the very Words of Consecration, that is, the Bread of Life Itself, forcing this with vast zeal, yea, with highest frenzy, in order that communicants should perform a good work by their own merit, and that they should not nourish and strengthen faith through the goodness of Christ. But those who are not able to answer after the manner mentioned above, we desire such wholly excluded and banished from the communion of this Supper, as being without the wedding garment.

Then when the bishop has perceived that they understand these things, he should also watch this, whether they evidence this faith and knowledge in life and conduct—for Satan also both perceives all these things and is able to talk about them —that is, if he should see some fornicator, adulterer, drunkard, gamester, usurer, slanderer, or one made infamous by some manifest crime, let him be excluded absolutely from this Supper, unless by evident proof he shall have witnessed that his life has been changed. For the Supper should not be denied those who sometimes fall away and return, sorrowing over the lapse; indeed we should realize that the Supper was instituted especially on account of just such as these so that they may be refreshed and strengthened; for we all offend in many things; and we carry each other's burdens while we also mutually burden ourselves. But I am speaking of those contemptuous ones who sin shamelessly and without fear, yet, nevertheless, boast glorious things about the Gospel.

Then when Mass is celebrated, it is fitting that those about to be communicated gather together by themselves in one place and in one group. For to this end the altar was invented, also the choir. Not that standing here or there matters anything with God or adds anything to faith, but that it is necessary that they be seen and known openly, both by those who commune and those who do not commune; thus then

their lives may be the better observed and proven and made
known. For participation in this Supper is part of the confession by which they confess before God and angels and
men that they are Christians. Therefore care must be taken
lest they carry off the Supper stealthily, and then mingled
with others it is not known whether they live well or badly.
However, I do not wish this to be made a law here, but to
point out this—what honorable and fitting (thing) may be
performed freely by free Christians.

Now concerning private confession before communion. I
still think as I have taught heretofore, namely, that it is
neither necessary nor to be demanded; nevertheless it is useful and not to be despised, since the Lord neither required
this Supper as necessary or established it by law, but left it
free to everyone, saying, As often as you do this, etc. So concerning the preparation for the Supper, we think that preparing oneself by fasting and prayers is a matter of liberty. Certainly it behooves us to approach in soberness of mind and
earnestly and diligently, whether you fast nothing at best or
pray ever so little. In truth, I say, moderation in drinking,
not that superstitious practice of the papists;[6] but moderation,
lest you belch drunkenly and become sluggish and dull from
a distended belly. For the best preparation is, as I have said,
a soul moved and vexed by sins, death, temptations, and
hungering and thirsting for healing and strength. Whatever
of these things is true, these are the concern of the bishop and
it rests with him that he may teach the people.

This now remains to be considered, whether both forms,
as they call them, should be ministered to the people. So here
I say, Now that the Gospel has been inculcated among us
these two whole years, at the same time sufficient indulgence
also has been granted to infirmity. Hereafter one must act
according to that saying of Paul: He who is ignorant, let him
be ignorant. For it does not matter, if they, who for so long
a time have not known the Gospel, do not receive again
neither of the two forms, lest perchance bearing with infirmity
perpetually may nourish obstinacy and result in proscription
contrary to the Gospel. Wherefore simply according to the
institution of Christ, let both forms be both sought and
ministered. Those who do not desire this, let them have their
way; and let nothing be ministered to them. For we point out
this form of the Mass to those to whom it is known in some
part. But those who have not heard as yet, or who have ability

to know, it is not yet possible to offer them any counsel concerning this matter.

Nor should this matter be delayed at all in order that they may call together a Council, in which this may again be sanctioned as allowable. We have the law of Christ and we do not want either to be hindered by or to hear a Council in those matters which manifestly are of the Gospel. Yea, we say more. And if by chance a Council would decide and permit this, then least of all do we want to partake of both forms; nay, on the contrary, then first in contempt both of the Council and its statute, we would wish to partake either of one or neither, but never of both; and we would hold those to be wholly anathema who would partake of both on the authority of such Council and statute. Do you wonder at this and ask the reason? Hear!—if you know the bread and wine were instituted by Christ, and both are to be received by all, as the Gospel and Paul testify most clearly, and as the adversaries themselves are forced to admit; nevertheless you do not dare to believe and trust Him so that you receive, but you dare to receive if men decide this in a Council:—then are you not preferring men to Christ? Do you not extol sinful men above Him who is named and worshiped, God? Do you not trust in the words of men more than in the words of God? Nay rather, do you not utterly distrust the words of God and believe only the words of men? Moreover, how great is such hatred and denial of the most high God? What idolatry then can equal your religious obedience of a Council of men? Should you not the rather die a thousand times? Should you not the rather receive one or no form, than receive under such sacrilegious obedience and apostasy from the faith?

Therefore let them stop talking about their councils continually; but let them do this first, let them replace their sacrilege with the divine glory; let them confess that with Satan their master they have held back one form; that they have lifted themselves up above God; that they have condemned the Word, and destroyed so many people through so many ages; and let them do penance for this unspeakable tyranny of inhumanity and impiety. Then let them solemnly declare that we have done right when on our part and even against their dogmas we have taught and received both forms and have not waited for their Council, and let them give thanks because we refused to follow their perdition and abomination. After they have done this, we will be willing and well-disposed to honor and welcome their Council and ordinance. In the meantime should they not do this, but continue to demand that we await their authorization (for our action), we will listen to nothing; but we will continue both to teach and to do things which are opposed to them; in particular, those things which we know are especially displeasing to them. For what do they exact by this diabolical demand save that we exalt them above God, their words above His words, and erect the abominable monsters of their spectres as idols in the place of God, when we want the whole world to be put under God and made subject to Him.

I also wish as many of the songs as possible to be in the vernacular, which the people should sing during Mass either immediately after the *Gradual*, and immediately after the *Sanctus* and *Agnus dei*. For who doubts that once upon a time all the people sang these, which now only the choir sings or responds when the bishop is consecrating? But these songs may be ordered by the bishops in this manner, they may be sung either right after the Latin songs, or on alternate days, now Latin, now the vernacular, until the entire Mass shall be made vernacular. But poets are wanting among us, —or they are not known as yet,—who can put together pleasingly pious and spiritual songs, as Paul calls them, which are worthy to be used by all the people in the Church of God. In the meantime it is proper to sing this after communion: *Gott sey gelobet und gebenedeyet der uns selber hatt gespeyset, etc.*; omitting this small part: *Und das heylige sacramente, an unserm letzten ende, aus des geweyeten priesters hende,* which was added by someone of the cult of St. Barbara, who, holding the sacrament during his whole life as of little value, in death hopes, without faith, by this good work to enter into life. For both the meter and the manner of the music prove this part of the song is superfluous. In addition to that, this is good: *Nu bitten wyr den heyligen geist.* Also: *Eyn kindelin so lobelich.* For you will not find many, which in some respect taste of a dignified spirit. I say this, so that if there are any German poets, they may be moved to and work out, pious poems for us.

Let these things said concerning the mass and communion suffice for the time being; other matters, use and the thing itself will teach; only let the Word of God be announced in the church actively and faithfully. For that which some require so strongly, namely, that all these things be proved

119

by the Scriptures and the example of the fathers, does not disturb us greatly; because we have said above, that in these matters liberty ought to rule, and it is not allowable to captivate Christian consciences either by laws or orders. For this reason the Scriptures define nothing of these things but permit the liberty of the spirit to abound according to its own perception in the matter, according to the fitness of places, times, and persons. Indeed the examples of the fathers are in part unknown; those which really are known are so varied that nothing definite can be established about them, evidently because they themselves used their own liberty. And even if they would be altogether definite and simple, nevertheless they could not impose upon us either law or necessity of imitating them.

In connection with the rest of the days, which we call *feriae,* I see nothing which cannot be continued, only discontinue the Mass; for Matins of three lessons and the Hours, including Vespers and Compline de tempore, excluding the *feriae* of saints, are nothing other than words of divine Scripture. And it is fitting, nay necessary, that the boys be accustomed to reading and hearing the Psalms and lections of Holy Scripture. But if anything here ought to be made new, the prolixity of things can be changed according to and at the will of the bishop; however after this fashion, that three Psalms be appointed for Matins, three for Vespers, together with one or two Responsories. These matters cannot be ordered better than at the will of the bishop whose duty it is to choose the best of the Responsories and Antiphons and to appoint their use from Lord's Day to Lord's Day throughout the week, so that neither excessive repetition of the same things cause aversion, nor too much variety and multitudinous singing and reading generate weariness of spirit. But let the entire Psalter, divided in parts, remain in use and the entire Scriptures, divided into lections, let this be preserved in the ears of the Church.

Here, too, must be noted what I have suggested elsewhere, in order that this singing may not be a matter merely of tongue and of speech, or without sense like the sound of a pipe or harp. Therefore, daily lections must be appointed, one for the morning in the New or Old Testament, another for Vespers in one or the other testament with vernacular exposition. This rite is an ancient one, as is proven by both the custom itself and the word *Homilia* in Matins, and

Capitulum in Vespers and the other Hours, namely, that the Christians, as often as they gathered together, read something and then it was interpreted in the vernacular, after the custom which St. Paul describes in I Corinthians 14. Then when more evil times came, when prophets and interpreters were wanting, only this voice was left remaining after the lections and capitula, *Deo gratias*. Then in place of the interpretation, lections, psalms and hymns were multiplied and other things also in this wearying verbosity and superabundance. Although the hymns and *Te deum laudamus* bear testimony to this as does *Deo gratias* also, namely, that after the expositions and homilies they praised God and gave Him thanks for the true revelation of the Word of God. Such also I wish our vernacular songs to do.

This much, O best Nicolas, I have for you in writing about the rites and ceremonies of our Wittenberg church, already partly instituted and, Christ willing, to be completed at an early day; which example, if it pleases you and others, you may imitate. If not, we will give place to your wisdom, being prepared to accept what is more fitting from you and any others. Let it not frighten either you or any others because that sacrilegious Tophet still persists in our Wittenberg, which is impious and wretched gain to the princes of Saxony; I speak of the Church of All Saints. For by the mercy of God there is antidote aplenty among us through the abundance of the Word of God, so that the pest, weary and faint in its own corner, may not be a pestilence to any save itself. And there are scarcely three or four swine and gourmands in that same house of perdition who worship that wealth; to all others and at the same time to all the people, it is a notable cause of loathing and an abomination.

Nor is it allowed to proceed against them by force or command, as you know it is not fitting for Christians to fight save with the power of the sword of the Spirit. For in this way I hold the people back daily, otherwise that house, now, for a long time, the House of All Saints,—nay rather the House of All Devils,—would be known by some other name in the earth. But I have not exercised the power of the Spirit, which God has given us, against that, patiently bearing that reproach, if perchance God may give them penitence; meanwhile I am content, because our house, which more truly is the House of All Saints, may reign here and stand as a tower of Lebanon against the House of All Devils. Thus we torment Satan with the Word, although he simulates a laugh; but Christ will grant that his hope will fail him and that he will be overthrown with all beholding.

Pray for me, O holy one of God.

Grace be with you and with all yours. Amen.

NOTES

1. Transcribed from *Works of Martin Luther* (Philadelphia: Muhlenberg, 1932), VI, 83-101. The editor of this text, Paul Z. Strodach, has supplied voluminous notes on pp. 101-17.
2. *non:* not; omitted in original print.
3. Cf. Weimar Ausgabe, 6: 365ff., 512ff.; 8: 431ff., 506ff.
4. Luther means the Words of Institution.
5. Latin: *post Canonem.* Probably a printer's error for *Concionem,* "sermon."
6. Luther means rigorous fasting.

DEUDSCHE MESSE VND ORDNUNG
GOTTIS DIENSTS

THE GERMAN MASS AND ORDER OF SERVICE [1]
1526

Martin Luther's Preface

In the first place, I want to make a request, in all kindness, and in God's name, too, that all who see this Order of Service or desire to adopt it, shall not impose it as a law or cause anyone's conscience to be distressed or bound by it, but shall use it in Christian freedom as they may please, as, where, when, and as long as conditions warrant or call for it. For we do not publish this with the intent of correcting anyone or legislating for him, but because there is clamor for German masses and services everywhere, and widespread lament and offense has been caused by the different usages in the new masses. For everyone is constructing his own: some with good intentions, others again with presumption, in order that they may shine as also having produced something new to prove that they are not ordinary leaders. Such is the fate of Christian freedom. Few use it save for their own pleasure or advantage, not for the honor of God and the welfare of the neighbor.

Although the exercise of such freedom is a matter for everyone's conscience and no one should seek to forbid or limit it, yet we must see to it that freedom is and shall ever be the servant of love and of the neighbor. And where men take offence or are led astray by the differences in usage we are bound, in truth, to forego our freedom and, as far as possible, to seek the improvement of the people and not cause offense by what we do or omit to do. Since this external order of service may serve the neighbor and there is nothing here affecting matters of conscience before God, we should seek to be of one mind in Christian love, as St. Paul teaches, and, as far as feasible, have like usages and ceremonies, even as all Christians have the one Baptism and the one Sacrament; nobody has received from God a special one of his own.

This is not to say that those who are already provided with a proper Order, or by God's grace can do better than I, shall abandon theirs and give place to ours. For it is not my thought that all Germany must immediately adopt our Wittenberg Order. It has never been so that all foundations, monasteries and parishes had a uniformity of observance. But it would be well if in every jurisdiction public worship were uniform and neighboring towns and villages observed the same ceremonies as the city. Nor should there by any constraint or reproof if in other jurisdictions they wished to observe the same ceremonies or make additions of their own. In short, we do not introduce any Order for the sake of those who already are Christians. They do not need them, for one does not live for such things. But they live for our sake, who are not yet Christians, that they may make Christians out of us. Their worship is in the spirit.

We need such Orders for those who either must still become Christians or need to be strengthened, since a Christian does not need Baptism, the Word of the Sacrament as a Christian—it is all his—but as a sinner. They are needed, most of all, for the sake of the simple minded and the youth, who shall and must be drilled and trained in the Scriptures and God's Word every day so that they may become familiar with the Scriptures, apt, well-versed and learned in them, enabled to defend their faith and in due time may teach others and help to increase the Kingdom of Christ. For their sake we must read, sing, preach, write and compose, and if it would help the matter along, I would have all the bells pealing, and all the organs playing, and let everything chime in that has a clapper. For this is damnable thing in the papal services, that they have been changed into laws, works and merits to the utter destruction of faith.

Nor did they use them to educate the youth and the simple minded, to drill them in the Scriptures and God's Word, but became so enmeshed in them as to regard them as themselves useful and necessary for salvation. That is the devil himself. The ancients did not institute nor order them with such intentions.

There are three kinds of services and masses. First the Latin, which we have published under the title: *Formula missae*.

This service I do not wish hereby to abrogate or change. As it has been in use by us hitherto, so shall it remain available for use where and when it pleases us or occasion calls for it. For I would in no wise banish the Latin tongue entirely from the Service, for the youth is my chiefest concern. If I could bring it to pass and Greek and Hebrew were as familiar to us as the Latin, and offered as much good music and song, we would hold mass, sing and read on successive Sundays in all four languages, German, Latin, Greek and Hebrew.

I am not at all in sympathy with those who cling to one language and despise all others. I would rather train the youth and folks who could also be of service to Christ in foreign lands and able to converse with the natives there, in order to avoid the experience of the Waldensians in Bohemia, who confined their faith to one language so completely, that they cannot speak correctly and intelligently with anyone, unless he first learn their language. This was not the method of the Holy Spirit at the beginning. He did not tarry until all the world came to Jerusalem and studied Hebrew, but gave manifold tongues for the office of the ministry, so that the apostles could preach wherever they went. I would rather follow this example. It is proper that the youth should be trained in many languages, for who knows how God may use them in time to come. For this our schools have been established.

The second is the German Mass and Order of Service, with which we are concerned here and which should be introduced for the sake of the simple laymen. These two Orders of Service must be used publicly, in the churches, for all the people. For among them are many who do not believe and are not yet Christians. The greater part stands around and gapes, hoping to see something new, just as if we were holding a service among the Turks or the heathen in a public square or out in a field. For there is as yet no well-ordered and organized congregation here, in which the Christians could be ruled according to the Gospel. Our Service is a public provocation to faith and to Christianity.

The third kind of Service which a truly Evangelical Church Order should have would not be held in a public place for all sorts of people, but for those who mean to be real Christians and profess the Gospel with hand and mouth. They would record their names on a list and meet by themselves in some house in order to pray, read, baptize, receive the Sacrament and do other Christian works. In this manner those who do not lead Christian lives could be known, reproved, reclaimed, cast out or excommunicated, according to the rule of Christ in Matthew XVIII. Here one could also establish a common benevolent fund among the Christians, which should be willingly given and distributed among the poor, according to the example of St. Paul, II Corinthians ix. The many and elaborate chants would be unnecessary. There could be a short, appropriate Order for Baptism and the Sacrament and everything centered on the Word and Prayer and Love. There would be need of a good brief catechism on the Creed, the Ten Commandments and the Our Father. In short, if one had the people and persons who wanted to be Christians in fact, the rules and regulations could easily be supplied.

But as yet I neither can nor desire to begin, or to make rules for such a congregation or assembly. I have not yet the persons necessary to accomplish it; nor do I observe many who strongly urge it. If circumstances should force me to it and I can no longer refuse with a good conscience, I shall gladly do my part and help as best I may. In the meanwhile the two kinds of service mentioned must suffice and I shall publicly help to foster, in addition to the preaching, such services for all the people as shall train the youth and call and provoke others to faith, until the Christians who take the Word seriously, find themselves and become insistent. If I should begin it by myself, it may result in a revolt. For we Germans are an untamed, crude, boisterous folk with whom one ought not lightly start anything except under the compulsion of a very great need.

Let us to it, in God's Name. First, the German Service needs an easily understood, plain, simple catechism. Catechism means instruction, in which heathen who want to be Christians are taught and directed in what they should believe, do, omit to do, and know in the Christian religion. For this reason beginners, who were admitted to such instruction and studied the Creed before they were baptized, were called *Catechumenos*. This instruction or direction I know not how to put in a clearer or better way than has been done since the beginning of Christendom and retained to our own day, namely in these three, the Ten Commandments, the Creed and the Our Father. These three contain, simply and briefly, about everything a Christian needs to know. This instruction must be given, as long as there is no special congregation, from the pulpit at stated times or daily as may be needed, and repeated or read aloud evenings and mornings in the homes for the children and the servants, if we want

126

to train them as Christians. They should not merely learn to say the words by heart, as heretofore, but with each part they should be asked questions and give answer, what each part means and how they understand it. If everything cannot be covered at once, one part should be taken up and the next day another. For if the parents and guardians of youth will not take the pains to do this themselves or secure others to do it, there will never be a catechism, unless it should come to pass that separate congregations were organized, as stated above.

They should be questioned like this: What do you pray? Answer: The Our Father. What does it mean when you say, Our Father in heaven? Answer: That God is not an earthly but a heavenly Father who would make us rich and blessed in heaven. What does this mean: Thy Name be hallowed? Answer: That we should honor His Name and keep it from being profaned. How is His Name dishonored and profaned? Answer: When we, who should be His children, live evil lives and teach and believe what is wrong. And so on, what the Kingdom of God means; how it comes; what God's Will is; what Daily Bread means; etc.

So in the Creed; What do you believe? Answer: I believe in God the Father, to the end. Thereafter one part after the other as time permits, one part or two at once. For instance; What does it mean to believe in God the Father Almighty? Answer: It means to trust in Him with all the heart and with assurance to expect all grace, favor, help and comfort from Him in time and in eternity. What does it mean to believe in Jesus Christ His Son? Answer: It means to believe in the heart that we would all be eternally lost if Christ had not died for us, etc.

Likewise in the Ten Commandments; one must ask, What does the first Commandment mean, the second, the third and the other Commandments? These questions can be taken from our *Betbuechlein* where the three chief parts are briefly explained, or one can follow his own method, until all Christian teaching is summed up for the heart in two portions, as it were two pouches, which are faith and love. Faith's pouch may have two purses. Into the one we put this, that we believe that through the sin of Adam we are all corrupt, sinners, and under condemnation, Romans v, Psalm li. Into the other purse we put this, that we are all saved through Jesus Christ from such corruption, sin and condemnation,

127

Romans v, John iii. Love's pouch may also have two purses. One shall contain this, that we should serve and do good to everyone, even as Christ hath done for us, Romans xiii; the other shall have this, that we should suffer and endure all kinds of evil with joy.

When a child begins to understand this, it should be encouraged to bring home Scripture texts from the sermons and repeat them at meal-time for the parents, as was formerly the custom with the Latin lesson. Then those texts should be put into the pouches and purses just as the Pfennige, Groschen or Gulden are put into the pockets. For instance: let faith's pouch be the golden pouch. Into the first purse this text shall go, Romans v: Through one man's sin all men are sinners and have passed under condemnation. Also this one, Psalm li: Behold, I was shapen in inquity, and in sin did my mother conceive me. These are two Rhenish Gulden for this purse. The Hungarian Gulden go into the other purse, as this text, Romans iv: Christ was delivered up for our trespasses and was raised again for our justification. Again, John I: Behold the Lamb of God, that beareth the sin of the world. These are two precious Hungarian Gulden for that purse.

Let love's pouch be the silver pouch. Into the first purse shall go the texts concerning welldoing, such as Galatians v: Through love be servants one to another. Matthew xxv: What ye have done unto one of the least of these my brethren, ye have done unto Me. They would be two silver Groschen for that purse. Into the other purse shall go this text, Matthew v: Blessed are ye, when men shall persecute you for my sake. Hebrews xii: Whom the Lord loveth he chasteneth, and scourgeth every son whom he receiveth. These are two Schreckenberger for that purse.

Let none think himself too wise for this and despise such child's play. Christ, in order to train men, must needs become a man himself. If we wish to train children, we must become children with them. Would to God such child's play were widely practiced. In a short time we would have a wealth of Christian people, souls becoming rich in Scripture and the knowledge of God, until they would, of their own accord add more of such purses as *Locos communes* and comprehend all Scripture in them. Otherwise things will remain as they have been, a daily going to church and a coming away again. For no one thinks that it makes any difference except for the time it takes. No one expects to learn anything there.

A man listens to preaching three or four years and does not learn enough to give answer concerning one article of the Creed; this I know from daily experience. Enough is written in the books, yes; but it has not been driven home to the hearts.

Concerning the Service

Since the chief and greatest aim of any Service is to preach and teach God's Word, we have arranged for sermons and lessons as follows: For the holy day or Sunday we retain the customary Epistles and Gospels and have three sermons. Early at five or six o'clock a few Psalms are chanted for Matins. A sermon follows on the Epistle of the day, chiefly for the sake of the servants, so that they too, may be cared for and hear God's Word, if perchance they cannot be present at the other sermons. After this an antiphon and the Te Deum or the Benedictus, alternately, concluding with the Lord's Prayer, Collect and Benedicamus Domino.

At the Mass, at eight or nine o'clock there is preaching on the Gospel appointed for the day. At Vespers in the afternoon there is preaching before the Magnificat, on the Old Testament, taken in proper order. The customary Epistles and Gospels of the various days of the year are retained by us because there is nothing specially censurable in this custom. This is the arrangement at Wittenberg at the present time when many are here who must learn to preach in the places where the system of Epistles and Gospels still is and may remain in vogue. Since in this matter we can be of service to others without loss to ourselves, we have made no change, without thereby implying any criticism of those who would take the complete books of the Evangelists in hand. This, we think, provides sufficient preaching and teaching for the layman; he who desires more, will find an abundance on the other days.

On Monday and Tuesday, early, we have a German lesson on the Ten Commandments, the Creed and the Lord's Prayer, Baptism and the Sacrament, so that these two days shall preserve the Catechism and deepen its understanding. On Wednesday, early, again a German lesson for which the Evangelist Matthew has been appointed, so that the day shall be his very own, especially since he is an excellent evangelist for the instruction of the congregation, reports the great sermon of Christ on the mount, and strongly urges the exercise of love and good works. The Evangelist John, who is so mighty in teaching faith, has his own day, too, on Saturday afternoon at Vespers. In this way we have a daily study of two evangelists. Thursday and Friday bring us, early in the morning, the weekday lessons from the Epistles of the Apostles and the rest of the New Testament. Thus enough lessons and sermons are appointed to give the Word of God free course among us. Then there are still the lectures given in the university for the scholars.

To exercise the boys and pupils in the Bible, this is done. Every day of the week they chant a few Psalms in Latin, before the Lesson, as customary at Matins hitherto. For we want to keep the youth in the knowledge and use of the Latin Bible, as was said above. After the Psalms a chapter from the New Testament is read in Latin by two or three of the boys in succession, depending on its length. Another boy then reads the same chapter in German, for the exercise, and for the benefit of any layman who might be present. Thereupon they proceed with an antiphon to the German lesson mentioned above. After the lesson the whole assembly sings a German hymn, the Lord's Prayer is said secretly, the pastor or chaplain reads a collect, closing with the Benedicamus Domino as usual.

At Vespers they chant a few of the Vesper Psalms in the same manner as heretofore in Latin with an antiphon, followed by a hymn, if one be available. Two or three of the boys, one after the other, again read a chapter in Latin from the Old Testament, or half a chapter, depending on the length. Another boy reads the same chapter in German, the Magnificat follows in Latin with an antiphon or hymn, the Lord's Prayer, said secretly, and the Collects with the Benedicamus. This is the daily week-day Service in the cities where there are schools.

The Sunday Service for the Laity

We allow the vestments, altars, and candles to remain in use until they are used up or it pleases us to make a change. But we do not oppose anyone who would herein do otherwise. In the true Mass, however, of real Christians, the altar could not remain where it is and the priest would always face the people as doubtless Christ did in the Last Supper. But let that await its own time.

To begin the Service we sing a hymn or a German Psalm in the first Tone[2] after this manner:

I will bless the Lord at all times: His praise shall continually be in my mouth. My soul shall make her boast in the Lord: The humble shall hear thereof and be glad, etc.

Then follows the Kyrie Eleison in the same Tone, three times and not nine times:

Kyrie Eleison.   Christe Eleison.   Kyrie Eleison.

Thereupon the priest reads a Collect in F faut in monotone as follows:

Almighty God, Who art the protector of all who trust in Thee, without Whose grace nothing is strong, nothing is holy, increase and multiply upon us Thy mercy, that by Thy holy inspiration we may think the things that are right and by Thy power may perform the same, through Jesus Christ, our Lord. Amen.

Thereafter the Epistle in the eighth Tone, in the same key as the Collect:

> The rules for this are these:
> Period is the end of a sentence.
> Colon is the part of a sentence.
> Comma is the subdivision within the colon.

Rules for this chant:

Beginning. Comma. Second Comma. Colon. Period. Question. Finale. Example: Thus writeth the holy Apostle Paul to the Corinthians. Dear Brethren, Let a man so account of us as of the ministers of Christ and stewards of the mysteries of Christ, etc.

He should read the Epistle facing the people, but the Collect facing the altar. After the Epistle a German hymn is sung: Nun bitten wir den heiligen Geist, or some other hymn by the full choir. Then he reads the Gospel in the fifth Tone, also facing the people.

The rules for chanting this are these:

Beginning. Comma. Second Comma. Colon. Period. Finale.

Voice of Persons:

Comma. Second Comma. Colon. Period. Question. Finale.

The Voice of Christ:

Comma. Colon. Period. Question. Finale.

Example: The Gospel of the Fourth Sunday in Advent would be chanted as follows: Thus writeth St. John in his Gospel. This is the witness of John when the Jews sent priests and Levites from Jerusalem to ask him, Who art thou? Etc.

After the Gospel the whole congregation sings the Creed in German: Wir glauben all an einen Gott.

The sermon on the Gospel for the Sunday or festival day follows. If we had a German Postil for the entire year, I think it would be best to direct that the sermon for the day, in whole or in part, should be read for the people out of the book, not only for the sake of the preachers who could not do any better, but also to prevent the rise of enthusiasts and sects. The homilies read at Matins seem to indicate that once such was the custom. For unless spiritual knowledge and the Spirit Himself speak through the preachers (whom I do not wish hereby to limit, for the Spirit teaches better how to preach than all the postils and homilies), the final result will be that everyone preaches his own whims and instead of the Gospel and its exposition we shall again have sermons on blue ducks. This is one of the reasons why we retain the Epistles and Gospels as they are given in the postils—there are so few gifted preachers who are able to give a powerful and practical exposition of a whole evangelist or some other book of the Bible.

After the sermon shall follow a public paraphrase of the Lord's Prayer and admonition for those who want to partake of the Sacrament, after this or a better fashion:

Dear Friends of Christ. Since we are here assembled in the Name of the Lord to receive His holy Testament, I admonish you first of all to lift up your hearts to God to pray with me the Lord's Prayer, as Christ our Lord has taught us and has given comfortable promise that it shall be heard.

That God, our Father in heaven, may look with mercy on us, His needy children on earth and grant us grace so that His holy Name be hallowed by us and all the world through the pure and righteous teaching of His Word and the fervent love of our lives; that He would graciously turn from us all

132

false doctrine and evil living whereby His precious Name is blasphemed and profaned.

That His Kingdom may come and be enlarged; that all transgressors, the sin-darkened, and those in the bonds of Satan's kingdom be brought to a knowledge of the true faith in Jesus Christ, His Son, and the number of Christians be increased.

That we may be strengthened by His Spirit to do His Will and suffer it to be done, both in life and in death, in good things and in evil, ever breaking, offering, slaying our own wills.

That He would also give us our daily bread, preserve us from avarice and gluttony, relying upon Him to grant us a sufficiency of all good things.

That He would forgive our debts as we forgive our debtors so that our heart may have a calm and joyful conscience before Him and no sin may frighten us nor make us afraid.

That He would not lead us into temptation but help us by His Spirit to subdue the flesh, despise the world and its ways and overcome the devil with all his wiles.

And finally, that He would deliver us from all evil, bodily, and spiritually, in time and in eternity.

All those who earnestly desire these things, will say, from their very hearts, Amen, believing without doubt that it is yea, and answered in heaven as Christ hath promised: Whatsoever things ye desire when ye pray, believe that ye shall receive them, and ye shall have then. Amen.

Secondly, I admonish you in Christ, that ye look upon the Testament of Christ in true faith above all having confident assurance in your hearts in the words by which Christ grants us His body and blood for the forgiveness of sins. That ye remember and give thanks to His boundless love, of which He gave proof when He redeemed us by His blood from God's wrath, sin, death, and hell, and thereupon take to yourselves externally the bread and wine, that is, His body and blood, as your guarantee and pledge. In His Name therefore, and according to His command, let us proceed by the use of His own words to the observance and administration of the Testament.

Whether such paraphrase and admonition should be read in the pulpit immediately after the sermon, or at the altar, I would leave to everyone's own decision. It seems as if the ancients did so in the pulpit, so that the custom still obtains to read General Prayers or to repeat the Lord's Prayer in the pulpit, but the former admonition has now become a Public Confession. But in this way the Lord's Prayer together with a short exposition of it would be current among the people, and the Lord would be remembered, even as He commanded at the Supper.

I want to stress this point, however, that the paraphrase and admonition be made in previously determined and prescribed words or be formulated in some definite manner for the sake of the common people. We cannot have one man do it one way today and tomorrow another do it some other way, everybody showing his art and confusing the people, so that they can neither learn nor abide by anything. What chiefly matters is the teaching and guiding of the people. Here it is necessary therefore to limit our freedom and keep to one form of such paraphrase and admonition, particularly in one church or congregation by itself, if, to retain its liberty, it will not follow the form used by another.

The Office and Consecration follows in this wise:

Example: Our Lord Jesus Christ, in the night in which He was betrayed, took bread; and when He had given thanks, He brake it and gave it to His disciples, saying, Take, eat; This is My Body, which is given for you; this do as oft as ye do it, in remembrance of Me.

After the same manner also, He took the cup, when He had supped, and said, Take and drink ye all of it, this is the Cup, a new Testament in My Blood, which is shed for you for the remission of sins: this do, as oft as ye drink it, in remembrance of Me.

It seems to me that it would be in accord with the institution of the Lord's Supper to administer the Sacrament immediately after the consecration of the Bread, before the Cup is blessed,[3] for both Luke and Paul say: He took the cup after they had supped, etc. During the distribution of the Bread the German Sanctus could be sung, or the hymn, Gott sei gelobet, or the hymn of John Hus: Jesus Christus unser Heiland. Then shall the Cup be blessed and administered; while the remainder of the hymns mentioned are sung, or the German Agnus Dei. Let there be a chaste and orderly approach, not men and women with each other but the women after the men, wherefore they should also stand separately at allotted places. What should be the attitude in respect to secret Confession, I have indicated in other writings and my opinion can be found in the *Betbuechlein*.

We do not want to abolish the Elevation but retain it because it goes well with the German Sanctus and signifies that Christ has commanded us to remember Him. For as the Sacrament is elevated in a material manner and yet Christ's body and blood are not seen in it, so He is remembered and elevated by the word of the sermon and is confessed and adored in the reception of the Sacrament. Yet it is all apprehended by faith, for we cannot see how Christ gives His body and blood for us and even now daily shows and offers it before God to obtain grace for us.

The German Sanctus

Isaiah, in a vision, saw the Lord
Enthroned, amid a heavenly light outpoured,
His garment's edge filled all the temple space,
The prophet's soul was filled with awe and grace.
Above the throne there stood two seraphim;
Each had six wings, his view disclosed to him.
With two they kept their faces veiled from view
And covered modestly their feet with two,
While two served them in flight. To praise His name
They sang this hymn to God with loud acclaim:
Holy is God, the Lord of Sabaoth,
Holy is God, the Lord of Sabaoth,
Holy is God, the Lord of Sabaoth,
His glory hath gone forth o'er all the earth.
The clamor of their voices shook the place,
With haze and smoke the temple filled apace.

The Collect follows with the Benediction.

We give thanks to Thee, Almighty God, that Thou hast refreshed us with this Thy salutary gift; and we beseech Thee, of Thy mercy, to strengthen us through the same in faith toward Thee, and in fervent love toward one another; through Jesus Christ, our Lord. Amen.

The Lord bless thee and keep thee.
The Lord make His face shine upon thee,
    and be gracious unto thee.
The Lord lift up His countenance upon thee,
    and give thee peace.

Exercitation or Practice for the Intoning

In order to increase proficiency in intoning and greater familiarity with the colons, commas, and similar pauses, I add another illustration. Some one else may choose another.

The Epistle

Thus writeth St. Paul, the holy apostle of Jesus Christ to the Corinthians: Let a man so account of us, as of the ministers of Christ, and stewards of the mysteries of God.

The Gospel

Hear the Holy Gospel. Thus saith Jesus Christ to His disciples: No man can serve two masters, for either he will hate the one and love the other; or else he will hold to the one and despise the other.

This is what I have to say concerning the daily Service and the teaching of God's Word, which is primarily for the training of the young and the encouragement of the simpleminded; for they who come out of curiosity and the desire for new things will soon tire of it and become indifferent. This has been the case with the Latin services; there was singing and reading in the churches every day and yet the churches remained bare and empty. It is beginning to be so in the German services, too. Therefore, it is best to plan the services in the interest of the young and such of the simpleminded as may happen to come. With all others, neither law nor order, admonition or urging will help: let them go, so that they may grant and consent to the things in the service, which they dislike and are unwilling to do. God is not pleased with forced service; it is hopeless and in vain.

On festivals like Christmas, Easter, Pentecost, St. Michael's Day, Purification, and the like, we must continue with the Latin services until enough German hymns become available for them. This work is only in its beginning: not everything required for it is ready. But it is needful to know how we should and could have a uniform usage, so that the differences in usage may be regulated and restrained.

Lent, Palm Sunday and Holy Week are continued, not to force anyone to fast, but to retain the Passion History and the Gospels appointed for that season. Not in such fashion, however, that we still have the Lenten Veil, Throwing of Palms, Veiling of Pictures, and whatever else of such trickery there is; nor do we continue the singing of four Passions, or

136

preaching on the Passion for eight hours on Good Friday. Holy Week shall be like any other week save that the Passion History be explained every day for an hour, throughout the week or on as many days as may be desirable, and that the Sacrament be given to everyone who desires it. For among Christians the whole service should center in the Word and Sacrament.

In short, this or any other Order shall be so used that whenever it becomes an abuse, it shall be straightway abolished and replaced by another, even as King Hezekiah put away and destroyed the brazen serpent, made by command of God Himself, because the children of Israel made an abuse of it. The Orders must serve for the improvement of faith and love and not cause any injury to faith. If they no longer serve their purpose, they are already dead and gone, of no value whatever; just as a good coin, when counterfeited, is cancelled and changed because of the abuse, or as new shoes become old and uncomfortable and are worn no longer but are thrown away and new ones bought. An Order is an external thing, no matter how good it is, it can be abused. Then it is no longer an Order but a Disorder. No Order exists, therefore, or is of any value, in and by itself, as the Papal Orders were held to be until now; but the life, worth, power and virtue of any Order is in its proper use; otherwise it is utterly worthless and good for nothing.

God's Spirit and grace be with us all. Amen.

NOTES

1. Transcribed from *Works of Martin Luther* (Philadelphia: Muhlenberg, 1932), VI, 170-86.
2. Of the eight Gregorian Psalm tones (chants), Luther mentions here and subsequently the first, fifth, and eighth.
3. This suggestion did not attain general acceptance. The Brunswick Liturgy of 1528 adopted it. In the Wittenberg order of 1533 it was no longer mentioned.

V
ULRICH ZWINGLI

The Zurich Liturgy
1525

ZWINGLI

Zwingli's first liturgical work was *An Attack on the Canon of the Mass* (*CR* 2: 556-608) which appeared in August, 1523, during the critical years of the reformation in Zurich. Aside from his impatience with the literary imperfections of the Mass, which led him to deny that it belonged to high antiquity, Zwingli's main point of contention was the sacrificial emphasis of the Canon. Having put its prayers through a searching analysis, he concluded that the Canon was "full of Godlessness," because it contradicted Scriptural evidence that "the Mass is not a sacrifice, but a memorial of *the* sacrifice, and a pledge of the redemption that Christ hath shown us." That part of the liturgy needed to be remodeled or completely done away.

Despite such radical pronouncements, Zwingli's policy of revision was one of conservatism "for the sake of the weaker brethren." He kept the first part of the Mass intact, except to simplify the lectionary, remove the Propers for saints' days, and to insist that the lessons and sermon must be given in the vernacular. Otherwise, Latin continued to rule the liturgy, which was still enhanced by the traditional vestments, ceremonies, and music. Zwingli's main interest in the liturgy of the Faithful was taken up by the Canon, which at first he tried to amend and keep; but he soon lost patience with its incoherence and barbarisms, and was finally defeated by its sacrificial emphasis. Rather than dispense with the Canon entirely, as Luther did, he put four of his own Latin prayers in its place. Those prayers suggest some insecurity in his thinking about the Lord's Supper. While he was convinced that the celebration was meant to be a memorial of Calvary, he also conceded that "the bread and wine become the body and blood of Christ to those who partake of them in faith" (*CR* 2: 604).

The conservatives scolded him for going too far; the radicals, for not going far enough. The latter element, shortly to become the Zurich Anabaptists, could not reconcile the clear mandate of Scripture with the slow pace Zwingli recommended. At length, in the summer of 1524, the "cleansing" of the churches began. Zwingli and his colleagues, accompanied by all manner of craftsmen, entered the churches and set to work. They disposed of the relics, raised their ladders against the walls and whitewashed the paintings and decorations, carted away the statues and ornaments, the gold and silver equipment, the costly vestments and splendidly bound service-books. They closed the organs in token that no music of any kind would resound in the churches again: the people were to give ear to the Word of God alone.

By Christmas, 1524, only the Mass remained, although it had become a source of great contention. Some pastors continued to use the Constance Missal, and some had taken up Zwingli's revision; but the Anabaptists preferred neither. Distressed by the confusion, Zwingli insisted upon the abolition of the Mass, first in his *Commentary on True and False Religion* (March, 1525) and then in vigorous representations to the Zurich Council. On April 11, 1525, which was Tuesday of Holy Week, the reformers appeared before the Council of Zurich to demand that the Roman liturgy be replaced by one agreeable to the Scriptures. Zwingli submitted such a service, *Action or Use of the Lord's Supper*, which he had recently prepared and published in German (*CR* 4: 13-24). The authorities abolished the Mass the next day, and agreed to the introduction of the new service, but with one qualification: they refused to allow the antiphonal recitations by the men and the women, which Zwingli had woven into his liturgy as a substitute for congregational singing; only the clergy were permitted to take part. Thus, on Maundy Thursday, Good Friday, and Easter, the faithful received the Lord's Supper according to Zwingli's service; and, as Bullinger remembered it, they did so "with great wonder and still greater joy."

At this time Zwingli made a decision that was of profound

significance to Protestantism. By 1525 he had arrived at a final doctrine of the Lord's Supper, in which he ruled out the possibility that Christians could participate in the substance of Christ's body. As if that were relevant in any case! "The flesh profiteth nothing," read the sixth chapter of John, which was the invariable Gospel lesson in the new Eucharistic liturgy. Zwingli was convinced that faith is given and nourished solely by the Holy Spirit, apart from any physical channels, any external means, especially anything so crass as eating. Thus the Supper remained to him a vivid spiritual exercise in which the elements of bread and wine were but reminders, not vehicles, of grace. As symbols of Christ's body and blood, their value lay in engaging the senses and fixing the mind upon the great moment of our redemption on Calvary, so that the believer might be brought "to consciousness of the actual thing through faith and contemplation." The Eucharist was above all a contemplative experience of the goodness of God manifest on the Cross of Christ—so vivid to the man of faith that he could "grasp the thing itself." Even so, Zwingli apparently decided that such an occasion need only be offered to Christians four times a year: at Easter, Pentecost, autumn, and Christmas. With that decision, the Eucharist was disconnected from the normal service of the Lord's Day; and Zwingli was left to devise a new type of Sunday worship around the sermon.

He based his liturgy of the Word (*CR* 4: 686-7) upon a vernacular preaching service in John Ulrich Surgant's *Manuale Curatorum* (Basel, 1502). Surgant, an eminent Basel pastor and professor at the university, developed the liturgy from the Medieval Prone in the interest of a liturgical reform that would revive biblical preaching and congregational worship. Intending no depreciation of the Roman rite, he designed the office to be preparatory to the Mass; but the split thus implicit between Word and Sacrament became exaggerated in the Zurich reformation. That Zwingli drew upon this source is apparent in both the structure and language of his own preaching service, as well as in the retention of such curious elements as the Ave Maria and the Commemoration of the Dead. He even accepted Surgant's practice of having the Confession of sins at the very end of the service, so that worship concluded abruptly on the note of penitence and lacked finality except in anticipation of the Mass.

For this reason, J. Schweizer contends that Zwingli never

meant to separate Word and Sacrament, precisely because his "Word-service cries for completion" in the Eucharist. Schweizer reasons that the Protestant Eucharist depended upon the actual communication of the people, and that Zwingli was thwarted by the popular reluctance to communicate often. If the Medieval Church found it difficult to bring the people to the altar once a year, then Zwingli actually made progress by requiring the Zurichers to partake quarterly. And if his premature death had not brought an end to this educational work, he might have persuaded them to go to the Lord's table every Sunday.

Schweizer's argument seems to depreciate the central importance that Zwingli assigned to preaching, and to overlook the fact that there is nothing in his Eucharistic doctrine to necessitate frequent Communion: the Supper did not convey grace, or mediate the divine life, or remit sins. Finally, Zwingli himself provided a sound theological reason for placing the Confession of sins last in the liturgy, holding that genuine confession could only be made after the sermon, *in response* to the Word that teaches men to recognize their misery and assures them of forgiveness (*CR* 3: 820-3).

The sermon was the solemn center of Zwingli's liturgy of the Word, to which everything else referred—from the first plea for the presence of the Spirit whò "opens" the Word, to the last act of Confession, made in the knowledge of human misery and divine mercy which only the Word affords. Silence and simplicity were the moods of this service, not because the Bible commanded such, but because these served the essential nature of worship as Zwingli understood it. Churchgoers were not expected to rush into the traditional activities of worship—seeing and doing, making adoration and oblation to the righteous God—but to wait in stillness and repose upon the loving heavenly Father, that they might *hear* His Word and *receive* His gift of forgiveness and sonship.

In the preparation of a Communion liturgy, Zwingli was thrown entirely upon his own creativity. He was not disposed to refer again to the Roman rite. Nor could Surgant help him in this instance, for he had never taken the liberty of improvising upon the Missal. In the "preface" to his liturgy, Zwingli set forth a sharp statement of policy: "It will be necessary to remove from Christ's Supper everything which does not conform to the divine Word." By that statement, however, Zwingli did not propose to have some sort of biblical worship, evolved wholly out of Scripture and purged of all things traditional. His real purpose—here and always—was to be rid of symbols that he deemed unscriptural or ambiguous, so as to make way for authentic symbols that would express the New Testament Gospel with simplicity, clarity, and power.

Thus a simple table was established at the front of the nave, in the midst of the people who were seated round about. It was not a place where man offered to God, but where God gave to man; and it was not the precinct of priests, but a congregational table for the new family of God. The ministers stood behind the table, facing the congregation, wearing the black academic habit used every day by men of letters. Their whole demeanor illustrated that they were not priests, nor guardians of the altar, still less actors who took the parts of Jesus and His disciples in a replica of the Last Supper. They were fellow members of the Body of Christ, servants of their brethren at this table of the Lord. They read the service in German, speaking in "a loud clear voice, so that all the people may know what is done." The congregation was privileged, through the direct medium of speech, to participate in genuinely "common worship." Moreover, if the civil authorities had not prevented him, Zwingli would have given the congregation a substantial part in the liturgy by having them engage in antiphonal recitation.

Zwingli's conception of the Eucharist in its liturgical setting is most clearly seen in the delivery of the elements. After the assistant had read the Words of Institution (I Cor. 11), there was no more speaking, and a profound stillness settled over the church. When the clergy had communicated, the assistants carried the elements to the people in wooden utensils. No Words of Delivery were spoken, no music sung or played; but the silence prevailed. The people remained in their places. They took the utensils in their hands, communicated, and passed them on to the rest. Meanwhile (according to the 1535 edition of the liturgy) another assistant read aloud from the Gospel of John, beginning at the thirteenth chapter.

Thus by a powerful, communal symbol, the congregation realized itself as the Body of Christ. Moreover this method made provision for "the contemplation of faith" to which Zwingli laid such importance. A stillness came over the

145

church, supported by the repose of the people who did not stir from their places. But Zwingli provided two aids to contemplation, so that the worshiper would not lapse into mere imagination or the wandering of his mind. One consisted of the Eucharistic elements, which Zwingli found to be powerful stimulants to the mind, enabling it to fix itself in contemplation more quickly and effectively. The other was the Word of the Lord, which the assistant read to the people as they communicated. And the people, in contemplation, looked through the Supper to "the thing itself": they laid hold of the goodness of God manifest on Calvary "as surely and undoubtedly as if it were shown to the natural eye." Whatever defects there may have been in Zwingli's Eucharistic theology and liturgy, the occasion was anything but a bare memorial. The Zurich liturgy of 1535 spoke of it as "a great holy mystery." Not in much speaking or teaching, not in a profusion of ceremonies, but in monumental simplicity and stillness, this liturgy gave expression to the central affirmations of Zwingli's Eucharistic theology: contemplation, fellowship, thanksgiving, and moral earnestness.

FOR FURTHER READING

CR = *Huldreich Zwinglis sämtliche Werke: Corpus Reformatorum,* edited by E. Egli and G. Finsler. 13 vols. Leipzig, 1905-35.

Yngve Brilioth, *Eucharistic Faith & Practice.* London, 1956.

Cyril C. Richardson, *Zwingli and Cranmer on the Eucharist.* Evanston, 1949.

F. Schmidt-Clausing, *Zwingli als Liturgiker.* Göttingen, 1952.

J. Schweizer, *Reformierte Abendmahlsgestaltung in der Schau Zwinglis.* Basel, n.d.

LITURGY OF THE WORD

1525 [1]

A form of prayer according to the teaching of Paul in I Tim. 2,[2] which is now used in Zurich at the beginning of the Sermon.

Let us earnestly beseech God that He will graciously open His holy and eternal Word to us poor men, and establish us in the knowledge of His will, and direct all who err in His Word to the right way again, so that we may live according to His divine pleasure.

Then let us pray God for all Christian rulers, for the honorable authorities of the common Confederacy, especially for the godly burgomasters, councils, and the whole community of this city and canton of Zurich, that it may please God to guide and direct them all according to His will, so that we may lead a god-fearing, peaceful and Christian life with one another, and rest in eternal peace when this miserable life is over.

Let us also pray that He will grant grace and perseverance to all who have come to be persecuted and oppressed for the sake of His Word, that they may remain firm and steadfast in their commitment to Him; and that He will mercifully grant us, out of His loving-kindness, all the necessities of body and soul.

Say: Our Father, which art in heaven. Hallowed be Thy name. Thy Kingdom come. Thy will be done, in earth as it is in heaven. Give us our daily bread. Forgive us our debt, as we forgive our debtors. And lead us not into temptation, but deliver us from evil. Amen.

Hail Mary, thou highly favored one. The Lord is with thee. Blessed art thou among women and blessed is the fruit of thy body: Jesus Christ. Amen.

¶ *If anyone has died during the week, it is announced after the Sermon on Sunday, in the following form.*

Since nothing warns man of himself more than death, it is fitting that we are notified about those of our congregation who have died in true Christian faith, in order that we may ever prepare ourselves and be on watch at all times, according to the warning of the Lord.[3] And these are the brothers and sisters whom God called away, out of this time, during the week: namely N.

Now let us praise and thank God that He has taken from this misery these brothers and sisters, our fellows in true faith and hope, and relieved them of all distress and toil, and placed them in everlasting joy. Then let us also pray God to grant us so to live our lives that we too will be led in true faith and His grace out of this vale of tears and into the eternal company of His world beyond. Amen.

¶ *At the end of the Sermon, after the General Confession of Sins,[4] the preacher says:*

Almighty, eternal God! Forgive us our sin and lead us to everlasting life; through Jesus Christ our Lord. Amen.

NOTES

1. *CR* 4: 686-7.
2. Cf. I Tim. 2:1-7.
3. Matt. 24:42; 25:13; Mk. 13:33.
4. Zwingli did not provide a form for confession. Apparently he meant to follow Leo Jud's liturgy of 1523 and have the people recite the brief plea of the prodigal son: "O Father, I have sinned in heaven and against thee and am not worthy to be called thy son." *CR* 4: 715.

ACTION OR USE OF THE LORD'S SUPPER

EASTER, 1525 [1]

To all who believe in Christ: We who administer God's Word and are Pastors in Zurich offer Grace and Peace from God.

Dearly beloved brethren, after a long time of error and darkness, we rejoice at the true way and light which God, our heavenly Father, has disclosed to us through His grace. And we esteem it so much more highly, we receive and embrace it with such exceeding desire, because there has been so much destructive and dangerous error. Though innumerable deceptions have occurred till now, to the detriment of faith and love, it still appears to us that not the least of them occurred in the abuse of this Supper. After a long captivity, we have reclaimed the Supper and re-established it in its proper use—by the help of God we hope—just as the children of Israel recovered the Passover lamb in the time of Hezekiah and Josiah the Kings.[2] So much for the Supper itself. Concerning the ceremonies which go with it, some people might suppose that we have perhaps done too much, others that we have done too little. In this matter, however, every congregation may hold its own opinion, for we do not wish to quarrel with anyone on this account. No doubt, all believers are well aware of how much damage and apostasy from God have resulted heretofore from the great mass of ceremonies. We therefore think it best to prescribe as little ceremonial and churchly custom as we can for our people's use of this Supper—which is also a ceremony, but instituted by Christ—lest we yield again, in time, to the old error. Nevertheless, to keep the action from being performed wholly without life and shape, and to make some concession to human weakness, we have authorized such ceremonies for the action—as appointed here—which we have deemed beneficial and appropriate to enhance in some degree the spiritual memorial of the death of Christ, the increase of faith and brotherly love, the reformation of life, and the prevention of the vices of the human heart.

But at the same time, we have no wish at all to condemn the additional ceremonies of other churches—singing and such—for perhaps they are suitable for them and beneficial to their devotion; for we hope that all pastors everywhere are constantly diligent to serve the Lord and to win many people.

We are also prepared, in keeping with divine ordinances, to exclude from this Supper all those who defile the body of Christ with intolerable stains and blemishes, because a communion of Christians and a pure, devout life ought to follow this memorial of Christ's passion and thanksgiving for His death. In what manner this shall be done will be explained in a separate booklet,[3] since time is not left to do it now.

The grace of Christ be with you all.

A PREFACE

That Christ's Supper is seriously abused has been brought out quite strongly and clearly from the Word of God for a long time: therefore, it will be necessary to remove from it everything which does not conform to the divine Word.

This memorial is a thanksgiving and a rejoicing before Almighty God for the benefit which He has manifested to us through His Son; and whoever appears at this feast, meal or thanksgiving bears witness that he belongs to those who believe that they are redeemed by the death and blood of our Lord Jesus Christ: Therefore, on Maundy Thursday,[4] the young people who now desire to come faithfully and in the knowledge of God and His Word and to celebrate this thanksgiving and Supper, shall repair to the nave of the church, between the choir and the transept-aisle, males to the right, females to the left; and the other people shall stay in the archway, the gallery, and other places. And while the Sermon takes place,[5] unleavened bread and wine shall be placed upon a table in the front of the nave. And then the intent and action of Christ—the way He instituted this memorial—shall be recited clearly, intelligibly, and in German (as follows hereafter). Thereupon the bread shall be carried round by the designated servers[6] on broad wooden plates from one seat to the next—to allow each person to break off a morsel or mouthful with his hand and eat it. In the same fashion, they shall go round with the wine, so that no one need move from his place.

And when that is done, praise and thanks shall be offered to God, with clear and distinct words, in a loud, intelligible voice. Then the whole multitude and congregation shall say

"Amen" at the end of the service. —On Good Friday, people of middle age shall assemble at the aforesaid place in the nave, and the thanksgiving shall take place in the same way, the men and women separated, as above. —On Easter Day, the old folk likewise.

The plates and cups are of wood, that pomp may not come back again.

And we shall use this order, so long as it pleases our churches, four times a year: at Easter, Pentecost, autumn,[7] and Christmas.

Action or Use of the Lord's Supper
A Memorial or Thanksgiving of Christ.
As It Will Be Begun in Zurich
At Easter in the Year 1525.

¶ *The overseer or pastor*[8] *turns toward the people and prays the following prayer with a loud, clear voice:*

A PRAYER

O Almighty, Eternal God, whom all creatures rightly honor, worship and praise as their Lord, Creator and Father: grant us poor sinners that with real constancy and faith we may perform thy praise and thanksgiving, which thine only begotten Son, our Lord and Savior Jesus Christ, hath commanded the faithful to do in memory of His death; through the same Jesus Christ, thy Son, our Lord, who liveth and reigneth with thee in unity with the Holy Spirit, God for ever and ever. Amen.

¶ *The server or lector says the following in a loud voice:*

The Lection[9] is found in the first Epistle of Paul to the Corinthians, the eleventh chapter.

"When ye come together therefore into one place [v. 20] . . . For he that eateth and drinketh unworthily, that is, improperly and not as one ought, eateth and drinketh judgment and damnation to himself, not discerning the Lord's body" [v. 29].

¶ *Here the servers say with the whole church:*

Praise be to God.

¶ *Now the pastor begins the first verse of the following hymn of praise, and then the people—men and women—say the verses alternately, one after the other.*

The pastor:	Glory be to God on high!
The men:	And peace on earth!
The women:	To men, a right will! [10]
The men:	We praise thee, we bless thee.
The women:	We worship thee, we glorify thee.
The men:	We give thanks to thee for thy great glory and goodness, O Lord God, heavenly King, Father Almighty!
The women:	O Lord, thou only-begotten Son, Jesus Christ, and the Holy Ghost.
The men:	O Lord God, thou Lamb of God, Son of the Father, thou that takest away the sin of the world, have mercy upon us!
The women:	Thou that takest away the sin of the world, receive our prayer!
The men:	Thou that sittest at the right hand of the Father, have mercy upon us.
The women:	For thou only art holy.
The men:	Thou only art the Lord.
The women:	Thou only, O Jesus Christ, with the Holy Ghost, art most high in the glory of God the Father.

Men and women: Amen.

¶ *Now the deacon or lector says:* The Lord be with you.

¶ *The people respond:* And with thy spirit.

¶ *The lector says the following:*

The following Lection from the Gospel [11] is found in John, the sixth chapter.

¶ *The people respond:* Praise be to God.

¶ *Now the lector begins as follows:*

"Verily, verily, I say unto you, He that believeth and trusteth in me hath everlasting life. I am the bread of life [vs. 47, 48] . . . It is the spirit that quickeneth; the flesh profiteth nothing: the words that I speak unto you, they are spirit, and they are life" [v. 63].

Ulrich Zwingli, The Zurich Liturgy

¶ Then the lector kisses the book and says:

Praise and thanks be to God. He willeth to forgive all our sins according to his holy Word.

¶ The people say: Amen!

¶ Now the first server begins the first line:

I believe in one God,

The men:	In the Father Almighty.
The women:	And in Jesus Christ, his only-begotten Son, our Lord.
The men:	Who was conceived by the Holy Ghost.
The women:	Born of the Virgin Mary.
The men:	Suffered under Pontius Pilate, was crucified, dead and buried.
The women:	He decended into hell.
The men:	The third day he rose again from the dead.
The women:	He ascended into heaven.
The men:	And sitteth on the right hand of God the Father Almighty.
The women:	From thence he shall come to judge the quick and the dead.
The men:	I believe in the Holy Ghost.
The women:	The holy, universal Christian Church, the Communion of Saints.
The men:	The forgiveness of sins.
The women:	The resurrection of the body.
The men:	And the life everlasting.
Men and women:	Amen.

¶ Then the server says:

Dear brothers, in keeping with observance and institution of our Lord Jesus Christ, we now desire to eat the bread and drink the cup which He has commanded us to use in commemoration, praise and thanksgiving that He suffered death for us and shed His blood to wash away our sin. Wherefore, let everyone call to mind, according to Paul's word, how much comfort, faith and assurance he has in the same Jesus Christ our Lord, lest anyone pretend to be a believer who is not, and so be guilty of the Lord's death. Neither let anyone commit offense against the whole Christian communion, which is the body of Christ.

Kneel, therefore, and pray:

Our Father, which art in heaven, hallowed be thy name. Thy kingdom come. Thy will be done, in earth as it is in heaven. Give us our daily bread. Forgive us our debt, as we forgive our debtors. And lead us not into temptation, but deliver us from evil.

¶ *The people say:* Amen.

¶ *Now the server prays further as follows:*

O Lord, God Almighty, who by thy Spirit hast brought us together into thy one body, in the unity of faith, and hast commanded that body to give thee praise and thanks for thy goodness and free gift in delivering thine only begotten Son, our Lord Jesus Christ, to death for our sins: grant that we may do the same so faithfully that we may not, by any pretense or deceit, provoke thee who art the truth which cannot be deceived.[12] Grant also that we may live as purely as becometh thy body, thy family and thy children, so that even the unbelieving may learn to recognize thy name and glory. Keep us, Lord, that thy name and glory may never be reviled because of our lives. O Lord, ever increase our faith, which is trust in thee, thou who livest and reignest, God for ever and ever. Amen.

THE WAY CHRIST INSTITUTED THIS SUPPER

¶ *The server reads as follows:*

"On the night in which He was betrayed and given up to death, Jesus took bread; and when he had given thanks, he brake it, and said, take, eat; this is my body: do this in remembrance of me. After the same manner also, he took the cup after supper, said thanks, and gave it to them, saying, Drink ye all of this: this cup is the new testament in my blood. This do ye, as oft as ye do it, in remembrance of me. For as often as ye shall eat this bread and drink this cup, ye should shew forth and glorify the Lord's death."

¶ *Then the designated servers carry round the unleavened bread, from which each one of the faithful takes a morsel or mouthful with his own hand, or has it offered to him by the server who carries the bread around.[13] And when*

154

those with the bread have proceeded so far that everyone has eaten his small piece, the other servers then follow with the cup, and in the same manner give it to each person to drink. And all of this takes place with such honor and propriety as well becomes the Church of God and the Supper of Christ.

¶ *Afterwards, the people having eaten and drunk, thanks is given according to the example of Christ, by the use of Psalm 112;[14] and the shepherd or pastor[15] begins:*

The pastor:	Praise, O ye servants of the Lord, Praise the name of the Lord.
The men:	Blessed be the name of the Lord, from this time forth and for evermore.
The women:	From the rising of the sun unto the going down of the same the Lord's name is highly praised.
The men:	The Lord is exalted above all nations and His glory above the heavens.
The women:	Who is like unto the Lord our God, who sitteth so high and bendeth down to have care for the things in heaven and earth? [16]
The men:	He raiseth up the humble out of the dust and lifteth the poor out of the filth,
The women:	That He may set him with princes, with the princes of his people.
The men:	He maketh the barren woman of the house to be a mother, who has the joy of children.[17]

¶ *Then the pastor says:*

We give thee thanks, O Lord, for all thy gifts and blessings: thou who livest and reignest, God for ever and ever.

¶ *The people respond:*

Amen.

¶ *The pastor says:*

Depart in peace.

NOTES

1. *CR* 4: 13-24.
2. II Kings 18:4; II Chron. 34:3-7.
3. *Ratschlag betreffend Ausschliessung vom Abendmahl für Ehebrecher, Hurer, Wucherer, uns.* (April, 1525). *CR* 4: 25-34.
4. April 13, 1525.
5. This translation is based upon the assumption that by the word "sermon" Zwingli meant the entire liturgy of the Word.
6. Durch verordnete diener. Zwingli rather consistently used *Diener* in German and *minister* in Latin to refer to the assistants or servers. In this instance, "verordnete" may mean either "designated" or "ordained."
7. Sept. 11, the day of SS. Felix and Regula.
8. Der wechter oder pfarrer. By "wechter" Zwingli may have meant "bishop."
9. Literally: Das yetz geläsen wirdt . . .
10. Den menschen ein recht gmüt!
11. Literally: Das harnach uss dem euangelio geläsen wirt . . .
12. Literally: die unbetrognenn warheyt erzürnind ("provoke the Truth which cannot be deceived"). In subsequent German editions: dich, die unbetrognen warheyt, erzürnind ("provoke thee, the truth which cannot be deceived"). *CR* 4: 692. In the Latin edition of 1536: te infallibilem veritatem . . . offendamus aut irritemus ("offend or provoke thee who art the infallible truth").
13. The 1536 edition clarifies the point: "If anyone does not wish to handle the bread, the assistant who carries it around serves it to him."
14. Psalm 113: 1-9. Zwingli used the Vulgate number, i.e., 112.
15. Der hirt oder pfarrer.
16. Wär ist wie der herr, unser gott, der so hoch sitzet und harnider ist ze sehen in himmel und erden.
17. Der da setzt die unfruchtbaren des huses zü einer müter, die mit kinden froüd hat. Zurich Bible (Christopher Froschauer, 1527): Der die unfruchtbarenn im hauss wonen machet, dass sy ein fröliche kindermüter ist. Vulgate: Qui habitare facit sterilem in domo matrem filiorum laetantem.

VI
MARTIN BUCER

The Strassburg Liturgy
1539

BUCER

Luther hesitated to publish a German Mass until 1526. Meanwhile certain impatient pastors ventured to produce their own vernacular services; • and among those who anticipated Luther in this respect was Diobald Schwarz, an assistant to Matthew Zell, the first reformer at Strassburg. On February 16, 1524, in a chapel at the cathedral, Schwarz read his own *Teutsche Messe*, a conservative adaptation of the Roman rite, which marked the beginning of the Strassburg liturgical tradition.

Schwarz retained much of the traditional cultus—vestments, the Elevation, and such; but the people were no longer dependent upon the ceremonial as the medium of their participation, since German was uniformly employed and loudly spoken. Everything related to the Roman doctrine of sacrifice was removed, discreetly however, by subtle alterations to the familiar text of the Mass. The Confiteor, which Schwarz adapted from the local breviary and renamed "The Common Confession," became a congregational confession of sin and thus a manifestation of the priesthood of all believers. The Absolution consisted merely of I Tim. 1:15, to which the celebrant added: "God have mercy upon us and bless us. Amen." In place of the Offertory with its sacrificial emphasis, an exhortation to self-oblation was devised out of Romans

• See Julius Smend, *Die evangelischen deutschen Messen bis zu Luthers Deutscher Messe.* (Göttingen: Vandenhoeck & Ruprecht, 1896.)

159

12:1. For the rest of the Mass, Schwarz held as closely and constructively to tradition as he could. He delivered both bread and wine to the communicants; and, while no one was forced to assume the chalice, the very option removed the exclusive privilege of the clergy. Still missing were two important evangelical elements: the sermon and congregational singing.

Schwarz's Mass established a precedent and was printed immediately. By 1539, the year of the liturgy reproduced below, some eighteen editions had been published, each containing variations, great or slight, from the previous. Especially did the simplification of worship proceed after 1525, when Martin Bucer, three years a resident of the city, began to make his influence felt. In the course of time, the word "Mass" gave way to "Lord's Supper." The "altar" became "altar-table" or simply "table." The celebrant was no longer described as "priest" but as "parson," or more often as "minister." He stood behind the table, facing the people, except to proclaim the Gospel from the pulpit. Finally vestments disappeared, and the minister wore some sort of black gown when he celebrated, as when he preached. The old ceremonial, including the Elevation, was eventually cast aside. The Epistle also disappeared, because the Gospel alone, as the "Crown of all Scripture," was deemed appropriate for the Sunday morning sermon. Even the Gospel was selected according to the method called *lectio continua:* chapter by chapter, Sunday after Sunday, so that the continuity and full meaning of each book might be brought out. And, since it involved the disuse of the lectionary, that method cost the church of Strassburg its association with the Christian Year; only the chief festivals were any longer observed. The sermon, which attained prominence by 1525, was based directly upon the lesson and lasted an hour. A host of daily and Sunday sermons were scheduled, such that only the most obdurate person could fail to find one of his convenience. Despite this emphasis upon preaching, the weekly observance of the Eucharist suffered but a slight decline: by 1539 Communion was celebrated every Sunday in the cathedral, elsewhere once a month. Congregational singing assumed increased importance as metrical psalms and hymns were introduced; but these also tended to displace such traditional elements as the Kyrie and Gloria in excelsis. Many other remains of the Mass were replaced by prayers and exhortations that were apt to be rather wordy and didactic. Nevertheless, the Strassburg rite remained a true Eucharist, immediately derived from the Mass, and neither conjured up by the Reformers nor drawn from the Medieval office of Prone. When the Lord's Supper was not celebrated, the Eucharistic portions were simply omitted, and the liturgy attained the character of the ancient Mass of the Catechumens, or Ante-Communion.

There is an important juxtaposition in the history of the Strassburg rite: While the liturgy itself began in the conservatism of the Mass and became increasingly evangelical, Bucer moved simultaneously from a radical view of worship and a Eucharistic doctrine only a hairsbreadth from Zwinglianism, to some of the most creative liturgical ideas enunciated in the Reformation and to a doctrine of the Supper very near to that of Melanchthon and Calvin. In 1524, the year that Schwarz slightly purified the Mass, Bucer published *Grund und Ursach,* in which he proposed the following radical shape of the liturgy:

When the congregation comes together on Sunday, the minister [*Diener*] admonishes them to make confession of their sins and to pray for pardon; and he confesses to God on behalf of the whole congregation, prays for pardon, and proclaims the remission of sins to those that believe. Then the whole congregation sings several short psalms or hymns of praise, after which the minister makes a brief prayer and reads to the congregation a passage from the writings of the Apostles, expounding the same as briefly as possible. Thereupon the congregation sings again: the Ten Commandments or something else. The priest [*Priester*] then proclaims the Gospel and delivers the sermon proper. After this the congregation sings the Articles of our Faith. The priest then offers a prayer for the civil authority, in which he prays for an increase of faith and love, and grace to keep the remembrance of Christ's death with profit.

Then he admonishes those who wish to observe the Lord's Supper with him, that they would do so in remembrance of Christ, to die to their sins, bear their cross willingly, and love their neighbor truly, being strengthened in faith, which must then come to pass when we consider with believing hearts what unlimited grace and goodness Christ hath shown us, in that He offered His body and blood to the Father on our behalf. After the exhortation he proclaims the Gospel of the Lord's Supper, as the three evangelists, Matthew, Mark, and Luke, have described it, together with Paul in I Cor. 11. Then the priest divides the bread and cup of the Lord amongst them, and also partakes of it himself. Presently the congregation sings another hymn of praise. After that the minister closes the Supper with a short prayer, blesses the people, and bids them go in the peace of the Lord. This is the manner and custom with which we now celebrate Christ's Supper on Sundays only.·

In the eleven chapters of *Grund und Ursach*, Bucer dealt with the entire scope of evangelical worship: sacraments, festivals, ceremonies, hymns, and prayers. He assailed both the Roman idea of sacrifice and the rich ceremonies of the Mass, and offered proposals for the restoration of the liturgy to that shape which is "old, true, and eternal." The *first principle* of liturgical recovery is adherence to "the clear and plain declarations" of Holy Scripture, for instance, the strictures of the Decalogue against the worship of idols, and the precept of our Lord (John 6:63) that "the flesh profiteth nothing." The Bible, which envelops the Word of God, must be authoritatively applied; it cannot be "set aside" as Rome had consistently done. Moreover, the preaching of the Word is the constitutive act of divine worship. True worship occurs when the Word goes forth to the church and the church makes its response of prayer and praise. It is in this context that the Spirit of the Lord does His work in the congregation, bringing men to faith and thence to true piety in Christ. The *second principle* is to give precedence, not to the physical and structural things of worship, but to the activity of the Holy Spirit. It is the Spirit who impresses the external Word of the sermon upon our hearts, making it the lively Word of God, who calls us to repentance, who impels us to prayer and assures us that we are heard, who provides us with the spiritual gifts for our mutual priesthood, that we may serve our neighbors in love. Taken seriously, the work of the Holy Spirit in the congregation negates the "sensual" worship of God that depends upon externals, and requires an "unsensual and true worship of God." The *third principle*—Christian liberty—stems partly

·Bucer insisted that Communion, by its very nature, was meant for the whole congregation. Therefore, it was held "on Sundays only" so that all the faithful could participate.

162

from Bucer's reaction to the prescribed liturgy of the Roman Church, but primarily from the stress he laid upon the presence and inspiration of the Holy Spirit among those who worshiped. "Except for the sermon," he counseled, "nothing should be dictated in the assembled congregation. Everyone may pray and praise without restraint." The *fourth principle* involves Bucer's conception of the church as a community of love. The whole life and work of the congregation are incited by the commandment of love; and that commandment is invested in the priesthood of believers, who, being freed from the fretful concern of working out their own salvation, are called to lead their neighbors into communion with God and with one another. That calling must be exercised in the congregation if worship is to be authentic. "For how can he praise God" who is indifferent to his neighbor? And what efficacy have intercessions "if praying and working do not go together through the inspiration of the Holy Spirit"?

Bucer worked out subsequent thoughts on the liturgy, sometimes elaborating, sometimes modifying, the principles of *Grund und Ursach.* By 1534 he began to plead for uniformity. While he still maintained that "the Spirit of Christ inspires the churches," he was now dismayed by "deplorable differences" of practice and "detestable changes" made upon an unfounded notion of freedom. This development in his thought coincided with his growing perception of the church, the ministry, the sacraments, and the liturgy as objective means of grace. In early writings he had rather depreciated the ministerial office, partly in reaction to the Roman priesthood, but mainly because of his strong reliance upon the inspiration of the Holy Spirit, invested in the priesthood of believers. But shortly he began to emphasize that the Lord uses the ministry as a special instrument to extend and restore His church. Thus, ministers were "overseers and dispensers of God's mysteries." Through the Word, which they alone were commissioned to offer in audible and visible tokens, God would inspire and strengthen faith, open and close heaven, forgive and condemn. Discipline also became a prominent feature of his thought in the 1530's. His view of the church as a community of love, in which one member lives for another in the mutual priesthood, strongly implied such a program: the love of one another involved the discipline of one another. But Bucer was only partially successful in his efforts to introduce *disciplina* at Strassburg. Even in the liturgy, where the power of the keys was implied, excommunication remained a sore omission. He was more successful in securing the preparation of evangelical hymns, that the people might have an instrument of praise and a voice in common worship; and he proposed the appointment of precentors—"specially decent singers"—to conduct the laity, so long untaught in the manner of congregational singing. His own notable *Gesangbuch* appeared in 1541 to replace a variety of hymnals found in the parishes. Bucer prized the hymn as a way to exercise both young and old in the knowledge of Christ and in true godliness.

In the liturgy of 1539 (below), worship commenced with the common Confession of sin, which Bucer used as a means to incite genuine repentance in the congregation. Such repentance, which he called *poenitentia evangelica,* involved more than contrition, but acceptance of grace through faith in Jesus Christ, and a hearty resolve to be supervised unremittingly by the Holy Spirit in the new life of godly obedience. Three forms of Confession were offered. The second, composed by Bucer for his own congregation, was the one adopted by Calvin. The third form, an interpolation of the Ten Commandments, reminds us of some Reformed liturgies (e.g., those of Farel and à Lasco) in which the law was used to convict sinners and drive them to repentance, and in which, therefore, the Decalogue immediately preceded Confession. In the main, however, as one can see in the liturgy of *Grund und Ursach,* Bucer used the law as Calvin also used it in worship: not to accuse sinners, but to bring the faithful to true piety by teaching them the divine will and exhorting them to obedience.

Then followed the Absolution, which was unmistakable in its authority. Bucer taught that when it is given "through the ministry of our Lord Jesus Christ," and when it is received with true repentance and a hearty desire for grace, the absolution imparts to the afflicted "a special and undoubted comfort and renewal, and also a special strength to avoid sins henceforth."

After the psalm, the minister offered the prayer for illumination, that God's holy Word might be truly heard "with all diligence and faith"; and then, having mounted the pulpit, he read the Gospel, taking up where he left off the preceding Sunday, and preached the sermon. Bucer drew a distinction between the "external" Word, which is preached abroad in the congregation, and the "internal" Word, which is heard in the heart through the inspiration of the Holy Spirit. "Without the operation of the Holy Spirit," he warned, "the external Word effects nothing." Yet the preaching of the Word and the inward work of the Spirit are by no means disconnected: "God does not give inner instruction to anybody without the outward instruction of his agents." While he thereby ascribed vital importance to the preaching of the Gospel, Bucer still assigned priority to the Spirit, who streams in from above, making the preached Word lively and effective in the human heart. Without this inner evidence, men cling to the external Word, which remains unconvincing, and to the letter, which kills.

When Holy Communion was scheduled, the minister appended to his sermon an exhortation of four points. These set forth in simple terms Bucer's finished doctrine of the Eucharist, which involved the spiritual real presence of Christ: "The Lord truly offers and gives His holy and sanctifying body and blood to us in the Holy Supper, with the visible things of bread and wine, through the ministry of the church."

After the sermon, the people sang the Apostles' Creed, which marked the transition from Word to Sacrament. As conceived by Bucer, the Creed was a genuine confession of faith; therefore it was both the proper response to the Word of God, and the expression of Christian renewal and commitment, which were essential for true participation in Holy Communion. To represent this meaning, the elements were brought to the table while the Creed was being sung.

Then followed the Great Prayer, which replaced the Roman Canon. At the end of the prayer, and as part of it, there occurred the Consecration—not of the elements precisely, but of those people who were about to communicate. Directly after the Lord's Prayer, the minister recited the Words of Institution, which now stood apart from the Canon, immediately before the Fraction and Delivery, as the warrant for the celebration of the Supper. The communicants came forward and knelt to receive, while one or another psalm was sung.

A century ago, when C. W. Baird published *Eutaxia*, a provocative little book on Reformed worship, Strassburg was not worth a chapter. Today, following the renaissance of Bucer and the prodigious scholarship devoted to his liturgy, Strassburg is acclaimed "a center of liturgical reformation," and her liturgy is pronounced "the norm of Sunday morning worship in the Reformed churches." Indeed, Bucer exercised a great influence upon the Reformed rite and upon the liturgies of Hesse, Cologne, and England. But the claims of his *singular* influence upon the Reformed tradition deserve to be modified. Such a judgment implies at once that the liturgies of Zwingli, Oecolampadius, Farel, and the church at Bern—none of which conformed to Strassburg—must be read out of the tradition, although that of Farel was the first used in Geneva. Neither did the later Reformed liturgies of the Dutch and German churches correspond impressively with the Strassburg rite. Perhaps even the indebtedness of Calvin to Bucer in liturgical matters has been exaggerated; but we shall turn to this problem in the next chapter.

FOR FURTHER READING

Hastings Eells, *Martin Bucer*. New Haven, 1931.

F. Hubert, *Die Strassburger liturgischen Ordnungen im Zeitalter der Reformation*. Göttingen, 1900.

W. D. Maxwell, *John Knox's Genevan Service Book, 1556*. Edinburgh, 1931.

G. J. Van de Poll, *Martin Bucer's Liturgical Ideas*. Assen, 1954.

PSALTER, WITH
COMPLETE CHURCH PRACTICE

STRASSBURG, MDXXXIX

Concerning the Lord's Supper, or Mass, and the Sermons[1]

¶ *First: there are three Sermons to be heard every day. In the morning at the time of early Mass, which is after 5 o'clock in winter and about 4 in summer, meetings are held in all parish churches, and so arranged that a person may surely be able to come to two of them. First at these services, the Public Confession of Sin is recited. It is followed by a Christian exhortation from Scripture. After that, an appropriate pause is observed for a special silent prayer, which the Minister brings to a close with a collect in keeping with the subject or according to the occasion and spirit, and then with the blessing. This is called The Morning Prayer.*

¶ *Second: there is a Sermon in the cathedral every day about 8 o'clock, summer and winter.*

¶ *Third: there is an evening Sermon in the cathedral at 4 o'clock in summer, or earlier if convenient, but at 3 in wintertime.*

¶ *Since, alas, the holy days are always misused by the common people to do wicked things, and since there are scarcely any days on which God is more disgraced and profaned, let us not insist that any holiday be kept the whole day except Sunday. It is desirable that that weekly day of rest might be kept holy by the worship of God. With regard to the other glorious days which commemorate the works of our redemption—such as the Incarnation and birth of our Lord Jesus, His Passion, Ascension and the like —these are observed in Sermons. Yet when those Sermons are over, no one is kept from his physical work. Moreover, the congregation is assisted daily by that which constitutes a true holiday, namely: Christian assemblies are held for the exercise of Word and prayer, and for the practice of spiritual works. But Christmas is generally a complete holiday, and a few other days as well.*

167

¶ *This is how Sundays are kept. First, early morning prayer is conducted in the cathedral as usual. After that, about 6 o'clock, the Assistants[2] hold a Sermon and exhortation for the domestic servants in the neighboring parish churches. Soon after, the congregation having assembled, the Pastor[3] comes in and goes before the Altar-Table,[4] which has been placed near the people, so that everyone may understand every word. And he begins the Common Worship with more or less the following words: he may add to it or abbreviate it according to the demands of time and occasion.*

THE CONFESSION

Make confession to God the Lord, and let everyone acknowledge with me his sin and iniquity.

Almighty, eternal God and Father, we confess and acknowledge unto thee that we were conceived in unrighteousness and are full of sin and transgression in all our life. We do not fully believe thy Word nor follow thy holy commandments. Remember thy goodness, we beseech thee, and for thy Name's sake be gracious unto us, and forgive us our iniquity which, alas, is great.

ANOTHER CONFESSION [5]

Almighty, eternal God and Father, we confess and acknowledge that we, alas, were conceived and born in sin, and are therefore inclined to all evil and slow to all good; that we transgress thy holy commandments without ceasing, and ever more corrupt ourselves. But we are sorry for the same, and beseech thy grace and help. Wherefore have mercy upon us, most gracious and merciful God and Father, through thy Son our Lord Jesus Christ. Grant to us and increase in us thy Holy Spirit, that we may recognize our sin and unrighteousness from the bottom of our hearts, attain true repentance and sorrow for them, die to them wholly, and please thee entirely by a new and godly life. Amen.

ANOTHER [6]

I poor sinner confess to thee, O Almighty, eternal, merciful God and Father, that I have sinned in manifold ways against thee and thy commandments.

I confess that I have not believed in thee, my one God and Father, but have put my faith and trust more in creatures than in thee, my God and Creator, because I have feared them more than thee. And for their benefit and pleasure, I have done and left undone many things in disobedience to thee and thy commandments.

I confess that I have taken thy holy Name in vain, that I have often sworn falsely and lightly by the same, that I have not always professed it nor kept it holy as I ought; but even more, I have slandered it often and grossly with all my life, words and deeds.

I confess that I have not kept thy Sabbath holy, that I have not heard thy holy Word with earnestness nor lived according to the same; moreover that I have not yielded myself fully to thy divine hand, nor rejoiced in thy work done in me and in others, but have often grumbled against it stoutly and have been impatient.

I confess that I have not honored my father and mother, that I have been disobedient to all whom I justly owe obedience, such as father and mother, my superiors, and all who have tried to guide and teach me faithfully.

I confess that I have taken life: that I have offended my neighbor often and grossly by word and deed, caused him harm, grown angry over him, borne envy and hatred toward him, deprived him of his honor and the like.

I confess that I have been unchaste. I acknowledge all my sins of the flesh and all the excess and extravagance of my whole life in eating, drinking, clothing and other things; my intemperance in seeing, hearing, speaking, etc., and in all my life; yea, even fornication, adultery and such.

I confess that I have stolen. I acknowledge my greed. I admit that in the use of my worldly goods I have set myself against thee and thy holy laws. Greedily and against charity have I grasped them. And scarcely, if at all, have I given of them when the need of my neighbor required it.

I confess that I have born false witness, that I have been untrue and unfaithful toward my neighbor. I have lied to him, I have told lies about him, and I have failed to defend his honor and reputation as my own.

And finally I confess that I have coveted the possessions and spouses of others. I acknowledge in summary that my whole life is nothing else than sin and transgression of thy holy commandments and an inclination toward all evil.

Wherefore I beseech thee, O heavenly Father, that, thou wouldst graciously forgive me these and all my sins. Keep and preserve me henceforth that I may walk only in thy way and live according to thy will; and all of this through Jesus Christ, thy dear Son, our Saviour. Amen.

AN ABSOLUTION OR WORD OF COMFORT: I TIM. I

This is a faithful saying, and worthy of all acceptation, that Christ Jesus came into the world to save sinners.

Let everyone, with St. Paul, truly acknowledge this in his heart and believe in Christ. Thus, in His name, I proclaim unto you the forgiveness of all your sins, and declare you to be loosed of them on earth, that you be loosed of them also in heaven, in eternity. Amen.

¶ *Sometimes he uses other passages which assure us of the forgiveness of sins and of Christ's ransom for our sin,*
   such as John III [16]
   or in the forementioned place [John 3:35f.]
   or Acts X [43]
   or I John II [1f.]

¶ *Thereafter the church begins to sing a Psalm or hymn instead of the Introit; and sometimes the Kyrie eleison and the Gloria in excelsis.*

¶ *When the singing is over, the Minister[7] offers a short prayer for grace and a right spirit, that the Sermon and Word of God which are to follow may be heard with profit. The prayer is to this effect:*

The Lord be with you.
Let us pray.

Almighty, gracious Father, forasmuch as our whole salvation depends upon our true understanding of thy holy Word, grant to all of us that our hearts, being freed from worldly affairs, may hear and apprehend thy holy Word with all diligence and faith, that we may rightly understand thy gracious will, cherish it, and live by it with all earnestness, to thy praise and honor; through our Lord Jesus Christ. Amen.

¶ *Then the church sings a Psalm or, if it is too long, several verses at the direction of the precentor.[8] And the Minister goes to the pulpit and reads out of one of the Gospels[9] as*

*much as he proposes to expound in a single sermon, treat-
ing the book in succession. Since the Gospels have described the words and works of our Lord quite clearly, it
is the custom of Sunday morning generally to preach from
one of the Gospels, more than from other books; and they
should be dealt with in their order, not as heretofore by
picking out several pieces, often without particular skill,
so that all the other things given in the Gospels have been
withheld from the congregation. In the afternoon and at
other hours, the other biblical books are also expounded.*

¶ *Near the end of the Sermon, the Minister explains the
action of the Lord's Supper and exhorts the people to observe the same with right faith and true devotion. This
said exhortation usually contains four points:*

The first: that, since the Lord now wishes to communicate
his body and blood to us, we should reflect upon the fact
that our body and blood—which means, our whole nature—
are corrupted to all evil and thus to eternal death, so that
they of themselves may nevermore share in the Kingdom of
God. I Cor. XV.

The second: that to deliver us from such corruption, the
eternal Word of God became flesh, so that there might be a
holy flesh and blood: this is to say, a truly divine man,
through whom the flesh and blood of us all would be restored
and sanctified. And this happens as we truly eat and drink of
His body and blood.

The third: that the Lord truly offers and gi es His ho'y
and sanctifying body and blood to us in the Holy Supper,
with the visible things of bread and wine, through the ministry of the Church, as His holy Word declares: "Take and
eat, this is my body which is given for you; Drink ye all of
it, this is my blood which is shed for you for the forgiveness
of sin." And we must accept this Word of the Lord with simple faith, and doubt not that He, the Lord Himself, is in the
midst of us through the external ministry of the Church
which He Himself has ordained for that purpose. Such does
He proclaim to us with His own words: that the bread
which we break may truly be, even for us, the communion of
His body, and the cup with which we give thanks, the communion of His blood. I Cor. X. But we must always diligently
consider why the Lord thus imparts to us His holy, sanctifying communion in the holy sacrament: namely, that He may

ever more live in us, and that we may be one body in Him our Head, even as we all partake here of one bread. I Cor. X.

The fourth: that in this action, we keep the Lord's memorial and feast with true devotion and thankfulness, so that we always laud and praise Him in all our words and deeds, yea with our whole life, for all His benefits: for his Incarnation and bitter death whereby He has paid for our sin; for this blessed communion of His body and blood; that is, for Himself entire, who is true God and man, through whom alone we obtain the true and blessed life and live both here and in eternity.

¶ *When, however, the holy Supper is not held—as in the case of the neighboring parish churches where it is now observed but once a month (though in the cathedral, every Sunday)—but children are there to be baptized, the mystery of Baptism is explained and the people are exhorted to a truly sacred use of this holy sacrament.*

¶ *At the conclusion of the Sermon, the people sing the Creed* [10] *or else, according to the occasion, a Psalm or hymn. Thereafter, if the holy Supper is to be observed, the Minister stands behind the Table and speaks to the people.* [11]

The Lord be with you.
Let us pray.

¶ *Then he leads the prayer, with these or similar words:*

Almighty, merciful God and Father, thou who hast promised us through thy Son that whatsoever we ask of thee in His name thou wilt grant unto us, and hast also commanded us through thy Spirit to pray for those in authority and for all men: We do heartily beseech thee through Jesus Christ, thy most-beloved Son our Saviour, to enlighten with the knowledge of thy Gospel the hearts of our lord Emperor and King, all princes and nobles, and the magistrates and ruling body of this city, that they and all those in power may acknowledge thee as their sovereign and true Lord, serve thee with fear and trembling, and rule over us, who are the work of thy hand and the sheep of thy pasture, according to thy will and good pleasure.

Grant that all men everywhere may come to knowledge of the truth. Especially to this congregation, being assembled in thy name, send forth thy Holy Spirit, the Master and Teacher, who may write thy law upon our hearts, take away our blindness, and lead us to recognize our sin, which otherwise, alas, is death, and its baseness and shame is concealed.[12] Make it vivid to us, O Lord, and enlighten our eyes that we may see the truth and recognize indeed that there is nothing in us except mere sin, death, hell and the deserved wrath of God, So, may we hunger and thirst after the rich well-spring of thy goodness and grace, and gratefully accept the same which thou hast delivered to us through thine only-begotten Son, who, having become like unto men and us poor sinners, suffered and died and rose from the dead, in order that He may save us from sin, death, and hell, and bring us to the resurrection and our inheritance of the Kingdom of God.

And grant us, O Lord and Father, that with true faith we may keep this Supper of thy dear Son, our Lord Jesus, as He hath ordained it, so that we verily receive and enjoy the true communion of His body and blood, of our Saviour Himself, who is the only saving bread of heaven. In this holy sacrament, He wishes to offer and give Himself so that He may live in us, and we in Him, being members of His body and serving thee fruitfully in every way to the common edification of thy Church, being set free from every passion of our evil, corrupted flesh, from all anger, vexation, envy, hatred, selfishness, lewdness, unchastity, and what more there may be of the damned work of the flesh: To the end that, by all means, we as thine obedient children may ever lift our hearts and souls unto thee in true childlike trust, and always call upon thee, saying as our only Master and Saviour, our Lord Jesus Christ, hath taught us:

Our Father . . .

ANOTHER PRAYER [13]

Almighty, heavenly Father, thou hast promised us through thy Son, our Lord Jesus Christ, that whatsoever we ask in His name, thou wilt grant unto us, and hast commanded us to petition thee for all men, and especially for those in authority: we do therefore beseech thee, dear faithful Father, through thy Son our Saviour, for our lord Emperor and king, all princes and nobles, and also for the magistrates of this city. Grant thy Spirit and a godly fear unto those whom thou hast surely set over us as lords in thy stead, that they may administer their office to thine honor and according to thy will, in order that thy children everywhere may lead a calm and quiet life, in all godliness and propriety.

We pray thee moreover for all whose duty it is to proclaim thy holy Word and be pastors of thy Church. Grant them thy Word and Spirit that they may serve thee in such wise that all of thine elect may be gathered unto thee, and that those who already bear thy name and are counted as Christians may live agreeably to their call, to thy glory and the edification of thy Church.

We beseech thee also for those whom thou dost chasten through sickness and other adversity. Enable them to perceive thy gracious hand and accept thy discipline for their amendment, that in thy grace thou mayest also impart to them thy comfort and help.

We pray thee moreover for those who do not yet apprehend thy holy Gospel, but remain in error and depravity. Enlighten their eyes that they also may recognize thee as their God and Creator, and be converted to thy will.

Heavenly Father, we pray thee even for ourselves who are gathered here. Grant that we may be gathered in thy name. Drive from our hearts and souls all things which displease thee. Enable us to understand that we live and move and have our being in thee, also that our sins are so great and so abominable before thee that neither thy grace nor the life could have been restored to us except through the death of thy Son, our Lord Jesus Christ. Enable us to grasp by true faith that such love dost thou have for us that thou hast given thy dear Son in death for us, so that when we believe in Him we shall not perish but have everlasting life. Merciful God and Father, draw our hearts and souls to this thy Son, so that—as He presents Himself to us in His holy Gospel and sacraments, and bestows His body and blood that we who are corrupt in ourselves may live in Him—we may receive such a love as His with living faith and eternal gratitude, and therefore die to all evil more and more each day, grow and increase in all goodness, and lead our lives in all propriety, patience, and love toward our neighbor. Thereto doth our Lord call and incite us so kindly through His holy Gospel and the sacraments. Wherefore grant us, O heavenly Father, that we may now receive and enjoy the same in sincere faith to our salvation, and always as true and living members of Him who is our Lord and thy dear Son, and be through Him thy true and obedient children who ever call upon thee and pray to thee in a right spirit and from truly believing hearts: saying as He Himself hath taught us:

Our Father . . .

ANOTHER PRAYER [18]

Almighty God, heavenly Father, thou hast promised us through thy dear Son, our Lord Jesus Christ, that whatsoever we ask of thee in His name thou wilt grant unto us. Thy very Son our Lord hath taught us, by Himself and by His beloved apostles, to assemble in His name, and hath promised to be there in the midst of us, and to procure and obtain for us at thy hand whatever we agree to ask of thee on earth. And especially hath He commanded us to pray for those whom thou hast set over us as magistrates and rulers; and then for all the desires both of thy people and of all men. Forasmuch as we have all come together, before thine eyes, to thy praise, and in the name of thy Son our Lord Jesus: we do heartily beseech thee, merciful God and Father, through thy most-beloved Son our only Saviour, graciously to forgive us all our sin and iniquity; and lift our hearts and souls unto thee that we may be able to beseech and implore thee with all our heart, according to thy will and pleasure which alone are righteous.

Wherefore we beseech thee, O heavenly Father, for our most gracious rulers, thy servants: our lord Emperor and King, and all princes and nobles, and the magistrates of this city. Grant unto them thy holy and right-sovereign Spirit, and ever increase the same in them, that they may acknowledge thee in true faith as the King of all kings and Lord of all lords, and thy Son our Lord Jesus as Him to whom thou hast given all power in heaven and earth; and so may they rule over their subjects, the work of thy hand and the sheep of thy pasture, according to thy good pleasure, that we here and everywhere may lead a quiet, peaceful life in all godliness and propriety, and, being delivered from the fear of our enemies, serve thee in all righteousness and holiness.

Moreover we beseech thee, O faithful Father and Saviour, for all those whom thou hast established over thy faithful people as pastors and curates of souls, and to whom thou hast intrusted the ministration of thy holy Gospel. Grant them thy Holy Spirit and increase the same in them, that they will be found faithful, and will always serve thee in such wise that thy poor erring lambs everywhere will be gathered to Christ thy Son, their chief Shepherd and Bishop, and daily be raised up in Him unto all holiness and righteousness, to the eternal praise of thy name.

Merciful God and gracious Father, we beseech thee further for all mankind. As it is thy will to be known as a Saviour to all the world, draw to thy Son, our Lord Jesus, those who are still estranged from Him. And those whom thou hast drawn to Him and taught that through Him alone, our only Mediator, thou wilt pardon our sin and show every grace: grant that they may prosper daily in such knowledge, that, being filled with the fruit of all good works, they may live without scandal, to thy praise and the edification of their neighbor, and await with sure hope the advent and the day of thy Son our Lord. And those whom thou holdest in special discipline, whom thou dost visit and chasten with poverty, misery, sickness, imprisonment, and other adversity: O Father of mercy and Lord of all consolation, enable them to perceive thy gracious, fatherly hand, that they may turn their whole hearts to thee who alone dost chasten them, so that thou wilt comfort them as a Father and finally deliver them from all evil.

And to all of us here gathered before thee, in the name of thy Son and at His Table, grant, O God and Father, that we may truly and profoundly recognize the sin and depravity in which we were born, and into which we thrust ourselves deeper and deeper by our sinful life. And as there is nothing good in our flesh, yea, as our flesh and blood cannot inherit thy kingdom, grant that we may yield ourselves with all our heart in true faith to thy Son, our only Redeemer and Saviour. And since, for our sake, He hath not only sacrificed to thee His own body and blood upon the Cross for our sin, but also wishes to give them to us for food and drink unto eternal life, grant that we may now accept with entire longing and devotion His goodness and gift, and with right faith receive and enjoy His true body and true blood, yea, Himself our Saviour, true God and man, the only true bread of heaven: That we may live no more our sinful and depraved life, but that He in us and we in Him may live His holy, blessed and eternal life, being verily the partakers of the true and eternal testament, the covenant of grace, sure and certain that thou wilt be our gracious Father forever, who nevermore reckons our sins against us and makes all manner of provision for us in body and soul as thy dear children and heirs: so that we may at all times render praise and thanks to thee, and glorify thy holy name with all our words and deeds. Wherefore, O heavenly Father, grant that we may celebrate today the glorious and blessed memorial of thy dear Son our Lord, and shew forth His death, that we shall ever grow and be strengthened in faith to thee and in all good works. And so, greatly comforted, we do now and always call upon thee, our God and Father, and pray to thee as our Lord hath taught us to pray, saying:

Our Father . . .[14]

¶ *At the conclusion of this prayer, the Minister makes a short exhortation, if he has not done so at the end of the Sermon, to the effect that the Holy Supper is to be observed with true faith and meet devotion; and he explains this Mystery.*

¶ *After such an exhortation and explanation, the Minister reads the words of the Lord, as the holy Evangelists and Paul have recorded them.*

THE INSTITUTION OF THE LORD'S SUPPER

In the same night in which the Lord Jesus was betrayed, while they were eating, He took the bread, and brake it, and gave it to His disciples, and said: Take, eat, this is my body which is given for you; do this in remembrance of me. In the same manner He also took the cup after the supper, gave thanks, and offered it to them, and said: Drink ye all of it; this is the new testament in my blood, which is shed for you and for many for the forgiveness of sins; this do ye, as oft as ye drink it, in remembrance of me.

¶ *Forthwith the Minister speaks in these words:*

Believe in the Lord, and give eternal praise and thanks unto Him!

¶ *Herewith he distributes the bread and cup of the Lord, first saying these words:*

177

Remember, believe and proclaim that Christ the Lord has died for you.[15]

¶ *Thereupon the church sings "Gott sey gelobet"* [16] *or another Psalm appropriate to the occasion.*

¶ *After the singing, he once again offers a prayer, in this wise:*

The Lord be with you.
Let us pray.

Grant unto us, O heavenly Father, that the remembrance of our redemption may never leave our hearts, but that we may walk in Christ, the Light of the world, far removed from our foolish reason and blind wills, which are vain and injurious darkness; through Christ Jesus our Lord. Amen.

Almighty God, heavenly Father, we give thee eternal praise and thanks that thou hast been so gracious unto us poor sinners, having drawn us to thy Son our Lord Jesus, whom thou hast delivered to death for us and given to be our nourishment and our dwelling unto eternal life. Grant that we may never relinquish these things from our hearts, but ever grow and increase in faith to thee, which, through love, is effective of all good works. And so may our whole life be devoted to thy praise and the edification of our neighbor; through the same Jesus Christ, thy Son, our Lord. Amen.[17]

ANOTHER THANKSGIVING

Almighty, gracious, heavenly Father, we give thee eternal praise and thanks that, through thy holy Gospel and Sacrament, thou hast again offered and presented to us thy most precious treasure: the true bread of heaven and food of eternal life, our Lord Jesus Christ. And we heartily beseech thee to grant that we may receive Him and partake of Him in true faith now and forever, and be so nourished by His flesh and blood that we may be set free from all evil and increase daily in all goodness, to thy glory; through the same Jesus Christ our Lord. Amen.

ANOTHER THANKSGIVING

We give thee eternal praise and thanks, O heavenly Father, that thou hast drawn us poor sinners to thy dear Son, our

Lord Jesus Christ, and hast again imparted to us His true communion. And we beseech thee, grant to us that this holy communion may always be effective and strong in us, so that in true faith, propriety, patience and love, sparing no diligence, we may lead a new and heavenly life wholly pleasing unto thee, to thy praise and honor and to the edification of our neighbor; through the same, &c.

The Blessing: Num. in the VI chap. The Lord bless you and keep you; the Lord make His face to shine upon you, and be gracious unto you; the Lord lift up His countenance upon you and give you peace.

Depart! The Spirit of the Lord go with you unto eternal life! Amen.

¶ *Following the meal* [18] *on Sunday, there is another Sermon in the cathedral, before and after which the holy psalms are also sung and common prayer conducted. Shortly after this Sermon, the Minister holds instruction for the children in the cathedral, except in wintertime, namely, when the children might suffer on account of the cold. He explains to them the Ten Commandments, the Creed and the Lord's Prayer in succession, about which he asks them questions, and thus drills them in the knowledge of our Lord Jesus Christ.*

¶ *A similar exercise is also held in the other parish churches at the time of Vesper Prayer, which comes after the two services. Psalms are sung at the beginning and the end, and the prayer is concluded with a collect which is directed to the subject of discussion.*[19] *At this time, provision is also made for the observance of Holy Baptism, if children are present to be baptized.*

¶ *Four times a year, congregational catechization*[20] *takes place in all the parish churches, morning and afternoon. The common matters of our Christian religion are treated, and expounded with a short and simple explanation: the Articles of our holy Christian faith, the Ten Commandments and Lord's Prayer, the understanding of the holy sacraments, and whatever else may be fruitfully brought up in connection with the elementary instruction of our Christian religion within the allotted time.*

NOTES

1. F. Hubert, *Die Strassburger liturgischen Ordnungen im Zeitalter der Reformation.* Critical text: pp. 90-114.
2. die helffer.
3. pfarrer.
4. altartisch. For a description of this "altar-table," written by Gerard Roussel in 1525, cf. A. L. Herminjard *Correspondance des Réformateurs,* I, 412.
5. This Confiteor was probably written by Bucer himself. It was the one that Calvin used. An enlarged, English version first appeared in John Knox's Genevan Service Book, 1556.
6. The third Confiteor is based upon the Ten Commandments, each of which prompts a paragraph of confession. Perhaps Bucer's use of the Commandments invited Calvin to introduce the singing of the Law in the first part of his own Strassburg liturgy.
7. diener.
8. Volgends singt die kirche aber ein psalmen oder uss dem vorgesungnen, so der lang, etliche vers. By "vorgesungnen," Bucer may have meant a precentor. As early as 1525 he urged the appointment of qualified men to lead congregational singing in every parish. They were to be "sondern ordentlichen senger": men who knew how to enhance the value of the evangelical hymn. Cf. G. J. Van de Poll, *Martin Bucer's Liturgical Ideas,* pp. 22, 29.
9. evangelisten; literally: "the evangelists."
10. The Apostles' Creed. Immediately after the Creed, the bread and wine were brought to the Table.
11. Spricht der diener ob dem tisch zum volck.
12. Sende deinen heyligen geyst, den meyster vnd lerer, welcher dein gesatz in vnsere hertzen schreibe, unsere blindheyt hynneme, unsere sünd vns gebe zü erkennen, die sunst leyder todt, vnd jr schnödigkeit vnd schand vnbekant ist. O herr, mach sye lebendig vnd erleuchte vnsere augen. . . .
13. An alternate form. Bucer provided three alternates of the Great Prayer. The first was traditional in Strassburg. The second and third were added *ca.* 1536. It was the third that Calvin adopted with slight alterations.
14. Matt. 6:9-13, including the Matthean doxology.
15. In some editions, these words were added: vnd sich selb euch gibt zur speis vnd tranck ins ewig leben.
16. This Communion hymn was customary elsewhere, e.g., Cologne (1543) and Würtemberg (1553).
17. Calvin's Post-Communion thanksgiving is an adaptation of this prayer. An expanded version is found in the *Book of Common Order.*

18. That is, the midday meal.
19. mit psalmensingen vor und noch, vnd dem gebet auch beschluss mit einer collect, die vff dis, dauon dehandlet, gerichtet ist.
20. gemeyne catechismos.

VII
JOHN CALVIN

The Form of Church Prayers
Strassburg, 1545, & Geneva, 1542

APPENDICES:

John Oecolampadius, *Form and Manner,* 1525?
William Farel, *La Maniere et fasson,* 1524?

CALVIN

Having had no priestly tenure, John Calvin cherished nothing of the Mass, but denounced it with raw invective. Of all the idols, he knew none so grotesque as that in which the priest called down Christ into his hands by "magical mumblings" and offered him anew on the sacrificial altar, while the people looked on in "stupid amazement." Having renounced the Roman rite in such categorical terms, Calvin resorted to a liturgical policy based upon the warrant of Scripture and "the custom of the ancient church." His first effort at reconstruction came in the *Institutes* of 1536 (Ch. IV):

Now as far as the Lord's Supper is concerned, it could have been administered most becomingly if it were offered to the church quite often, and at least once a week. First then, it should commence with common prayers, after which a sermon should be delivered. Then, the bread and wine having been placed on the table, the minister should recite the Institution of the Supper, after which he should expound the promises which are left to us in it; at the same time he should excommunicate all those who are excluded from it by the Lord's prohibition. Afterward, prayer should be offered that the Lord, with the kindness wherewith he has given us this sacred food, would also teach and prepare us to receive it with faith and thankfulness of heart, and in his mercy make us worthy of such a feast, inasmuch as we are not so of ourselves. At this time, either psalms should be sung or something should be read; and in becoming order the faithful should partake of the most holy banquet, the ministers breaking the bread and giving the cup. When the Supper is finished, there should be an exhortation to sincere faith and the witness of the same, to love, and to a manner of life worthy of Christians. At the last, thanks should be given and praises sung to God. When these things are ended, the church should be dismissed in peace.

Thus, in the primitive edition of the *Institutes*, Calvin conceived of ideas that were to be characteristic of his later Communion service—namely, the rehearsal of the Lord's Institution as the warrant of the sacrament; the proclamation of the Lord's promises, which relate to his ordinance and supply meaning and reality to its signs; the excommunication of obdurate sinners; and the stress upon worthy participation and holiness of life. These uses suggest the milieu of Basel, where Calvin repaired to complete and publish the *Institutes*.

On All Saints' day, 1525, the venerable John Oecolampadius of Basel introduced *Form und Gstalt*, a simple German liturgy, fashioned on Zwinglian principles. The Communion service had two notable characteristics. By the meditative use of Scripture, Oecolampadius made provision for the profound contemplation of Christ's passion, which was the crux of the Zwinglian Eucharist. And by a parallel emphasis upon self-examination and excommunication, he expressed a grave concern, which found its way into the Calvinist rite: those who would celebrate their redemption at the Lord's table must be distinguished, as members of his Body, by sincerity of faith and holiness of life, else the church is not the church, the sacrament is profaned, and the offenders are liable for the Lord's body and blood.

Associated with the theologians at Basel was the fiery evangelist Guillaume Farel, apostle to French-speaking Switzerland. It was in 1524, apparently, while he labored at Montbéliard, that Farel prepared *La Maniere et fasson*, the first manual of evangelical worship in the French language. This was a suitable instrument for his evangelism: simple, didactic, replete with Scriptural marginalia, and typical of the liturgies of Basel and Zurich. The service of the Word, called "The Order Observed in Preaching," was an adaptation of Prone, rather like that of Zwingli; its title was eloquent of the

Zwinglian conception of Sunday Morning Worship, in which the sermon was exalted and the sacrament disconnected. (Farel's constituents spoke of "going to church" as *aller au sermon*.) He also conceived of the Eucharist in Zwinglian terms, which he expounded in a "Brief Interpretation of the Holy Supper," printed with *La Maniere*. When he described the sacrament as "a visible communion of the members of Jesus Christ," he meant that it was: (1) a testimony of our faith, by which we are "grafted" into Christ as members of his Body, and (2) a realization of the fellowship and love that shall exist among those who belong to Christ and hence to one another. It was this very doctrine that caused him to guard the Supper so assiduously against unbelievers and scandalous sinners, both of whom would shortly reduce this "communion" to a sham. As he proceeded to give these ideas liturgical expression, Farel laid down the broad lines of the Reformed Communion Exhortation. His Eucharistic liturgy contained the following elements: (1) the recital of God's promises, which heighten the meaning of the sacrament; (2) an invitation to the faithful to share the Lord's board, though they be not blameless; (3) self-examination; (4) excommunication of the unworthy; (5) the rehearsal of the Lord's Institution as the warrant of the Supper; and (6) the Reformed *Sursum corda:*

> Therefore lift up your hearts on high, seeking the heavenly things in heaven, where Jesus Christ is seated at the right hand of the Father; and do not fix your eyes on the visible signs, which are corrupted through usage. . . .

That final admonition, which is found in Calvinist liturgies to the time of the Westminster *Directory* (1644), was apparently the creation of Farel. It warned the worshiper not to look for Christ on the altar nor cleave to the signs that had been spoiled by the Mass. Farel was even afraid of Zwingli's idea that the bread and wine were stirring pictures of Christ's passion and hence powerful aids to the mind in contemplation. Instead he employed the signs in an incongruous way, which the Calvinist tradition tended to follow. These creatures of *earth*, these signs of God's redemptive *condescension* were supposed to transport the believer *above* the material realm, to the Risen Lord in the far reaches of heaven.

The crowning achievement of the redoubtable Farel was the conversion of Geneva in 1536. It came after four years of struggle, which were marked by provocative evangelism and the development of an evangelical cultus, based, no doubt, upon *La Maniere*. In July, 1536, Calvin chanced to lodge overnight in Geneva, intent upon proceeding to Strassburg, there to find a safe, scholarly retreat. Discovering the whereabouts of this visitor, and assuming that his presence was providential, Farel confronted Calvin in his chambers, dispelled his reluctance by dreadful pronouncements of God's wrath, and thus enlisted him in the meaner business of transforming Geneva into a model of piety.

At the start of 1537, the Reformers submitted "Articles Concerning the Organization of the Church and of Worship at Geneva," in which they proposed to edify the community by two means: the frequent celebration of the Lord's Supper and the exercise of discipline. They declared that the Supper ought to be celebrated "every Sunday" because of its exceeding profit: "We are really made participants of the body and blood of Jesus, of his death, of his life, of his Spirit, and of all his benefits." These were the views in which Calvin persisted (and to which Farel now subscribed); but such was the "frailty of the people" in prospect of this "mystery," that the Reformers compromised on a schedule of monthly Communion.

Moreover, as the Supper intended "to join the members of our Lord Jesus Christ with their Head and with each other in one Body," it must be protected against profanation by faithless and profligate persons who manifestly did not belong to Christ. Such was the purpose of discipline, which preserved the integrity of both sacrament and church. Those who were "ex-communicated" from Holy Communion were by the same token cut off from the constituency of the church until they repented the error of their ways. The critical issue of the whole Christian life was fitness to approach the Lord's table.

The Reformers also urged the singing of psalms in church as an instrument of praise and a means of attaining "common" worship. *La Maniere* was deficient in this respect, although Farel stated at the Disputation of Rive (1535) that he had no qualms about congregational singing, especially if psalms were sung in the vernacular.

The implementation of the "Articles" was attended by multiple difficulties, none being so grave as the resistance to discipline. In April, 1538, the Reformers were harried out of the city. Calvin retreated to Basel for scholarly endeavor;

but Martin Bucer summoned him to Strassburg, and by heavy persuasion, including further mention of God's wrath, prevailed upon him to accept. In September, 1538, he commenced his ministry to the congregation of French refugees in that city.

The parishes of Strassburg, both French and German, had enjoyed congregational singing since 1525. Moved at hearing the voices of men and women raised in psalmody, Calvin set his hand to a French psalter—*Aulcuns psaulmes et cantiques* (1539)—which supplied his parishioners with seventeen metrical psalms, five of his own preparation, the rest by Clément Marot. This work reached its culmination in the Genevan Psalter of 1562. A more pressing assignment, however, was the production of a liturgy for the French church, which now celebrated the Lord's Supper on a monthly schedule. Impressed by the Strassburg rite, Calvin appropriated it as his model: "As for the Sunday prayers, I took the form of Strassburg and borrowed the greater part of it." His service-book came from the press in 1540.·

If the Strassburg rite was derived from the Mass, Calvin preferred not to stare at that misfortune, but rather to believe that the work of Schwarz and Bucer conformed to the practice of the primitive church. Indeed, the Sunday service preserved the ancient union of Word and Sacrament, being constructed so that on those days when the Supper was not celebrated, the Eucharistic portions could be omitted, leaving the liturgy an Ante-Communion. Such a plan was most agreeable to Calvin's insistence upon frequent Communion. Moreover, in contrast to the stark simplicity and didactic tyranny of Farel's manual, the Strassburg book offered liturgical action and provided congregational singing, thereby engaging the passive people and filling worship with the note of adoration, which was to Calvin *le premier poinct* of religion. Finally, Bucer shaped or confirmed many of Calvin's liturgical ideas, as one can readily see by the text and sequence of their respective services. In view of all this, most scholars have said that Calvin did no more than alter Bucer's work here and there, reducing the number of variants, adding the Decalogue, and such. But we must not overlook the Communion Exhortation of Calvin's rite; in that important realm

The first edition is lost. A second was published by Calvin's successor, Pierre Brully, in 1542; and a third (below), edited by Calvin himself, was printed at Strassburg in 1545.

he adhered mainly to the plan of Farel and to his own outline in the 1536 *Institutes*.

Upon his return to Geneva in 1541, Calvin replaced *La Maniere et fasson* with the French liturgy he had prepared abroad. It was published in the following year as *The Form of Prayers*, to which the imprimatur was affixed: *According to the Custom of the Ancient Church*.

Again the schedule of Communion became an issue. In Strassburg, where Bucer had labored to restore the weekly observance of the primitive Eucharist, the sacrament was celebrated every Sunday in the cathedral and once a month in the parishes. As the "ancient church" was his witness, Calvin would have no less in Geneva (*Institutes* 4:17:44ff.). Clearly, the Roman practice of having the people communicate once a year was an "invention of the devil," while a Zwinglian "commemoration two or three times a year" was equally intolerable; for there was "nothing more useful" in the church than the Lord's Supper (*Institutes* 4:14:7ff.). God himself added the Supper to his Word; it was a perilous matter to separate them.

In the pursuit of this lifelong desire, Calvin was continually rebuffed by the Genevan Council. The monthly schedule he proposed in the "Articles" of 1537 was overruled by the authorities, who preferred a quarterly observance. And now again, when he presented the *Ecclesiastical Ordinances* in 1541, the magistrates rejected his scheme for a monthly Communion, but ordained that it "be administered four times a year." And there the matter remained. He continued to express dissatisfaction, and as late as 1561 declared: "Our custom is defective." But the structure of his Sunday Service remained an Ante-Communion, standing in anticipation of the Holy Supper.

The liturgy (below) began with the solemn declaration of God's glory and man's frailty: "Our help is in the name of the Lord." Directly, the minister led the people in the Confession of sin, using a revised form of Bucer's second Confiteor. In "well-ordered churches" Confession was the proper beginning of worship. It brought men to "a true estimation" of themselves; and by the very acknowledgment of their wretchedness, they paid testimony to "the goodness and mercy of our God." So the "gate of prayer is opened" (*Institutes* 3:4:10f.).

Confession deserved to be followed by Absolution. When the people have thrown themselves on God's mercy, said Calvin, "it is no mean or trivial consolation to have Christ's ambassador present, furnished with the mandate of reconciliation." It was the minister's office to "seal" in the hearts of believers the gracious promises of the Word, with which the power of the keys is inseparably bound (*Institutes* 3:4:12ff.). In Strassburg Calvin supplied an Absolution no less forthright than that of Bucer; but when he returned to Geneva, the people objected to this "novelty," illustrating their hostility by jumping up before the end of Confession to forestall an Absolution. Thus he yielded to their scruples.

In his Strassburg text, Calvin appointed the Ten Commandments to be sung after Confession, even as Bucer had suggested in *Grund und Ursach*. Here he employed the Law according to its "third and principal use": not to accuse and convict the sinner (in which case the Commandments would likely precede Confession) but to bring the penitents to true piety by teaching them the will of God and exhorting them to obey. "In this way the saints must press on" (*Institutes* 2:7:12).

Leaving the Communion table, the minister entered the pulpit and made extempore prayer for the illumination of the Holy Spirit, that the Word might be truly published and heard in the congregation. He proceeded to the *lecture et explication de L'evangile*—the reading and explication of the Gospel—one inseparable element, which Calvin called "the incomparable treasure of the church." Through the sovereign action of the Spirit, the words of the minister, be they ever so frail, might be heard as *Deus loquens,* God speaking, calling men to faith.

In response to the Word, the church made Intercessions for those in authority and for all sorts and conditions of men (I Tim. 2:1ff.). To this "Great Prayer," Calvin added an edifying paraphrase of the Lord's Prayer, which dwelt upon the high themes of his piety: the glory of God who requires of men their obedience and sanctity.

Then the congregation confessed the Apostles' Creed and offered a prayer of Humble Access, beseeching God that they might receive the Supper worthily and to their spiritual benefit. (The order of these elements was reversed in Geneva.) The Creed marked the transition of the liturgy. As a testimony that the people wished "to live and die in the Christian doctrine and religion," it was a response to the sermon and a sign of commitment essential for Holy Communion. Now the bread and wine were brought to the table. Calvin did not think it appropiate to expose the elements until the Word could be added to validate the sacrament: "The Word ought to sound in our ears as soon as the sign itself meets our eyes." The Creed was a proper point to furnish the table; for the sermon, which preceded it, had already made reference to the Eucharist, while the Exhortation, which directly followed it, contained the Words of Institution and the rehearsal of Christ's promises.

At his station behind the table, the minister recited the Words of Institution which served three purposes. First, they published the command of Christ to which the sacrament owes its origin, and the promise of Christ in the hope of which the church fulfills his ordinance (*Short Treatise,* IV). Second, they set forth the manner in which the Supper is to be celebrated, namely, in accord with "the pure institution of Jesus Christ"—a matter of no small importance, since "the promises of the Lord extend only to the uses he has authorised" (*Short Treatise,* IV). Finally, they were part of the Word which must be added to the sacrament for its efficacy.

How then did Calvin conceive of the relationship between Word and Sacrament? Apart from the Word, he said, the Lord's Supper has no power, but remains "a lifeless and bare phantom." This is the prime error of Roman priests, who, leaving the Word aside, aim to effect the consecration of *elements* "by murmuring and gesticulating in the manner of sorcerers." Their means and their end are both wrong. What is required to season the sacrament is not an "incantation" over the bread and wine, but a "lively preaching," addressed to the *people,* setting forth the promises of Christ, which are antecedent to the Lord's Supper and which supply meaning and reality to its signs (*Institutes* 4:17:39). It is the very nature of a sacrament, not to stand dissevered from the Word, but to "confirm and seal" a divine promise annexed to it. Unless that promise is proclaimed in the church, the Supper has nothing to convey, but is an insipid ceremony in which the participants "taste a little bread and wine" (*Institutes* 4:14:3ff.). Such "lively preaching" is to be accomplished in the sermon, in the Words of Institution, and in a particular fashion in the liturgy, beginning:

Above all, therefore, let us believe those promises which Jesus Christ has spoken with his own lips: He is truly willing to make us partakers of his body and blood, in order that we may possess him wholly. . . .

After the Words of Institution, the minister reiterated Paul's warning against unworthy participation; and on that basis he proceeded to a twofold action. All men whose demeanor disqualified them as "disciples" were fenced from the table. The rest of the people were admonished to search their hearts; and those were invited to partake who sought their life in Christ, knowing that they lived in the midst of death. Then the minister proclaimed the promises of Christ (of which we have spoken), and, using the *Sursum corda* devised by Farel, exhorted the communicants not to cleave to the "earthly and corruptible elements," but to lift their "hearts on high where Jesus Christ is in the glory of his Father." That exhortation led directly to the Administration of the elements.

Two problems pertain to this part of the liturgy: (1) The emphasis on introspection and exclusion appears to spoil the Eucharistic spirit and social character of the meal—until we recognize that what Calvin had in mind was not a random gathering of Christians, but the holy, elect people of God, whose integrity must be maintained in this moment of their communion with Christ and with one another. (2) The arbitrary (rather than essential) connection which Calvin found to exist between the elements and the fruit of the sacrament proved difficult of liturgical expression, leaving the worshiper in a quandary over the sense of the bread and wine. For the sake of clarity at this point, the *Short Treatise on the Holy Supper* should be read alongside the liturgy.

The Form of Prayers reflected the chief doctrines of Calvin. The Christian life in all its expressions was meant to serve the glory of God, who is of infinite greatness, incomprehensible essence, boundless might, and everlasting immortality, yet deigns to extend his providence even to us and to take care for our salvation (*Institutes* 3:20:40). The liturgy itself was directed *soli Deo gloria,* though in the same subdued and austere fashion that shaped all of Calvinist piety. Moreover, on the other side of the same theological coin was the creatureliness of man—a theme that informed and subdued Calvin's liturgical work even more.

The adoration of God received its highest expression in man's obedience and sanctity. "We ourselves and all our works," said Calvin, "should be sanctified and dedicated to him, that everything within us may minister to his praise and shew forth his glory." While Luther emphasized the consolations of grace, Calvin dwelt upon the demands of grace. And while the one found the Bible to be a "book of comfort," wherein the joy and peace of the Gospel is laid, the other saw it as "the holy Law and Word of God," which is confirmed in the believer's heart by the Holy Spirit, and which commands his obedience.· There were reflections of this theme throughout the liturgy: in the use of the Decalogue, in the paraphrase of the Lord's Prayer, in the excommunication of the unworthy.

According to his doctrine of election, Calvin conceived of the church as the company of the predestined, the holy people of God. The liturgy was not fashioned for individual comforts; it was rather the corporate instrument of this chosen people, by which they received God's most holy Word and published his most worthy praise, well knowing that he had not elected them for their "handsomeness." And surely the doctrine of election incited Calvin's desire for the weekly celebration of Holy Communion, which had ever been deemed "the liturgy of the Faithful," wherein God sealed his promises to his chosen people.

Simplicity was the hallmark of Calvin's liturgical policy. His model was the "ancient church," by which he meant L'eglise ancienne des Apostres, des Martirs et des saintz Peres, in short, the church "prior to the papacy." Behind this principle lay his adherence to the divine will given in Scripture. To exceed that will is presumption, ingratitude, impiety, rank disobedience. True worship, as true religion, begins with docility, the quality of being teachable by God's Word. Men who improvise upon the Word, "though they toil much in outward rites," are yet impious and contumacious, "because they will not suffer themselves to be ruled by God's authority" (Commentary on Zephaniah 3:2). To the ways of worship set forth in Scripture, the church must adhere with "the least possible admixture of human invention." Moreover, such contrivances, however well intended, are inevitably vitiated by sin and vanity: "Men can do nothing but err when they are guided by their own opinion" (Commentary on John

· Whale, p. 156.

194

4:22); and those "who introduce newly invented methods of worshiping God really worship and adore the creature of their own distempered imaginations" (*Institutes* 1:4:3). For this reason, chiefly, Calvin favored a liturgy "from which ministers be not allowed to vary": it would curtail "the capricious giddiness and levity of such as effect innovations."

He condoned the use of those ceremonies that served decency, order, and reverence, conceding the value of such to the "stimulus" and "expression" of religion. But in the main, he crammed his writings with the damnation of "lifeless and theatrical trifles" and feared nothing more than that the floodgate of ceremonies would be reopened.

For Calvin, a profusion of external forms was an encumbrance upon the "spiritual" worship of God, a service of the "heart." He expressed this in a variety of ways. In *The Necessity of Reforming the Church*, he argued that external worship is an evasion; by performing all manner of ceremonial "subterfuges," men really hope to escape the need of giving *themselves* to God. In the *Short Treatise*, he insisted that the Incarnation was meant to deliver us from the shadowy symbols of the old dispensation, and that a reversion to ceremonies would serve no other end than to "obscure the clarity of the Gospel." And in the *Institutes* (1:11:7) he reasoned that those churches that clamor for bric-a-brac suffer from a lack of sound preaching. Idols arise when preaching declines. The true "painter" does not embellish the sanctuary; he proclaims the Crucifixion more eloquently than "a thousand crosses of wood and stone."

FOR FURTHER READING

J. G. Baum (ed.), *La Maniere et fasson* (Neuchâtel, 1533). Strasbourg, 1859.

Yngve Brilioth, *Eucharistic Faith & Practice*. London, 1956.

E. Doumergue, *Jean Calvin*, II. Lausanne, 1902.

T. H. L. Parker, *The Oracles of God: An Introduction to the Preaching of John Calvin*. London, 1947.

Julius Smend (ed.), *Die evangelischen deutschen Messen bis zu Luthers Deutscher Messe*. Göttingen, 1896. Contains Oecolampadius' *Form und Gstalt*, pp. 214-21.

Bard Thompson, "Reformed Liturgies in Translation" (pt. III, Calvin; pt. IV, Farel), *Bulletin of the Theological Seminary of* the *Evangelical and Reformed Church,* XXVIII/3, 42-62; XXVIII/4, 28-42.

R. S. Wallace, *Calvin's Doctrine of the Word and Sacrament.* Edinburgh, 1953.

J. S. Whale, "Calvin" in *Christian Worship,* edited by Nathaniel Micklem. London, 1936.

THE FORM OF CHURCH PRAYERS AND HYMNS WITH THE MANNER OF ADMINISTERING THE SACRAMENTS AND CONSECRATING MARRIAGE ACCORDING TO THE CUSTOM OF THE ANCIENT CHURCH[1]

Strassburg, 1545   *Geneva, 1542*

The Form of Church Prayers

¶ *On working days, the Minister[2] frames the sort of exhortation to prayer which may seem suitable to him, adapting it to the times and to the topic of his Sermon.*

¶ *On Sunday morning [and on the day of prayers], the following form is generally used.*

Our help is in the name of the Lord, who made heaven and earth. Amen.

CONFESSION

My brethren, let each of you present himself before the face of the Lord, and confess his faults and sins, following my words in his heart.

O Lord God, eternal and almighty Father, we confess and acknowledge unfeignedly before thy holy majesty that we are poor sinners, conceived and born in iniquity and corruption, prone to do evil, incapable of any good, and that in our depravity we transgress thy holy commandments without end or ceasing: Wherefore we purchase for ourselves, through thy righteous judgment, our ruin and perdition. Nevertheless, O Lord, we are grieved that we have offended thee; and we condemn ourselves and our sins with true repentance, beseeching thy grace to relieve our distress. O God and Father most gracious and full of compassion, have mercy upon us in the name of thy Son, our Lord Jesus Christ. And as thou dost blot out our sins and stains, magnify and increase in us day by day the grace of thy Holy Spirit: that as we acknowledge our unrighteousness with all our heart, we may be moved by that sorrow which shall bring forth true repentance in us, mortifying all our sins, and producing in us the fruits of righteousness and innocence which are pleasing unto thee; through the same Jesus Christ &c. [our Lord. Amen.]

Strassburg only

¶ *Now the Minister delivers some word of Scripture to console the conscience; and then he pronounces the Absolution in this manner:*

Let each of you truly acknowledge that he is a sinner, humbling himself before God, and believe that the heavenly Father wills to be gracious unto him in Jesus Christ.

To all those that repent in this wise, and look to Jesus Christ for their salvation, I declare that the absolution of sins is effected, in the name of the Father, and of the Son, and of the Holy Spirit. Amen.

¶ *Now the Congregation sings the first table of the Commandments, after which the Minister says:*

The Lord be with us. Let us pray to the Lord.

Heavenly Father, full of goodness and grace, as thou art pleased to declare thy holy will unto thy poor servants, and to instruct them in the righteousness of thy law, grant that it may also be inscribed and impressed upon our hearts in such wise, that in all our life we may endeavor to serve and obey none beside thee. Neither impute to us at all the transgressions which we have committed against thy law: that, perceiving thy manifold grace upon us in such abundance, we may have cause to praise and glorify thee through Jesus Christ, thy Son, our Lord. Amen.[3]

Strassburg	Geneva
¶ *While the Congregation sings the rest of the Commandments, the Minister goes into the pulpit; and then he offers prayers of the type which follows.*[4]	¶ *That done, a Psalm is sung by the Congregation. Then the Minister commences again to pray, beseeching God for the grace of His Holy Spirit, that His Word may be faithfully expounded to the honor of His name and the edifica-*

> *tion of the Church, and be received with such humility and obedience which it deserves. The form is left to the discretion of the Minister.*

COLLECT FOR ILLUMINATION. LESSON AND SERMON

¶ *At the end of the Sermon, the Minister, having made exhortations to prayer, commences in this manner:*

Almighty God, heavenly Father, thou has promised to grant our requests which we make unto thee in the name of thy well-beloved Son, Jesus Christ our Lord: by whose teaching and that of His apostles we have also been taught to gather together in His name, with the promise that He will be in the midst of us, and will be our intercessor with thee, to obtain all those things for which we agree to ask on earth.

First we have thy commandment to pray for those whom thou hast established over us as rulers and governors; and then, for all the needs of thy people, and indeed of all mankind. Wherefore, with trust in thy holy doctrine and promises, and now especially that we are gathered here before thy face and in the name of thy Son, our Lord Jesus, we do heartily beseech thee, our gracious God and Father, in the name of our only Saviour and Mediator, to grant us the free pardon of our [faults and] offenses through thine infinite mercy, and to draw and lift up our thoughts and desires unto thee in such wise that we may be able to call upon thee with all our heart, yea agreeably to thy good pleasure and only-reasonable will.

Wherefore we pray thee, O heavenly Father, for all princes and lords, thy servants, to whom thou hast intrusted the administration of thy justice, and especially for the magistrates of this city. May it please thee to impart to them thy Spirit, who alone is good and truly sovereign, and daily stablish them in the same, that with true faith they may acknowledge Jesus Christ, thy Son, our Lord, to be the King of kings and Lord of lords, as thou hast given Him all power in heaven and earth. May they seek to serve Him and to exalt His kingdom in their government, guiding and ruling their subjects, who are the work of thy hands and the sheep of thy pasture, in accordance with thy good pleasure. So may all of us both here and throughout the earth, being kept in perfect peace and quietness, serve thee in all godliness and virtue, and being delivered and protected from the fear of our enemies, give praise unto thee all the days of our life.[5]

We pray thee also, O faithful Father and Saviour, for all those whom thou hast ordained pastors of thy faithful people, to whom thou hast intrusted the care of souls and the ministry of thy holy Gospel. Direct and guide them by thy Holy Spirit, that they may be found faithful and loyal ministers of thy glory, having but one goal: that all the poor, wandering, and lost sheep be gathered and restored to the Lord Jesus Christ, the chief Shepherd and Prince of bishops, so that they may grow and increase in Him daily unto all righteousness and holiness. Wilt thou, on the contrary, deliver all the churches from the mouths of ravening wolves and from all mercenaries who seek their own ambition or profit, but never the exaltation of thy holy name alone, nor the salvation of thy flock.[6]

We pray thee now, O most gracious and merciful Father, for all men everywhere. As it is thy will to be acknowledged the Saviour of the whole world, through the redemption wrought by thy Son Jesus Christ, grant that those who are still estranged from the knowledge of Him, being in the darkness and captivity of error and ignorance, may be brought by the illumination of thy Holy Spirit and the preaching of thy Gospel to the straight way of salvation, which is to know thee, the only true God, and Jesus Christ whom thou hast sent. Grant that those whom thou hast already visited with thy grace and enlightened with the knowledge of thy Word may grow in goodness day by day, enriched by thy spiritual blessings: so that all together we may worship thee with one heart and one voice, giving honor and reverence to thy [Son Jesus] Christ, our Master, King, and Lawgiver.

Likewise, O God of all comfort, we commend unto thee all those whom thou dost visit and chasten with cross and tribulation, whether by poverty, prison, sickness, or banishment, or any other misery of the body or affliction of the spirit. Enable them to perceive and understand thy fatherly affection which doth chasten them unto their correction, that they may turn unto thee with their whole heart, and, having turned, receive full consolation and deliverance from every ill.

200

Finally, O God and Father, grant also to those who are gathered here in the name of thy Son Jesus, to hear[7] His Word (and to keep His holy Supper),• that we may acknowledge truly, without hypocrisy, what perdition is ours by nature, what condemnation we deserve and heap upon ourselves from day to day by our unhappy and disordered life. Wherefore, seeing that there is nothing of good in us and that our flesh and blood cannot inherit thy kingdom, may we yield ourselves completely, with all our love and steadfast faith, to thy dear Son, our Lord, the only Saviour and Redeemer:

[8] To the end that He, dwelling in us, may mortify our old Adam, renewing us for a better life, by which thy name, according as it is holy and worthy, may be exalted and glorified everywhere and in all places, and that we with all creatures may give thee true and perfect obedience, even as thine angels and heavenly messengers have no desire but to fulfil thy commandments. Thus may thy will be done without any contradiction, and all men apply themselves to serve and please thee, renouncing their own will and all the desires of their flesh. In this manner mayest thou have lordship and dominion over us all, and may we learn more and more each day to submit and subject ourselves to thy majesty. In such wise mayest thou be King and Ruler over all the earth, guiding thy people by the sceptre of thy Word and the power of thy Spirit, confounding thine enemies by the might of thy truth and righteousness. And thus may every power and principality which stands against thy glory be destroyed and abolished day by day, till the fulfilment of thy kingdom be manifest, when thou shalt appear in judgment.

Grant that we who walk in the love and fear of thy name may be nourished by thy goodness; and supply us with all things necessary and expedient to eat our bread in peace. Then, seeing that thou carest for us, we may better acknowledge thee as our Father and await all good gifts from thy hand, withdrawing our trust from all creatures, to place it entirely in thee and thy goodness.

And since in this mortal life we are poor sinners, so full of weakness that we fail continually and stray from the right way, may it please thee to pardon our faults by which we are beholden to thy judgment; and through that remission,

• That which is enclosed by these two marks (   ) is not said except on the day of the Lord's Supper.

deliver us from the obligation of eternal death in which we stand. Be pleased, therefore, to turn aside thy wrath from us, neither impute to us the iniquity which is in us; even as we, by reason of thy commandment, forget the injuries done to us, and instead of seeking vengeance, solicit the good for our enemies.

Finally, may it please thee to sustain us by thy power for the time to come, that we may not stumble because of the weakness of our flesh. And especially as we of ourselves are so frail that we are not able to stand fast for a single moment, while, on the other hand, we are continually beset and assailed by so many enemies—the devil, the world, sin, and our own flesh never ceasing to make war upon us—wilt thou strengthen us by thy Holy Spirit and arm us with thy grace, that we may be able to resist all temptations firmly, and persevere in this spiritual battle until we shall attain full victory, to triumph at last in thy kingdom with our Captain and Protector, Jesus Christ our Lord.

Geneva only

¶ *On those days when the Lord's Supper is to be celebrated, that which follows is joined to the preceding:*

And as our Lord Jesus has not only offered His body and blood once on the Cross for the remission of our sins, but also desires to impart them to us as our nourishment unto everlasting life, grant us this grace: that we may receive at His hands such a great benefit and gift with true sincerity of heart and with ardent zeal. In steadfast faith may we receive His body and blood, yea Christ Himself entire, who being true God and true man, is verily the holy bread and heaven which gives us life. So may we live no longer in ourselves, after our nature which is entirely corrupt and vicious, but may He live in us and lead us to the life that is holy, blessed and everlasting: whereby we may truly become partakers of the new and eternal testament, the covenant of grace, assured that it is thy good pleasure to be our gracious Father forever, never reckoning our faults against us, and to provide for us, as thy well-beloved children and heirs, all our needs both of body and soul. Thus may we render praise and thanks unto thee without ceasing and magnify thy name in word and deed.

Grant us, therefore, O heavenly Father, so to celebrate

this day the blessed memorial and remembrance of thy dear Son, to exercise ourselves in the same, and to proclaim the benefit of His death, that, receiving new growth and strength in faith and in all things good, we may with so much greater confidence proclaim thee our Father and glory in thee. Amen.

¶ *When the Supper has been completed, this thanksgiving, or one similar, is used:*

Heavenly Father, we offer thee eternal praise and thanks that thou hast granted so great a benefit to us poor sinners, having drawn us into the Communion of thy Son, Jesus Christ our Lord, whom thou hast delivered to death for us, and whom thou givest us as the meat and drink of life eternal. Now grant us this other benefit: that thou wilt never allow us to forget these things; but having them imprinted on our hearts, may we grow and increase daily in the faith which is at work in every good deed. Thus may we order and pursue all our life to the exaltation of thy glory and the edification of our neighbor; through the same Jesus Christ, thy Son, who in the unity of the Holy Spirit liveth and reigneth with thee, O God, forever. Amen.

Strassburg	*Geneva*
¶ *At the end a Psalm is sung, after which the Minister dismisses the Congregation, saying:*	¶ *The blessing which is given at the departure of the people, according to our Lord's appointment. Num. 6.*

The Lord bless you and keep you. The Lord make His face to shine upon you and be merciful unto you. The Lord lift up His countenance upon you and keep you in virtuous prosperity.[9] Amen.

The Manner of Celebrating the Lord's Supper[10]

¶ *It is proper to observe that on the Sunday prior to the celebration of the Lord's Supper, the following admonitions are made to the people: first, that each person prepare and dispose himself to receive it worthily and with such reverence that it deserves; second, that children may certainly not be brought forward unless they are well in-*

structed and have made profession of their faith in church; third, that if strangers are there who may still be untaught and ignorant, they proceed to present themselves for private instruction. On the day of the Lord's Supper, the Minister touches upon it in the conclusion of his Sermon, or better, if there is occasion, preaches the whole Sermon about it, in order to explain to the people what our Lord wishes to say and signify by this mystery, and in what way it behooves us to receive it.

Strassburg

¶ Then, after the accustomed prayers have been offered, the Congregation, in making confession of the faith, sings the Apostles' Creed to testify that all wish to live and die in the Christian doctrine and religion. Meanwhile, the Minister prepares the bread and wine on the Table. Thereafter he prays in this fashion:

Geneva

¶ Then, having made the prayers and the Confession of Faith (which is to testify in the name of the people that they all wish to live and die in the Christian doctrine and religion), he says in a loud voice:

Strassburg only

Inasmuch as we have made confession of our faith to testify that we are children of God, hoping therefore that He will take heed of us as a gracious Father, let us pray to Him, saying:

Heavenly Father, full of all goodness and mercy, as our Lord Jesus Christ has not only offered His body and blood once on the Cross for the remission of our sins, but also desires to impart them to us as our nourishment unto everlasting life, we beseech thee to grant us this grace: that we may receive at His hands such a great gift and benefit with true sincerity of heart and with ardent zeal. In steadfast faith may we receive His body and blood, yea Christ Himself entire, who, being true God and true man, is verily the holy bread of heaven which gives us life. So may we live no longer in ourselves, after our nature which is entirely corrupt and vicious, but may He live in us and lead us to the life that

204

is holy, blessed and everlasting: whereby we may truly become partakers of the new and eternal testament, the covenant of grace, assured that it is thy good pleasure to be our gracious Father forever, never reckoning our faults against us, and to provide for us, as thy well-beloved children and heirs, all our needs both of soul and body. Thus may we render praise and thanks unto thee without ceasing, and magnify thy name in word and deed.

Grant us, therefore, O heavenly Father, so to celebrate this day the blessed memorial and remembrance of thy dear Son, to exercise ourselves in the same, and to proclaim the benefit of His death, that, receiving new growth and strength in faith and in all things good, we may with so much greater confidence proclaim thee our Father and glory in thee; through the same Jesus Christ, thy Son, our Lord, in whose name we pray unto thee, as He hath taught us.

Our Father which art in, etc.

Strassburg & Geneva

¶ *Then the Minister says:*

Let us hear how Jesus Christ instituted His holy Supper for us, as St. Paul relates it in the eleventh chapter of First Corinthians:

I have received of the Lord, he says, that which I have delivered unto you: That the Lord Jesus, on the night in which He was betrayed, took bread: And when He had given thanks, He brake it and said, Take, eat, this is my body which is broken for you: this do in remembrance of me. After the same manner, when He had supped, He took the cup saying, This cup is the new testament in my blood: this do ye, as oft as ye shall drink it, in remembrance of me. For as often as ye eat this bread and drink this cup, ye do proclaim the Lord's death till He come. Therefore, whosoever shall eat this bread and drink of this cup unworthily shall be guilty of the body and blood of the Lord. But let a man examine himself and so let him eat of this bread and drink of this cup. For whosoever eateth and drinketh unworthily, taketh his own condemnation, not discerning the Lord's body.

We have heard, my brethren, how our Lord observed His Supper with His disciples, from which we learn that strangers and those who do not belong to the company of His faithful people must not be admitted. Therefore, following that precept, in the name and by the authority of our Lord Jesus

Christ, I excommunicate all idolaters, blasphemers and despisers of God, all heretics and those who create private sects in order to break the unity of the Church, all perjurers, all who rebel against father or mother or superior, all who promote sedition or mutiny; brutal and disorderly persons, adulterers, lewd and lustful men, thieves, ravishers, greedy and grasping people, drunkards, gluttons, and all those who lead a scandalous and dissolute life. I warn them to abstain from this Holy Table, lest they defile and contaminate the holy food which our Lord Jesus Christ gives to none except they belong to His household of faith.

Moreover, in accordance with the exhortation of St. Paul, let every man examine and prove his own conscience to see whether he truly repents of his faults and grieves over his sins, desiring to live henceforth a holy life according to God. Above all, let him see whether he has his trust in the mercy of God and seeks his salvation wholly in Jesus Christ and, renouncing all hatred and rancor, has high resolve and courage to live in peace and brotherly love with his neighbors.

If we have this witness in our hearts before God, never doubt that He claims us as His children, and that the Lord Jesus addresses His Word to us, to invite us to His Table and to give us this holy Sacrament which He imparted to His disciples.

And yet, we may be conscious of much frailty and misery in ourselves, such that we do not have perfect faith, but are inclined toward defiance and unbelief, or that we do not devote ourselves wholly to the service of God and with such zeal as we ought, but have to fight daily against the lusts of our flesh. Nevertheless, since our Lord has granted us the grace of having His Gospel graven on our hearts, so that we may withstand all unbelief, and has given us the desire and longing to renounce our own wishes, that we may follow His righteousness and His holy commandments: let us be assured that the sins and imperfections which remain in us will not prevent Him from receiving us and making us worthy partakers of this spiritual Table. For we do not come here to testify that we are perfect or righteous in ourselves: On the contrary, by seeking our life in Jesus Christ we confess that we are in death. Know, therefore, that this Sacrament is a medicine for the poor sick souls, and that the only worthiness which our Lord requires of us is to know ourselves sufficiently to deplore our sins, and to find all our pleasure, joy and satisfaction in Him alone.

Above all, therefore, let us believe those promises which Jesus Christ, who is the unfailing truth, has spoken with His own lips: He is truly willing to make us partakers of His body and blood, in order that we may possess Him wholly and in such wise that He may live in us and we in Him. And though we see but bread and wine, we must not doubt that He accomplishes spiritually in our souls all that He shows us outwardly by these visible signs, namely, that He is the bread of heaven to feed and nourish us unto eternal life. So, let us never be unmindful of the infinite goodness of our Saviour who spreads out all His riches and blessings on this Table, to impart them to us. For in giving Himself to us, He makes a testimony to us that all that He has is ours. Therefore, let us receive this Sacrament as a pledge that the virtue of His death and passion is imputed to us for righteousness, even as though we had suffered them in our own persons. May we never be so perverse as to draw away when Jesus Christ invites us so gently by His Word. But accounting the worthiness of this precious gift which He gives, let us present ourselves to Him with ardent zeal, that He may make us capable of receiving it.

To do so, let us lift our spirits and hearts on high where Jesus Christ is in the glory of His Father, whence we expect Him at our redemption. Let us not be fascinated by these earthly and corruptible elements which we see with our eyes and touch with our hands, seeking Him there as though He were enclosed in the bread or wine. Then only shall our souls be disposed to be nourished and vivified by His substance when they are lifted up above all earthly things, attaining even to heaven, and entering the Kingdom of God where He dwells. Therefore let us be content to have the bread and wine as signs and witnesses, seeking the truth spiritually where the Word of God promises that we shall find it.[11]

Strassburg	Geneva
¶ *That done, the Minister, having informed the people that they are to come to the holy Table in rever-*	¶ *That done, the Ministers distribute the bread and the chalice to the people, having admonished them*

ence, good order, and Christian humility, first partakes himself of the bread and wine, then administers it to the deacon,[12] and subsequently to the whole congregation, saying:

Take, eat, the body of Jesus which has been delivered unto death for you.

to come forward with reverence and in good order. Meanwhile some Psalms are sung; or some portion of Scripture is read, appropriate to the significance of the sacrament. At the conclusion, Thanksgiving is offered, as it has been stated.

Strassburg only

¶ And the deacon offers the cup, saying:

This is the cup of the new testament in the blood of Jesus which has been shed for you.

¶ Meanwhile, the Congregation sings the Psalm: Louang' et Grâce [138].

THANKSGIVING AFTER THE SUPPER

Heavenly Father, we offer thee eternal praise and thanks that thou hast granted so great a benefit to us poor sinners, having drawn us into the Communion of thy Son, Jesus Christ our Lord, whom thou hast delivered to death for us, and whom thou givest us as the meat and drink of life eternal. Now grant us this other benefit: that thou wilt never allow us to forget these things; but having them imprinted on our hearts, may we grow and increase daily in the faith which is at work in every good deed. Thus may we order and pursue all our life to the exaltation of thy glory and the edification of our neighbor; through the same Jesus Christ, thy Son, who in the unity of the Holy Spirit liveth and reigneth with thee, O God, forever. Amen.

¶ After thanks has been given, the Canticle of Simeon is sung: Maintenant Seigneur Dieu.

¶ Then the Minister dismisses the Congregation by pronouncing the Benediction used on Sunday.

NOTES

1. Both editions of Calvin's liturgy—Strassburg and Genevan—
   are given in *Calvini opera*, VI, 173-84. The Strassburg edition
   has been edited separately by Stephen A. Hurlbut in *The
   Liturgy of the Church of Scotland* (Charleston: St. Albans
   Press, 1954), pp. 8-23. Where differences occur between the
   two texts the Strassburg version is given in the left column,
   or is set apart in brackets. Major differences are noted by
   italicized titles.
2. le ministre.
3. Ainsi soit il. So be it.
4. This is the example given:

   Let us call upon our Heavenly Father, Father of all goodness and mercy, beseeching Him to cast the eye of His
   clemency upon us, His poor servants, neither impute to us
   the many faults and offenses which we have committed, provoking His wrath against us. But as we look into the face of
   the Son, Jesus Christ our Lord, whom He hath appointed
   Mediator between Himself and us, let us beseech Him, in
   whom is all fulness of wisdom and light, to vouchsafe to guide
   us by His Holy Spirit into the true understanding of His
   holy doctrine, making it productive in us of all the fruits of
   righteousness: to the glory and exaltation of His name, and
   to the instruction and edification of His Church. And let us
   pray unto Him in the name and favor of His well-beloved Son,
   Jesus Christ, as He hath taught us to pray, saying: Our Father,
   which art in heaven, etc.

   Calvin employed several other Collects for Illumination. He
   derived the following from Bucer:

   Almighty and gracious Father, since our whole salvation
   standeth in our knowledge of thy Holy Word, strengthen us
   now by thy Holy Spirit that our hearts may be set free from
   all worldly thoughts and attachments of the flesh, so that we
   may hear and receive that same Word, and, recognizing thy
   gracious will for us, may love and serve thee with earnest
   delight, praising and glorifying thee in Jesus Christ our Lord.
   Amen.
5. "Amen" omitted in translation.
6. This sentence, while not in the 1539 edition of Bucer's liturgy,
   is found in certain earlier and later editions of that liturgy.
7. à cause de sa Parolle (et de sa saincte Cene).

8. Here Calvin departs from Bucer's text to insert a long paraphrase of the Lord's Prayer. In the Genevan version, he returns to Bucer's text immediately after the next rubric; in the Strassburg version, with the opening prayer of the Communion liturgy.
9. et vous maintienne en bonne prosperité.
10. *Calvini opera*, VI, 193-200.
11. This final paragraph of the Exhortation probably came from Farel's liturgy: *La Maniere et fasson*, edited by J. G. Baum (Strasbourg: Treuttel et Wurtz, 1859), pp. 64-5.
12. diacre.

FORM AND MANNER
OF THE LORD'S SUPPER,
INFANT BAPTISM, AND
THE VISITATION OF THE SICK
AS THEY ARE USED
AND OBSERVED IN BASEL[1]

(1525?)

The truth abideth forever.

Use for the Administration of the Holy Sacrament of Christ's Body and Blood [2]

¶ *After the proclamation of God's Word in the Sermon, the Preacher[3] delivers an admonition to this effect:*

I admonish all who now desire to receive this sacrament to prove themselves beforehand, whether they understand and hold the mystery of the sacrament, lest the pearls be cast before swine, and they be guilty of the body and blood of Christ.

Our mystery is: that Christ is for us the bread of life: which we attest with thanksgiving by this sacramental bread. Above all, therefore, each communicant of the Supper ought to know that his sins are forgiven through the passion of Christ. He should likewise verify in himself that such faith and trust now incites him to a new, peaceful, and God-fearing life. Furthermore, we declare ourselves to be united here in the one body of Christ, as disclosed in the unity of faith; and the substance of our faith is this:

We believe in one God, the Father Almighty, Maker of heaven and earth. We believe in His Son, our Lord Jesus Christ: Who was conceived by the Holy Ghost, born of the Virgin Mary: Who suffered under the judge, Pontius Pilate, was crucified, dead, and buried: Who descended into hell, the third day rose from the dead, ascended into heaven: Who sitteth there on the right hand of His heavenly Father: From thence He shall come to judge the living and the dead. We believe in the Holy Ghost. We believe in one Christian Church, that is, the Communion of Saints. We believe in the

211

forgiveness of sins, the resurrection of the flesh, and, after this life, the life everlasting.

By this Creed let us be satisfied, no one forming irresponsible judgments on account of other matters.[4] Likewise, we have excluded those who are banned by the Word of God and who rack the body of Christ as unsound and withered members. Here in this Supper, we should not and cannot have fellowship with idolaters, sorcerers, blasphemers, despisers of God's Word and of the holy sacraments of Baptism and the Lord's Supper. Let those be excluded from us who do not honor their father and mother, who are disobedient to the civil authority, being rebellious and loath to meet their interest, taxes, etc., those who are not willing in matters of faith to be guided by the Word alone. Excluded are: all murderers and those who do not put aside their envy, all who cause strife for the sake of mischief, fornicators, adulterers, drunkards and gluttons, thieves, robbers, usurers or those who promote improper gain, business or trade, those who look only to themselves,[5] idlers who by their sloth are a burden upon their neighbors, all false witnesses[6] and oppressors of righteousness. For they all lack faith and are mockers of God, who desires to have a holy courageous people. Likewise, if anyone ventures to be caught in these or similar vices henceforth, he shall submit to brotherly correction in a good spirit, and since he has offended the Congregation, shall reconcile himself to it by a new life.

Now, as before,[7] we should pray for all who rule the Christian community: First, that God may endow, govern, and protect His Church and His people with the spirit of wisdom, strength, and the godly profession and knowledge of our Lord Jesus. We[8] pray also for the public authority, namely for the whole common Confederacy, for the honorable burgomaster, guildmaster, council, and general city and canton of Basel: that God wilt direct and govern them all according to His will, so that we may lead a God-fearing, peaceful, and Christian life with one another, and attain eternal life when this existence is over. Likewise, let all those be commended unto you who are tormented and persecuted for the sake of His Word, that God help them, so that they may persevere in the affirmation of the truth. We also pray that of His loving-kindness, He will attend all our needs of both body and soul. Amen.

Recite the Lord's Prayer.

¶ *Hereafter the liturgy proceeds before the altar, where bread and wine are prepared and candles burn, but without any further ceremonies.*

Beloved in Christ, that we may partake to greater advantage of the holy sacrament of Christ's body and blood with thanksgiving, we would first make confession of our guilt:

O Almighty God and heavenly Father, we poor, miserable sinners confess that we have sinned against thy law from our childhood till this hour, by evil thoughts, words, inclinations and deeds which we cannot count, and above all by gross unbelief. Wherefore we are not worthy to be called thy children, or to lift our eyes up to heaven. O God and Father, would that we had never offended thee! We beseech thee, for the sake of thy loving-kindness and the honor of thy name, to receive us into thy grace, with the forgiveness of our sin.

Hearken to a Psalm:

Out of a deep heart I cried unto thee. O Lord, O Lord, hear my voice. . . . [Here follow the penitential, yet comforting words of Psalm 130:1-8.]

Lord, have mercy. Christ, have mercy. O Lord, have mercy and be gracious unto us forever and ever.

Hear the Absolution:

The Almighty God will have mercy upon us. As an undoubted pledge to us, He hath sent His Son into the world, who was sacrificed as the innocent lamb, bore our sin, and made satisfaction for it. Then, whosoever believeth in our Lord Christ will have the forgiveness of his sin and everlasting life. As you hold this faith, I absolve you of all sins through the power of such faith: in the name of the Father, and of the Son, and of the Holy Spirit. Amen.

Inasmuch as one of the principal points in the reception of the sacrament—yea, the whole matter—is to meditate upon the passion of Christ: therefore hear and contemplate that which Isaiah hath perceived in spirit long ago, when he says: O Lord, how very few believe this our report. . . . [Isaiah 53:1-7].

Hearken to a portion of the Gospel of Matthew and reflect upon it:

When they had crucified Jesus . . . [Matthew 27:35-50]. But Jesus cried once more and yielded up His spirit.

O beloved, you have heard the unspeakable mercy of God. The heavenly Father hath given His only-begotten Son for us in the most despicable death. The Shepherd hath died for the lambs; the Innocent hath suffered for the sinners, the Head for the members. By ineffable love, the High Priest hath sacrificed Himself to the Father as a burnt[9] offering on our behalf, and with His blood hath sufficiently secured and sealed our union with God the Father. Therefore let us hold these benefits in an everlasting and lively remembrance. His blood touch our heart! To Him be praise forevermore! No longer do we desire to be our own, but the Lord's, and servants of His servants.[10] Now we wish to live and aspire unto Christ, and not to ourselves, thus to be incorporated with Him as members, redeemed and purified by His blood. Wherefore we remember with thanksgiving the benefit of His body and blood, even as He hath willed us to recall by the holiest of all services—His Supper.[11] Think upon it now, as you sit near Christ and hear of Him.

Who, on the day before He suffered, took bread in His hand: And when He had given thanks, He brake it, and said, Take, eat: this is my body which is given for you: this do in remembrance of me. After the same manner He also took the cup after supper, gave thanks, offered it to them, and said, Drink ye all of this: the cup of the new testament is in my blood: this do ye, as oft as ye do it, in remembrance of me. For as often as ye shall eat this bread and drink of this cup, ye shall proclaim and extol the Lord's death.

That our thanksgiving be still more truthful, let us pray:

Our Father, which art in heaven, Hallowed be thy name. Thy kingdom come to us. Thy will be done, On earth as it is in heaven. Give us this day our daily bread. And forgive us our debt, as we forgive our debtors. Lead us not into temptation, But deliver us from evil. Amen.

Let each one prove himself, as before, lest he receive judgment: for God desires a holy and courageous people, in all discipline and devotion. Be diligent to show love and concord without any hypocrisy, that the name of God may be hallowed through you.

¶ *As he administers the bread to them, he says:*

The undoubted faith, which you have in the death of Christ, lead you into eternal life.[12]

John Calvin, The Form of Church Prayers

¶ *After the same manner also with the wine:*

The faith, which you have in the spilt blood of Jesus Christ, lead you into eternal life.[13]

You are commended to have love among yourselves, and especially toward the poor.[14] The peace of Christ be with you. Amen.

NOTES

1. *Form und gstalt Wie das Herren Nachtmal / Der kinder Tauff / Der Krancken haymsüchung / zu Basel gebraucht vnd gehalten werden.* Baseler Univ.-Bibl. and Ratsschulbibl., Zwickau. Undated, but presumably 1525.
2. Julius Smend (ed.), *Die evangelischen deutschen Messen bis zu Luthers Deutscher Messe* (Göttingen, 1896), pp. 213-19.
3. Predicant.
4. Bey disem Artikel lassen wir es bleyben, nyemand andersach halben frevenlich urtaylen.
5. die nit zu geben oder nemen. In a footnote, Smend suggests: die nicht aufzutragen noch zu übernehmen.
6. falsch zungen: deceitful tongues.
7. A reference, apparently, to the Intercessions made in the service of the Word.
8. The following passage corresponds to the Intercessions at the beginning of Zwingli's service of the Word. *CR* 4: 686.
9. zu ainem brinnenden opfer.
10. und knecht und diener seiner knecht.
11. Darumb auch wir mit danksagung ingedenk sein der gutthat seynes leybs und bluts, wie er uns des aller hailigsten brauchs hat wöllen erinneren, seynes Nachtmals.
12. Der ungezweyfelt glaub, so jr hond in den tod Christi, für euch in das ewig leben.
13. Der glaub, so jr hond in das vergossen blut Jesu Christi, für dich in das ewig leben.
14. Lassend euch die lieb befolhen seyn under ainander, und zuvorab die armen.

215

LA MANIÈRE ET FASSON

*The Manner Observed in Preaching
When the People Are Assembled
to Hear the Word of God* [1]

Bidding Prayer. He who serves the people with the Word admonishes everyone to turn unto God, our most merciful Father, beseeching Him to send His Holy Spirit upon all men. They pray that He may delight to have mercy upon all kings, princes and lords, upon all those whom He has established in dignity and authority by giving them the sword to punish the wicked and defend the good: that of His grace He may show compassion upon them, granting them His Holy Spirit, so that they exercise their office in a godly way, to the honor and glory of our Lord [2] and to the benefit and welfare of their subjects. They pray for all who are gathered to hear the Word of truth: that our Lord may forgive every fault and sin, and grant His grace and His Spirit through whom comes the full understanding of all truth. Thus, in a pure and holy way one may be able to treat, expound and proclaim His Holy Word, and to hear, understand, receive and keep the same, accomplishing the will of this good Father. Of Him they ask all things in the name of His only Son Jesus, saying as He has taught:

Our Father, who art in heaven. Hallowed be thy name, etc.

Proclamation of the Word. After the prayer, the preacher[3] commences by taking some text of the Holy Scripture, which he reads as clearly as did our Lord in Nazareth, and, having read it, expounds word for word without skipping, using scriptural passages to clarify the subject which he is explaining. He does not depart from Holy Scripture lest the pure Word of God be obscured by the filth of men, but bears the Word faithfully and speaks only the Word of God. And having expounded his text as simply as possible and without deviating from Scripture, as God gives grace he exhorts and admonishes the hearers, in keeping with the text, to depart from all sin and error, superstition and vanity, and return wholly to God. He exhorts them to have complete faith and perfect trust in Him, to give their whole heart to God, loving Him above all things, and, for the love of Him, our neighbor as ourselves, to live honorably without doing wrong to any man or hindering anyone by slandering him, to strive to edify all men and lead them to our Lord, to obey the lords and princes (whether they be good or bad) in all things which are not against God, giving and paying them everything ordered and due. One should obey the rulers not simply out of the fear of the sword which they have from God, or of being punished and tormented by them, but indeed for conscience' sake. For everyone who resists authority resists God's ordinance, because there is no authority apart from His ordinance and disposition. Sometimes, to show mercy, He gives us good princes who are confronted by the fear of God, who obey His Word and take to heart the advancement of His honor and the welfare of their subjects; and sometimes, in wrath over the sins of the people, He gives us iniquitous tyrants who have their own way and do what pleases them. Of whatever sort they may be, one must obey them and desire their welfare and peace—so far as our Lord commands, who raises up the princes and casts them down and transfers kingdoms according to His good pleasure. Wherefore, the Minister must exhort the Christian people to seek the liberty and freedom, not of the flesh, but of the spirit and soul. For if our King Jesus was a subject and rendered unto Caesar the things which were Caesar's,[4] all true Christians and faithful ones must do the same. In such wise, every preacher of the truth should teach, admonishing the princes too, if need be, that having power, they do their duty and treat their subjects as their brethren and children, knowing that God is above all princes and that He shall judge all men according to their deserts.

The Law of God. In like manner, he admonishes everyone to keep God's holy commandments, beseeching our Lord to bestow the grace to obey them. He proclaims the law of God and the holy commandments which are written in the twentieth chapter of Exodus and which are applied at Baptism.[5]

The Confession of Sin. After that, he incites all of them to seek the mercy of God as they confess their sins, following the form which is contained in the Order for the Lord's Supper.[6]

The Apostles' Creed. And thus, having said the Lord's Prayer,[7] he exhorts the people to beseech our Lord for grace to be firm in the faith, which they all confess by saying the Creed:

I believe in God the Father, etc.

Intercessions. Likewise, he exhorts everyone to offer prayer: for all who are untaught, that God in His mercy may inspire them and lead them to the knowledge of truth; for all who bear the sword, that He may grant them grace and power to exercise it in a godly way; for all who are in distress, that He comfort them; and, above all, for those who suffer for the faith of our Lord Jesus, for His Holy Gospel, that God may help and strengthen them, and in His grace cause them to persevere in the confession of His name, so that nothing may induce them to do or say anything which is not in keeping with the Word of our Lord. Thus, the people are dismissed in peace.

NOTES

1. J. G. Baum (ed.), *La Maniere et fasson* (Strasbourg: Treuttel et Wurtz, 1859), pp. 69-77. The original edition (if such existed) is now lost. This, the extant text, was published at Neuchâtel in 1533. Farel himself noted that he had prepared some services at Montbéliard in 1524: *Epistre aux lecteurs fideles* (in the 6th edition of Farel's *Le Sommaire,* 1552), p. 226. Upon this evidence, J. Meyhoffer argues that a primitive edition was printed at Basel *ca.* 1525. He notes the similarity between the liturgy of Oecolampadius and that of Farel, but hesitates to say which preceded the other. Cf. *Guillaume Farel: Une Biographie Nouvelle,* prepared by Le Comité Farel (Neuchâtel, 1930), pp. 141-2. On the contrary, H. Vuilleumier submits that the first edition was published at Neuchâtel in 1533, there being no earlier one, and that it came from the Bernese *Agendbuchly* of 1529, since Farel was then an agent of Bern: *Histoire de l'Eglise Réformée de Pays de Vaud* (Lausanne, 1927), I, 309ff. Meyhoffer concedes the similarity, but reverses the order of dependence: the *Agendbuchly* was an abridgment of *La Maniere.* Also see: Baum's introduction, pp. xv, xvi; and G. J. Van de Poll, *Martin Bucer's Liturgical Ideas* (Assen, 1954), pp. 110f.
2. By the expression, "our Lord," Farel usually means God the Father.

218

3. le prescheur.
4. Literally: "and paid to Caesar that which he [Caesar] was receiving from others."
5. et mis la sus au baptesme.
6. Cf. p. 221, below.
7. The Lord's Prayer was one of the elements in the Office of Confession.

Our Lord's Supper[1]

Exhortation. Our God and most merciful Father does not think thoughts of affliction (which is to say, punishment), but those of peace, grace and forgiveness, for the sake of His own love instead of our good works or righteousness. He wills to blot out our sins and be gracious unto us and to accomplish His holy promises, granting us clean water and His Holy Spirit to cleanse us from all our filth and defilement, and giving us a new heart by writing His holy law thereon. When the fulness of time was come, He sent his dearly beloved Son, revealing the very great love and affection which He has had for us. He did not even spare His only and most beloved Son, our Lord Jesus Christ, but gave Him for us. Thus, according to the good purpose of His Father that we be reconciled to Him, this good Saviour offered Himself to His Father once for our redemption; He died to gather all of us who were scattered, that all might be united in one body, even as He and the Father are one. Far more than we can possibly express, our Father has thereby revealed the great treasures of His goodness and mercy: For the sake of us who were dead through sin and who were His enemies, He willed that His Son should die to give us life and make us children who are pleasing to this good Father. Likewise, our blessed Saviour has abundantly expressed His very great love, by giving His life for us, washing and purging us by His blood. Thus, before He suffered, He instituted His Holy Supper in that last meal which He held in this mortal life and which He said He deeply desired. It was His will that, in memory of His profound love, in which He gave His body for us on the Cross and spent His blood for the remission of our sins, we should partake of the same bread and drink of the same cup, without any discrimination, even as He died for all men without discrimination. And He bade all men to take, eat, and drink in His Supper.

219

Invitation. Therefore, let all true Christians and faithful ones, who believe steadfastly in our Lord Jesus Christ, having true faith that He died for us, come to this Holy Table, all together giving thanks unto God for the great goodness which He has shown us, and bearing witness to their faith, inasmuch as they believe that, through the death of the Lamb without blemish, we are delivered from the enemy. So they give thanks to this blessed Saviour Jesus, who of His good pleasure died for our sake, through the very great love which He had toward us. It is a love which all do imitate and follow, loving one another with a perfect love, even as our gentle and blessed Saviour Jesus loved us by offering and giving His life for our sake.

Self-examination. Let everyone take heed of himself and inquire whether he has true faith in our Lord Jesus Christ, whether he believes completely that peace is made between God and us through the death and passion of Jesus, that God is gracious unto us, that His wrath is appeased by the blessed Saviour Jesus, through whom we are made sons and heirs of God, heirs with Jesus Christ by whose blood we are all purged and cleansed, our sins blotted out and plainly forgiven, and that Jesus, our Saviour, has made satisfaction for everything.

Excommunication. On the other hand, all those who do not have true faith must not presume at all to come to the Holy Table, pretending and falsely testifying to be members of the body of Jesus Christ to which they do not belong. Such are: all idolaters who worship and serve other than the one God; all perjurers; the slothful who serve no purpose and are of no account, though they could be; all who are disobedient to their father and mother and to those whom God has purposely appointed to rule over us without contravening His authority; all ruffians, quarrelsome persons who unjustly beat and smite their neighbors, whom they hate; all lechers; the intemperate who live dissolutely in their eating and drinking; all thieves who work damage and injury upon their neighbors; all false witnesses and perpetrators of crimes; and all those who live wickedly and contrary to the holy commandments of God, who do not intend to obey His holy law nor live according to His Word by following the holy Gospel, like true children of God. Let them not presume to approach this Holy Table, to which only those are to come who really belong to the body of Christ, united and rooted in Him by true and living faith which works through love. For it shall be to their judgment and condemnation if they come here; and they shall be rejected as traitors and the successors of Judas.

Confession. Yet, while we abide in this world, surrounded by this body of death and sin, we are all poor sinners and cannot say that we are without sin. So, ere we come to this Holy Table, to keep the memorial of our Saviour who died for our sins and was raised for our justification, we will present ourselves, humbly and lowly in heart, confessing our faults, and will cast ourselves before the exalted majesty of our God in complete trust and true faith through Jesus our Saviour and Redeemer, beseeching His grace as we confess before Him that we have offended Him very grievously and profoundly by breaking His holy law: We do not worship Him sincerely in spirit and in truth, nor serve Him alone, nor love Him above all else by honoring His holy name without taking it in vain; we do not live a holy life to the glory of God and the aid and succor of our neighbors; we do not achieve the true and holy repose from saying evil, doing evil and thinking evil; we do not honor those who have power over us; we do not shun all hatred, lewdness, theft, untruth, and all things which go against the love of God and of our neighbors; but we do unto others those things which we would not have them do unto us. By transgressing the holy law of our good Father, we have all sinned greatly and deserve the wrath and indignation of our God more than we can express or say. With such gross ingratitude do we work against His holy will. Yet, for all our faults and sins—which. are too many to count—humbly and lowly in heart do we ask mercy and compassion of our very good Father, beseeching Him not to look at all upon our faults, ignorance and iniquities, but upon the righteousness, holiness, purity and innocence of His very dear Son, our Lord Jesus, who died for us: and for the love of Him to forgive us all our offenses and errors, keep up from falling deeper into sin, magnify His holy name in us, reign in us, perfect His holy will in us, and grant us what the gentle Saviour has taught to ask by saying:

Our Father, who art in heaven, hallowed be thy name, etc.

The Creed. We shall beseech our Father to give us steadfast, living, and perfect faith, and to increase and enlarge the same in us, by which we may be able to overcome all the malice of our enemy. We shall express our desire to live in that faith by making our confession of it, saying:

I believe in God the Father Almighty, Maker of heaven, etc.

Assurance of Pardon. My dearly beloved brothers and sisters, you know that our very good Father does not desire the death of sinners, but that they turn and live. For He, being full of all goodness and mercy, loved the world with such great love that, in order to save it, He gave His only Son, who said plainly that He had come to save that which had been lost. For the Word is very clear that Jesus Christ has come to save the sinners. And that good Saviour has promised us that everything we shall ask in His name we shall obtain, and that if we forgive others their sins, the Father shall forgive our own. Believe, therefore, that when we ask God's mercy in the name of our Lord Jesus, and when everyone heartily forgives his neighbor, our Lord forgives us, and, through the faith we have in Jesus Christ, our hearts are cleansed.

Words of Institution. Hear how our Lord Jesus Christ has instituted His Holy Supper, as it is written in I Corinthians, the eleventh chapter:

The Lord Jesus, on the night in which He was betrayed, took the bread and, giving thanks, He brake it, saying, Take, eat, this is my body which is delivered for you: this do in remembrance of me. After the same manner He also took the cup, when He had supped, saying, This cup is the new testament in my blood: this do ye, as oft as ye drink it, in remembrance of me. For as oft as ye shall eat this bread and drink this cup, ye shall proclaim the Lord's death till He come.

Hearken now, all of you, to the institution of our Lord's Holy Table, as it has been ordained by the only Saviour, who ought not to be reproved nor presumed upon, with the intention of teaching or doing something other than He has commanded. He breaks the bread for His disciples and gives it to them: which shows us that all those who come to the Table must be of His disciples, who deny themselves and follow Jesus Christ in true love. He prescribes that when we eat and drink at His Table, we do so in His memory; so that, as oft as we take the bread and drink of the cup, we do proclaim the death of our Lord Jesus Christ: who died for us by giving His body (as the bread signifies) and shed His blood for us (as the cup signifies).

The Sursum corda. Therefore, lift up your hearts on high, seeking the heavenly things in heaven, where Jesus Christ is seated at the right hand of the Father; and do not fix your eyes on the visible signs which are corrupted through usage. In joy of heart, in brotherly union, come, everyone, to partake of our Lord's Table, giving thanks unto Him for the very great love which He has shown us. Have the death of this good Saviour graven on your hearts in eternal remembrance, so that you are set afire, so also that you incite others to love God and follow His holy Word.

COMMUNION

¶ *In giving the bread, which shall be without image, the Minister does not suffer it to be adored. As he distributes it into the hands of everyone, so that they may take it and eat, the Minister may say:*

Jesus, the true Saviour of the world, who died for us and is seated in glory at the right hand of the Father, dwell in your hearts through His Holy Spirit, that you be wholly alive in Him, through living faith and perfect love.

POST-COMMUNION

¶ *When all have communicated:*

Dearly beloved brothers and sisters in our Lord Jesus, who have come to the Holy Table of our Lord to give Him thanks for the very great blessings which He has bestowed upon us: we shall pray the Father all-merciful for everyone on earth; we shall beseech Him for all kings, princes, lords, and all who are established in authority, to whom He has given the sword and the government of the people, for the purpose of defending the good and punishing the wicked. May the good God give His grace to everyone and have mercy upon all.

We beseech Him, of His very great goodness and kindness, that He will fill us with His Holy Spirit, so that all of us may be truly united in one body by living and unfeigned faith, which it may please Him to increase in us. And even as we have borne witness externally and outwardly, at the Holy Table, that we are disciples of Jesus, He bestows upon us grace

223

to be His disciples truly, which is to persevere in His holy doctrine, separated from all infidelity and from the world, everyone living in true love, rushing to one another in all good things of heart, word and deed. For the love of Him who has loved us so much, strive and labor to that end. And being partakers of our Lord's Table as members of Jesus, be not partakers with the unfaithful in their infidelity, and be not conformed to the world; but walk ye in all purity, sanctity, and innocence, living soberly and worthily as children of God, being merciful and charitable to everyone, especially to the faithful. Allow none to remain in poverty, but attend to the comfort of all. In such wise, may your whole life and conversation be in accord with God and His holy Word, to the edification of every man and the advancement of the Holy Gospel, according to which our Lord would have us all to live. Amen.

Go in peace. The grace, peace and blessing of God be upon you all. Amen.

NOTES

1. *La Maniere,* pp. 50-69.

VIII

THE FIRST AND SECOND
PRAYER BOOKS
OF KING EDWARD VI

London: 1549 & 1552

THE ENGLISH RITE

Although he abolished the pope in England, Henry VIII was scarcely a hot gospeler. Not even the Ten Articles (1536), which were designed to allure support from the Lutherans, drew him far from orthodoxy. And when that fancy had cooled, he inaugurated a catholic reaction by the Six Articles of 1539 which, among other conservative provisions, enjoined his subjects to confess to transubstantiation on pain of being burnt. Neither his doctrine nor his piety impelled Henry to overturn the Latin Mass. Yet there were two developments in his reign that affected the English rite.

Within fifteen years of the burning of Tyndale's New Testament (*ca.* 1525), the English Bible had been successively outlawed, tolerated, licensed, and appointed to be read in the parishes of the realm. In 1534 the Convocation of Canterbury petitioned the Crown to provide an authorized translation of Holy Writ; and that desire was ultimately realized with the appearance of the Great Bible (1539) which became, and in part continues to be, the text of Scripture used in the Prayer Book. By royal injunction it was assigned a place in every parish, so that all men would have access to "the lively word of God." In 1543, Convocation required the English Scriptures to be read "in course" after the *Te Deum* and *Magnificat* on Sundays and holy days. Thus, the first step was taken in the reform of worship and the way opened for the further use of English in the liturgy.

In this era Thomas Cranmer, Archbishop of Canterbury

and leader of the reform party, proposed on several occasions to amend the service-books. He himself attempted two separate revisions of the Breviary and experimented with vernacular forms of other sorts. After 1546, the year in which he was delivered from "the error of the Real Presence" by his colleague Nicholas Ridley,· Cranmer was intent upon the preparation of an English order of Holy Communion to replace the Mass. But of all these liturgical productions, only one was used in Henry's time, namely, the "Letanie with suffrages," which has been preserved to a considerable extent in the modern Prayer Book.

The old king died in January, 1547. To the throne of England came Edward VI, a precocious boy of ten, reared in the "new learning." Cranmer hailed him at his coronation as the "second Josiah" and illustrated that title by saying: "I shall most humbly admonish your royal majesty what things your highness is to perform." The lad's uncle, Somerset, who was a patron of reform, assumed control of the government as Protector, while the Privy Council was divested of notorious conservatives, chiefly Gardiner, bishop of Winchester.

Neither Cranmer nor Somerset cherished a drastic breach with tradition. The initial steps were rather designed to encourage sound preaching and to establish men in the English Bible. In July there appeared the first *Book of Homilies* which promised to raise the standard of sermons. The next month, injunctions were issued requiring each parish to furnish a Bible and Erasmus' Paraphrase of the Gospels; the lessons at High Mass were now to be read "in English and not in Latin"; and one of the homilies was to be used every Sunday. The first Parliament of the new reign enacted a statute, in December, that required Communion to be given in both bread and wine, agreeably to the custom "of the Apostles and the primitive Church."

· At his trial, Cranmer was accused of having taught three successive doctrines of the Eucharist: Roman, Lutheran, Zwinglian. He protested that he had never "taught but two contrary doctrines": the Roman and one other. Smyth (pp. 48-74) maintains that, having renounced the Roman view, he kept consistently to "Suvermerianism" (i.e., the spiritual real presence as taught by Bucer). Yet Dix (pp. 645-56) is "quite unable to distinguish the substance of his doctrine from that of Zwingli." Richardson (pp. 20-44), while redressing Dix's defective understanding of Zwingli, agrees nonetheless that Cranmer's view lay "within the basic framework" of Zwinglianism; but he doubts that the Archbishop was fully confirmed in that doctrine until December, 1548.

To make provision for that statute, a commission of "prelates and other learned men in the Scriptures" sat at Windsor Castle over the winter and prepared *The Order of the Communion*, which was issued by royal proclamation on March 8, 1548. It consisted of two parts: (1) an Exhortation to be delivered to the people within the week before the Eucharist, admonishing them to prepare themselves; and (2) an English form of Communion to be inserted into the Mass, which was otherwise left completely intact. This method was a concession to the conservative bishops who deemed it "neither expedient nor convenient to have the whole Mass in English." It represented, on the other hand, a modest victory for the reformers who insisted that the Lord's Supper was not a sacrifice, but a communion of the people of God, efficacious to those alone who received it.

While it preserved much of the traditional language, the preliminary Exhortation described the sacrament in terms that were not wholly decisive. What did Cranmer mean: "to feed and drink upon" the body and blood of Christ? Dix is prepared to say that here and hereafter he gave that expression a purely Zwinglian definition: "to remember the Passion with confidence in the merits of Christ." Richardson allows Cranmer some additional months of indecision before he came finally to the Zwinglian doctrine, which was fully expressed only in the 1552 Prayer Book.

The body of the *Order* consisted of an English form of Administration to be inserted into the Latin rite immediately after the priest's Communion. It included the following elements virtually as they would appear in the first Prayer Book: an Exhortation to self-examination, in the course of which the obdurate sinners were fenced from the Lord's table; the Invitation ("You that do truely and earnestly repente"); the General Confession ("Almightie GOD, father of oure Lorde Iesus Christ"); the Absolution and Comfortable Words; the Prayer of Humble Access ("We doe not presume"); and the Administration of Communion by the words: "The body of our Lord Iesus Christ whiche was geuen for thee, preserue thy bodye unto euerlasting lyfe" and "The bloud of our Lord Iesus Christe whiche was shed for thee, preserue thy soule unto euerlastynge lyfe."

The Confession, Absolution, and Comfortable Words in the *Order* were evidently inspired by the Lutheran liturgy of Cologne, which was the creature of Bucer and Melanchthon. Incited by the Imperial Diet of Regensburg (1541), which bade the German prelates to proceed with a reform of their dioceses, Archbishop Hermann von Wied determined upon a reformation of Cologne. He summoned Bucer and Hedio of Strassburg, Pistorius of Hesse, and Melanchthon of Wittenberg to prepare the necessary ordinances, which were subsequently published in August, 1543, under the title *Einfaltigs bedencken*. A Latin edition, *Simplex ac pia deliberatio,* appeared in 1545 and is known to have been used by Cranmer; while two English editions followed in 1547 and 1548 as *A Simple and Religious consultatiō.*

In the course of three hundred pages this book offered a compendium of doctrine, and liturgical services for the several ministries of the church. Melanchthon, who took charge of the doctrinal articles, incorporated Bucer's statement of the Eucharist, judging it to be entirely wholesome—a circumstance that did not endear the book to Luther, who was not currently *gemütlich* toward the Strassburg Reformer or his sacramental theology. At the Archbishop's request, the liturgical sections were molded after the Brandenburg-Nürnberg rite of 1533, although Bucer and his committee did not hesitate to draw upon the Saxon liturgy (1539) and upon the Hessian liturgy (1539), which was itself rich in the Strassburg liturgical tradition.

The Cologne reformation was swiftly overturned. Johann Gropper, a learned Catholic reformer who had only recently collaborated with Bucer in the interests of Christian reunion, led the Cologne chapter in giving resistance to the designs of Archbishop Hermann. In 1544 the chapter published *Antididagma,* which means, "against the teaching" of the *Consultation;* and that creative statement of Roman liturgical ideas and forms contributed in a modest way to the English rite.

The Order of the Communion was an interim arrangement. In the very proclamation by which it was issued, the Boy King was made to say that there would be still further "travail for the reformation" and that other "godly orders" would be brought to effect. Thus, at Pentecost 1549, it was superseded by *The Booke of the Common Prayer,* which kept the struc-

230

ture of the Latin rite and preserved many prayers of traditional English usage. The preparation of that Book was
undertaken by "the Archbishop of Canterbury and certain
of the most learned and discreet bishops and other learned
men of this realm." Inasmuch as their high responsibility
transcended the egotism of authorship, they are known to us
only as the Windsor Commission.• Cranmer did confide that
they were representative men, "some favouring the old, some
the new learning." Yet all were agreed "that the service of the
church ought to be in the mother-tongue."

The principles that governed the new Book were set forth
in its Preface. First, it was designed to exercise both clergy
and people in "the whole Bible" according to the intention
of the "auncient fathers." If the Church of Rome had seen
fit to parcel out a few broken pieces of Scripture, suppress-
ing the rest, that defect would now be redressed by a new
and plain Kalendar which promised to conserve the continuity
of Scripture. Moreover, nothing was ordained to be read
save "the very pure worde of God . . . or that whiche is
euidently grounded upon the same."

Second, the English tongue was appointed to replace the
unedifying Latin, which failed to reach the "hartes, spirite,
and minde" of the people. Third, the quantity and rigidity
of liturgical rubrics and the complex character of the service,
requiring the use of many books, would be reduced to those
necessary rules which were "fewe in nombre . . . plain and
easy to be understanded." Fourth, the "great diuersitie" of
current English usage would yield to a wholesome uniformity,
which this Prayer Book afforded.

To these principles we may add three others that were implicit in the Book. First, it was meant to be as comprehensive˙
as possible of all the parties within the Anglican communion.
The very titles contained traditional phrases (The Booke of
the Common Prayer . . . *After the Use of the Churche of
England*, and, The Svpper of the Lorde . . . *Commonly
Called the Masse*), which invited the sympathy of conserva-

• There is evidence to suppose that Cranmer was assisted by bishops Ridley of Rochester; Holbeach of Lincoln; Thirlby of Westminster; Goodrich of Ely; and possibly Skip of Hereford; and Day
of Chichester; and by doctors William May, Dean of St. Paul's;
Simon Heynes, Dean of Exeter; Thomas Robertson, later Dean of
Durham; John Redman, Master of Trinity College, Cambridge;
and possibly Richard Cox, Chancellor of Oxford, later bishop of
Ely; and John Taylor, Dean, later bishop of Lincoln.

tive men. Perhaps the overarching principle of revision was stated in one of the Exhortations of Holy Communion: "In all thinges to folowe and kepe the rule of charitie, and euery man to be satisfied with his owne conscience, not iudgyng other mennes myndes or consciences." With respect to ceremonies, the Windsor committeemen were scarcely iconoclasts. They distinguished between those which were vain and superstitious and those which served order and edification; if the former deserved "to be cut awaye," the latter were to be retained, and indeed prized "for theyr antyquitye." "New-fangleness" did not contribute to the unity and concord of religion. Yet in giving warning against the "excessiue multitude of Ceremonies," the committeemen expressed a policy that was not appreciably different from that of Calvin:

Christes Gospell is not a Ceremoniall lawe (as muche of Moses lawe was), but it is a relygion to serue God, not in bondage of the figure or shadowe: but in the freedome of spirite, beeyng contente onely wyth those ceremonyes whyche dooe serue to a decente ordre and godlye discipline, and suche as bee apte to stirre uppe the dulle mynde of manne to the remembraunce of his duetie to God.

But, second, no concessions were made to the papists. Still the Litany made reference to "the tyrannye of the bishop of Rome and all his detestable enormities." The day of St. Thomas of Canterbury, that notorious champion of the church against royal power, disappeared from the Kalendar. And some of the chief marks of the Medieval cultus were abolished, notably, the Elevation, holy water, the veneration of images, the doctrine of purgatory, and the invocation of saints. Third, the liturgy was meant to be a congregational instrument, a book of *common* prayer, cast in the English language, ruled by the English Bible. It required Communion in both kinds and did not countenance private Mass. Its chief deficiency in this respect was the lack of congregational singing, which came from no hostility toward metrical psalms, but from their dearth in the vernacular. Thomas Sternhold's *Certayne Psalmes* (1547?) was merely the beginning of English hymnody.

These were the sources of the Communion order as it appeared in 1549:

1. *The Great Bible*, from which the Psalms and Lessons (save one) were taken.

2. *The Latin Rite according to the Use of Sarum.* The Preface to the Prayer Book stated that five diocesan "Uses" of the Latin rite were current in England at the Reformation: those of Salisbury, Hereford, Bangor, York, and Lincoln. Of these the most influential was the Use of Salisbury or Sarum, which tradition ascribes to the eleventh century, but which in fact did not attain definitive character until the opening of the thirteenth century. The Use of Sarum contributed both to the structure of the liturgy and to the text itself through the course of translation and adaptation. The Collect for Purity illustrates the relationship:

SARUM (from the Latin)	PRAYER BOOK
O God, to whom every heart is open, and every wish speaks, and from whom no secret is hid: cleanse the thoughts of our hearts by the inpouring of the Holy Spirit, that we may perfectly love thee, and worthily praise thee: through Christ.	Almightie God, unto whom all hartes bee open, and all desyres knowen, and from whom no secretes are hid: clense the thoughtes of our hartes, by the inspiracion of thy holy spirite: that we may perfectly loue thee, & worthely magnifie thy holy name: through Christ our Lorde.

3. *The Orthodox Liturgy* contributed some few elements (including the "Prayer of St. Chrysostom" in the Litany), the most important of which was the Invocation in the Prayer of Consecration: "And with thy holy spirite & worde, vouchsafe to blesse and sanctifie these thy gyftes, and creatures of bread and wyne, that they maie be unto us the bodye and bloude" of Jesus Christ.·

· Yet, several interpretations have been placed upon this prayer in the English Canon. Dix (p. 675n.) believes that it represents the Latin, *Quam oblationem*, in both position and meaning, combined perhaps with the dictum of Paschasius Radbertus that the sacrament is consecrated in the Word of the Creator and the power of the Holy Spirit. In Clarke and Harris (p. 342) the prayer is conceived to be "a combination of Western and Eastern views of consecration," Western insofar as it precedes the recital of the Institution and retains the "worde" as the "form" of the sacrament, Eastern insofar as it specifies the agency of the "holy spirite."

4. *The Antididagma of Cologne.*

5. *The Order of the Communion* was taken bodily into the new liturgy, the prayers being given exactly the position they had before. The Lutheran influence upon the Prayer Book came largely through this avenue.

The liturgy of 1549 (below) kept to the Medieval structure. The Introit, Kyrie eleison, Gloria in excelsis, Collect, Epistle, Gospel, Creed, and Sermon were all appointed in their traditional order. The first important change occurred in the Offertory, with which the Mass of the Faithful properly began. Prior to the eleventh century the people brought bread and wine for the Eucharistic sacrifice, and offered them at this time, while the choir chanted a psalm called the *Offertorium*. These gifts the prie commended unto God, setting them apart from common use in anticipation of the Consecration. In the Middle Ages prayers of devotion were added to heighten this formal act of oblation, which was integrally connected to the whole Eucharistic sacrifice. Cranmer and his colleagues were concerned to purge the Offertory of this association. Hence the elements (unleavened bread, and wine mixed with water) were now to be placed on the altar by the priest without prayer or ceremony. The Offertory sentences were directed rather to almsgiving; and the people presented their money, not at the altar, but into a chest, which was placed in the choir. Those who proposed to communicate remained in the choir.

After the Preface and Sanctus came the Canon, which refers to the body of venerable prayers and rites surrounding the Consecration. That portion of the Mass was odious to Luther, who pronounced it "a heap of filth" inasmuch as its sacrificial emphasis perverted the nature of Holy Communion and obscured the one, all-sufficient oblation of Christ on Calvary. The English reformers, however, were not disposed to abolish the Canon, as Luther had done, but merely to rid it of its sacrificial doctrine. Let us see how skillfully this was accomplished.

The Canon opened with the Intercessions. These commenced with an allusion to *Te igitur* of the Mass; but while the Latin prayer asked God to "accept and bless these offerings, these oblations, these holy, unblemished sacrificial gifts," the English prayer said pointedly: "receiue

234

these our praiers, which we offre unto thy diuine Maiestie."
The Intercessions also comprehended the sense of *Momento*
(commemoration of the living), *Communicantes* (commemoration of the saints), and *Memento etiam* (commemoration of the dead), the last prayer having been removed
from a place later in the Roman Canon.

Then came the Prayer of Consecration. The sense of
Hanc igitur ("We thy servants, and with us thy whole
household, make this peace-offering which we entreat thee
to accept") was deliberately overturned in the Prayer
Book, which labored the point of Christ's "one oblacion
once offered, a full, perfect, and sufficient sacrifyce."
Hence the Eucharist was a "perpetuall memory of that his
precious death." Then followed an adaptation of *Quam
oblationem;* yet instead of asking that the bread and wine
"may *become* for us the Body and Blood" of Jesus Christ,
the English version begged that "they maie *be* unto us the
bodye and bloude of" Christ, thus dispelling any exact
definition of the consecration. Finally, *Qui pridie* became
I Cor. 11:23ff., with the removal of all non-Scriptural additions. The elevation was forbidden.

The English Canon continued with the Prayer of Oblation. It contained an adaptation of *Unde et memores;* but
while the Latin prayer referred to the oblation as "a pure
victim, a holy victim, a spotless victim," the English text
dwelt entirely upon "the memoryall whyche thy sonne
hath wylled us to make" and upon "this our Sacrifice of
praise and thankes geuing." The prayer then proceeded to
define the new sense of "oblation." It was not an offering
of Christ to God; it was rather the self-offering of the
whole church: "oure selfe, oure soules, and bodies." There
followed a reflection of *Supplices te rogamus,* in which
God is asked to "bid these things be carried by the
hands of thy holy angel up to thy altar on high, into the
presence of thy divine majesty." By that means, the oblation attained its completion. Keeping virtually the same
wording, the English text interpreted "these things" to
mean "our prayers and supplicacions," while the expression
"to thy altar on high" was deftly changed to "thy holy
Tabernacle."

The Canon came to a close with the final words of *Nobis
quoque peccatoribus:* "not waiyng our merites, but pardonyng our offences, through Christe our Lorde." After

the Lord's Prayer and the *Pax*, there followed the several parts of *The Order of the Communion.*

Thus, the Book was a reverent adaptation of the Latin rite, possessed of liturgical fitness and a deep Eucharistic piety. But it was not scrupulously clear. Dryander informed Zurich that it harbored "every kind of deception by ambiguity or trickery of language." Cranmer's Zwinglianism (if such was then his doctrine) did not appear in such expressions as "vouchsafe to blesse and sanctifie these thy gyftes . . . that they maie be unto us the bodye and bloude" of Christ. Indeed, Gardiner seized upon five such items to prove that the Book taught "the most true and catholic doctrine of the substance of the sacrament," namely, that "we receive in the sacrament the body of Christ with our mouth."

So when *The Booke of the Common* Prayer was sent down upon England at Pentecost 1549, it had a bad reception all around. The laity mocked it as a frivolous novelty. The parish priests took every means to make it a Mass, even though it was of necessity celebrated in English. Foreign divines charged that "the Book speaks very obscurely," while home-grown reformers pronounced it "inadequate. . . ambiguous . . . impious." Cranmer himself indicated that it was a temporary arrangement. By Whit-Monday the tottering government of Somerset was faced by a serious rebellion in Cornwall and Devon and by uprisings, partly agrarian, over half the countryside. The insurgents of Devon stated their complaint in fifteen articles. Referring to the Prayer Book as a mere "Christmas game," they demanded that England be taken back to the religion of the Six Articles, with the Mass in Latin, Communion in one kind, the reservation of the sacrament, the restoration of ceremonies and images, and the recall of the English Bible. By the end of August the rebellion had been suppressed, but only at the expense of human life.

During these years a growing company of foreign divines took refuge in England from untoward circumstances abroad. In 1547, the year after Luther died, German Protestantism suffered a crushing defeat at the battle of Mühlberg, which allowed Charles V to impose an adverse religious settlement —the Augsburg *Interim* (1548)—on Lutheran lands. Among the first to arrive in England was Peter Martyr, lately of Strassburg, who was appointed Regius Professor of Divinity at Oxford in March, 1548, and promptly stirred up controversy over the Eucharist, with respect to which he was a latent Zwinglian. In the spring of 1549, when the *Interim* made his tenure hopeless in Strassburg, Martin Bucer arrived, even as the Prayer Book, to which he had indirectly contributed, was being readied for use. Presently he was appointed to the Regius professorship at Cambridge. A year hence came John à Lasco who had likewise been forced to abandon his work in East Friesland. An advocate of the Zwinglian doctrine of the Supper, his presence was apparently not without effect upon Cranmer. In July, 1550, he was appointed Superintendent of the Strangers' Church of London—a company of Protestant refugees who deported themselves autonomously in the midst of Ridley's diocese and to that bishop's great vexation. For the use of these "strangers," à Lasco prepared a complete church-manual, *Forma ac Ratio* (1551?), including services of worship that were Reformed, but not quite Genevan, in character. In the same era Valerand Pullain presided over a congregation of Flemish weavers at Glastonbury Abbey. Having been a presbyter in the French church of Strassburg soon after Calvin's tenure, he was concerned to translate Calvin's Strassburg liturgy into Latin as *Liturgia sacra* (1551), dedicating it to Edward VI, that perchance it would contribute to the revision of the *Common Prayer*. An English edition of Calvin's *Genevan* liturgy had been published the previous year by William Huycke; so that three separate texts of the Reformed rite were in circulation prior to the publication of the second Prayer Book.·

Meanwhile Somerset had fallen from power (October, 1549), and, under his successor, Warwick, the reformation was pursued with increased vigor. In April, 1550, John Hooper, the apostle of simplicity trained in Zurich, was offered the See of Gloucester. But inasmuch as he refused to

---

· The arrival of the divines—all told, twelve important preachers and theologians—coincided with Cranmer's plan to convene a "godly synod" in England (or elsewhere) in which an "entire system of true doctrine" could be arrived at by all parties to the Reformation. The presence of Melanchthon was deemed indispensable to this consensus; yet no amount of persuasion could secure his participation. Even Calvin, who applauded the venture, excused himself because of the "insignificance" of his capacity. Despite these efforts by Cranmer, the rumor persisted in the sixteenth century that the English never meant to fashion "an entire body of Christian doctrine" but merely to attend to "the right institution of Christian worship." So: Dryander to Bullinger, March 25, 1549.

swear by "all saints and the holy evangelists," as the form of Consecration required, and scrupled at the episcopal vestments, which would have made him appear a "magpie," Hooper stirred up the Vestiarian controversy, which presently brought à Lasco to his side and aroused no end of contention. At the same time Ridley began a systematic destruction of altars in the diocese of London, whereupon Hooper joined him in assailing the "altars of Baal." Warwick encouraged this wholesome iconoclasm; and in November the Council ordered the bishops to substitute tables for altars. Moreover, Calvin dispatched exhortations to Cranmer ("Do not imagine that you have reached the goal.") and to the young Josiah ("God does not allow anyone to sport with his name, mingling frivolities among his holy and sacred ordinances."). Given such stimulation, by the beginning of 1551 both Crown and Canterbury were determined upon a revision of the Prayer Book.

In the course of that year two documents appeared that illustrated the nature of the problem at hand. Gardiner, who languished in the Tower, prepared *An Explication and Assertion of the true Catholick Faith touching the most blessed Sacrament of the Aultar.* That treatise, published abroad in 1551, was directed against Cranmer's *Defence of the true and catholike doctrine of the sacrament* (1550); it was a cunning attempt to indict Cranmer's Eucharistic theology by citing his own Prayer Book against him. In order to succeed at that crafty business Gardiner had to show, of course, that the Prayer Book was "not distant from the catholic faith." This he tried to establish by five theses: (1) that the Words of Administration made allowance for transubstantiation; (2) that the Post-Communion rubric that taught that "the whole body of our sauiour Jesu Christ" was in each particle of the bread, was "agreeable to the catholic doctrine"; (3) that the commemoration of the dead in the Intercessions implied that the Mass was a propitiatory sacrifice; (4) that the Prayer of Consecration supported transubstantiation; and (5) that the Prayer of Humble Access, at which the priest was required to kneel, involved the adoration of the consecrated elements.

The second document was Bucer's *Censura,* a "judgment" of the Prayer Book, which that liturgical scholar had been asked to make; he submitted it in January, 1551, less than two months before his death. Commencing with praise, Bucer observed that the Book had indeed been reformed to a "pitch of purity," leaving him only a few "minor points" to raise (which yet required fifty pages). He urged the reduction of the Church Year and warned against those "popish gestures" held over from the Mass. Most of his notations dealt with the Holy Communion, which, in the main, he pronounced "scrupulously faithful to the Word of God." But some things needed to be "perfected or corrected."

Of the introductory rubrics he heartily approved of all but the last, on vestments, with respect to which he reiterated his opinion given in the Vestiarian controversy. While he refused to agree that vestments were unlawful or condemned in Scripture or irreparably spoiled by Rome, Bucer pleaded for their removal on the grounds that they were involved in superstition and had become a source of contention. Apostolic simplicity should govern all external things in the church.

Of the seven concluding rubrics he had more to say. The first, which required a "half-Mass" at certain times when there were no communicants, he judged to be a "dumb show," a counterfeit of the sacrament. The second, which allowed for the celebration of the Eucharist in side chapels and "other places," contradicted his strong opinion that Holy Communion pertained to the whole congregation and should never be celebrated in small gatherings, much less in private. The third, which specified the character of the wafer, prompted the notation that common (leavened) bread should also be permitted for the sake of Christian liberty; and he objected to the import of the last sentence, which declared that "the whole body" of Christ was received in each particle of the bread. The fifth, which allowed families to send substitutes to offer and communicate for them, he deemed an occasion for abuse (as indeed it was). The sixth he found "shocking" inasmuch as it required Christians to communicate but once a year, and then under legal compulsion; the liturgy would do better to set before the people "the greatness of their fault" if they did not communicate as often as the sacrament was provided. And the seventh, which required the sacrament to the delivered into the mouths of the people, rather than into their hands (lest they smuggle it home for adoration), he deemed unnecessary and liable to superstition; and it unduly exalted the priest above the people.

Of the Offertory rubrics, he objected to the one that cautioned the priest to prepare no more bread and wine than would suffice for the communicants. This implied that the nature of the elements would be changed by the Consecration and that Christ would be "interned" in the bread and wine. Such an impression was not to be conveyed. Indeed, the "remains" of Communion ought to revert to common use.

Bucer did not object to the shape of the liturgy nor recommend a remodeling of the Canon. He took exception to the commemoration of the dead in the Intercessions because it intimated (as Gardiner said) that the Eucharist was a propitiatory sacrifice. In the Prayer of Consecration, he proposed to remove the words: "Blesse and sanctifie these thy gyftes. . . ." and to supply a new formula: "Bless us and sanctify us by the Holy Spirit and word, that by true faith we may perceive in these mysteries the body and blood of thy Son." This was precisely the Reformed view of Consecration; and Bucer underscored it by saying that the Words of Institution were not addressed to the bread and wine, as if to change them, but "to the men present." Therefore the priest should not take the bread into his hand at the Consecration, lest some presume to adore it. Bucer expressed warm approval of the Prayer of Humble Access, suggesting only that it be said by the whole congregation.

Completed in the spring of 1552, the second Prayer Book was annexed to a new Act of Uniformity (April 14), which required its use by All Saints' day forthcoming. The Act spoke darkly of those "mistakers" who had abused the comprehensive character of the first Book, twisting it to their purposes. But the time for ambiguity had passed; and that "very godly order" had been "perused, explained, and made fully perfect," its "perfection" consisting in a more drastic reformation. Peter Martyr exclaimed to Bullinger that everything had been cast out of it that "could nourish superstition."

The main title of the new Book (below) no longer carried the clause, "after the Use of the Churche of England," which had implied the continuation of Medieval usage; and the expression, "commonly called the Masse" was stricken from the title of Holy Communion. Nearly all of the rubrics to which Bucer had taken exception were removed. The number of ceremonies was reduced and the use of vestments curtailed. The word "altar" was everywhere replaced by "table" or "Goddes borde." The Introit disappeared; and the Kyrie eleison and Gloria in excelsis were replaced by the Ten Commandments—a feature that may have been suggested by Calvin's Strassburg liturgy.

The Offertory underwent further change, such that it could not possibly be construed as an oblation in the traditional sense. The detailed rubric of 1549, requiring the priest to place the bread and wine on the altar at this time, was omitted, perhaps to obscure even the *appearance* of the old Offertory which had remained in the first Prayer Book. The alms of the people, never touching the hands of the priest, were collected by the church wardens and deposited into "the poremens boxe."

The Intercessions, having been removed from the Canon, were placed after the Sermon and Offertory, in the approximate position of the Great Prayer in the Reformed rite. The title of the Intercessions was made to read, "for the whole state of Christes Church *militant here in earth*," which emphasized the fact that the commemoration of the dead and of the saints had been stricken.

There followed the "Long Exhortation" ("Derely beloued in the Lorde"), to which were now joined the Invitation, General Confession, Absolution, and Comfortable Words. Dix suggests that by this sequence of the liturgy, Cranmer meant to express the true sense of the Eucharistic offering— "the sacrifice of praise and thanksgiving"—which involved our penitence, our joy at Christ's benefits, our faith and consolation in his passion, and our resolve to live in newness of life.

After the Preface and Sanctus came the Prayer of Humble Access, which may have been moved to this place, *before* the Consecration, to overrule Gardiner's inference that it was a prayer of adoration over the transubstantiated elements. Moreover, the words, "in these holy Misteries," were omitted, diminishing the reality of Christ's presence that this prayer formerly conveyed. In the Prayer of Consecration, the idea that the elements were "sanctified" by Word and Spirit was removed; and in its place a prayer was conceived which did not, in fact, authorize any single view of the Lord's Supper, yet, considered by itself, was rather patient of the "receptionist" doctrine: "Graunt that wee, receyuing these thy creatures of bread and wyne . . . in remembraunce of his death and passion, may be partakers of his most blessed body and bloud." Immediately after the recital of the Institution came the Communion of the ministers and of the people, no prayers or rites intervening. The Words of Administration in the 1549 Book were removed. Upon giving the bread, the minister now said: "Take and eate this, in remembraunce that Christ dyed for thee, and feede on him in thy hearte by faythe, with thankes geuinge." · To keep an unbroken continuity between the Consecration and Communion, the Lord's Prayer and the Prayer of Oblation were put *after* Communion, the latter being divested of one salient clause: "worthely receiue the moste precious body and bloude of thy sonne Jesus Christe." Either the Prayer of Oblation or the Prayer of Thanksgiving could thus be used as the Post-Communion; and, since the Gloria in excelsis was transferred to the end of the liturgy, the Lord's Supper closed on the prevailing theme of the church's "sacrifice of praise and thanksgiving."

"To take awaye the supersticion," household bread was deemed "sufficient" (but not mandatory) for sacramental use. It was delivered into the *hands* of the people. And whatever remained of the elements after Communion reverted to the curate for common use.

Even while the new Book was being printed, a commotion arose over kneeling to communicate. In the sixth of his court sermons on Jonas (March 27, 1550) John Hooper had already warned the young king that kneeling pertained to the "damned idolatry" of adoring the elements and had proposed that the people should be seated to receive the sacrament, according to apostolic practice. In the Strangers' Church of London, over which à Lasco presided, communicants sat down at the table to receive the Supper, according to elaborate directions given in *Forma ac Ratio.* A proposal to incorporate such a custom into the second Prayer Book was considered and flatly rejected by the committee of revision.

· In à Lasco's *Forma ac Ratio,* the following words were specified: "Take, eat, and remember that the body of our Lord Jesus Christ was delivered to death on the beams of the Cross for the remission of all our sins."

Presently, in the autumn of 1552, John Knox appeared at Court as a royal chaplain, having come lately from Berwick-on-Tweed where he had administered Communion after the fashion of John à Lasco. Preaching in the King's presence, Knox denounced the custom of kneeling to receive the sacrament. As All Saints' day was nearly at hand, these dreadful pronouncements by "Mr. Knocks" threw King and Court into confusion. Late in September the Council ordered the printer to refrain from "uttering" the Book until "certain faults" had been corrected. Cranmer objected to the biblicism, which he saw at the root of this matter, supposing that the entire liturgy would have to be scrapped if the Bible were so scrupulously followed. But Edward was (as Smyth observed) highly superstitious of superstition; and in the end the view of Knox prevailed. On October 27, the Council instructed the Lord Chancellor to append the "Black Rubric" to the Prayer Book. That final rubric in the Communion liturgy declared that kneeling was required for the sake of humility, reverence, and uniformity, but by no means implied the adoration of the elements that "remayne styll in theyr verye naturall substaunces."

The death of King Edward (July, 1553) was attended by the demise of his Prayer Book, the departure of the "strangers," the flight of the Marian exiles (Ch. IX), and, at last, the execution of Thomas Cranmer, to whom *The Book of Common Prayer* remains a living monument. Queen Mary, in whose time these things occurred, restored the Latin rite as it was used in the last year of Henry VIII, and re-established communion with Rome as it existed in 1529. The accession of Elizabeth was shortly followed by a new Act of Uniformity (April, 1559) to which was annexed the Elizabethan Prayer Book. It was the Second Book of Edward VI, with certain specified amendments. Of these, three pertained to Holy Communion: (1) the Black Rubric was omitted; (2) vestments and ornaments were to conform to those in use "in the second year of the reign of K. Edward VI"; and (3) the Words of Administration in the 1549 Book were prefixed to those of 1552:

The body of our Lord Jesus Christ, which was given for thee, preserve thy body and soul into everlasting life: and take and eat this in remembrance that Christ died for thee, and feed on him in thine heart by faith, with thanksgiving.

That formula served to reopen the whole matter of Eucharistic theology, in respect to which the Elizabethan churchmen and their seventeenth-century successors did not always suffer the Prayer Book to interpret itself. In their Articles and Catechisms, and in all manner of private utterance, they tended to profess a doctrine of the spiritual real presence in which the fruit of the sacrament was by no means dissociated from the reception of Holy Communion.

FOR FURTHER READING

F. E. Brightman (ed.), *The English Rite*. 2 vols. London, 1921.

W. K. L. Clarke and C. Harris (eds.), *Liturgy and Worship*. London, 1947.

Gregory Dix, *The Shape of the Liturgy*. Westminster, 1947.

C. W. Dugmore, *Eucharistic Doctrine from Hooker to Waterland*. London, 1942.

F. A. Gasquet and E. Bishop, *Edward VI and the Book of Common Prayer*. London, 1890.

Francis Proctor and W. H. Frere, *A History of the Book of Common Prayer*. London, 1949.

C. C. Richardson, *Zwingli and Cranmer on the Eucharist*. Evanston, 1949.

C. H. Smyth, *Cranmer and the Reformation under Edward VI*. Cambridge, 1926.

THE [1]
booke of the common
prayer and admi =
nistracion of
the
Sacramentes, and other
rites and ceremonies of
the Churche: after the
use of the Churche
of England.
LONDINI IN OFFICINA
Eduardi Whitchurche.
ANNO DO. 1549. Mense
Martii.
THE SVPPER
of the Lorde, and the holy Com =
munion, commonly cal =
led the Masse.

*SO many as intende to bee partakers of the holy Communion,
shall sygnifie their names to the Curate, ouer night: or els
in the morning, afore the beginning of Matins, or immediatly
after.*

*And if any of those be an open and notorious euill liuer,
so that the congregacion by hym is offended, or haue doen
any wrong to his neighbours, by worde, or dede: The Curate
shall call hym, & aduertise hym, in any wise not to presume
to the lordes table, untill he haue openly declared hymselfe,
to haue truly repented, and amended his former naughtie
life: that the congregacion maie thereby be satisfied, whiche
afore were offended: and that he haue recompensed the
parties, whom he hath dooen wrong unto, or at the least bee
in full purpose so to doo, as sone as he conueniently maie.*

¶ *The same ordre shall the Curate use, with those betwixt
whom he perceiueth malice, and hatred to reigne, not suffering them to bee partakers of the Lordes table, untill he
knowe them to bee reconciled. And yf one of the parties so
at variaunce, be content to forgeue from the botome of his*

harte, all that the other hath trespaced against hym, and to make amendes for that he hymself hath offended: and the other partie will not bee perswaded to a godly unitie, but remaigne still in his frowardnes and malice: The Minister in that case, ought to admit the penitent persone to the holy Communion, and not hym that is obstinate.

¶ *Upon the daie, and at the tyme appoincted for the ministracion of the holy Communion, the Priest that shal execute the holy ministery, shall put upon hym the vesture appoincted for that ministracion, that is to saye: A white ·Albe plain, with a vestement or Cope. And where there be many Priestes, or Decons, there so many shalbe ready to helpe the Priest, in the ministracion, as shalbee requisite: And shall haue upon theim lykewise, the vestures appointed for their ministery, that is to saye, Albes, with tunacles. Then shall the Clerkes syng in Englishe for the office, or Introite, (as they call it) a Psalme appointed for that daie.*

The Priest standing humbly afore the middes of the Altar, shall saie the Lordes praier, with this Collect.

ALmightie GOD, unto whom all hartes bee open, and all desyres knowen, and from whom no secretes are hid: clense the thoughtes of our hartes, by the inspiracion of thy holy spirite: that we may perfectly loue thee, & worthely magnifie thy holy name: Through Christ our Lorde. Amen.

Then shall he saie a Psalme appointed for the introite: whiche Psalme ended, the Priest shall saye, or els the Clerkes shal syng.

iii. Lorde haue mercie upon us.
iii. Christ haue mercie upon us.
iii. Lorde haue mercie upon us.

Then the Prieste standyng at Goddes borde shall begin.

Glory be to God on high.

The Clerkes.

And in Yearth peace, good will towardes men.

We praise thee, we blesse thee, we worship thee, we glorifie thee, wee geue tankes to thee for thy greate glory, O Lorde GOD heauenly kyng, God the father almightie.

O Lorde the onely begotten sonne Jesu Christe, O Lorde

God, Lambe of GOD, sonne of the father, that takest awaye the synnes of the worlde, haue mercie upon us: thou that takest awaye the synnes of the worlde, receiue our praier.

Thou that sittest at the right hande of GOD the father, haue mercie upon us: for thou onely art holy, thou onely art the Lorde, Thou onely (O Christ) with the holy Ghoste, art moste high in the glory of God the father. Amen.

Then the priest shall turne hym to the people and saye.

The Lorde be with you.

The aunswere.

And with thy spirite.

The Priest.

Let us praie.

Then shall folowe the Collect of the daie, with one of these two Collectes followyng, for the Kyng.

ALmighty God, whose kingdom is euerlasting, and power infinite, haue mercie upon the whole congregacion, and so rule the heart of thy chosen seruaunt Edward the sixt, our kyng and gouernour: that he (knowyng whose minister he is) maie aboue al thinges, seke thy honour and glory, & that we his subiectes (duely consydering whose auctoritie he hath) maye faithfully serue, honour, and humbly obeye him, in thee, and for thee, according to thy blessed word, and ordinaunce: Through Jesus Christe oure Lorde, who with thee, and the holy ghost, liueth, and reigneth, euer one God, worlde without ende. Amen.

ALmightie and euerlasting GOD, wee bee taught by thy holy worde, that the heartes of Kynges are in thy rule and gouernaunce, and that thou doest dispose, and turne them as it semeth best to thy godly wisedom: We humbly beseche thee, so to dispose and gouerne, the hart of Edward the sixt, thy seruaunt, our Kyng and gouernour, that in all his thoughtes, wordes, and workes, he maye euer seke thy honour and glory, and study to preserue thy people, committed to his charge, in wealth, peace, and Godlynes: Graunt this, O mercifull father, for thy dere sonnes sake, Jesus Christ our Lorde. Amen.

The Collectes ended, the priest, or he that is appointed, shall reade the Epistle, in a place assigned for the purpose, saying.

The Epistle of sainct Paule written in the   Chapiter of   to the.

The Minister then shall reade thepistle. Immediatly after the Epistle ended, the priest, or one appointed to reade the Gospel, shall saie.

The holy Gospell written in the   Chapiter of.

The Clearkes and people shall aunswere.

Glory be to thee, O Lorde.

The priest or deacon then shall reade the Gospel: after the Gospell ended, the priest shall begin.

I beleue in one God.

The clerkes shall syng the rest.

The father almightie maker of heauen and yearth, and of all thinges visible, and inuisible: And in one Lorde Jesu Christ, the onely begotten sonne of GOD, begotten of his father before all worldes, God of GOD, light of light, very God of very God, begotten, not made, beeyng of one substaunce with the father, by whom all thinges were made, who for us men, and for our saluacion, came doune from heauen, and was incarnate by the holy Ghoste, of the Virgin Mary, and was made manne, and was Crucified also for us under Poncius Pilate, he suffered and was buried, and the thirde daye he arose again according to the scriptures, and ascended into heauen, and sitteth at the right hande of the father: And he shall come again with glory, to iudge both the quicke and the dead.

And I beleue in the holy ghost, the Lorde and geuer of life, who procedeth from the father and the sonne, who with the father and the sonne together, is worshipped and glorified, who spake by the Prophetes. And I beleue one Catholike and Apostolike Churche. I acknowlege one Baptisme, for the remission of synnes. And I loke for the resurreccion of the deade: and the lyfe of the worlde to come. Amen.

After the Crede ended, shall folowe the Sermon or Homely, or some porciō of one of the Homelyes, as thei

shalbe herafter deuided: wherin if the people bee not
exhorted, to the worthy receiuyng of the holy Sacrament,
of the bodye & bloude of our sauior Christ: then shal
the Curate geue this exhortaciō, to those ye be minded
to receiue ye same.

DErely beloued in the Lord, ye that mynde to come to the
holy Communiō of the bodye & bloude of our sauior Christe,
must considre what S. Paule writeth to the Corinthiās, how
he exhorteth all persones diligently to trie & examine thēselues,
before they presume to eate of that breade, and drinke of
that cup: for as the benefite is great, if with a truly penitent
heart, & liuely faith, we receiue that holy Sacramēt: (for
then we spiritually eate the fleshe of Christ, & drinke his
bloude, then we dwell in Christ & Christ in us, wee bee made
one with Christ, and Christ with us) so is the daunger great,
yf wee receyue the same unworthely, for then wee become
gyltie of the body and bloud of Christ our sauior, we eate
and drinke our owne damnacion, not considering the Lordes
bodye. We kyndle Gods wrathe ouer us, we prouoke him to
plague us with diuerse dyseases, and sondery kyndes of death.
Therefore if any here be a blasphemer, aduouterer, or bee
in malyce or enuie, or in any other greuous cryme (excepte
he bee truly sory therefore, and earnestly mynded to leaue
the same vices, and do trust him selfe to bee reconciled to
almightie God, and in Charitie with all the worlde) lette him
bewayle his synnes, and not come to that holy table, lest after
taking of that most blessed breade: the deuyll enter into
him, as he dyd into Judas, to fyll him full of all iniquitie, and
brynge him to destruccion, bothe of body and soule. Judge
therefore your selfes (brethren) that ye bee not iudged of
the lorde. Let your mynde be without desire to synne, repent
you truely for your synnes past, haue an earnest & lyuely
faith in Christ our sauior, be in perfect charitie with all men,
so shall ye be mete partakers of those holy misteries. And
aboue all thynges: ye must geue moste humble and hartie
thankes to God the father, the sonne, and the holy ghost,
for the redempcion of the worlde, by the death and passion
of our sauior Christ, both God and man, who did humble
him self euen to the death upon the crosse, for us miserable
synners, whiche laie in darknes and shadowe of death, that
he myghte make us the children of God: and exalt us to
euerlasting life. And to thend that wee should alwaye remem-

bre the excedyng loue of oure master, and onely sauior Jesu Christe, thus diyng for us, and the innumerable benefites (whiche by his precious bloudshedyng) he hath obteigned to us, he hath lefte in those holy Misteries, as a pledge of his loue, & a continuall remēbraunce of the same his owne blessed body, & precious bloud, for us to fede upon spiritually, to our endles comfort & consolacion. To him therfore with the father and the holy ghost, let us geue (as we are most bounden) continual thankes, submittyng our selfes wholy to hys holy will and pleasure, & studying to serue hym in true holines and righteousnes, al the daies of our life. Amen.

> *In Cathedral churches or other places, where there is dailie Communion, it shal be sufficient to reade this exhortacion aboue written, once in a moneth. And in parish churches, upon the weke daies it may be lefte unsayed.*

> ¶ *And if upon the Sunday or holy daye, the people be negligent to come to the Communion: Then shall the Priest earnestly exhorte his parishoners, to dispose themselfes to the receiuing of the holy cōmunion more diligētly, saiyng these or like wordes unto thē.*

DEre frendes, and you especially upon whose soules I haue cure and charge, on　　　　　next, I do intende by Gods grace, to offre to all suche as shalbe godlye disposed, the moste comfortable Sacrament of the body and bloud of Christ, to be taken of them, in the remembraunce of his moste fruitfull and glorious Passyon: by the whiche passion, we haue obteigned remission of our synnes, and be made partakers of the kyngdom of heauen, whereof wee bee assured and asserteigned, yf wee come to the sayde Sacrament, with hartie repentaunce for our offences, stedfast faithe in Goddes mercye, and earnest mynde to obeye Goddes will, and to offende nomore. Wherefore our duetie is, to come to these holy misteries, with moste heartie thankes to bee geuen to almightie GOD, for his infinite mercie and benefites geuen and bestowed upon us his unworthye seruauntes, for whom he hath not onely geuen his body to death, and shed his bloude, but also doothe vouchsaue in a Sacrament and Mistery, to geue us his sayed bodye and bloud to feede upon spiritually. The whyche Sacrament beyng so Diuine and holy a thyng, and so comfortable to them whiche receyue it worthilye, and so daungerous to them that wyll presume to take the same unworthely: My duetie is to exhorte you in the meane season, to consider the greatnes of the thing, and to serche and examine your owne consciences, and that not lyghtly nor after the maner of dissimulers with GOD: But as they whiche shoulde come to a moste Godly and heauenly Banket, not to come but in the mariage garment required of God in scripture, that you may (so muche as lieth in you) be founde worthie to come to suche a table. The waies and meanes therto is.

First that you be truly repentaūt of your former euill life, and that you confesse with an unfained hearte to almightie God, youre synnes and unkyndnes towardes his Maiestie committed, either by will, worde or dede, infirmitie or ignoraunce, and that with inwarde sorowe & teares you bewaile your offences, & require of almightie god, mercie, & pardon, promising to him (from the botome of your hartes) thamendment of your former lyfe. And emonges all others, I am commaunded of God, especially to moue and exhorte you, to reconcile your selfes to your neighbors, whom you haue offended, or who hath offended yoù, putting out of your heartes al hatred and malice against them, and to be in loue and charitie with all the worlde, and to forgeue other, as you woulde that god should forgeue you. And yf any mā haue doen wrōg to any other: let him make satisfaccion, and due restitucion of all landes & goodes, wronfully taken awaye or with holden, before he come to Goddes borde, or at the least be in ful minde and purpose so to do, assone as he is able, or els let him not come to this holy table, thinking to deceyue God, who seeth al mēnes hartes. For neither the absolucion of the priest, can any thing auayle them, nor the receiuyng of this holy sacrament doth any thing but increase their damnacion. And yf there bee any of you, whose conscience is troubled & greued in any thing, lackyng comforte or counsaill, let him come to me, or to some other dyscrete and learned priest, taught in the law of God, and confesse and open his synne & griefe secretly, that he maye receiue suche ghostly counsaill, aduyse and comfort, that his conscience maye be releued, and that of us (as of the Ministers of GOD and of the churche) he may receiue comfort and absolucion, to the satisfaccion of his mynde, and auoyding of all scruple and doubtfulnes: requiryng suche as shalbe satisfied with a generall confession, not to be offended with them that doe use, to their further satisfiyng, the auriculer and secret confession to the Priest: nor those also whiche thinke nedefull or conuenient, for the quietnes of their awne cōsciences particuliarly to open their sinnes to the Priest: to bee offended with them that are satisfied, with their humble confession to GOD, and the generall confession to the churche. But in all thinges to folowe and kepe the rule of charitie, and euery man to be satisfied with his owne conscience, not iudgyng other mennes myndes or consciences: where as he hath no warrant of Goddes word to the same.

¶ *Then shall folowe for the Offertory, one or mo, of these Sentences of holy scripture, to bee song whiles the people doo offer, or els one of theim to bee saied by the minister, immediatly afore the offeryng.*

Let your light so shine before men, that they maye see your good woorkes, and glorify your father whiche is in heauen. (Math. v.)

Laie not up for your selfes treasure upon the yearth, where the rust and mothe doth corrupt, and where theues breake through and steale: But laie up for your selfes treasures in heauen, where neyther rust nor mothe doth corrupt, and where theues do not breake through nor steale. (Math. vi[.])

Whatsoeuer you would that menne should do unto you, euen so do you unto them, for this is the Lawe and the Prophetes. (Math. vi[i.])

Not euery one that saieth unto me, lorde, lorde, shall entre into the kyngdom of heauen, but he that doth the will of my father whiche is in heauen. (Math. v[ii.])

Zache stode furthe, and saied unto the Lorde: beholde Lorde, the halfe of my goodes I geue to the poore, and if I haue doen any wrong to any man, I restore foure fold. (Luc. xix.)

Who goeth a warfare at any tyme at his owne cost? who planteth a vineyarde, and eateth not of the fruite thereof? Or who fedeth a flock, and eateth not of the milk of the flocke? (i. Cor. ix.)

If we haue sowen unto you spirituall thinges, is it a great matter yf we shall reape your worldly thynges? (i. Cor. ix.)

Dooe ye not knowe, that they whiche minister aboute holy thinges, lyue of the Sacrifice? They which waite of the alter, are partakers with the alter? euen so hath the lorde

252

also ordained: that they whiche preache the Gospell, should liue of the Gospell. (i. Cor. ix.)

He whiche soweth litle, shall reape litle, and he that soweth plenteously, shall reape plenteously. Let euery manne do accordyng as he is disposed in his hearte, not grudgyngly, or of necessitie, for God loueth a cherefull geuer. ([ii. C]or. ix.)

Let him that is taught in the woorde, minister unto hym that teacheth, in all good thinges. Be not deceiued, GOD is not mocked. For whatsoeuer a man soweth, that shall he reape. ([Gal]a. vi.)

While we haue tyme, let us do good unto all men, and specially unto them, whiche are of the household of fayth. ([Ga]lla. vi.)

Godlynes is greate riches, if a man be contented with that he hath: For we brought nothing into the worlde, neither maie we cary any thing out. ([i T]imo. vi.)

Charge them whiche are riche in this worlde, that they bee ready to geue, and glad to distribute, laying up in stoare for theimselfes a good foundacion, against the time to come, that they maie attain eternall lyfe. ([i.] Timo. vi.)

GOD is not unrighteous, that he will forget youre woorkes and labor, that procedeth of loue, whiche loue ye haue shewed for his names sake, which haue ministered unto the sainctes, and yet do minister. ([H]ebre. vi.)

To do good, & to distribute, forget not, for with suche Sacrifices God is pleased. (Hebre. xiii.)

Whoso hath this worldes good, and seeth his brother haue nede, & shutteth up his compassion from hym, how dwelleth the loue of God in him? (Jhon. iii.)

Geue almose of thy goodes, and turne neuer thy face from any poore man, and then the face of the lorde shall not be turned awaye from thee. ([T]oby. iiii.)

Bee mercifull after thy power: if thou hast muche, geue plenteously, if thou hast litle, do thy diligence gladly to geue of that litle, for so gathereste thou thy selfe a good reward, in the daie of necessitie. (Toby. iiii.)

He that hath pitie upon the poore, lendeth unto the Lorde: and loke what he laieth out, it shalbe paied hym again. (Prouerbes x[ix.])

Blessed be the man that prouideth for the sicke and nedy, the lorde shall deliuer hym, in the tyme of trouble. (Psal. lxiiii)

Where there be Clerkes, thei shall syng one, or many of the sentences aboue written, accordyng to the length and shortenesse of the tyme, that the people be offeryng. In the meane tyme, whyles the Clerkes do syng the Offertory, so many as are disposed, shall offer unto the poore mennes boxe euery one accordynge to his habilitie and charitable mynde. And at the offeryng daies appoynted: euery manne and woman shall Paie to the Curate, the due and accustomed offerynges. Then so manye as shalbe partakers of the holy Communion, shall tary still in the quire, or in some conuenient place, nigh the quire, the men on the one side, and the women on the other syde. All other (that mynde not to receiue the said holy Communion) shall departe out of the quire, except the ministers and Clerkes.

Than shall the minister take so much Bread and Wine, as shall suffice for the persons appoynted to receiue the holy Communion, laying the breade upon the corporas, or els in the paten, or in some other comely thyng, prepared for that purpose. And puttyng ye wyne into the Chalice, or els in some faire or cōueniente cup, prepared for that use (if the Chalice will not serue) puttyng thereto a litle pure and cleane water: And settyng both the breade and wyne upon the Alter: Then the Prieste shall saye.

The Lorde be with you.

Aunswere.

And with thy spirite.

Priest.

Lift up your heartes.

Aunswere.

we lift them up unto the Lorde.

Priest.

Let us geue thankes to our Lorde God.

Aunswere.

It is mete and right so to do.

The Priest.

IT is very mete, righte, and our boūden dutie that wee shoulde at all tymes, and in all places, geue thankes to thee, O Lorde, holy father, almightie euerlastyng God.

⁋ *Here shall folowe the proper preface, accordyng to the tyme (if there bee any specially appoynted) or els immediatly shall folowe. Therefore with Angelles. &c.*

PROPRE

Prefaces.

⁋ *Upon Christmas daie.*

BEcause thou diddeste geue Jesus Christe, thyne onely sonne to bee borne as this daye for us, who by the operacion of the holy ghoste, was made very man, of the substaunce of the Virgin Mari his mother, and that without spot of sinne, to make us cleane from all synne. Therefore. &c.

⁋ *Upon Easter daie.*

BUt chiefly are we bound to praise thee, for the glorious resurreccion of thy sonne Jesus Christe, our Lorde, for he is the very Pascall Lambe, whiche was offered for us, & hath taken awaie the synne of the worlde, who by his death hath destroyed death, and by his risyng to life againe, hath restored to us euerlastynge life. Therefore. &c.

⁋ *Upon the Assencion daye.*

THrough thy most dere beloued sonne, Jesus Christ our Lorde, who after his moste glorious resurreccion, manifestly appered to all his disciples, and in their sight ascended up into heauen, to prepare a place for us, that where he is, thither mighte we also ascende, and reigne with hym in glory. Therefore. &c.

⁋ *Upon Whitsondaye.*

THrough Jesus Christe our Lorde, accordyng to whose moste true promise, the holy Ghoste came doune this daye frō heauen, with a sodain great sound, as it had been a mightie wynde, in the likenes of fiery tounges, lightyng upon the Apostles, to teache them, and to leade them to all trueth, geuyng them bothe the gifte of diuerse languages, and also boldnes with feruent zeale, constantly to preache the Gospell unto all nacions, whereby we are brought out of darkenes and error, into the cleare light and true knowlege of thee, and of thy sonne Jesus Christ. Therefore. &c.

¶ *Upon the feast of the Trinitie.*

IT is very meete, righte, and oure bounden duetie, that we should at al tymes, and in al places, geue thankes to thee O Lorde, almightye euerlasting God, whiche arte one God, one Lorde, not one onely person, but three persones in one substaunce: For that which we beleue of the glory of the father, the same we beleue of the sōne, and of the holy ghost, without any difference, or inequalitie, whom the Angels. &c.

After whiche preface shall folowe immediatly.

Therfore with Angels and Archangels, and with all the holy companye of heauen: we laude and magnify thy glorious name, euermore praisyng thee, and saying:

Holy, holy, holy, Lorde God of Hostes: heauen & earth are full of thy glory: Osanna in the highest. Blessed is he that commeth in the name of the Lorde: Glory to thee O lorde in the highest. *This the Clerkes shal also syng.*

¶ *When the Clerkes haue dooen syngyng, then shall the Priest, or Deacon, turne hym to the people and saye.*

Let us praie for the whole state of Christes churche.

¶ *Then the Priest turnyng him to the Altar, shall saye or syng, playnly and distinctly, this prayer folowyng.*

ALmightie and euerliuyng God, whiche by thy holy Apostle haste taught us to make prayers and supplicacions, and to geue thankes for al menne: We humbly beseche thee moste mercyfully to receiue these our praiers, which we offre unto thy diuine Maiestie, beseching thee to inspire cōtinually the uniuersal churche, with the spirite of trueth, unitie and concorde: And graunt that al they that do cōfesse thy holy name, maye agree in the trueth of thy holye worde, and liue in unitie and godly loue. Speciallye we beseche thee to saue and defende thy seruaunt, Edwarde our Kyng, that under hym we maye be Godly and quietly gouerned. And graunt unto his whole coūsaile, and to all that be put in aucthoritie under hym, that they maye truely and indifferently minister iustice, to the punishemente of wickednesse and vice, and to the maintenaunce of Goddes true religion and vertue. Geue grace (O heauenly father) to all Bishoppes, Pastors, and

256

Curates, that thei maie bothe by their life and doctrine, set furthe thy true and liuely worde, and rightely and duely administer thy holy Sacramentes. And to al thy people geue thy heauenly grace, that with meke heart and due reuerence, they may heare and receiue thy holy worde, truely seruyng thee in holyness and righteousnes, all the dayes of their life: And we most hūbly beseche thee of thy goodnes (O Lorde) to coumfort and succour all them, whyche in thys transytory life be in trouble, sorowe, nede, syckenes, or any other aduersitie. And especially we commend unto thy mercifull goodnes, this congregacion which is here assembled in thy name, to celebrate the commemoracion of the most glorious death of thy sonne: And here we do geue unto thee moste high praise, and hartie thankes for the wonderfull grace and vertue, declared in all thy sainctes, from the begynning of the worlde: And chiefly in the glorious and most blessed virgin Mary, mother of thy sonne Jesu Christe our Lorde and God, and in the holy Patriarches, Prophetes, Apostles and Martyrs, whose examples (O Lorde) and stedfastnes in thy fayth, and kepyng thy holy commaundementes: graunt us to folowe. We commend unto thy mercye (O Lorde) all other thy seruauntes, which are departed hence from us, with the signe of faith, and nowe do reste in the slepe of peace: Graūt unto them, we beseche thee, thy mercy, and euerlasting peace, and that at the day of the generall resurreccion, we and all they which bee of the misticall body of thy sonne, may altogether be set on his right hand, and heare that his most ioyfull voyce: Come unto me, O ye that be blessed of my father, and possesse the kingdom, whiche is prepared for you, from the begynning of the worlde: Graunt this, O father, for Jesus Christes sake, our onely mediatour and aduocate.

O God heauenly father, which of thy tender mercie, diddest geue thine only sonne Jesu Christ, to suffre death upon the crosse for our redempcion, who made there (by his one oblacion once offered) a full, perfect, and sufficient sacrifyce, oblacion, and satysfacyon, for the sinnes of the whole worlde, and did institute, and in his holy Gospell commaund us, to celebrate a perpetuall memory, of that his precious death, untyll his comming again: Heare us (o merciful father) we besech thee: and with thy holy spirite & worde, vouchsafe

Here the [Pri]este must

to bl✠esse and sanc✠tifie these thy gyftes, and creatures of bread and wyne, that they maie be unto us the bodye and bloude of thy moste

[ta]ke the
[bre]ad
into
[his] hādes.
Here the
[Pr]iest
shall
[ta]ke the
[cu]ppe
into
[hi]s
hādes.

derely beloued sonne Jesus Christe. Who in the same nyght that he was betrayed: tooke breade, and when he had blessed, and geuen thankes: he brake it, and gaue it to his disciples, saiyng: Take, eate, this is my bodye which is geuen for you, do this in remembraunce of me.

Likewyse after supper he toke the cuppe, and when he had geuen thankes, he gaue it to them, saiyng: drynk ye all of this, for this is my bloude of the newe Testament, whyche is shed for you and for many, for remission of synnes: do this as oft as you shall drinke it in remembraunce of me.

These wordes before rehersed are to be saied, turning still to the Altar, without any eleuacion, or shewing the Sacrament to the people.

WHerfore, O Lorde and heauenly father, accordyng to the Instytucyon of thy derely beloued sonne, our sauiour Jesu Christ, we thy humble seruauntes do celebrate, and make here before thy diuine Maiestie, with these thy holy giftes, the memoryall whyche thy sonne hath wylled us to make, hauing in remembraunce his blessed passion, mightie resur-receyon, and gloryous ascencion, renderyng unto thee most hartie thankes, for the innumerable benefites procured untc us by thesame, entierely desiryng thy fatherly goodnes, mercifully to accepte this our Sacrifice of praise and thankes geuing: most humbly beseching thee to graunt, that by the merites and death of thy sōne Jesus Christ, and through faith in his bloud, we and al thy whole church, may obteigne remission of our sinnes, and all other benefites of hys passyon. And here wee offre and present unto the (O Lorde) oure selfe, oure soules, and bodies, to be a reasonable, holy, and liuely sacrifice unto thee: humbly besechyng thee, that who-soeuer shalbee partakers of thys holy Communion, maye worthely receiue the moste precious body and bloude of thy sonne Jesus Christe: and bee fulfilled with thy grace and heauenly benediccion, and made one bodye with thy sonne Jesu Christe, that he maye dwell in them, and they in hym. And although we be unworthy (through our manyfolde synnes) to offre unto thee any Sacryfice: Yet we besche thee to accepte thys our bounden duetie and seruice, and com-maunde these our prayers and supplicacions, by the Ministery of thy holy Angels, to be brought up into thy holy Tabernacle before the syght of thy dyuine maiestie: not waiyng our merites, but pardonyng our offences, through Christe our Lorde, by whome, and with whome, in the unitie of the holy Ghost: all honour and glory, be unto thee, O father almightie, world without ende. Amen.

Let us praye.

AS our sauior Christe hath commaunded and taught us, we are bolde to saye. Our father whyche art in heauen, halowed be thy name. Thy Kyngdome come. Thy wyll be doen in yearth, as it is in heauen. Geue us this daye our dayly breade. And forgeue us our trespaces, as wee forgeue them that trespasse agaynst us. And leade us not into temptacion.

The aunswere.

But deliuer us from euill. Amen.

Then shall the priest saye.

The peace of the Lorde be alwaye with you.

The Clerkes.

And with thy spirite.

The Priest.

CHrist our Pascall lambe is offred up for us, once for al, when he bare our sinnes on hys body upon the crosse, for he is the very lambe of God, that taketh away the sinnes of the worlde: wherfore let us kepe a ioyfull and holy feast with the Lorde.

Here the priest shall turne hym toward those that come to the holy Communion, and shall saye.

YOu that do truly and earnestly repent you of your synnes to almightie God, and be in loue and charitie with your neighbors, and entende to lede a newe life, folowyng the commaundementes of God, and walkyng from hencefurth in his holy wayes: draw nere and take this holy Sacrament to your comforte, make your humble confession to almightie God, and to his holy church here gathered together in hys name, mekely knelyng upon your knees.

Then shall thys generall Confession bee made, in the name of al those that are minded to receiue the holy

Communion, eyther by one of them, or els by one of the ministers, or by the prieste hymselfe, all kneling humbly upon their knees.

ALmyghtie GOD father of oure Lord Jesus Christ, maker of all thynges, iudge of all men, we knowlege and bewaile our manyfold synnes and wyckednes, which we from tyme to tyme, most greuously haue committed, by thought, word and dede, agaynst thy diuine maiestie, prouokyng most iustly thy wrath and indignacion against us, we do earnestly repent & be hartely sory for these our misdoinges, the remembrance of them is greuous unto us, the burthen of them is intollerable: haue mercye upon us, haue mercie upon us, moste mercifull father, for thy sonne our Lorde Jesus Christes sake, forgeue us all' that is past, and graunt that we may euer hereafter, serue and please thee in neunes of life, to the honor and glory of thy name: Through Jesus Christe our Lorde.

Then shall the Prieste stande up, and turnyng himselfe to the people, say thus.

ALmightie GOD our heauenly father, who of his great mercie, hath promysed forgeuenesse of synnes to all them, whiche with hartye repentaunce and true fayth, turne unto him: haue mercy upon you, pardon and delyuer you from all youre sinnes, confirme and strēgthen you in all goodnes, and bring you to euerlasting lyfe: through Jesus Christ our Lord. Amen.

Then shall the Priest also say.

Heare what coumfortable woordes our sauiour Christ sayeth, to all that truely turne to him.

Come unto me all that trauell and bee heauy laden, and I shall refreshe you. So God loued the worlde that he gaue his onely begotten sonne, to the ende that al that beleue in hym, shoulde not perishe, but haue lyfe euerlasting.

Heare also what saint Paul sayeth.

This is a true saying, and woorthie of all men to bee receiued, that Jesus Christe came into thys worlde to saue sinners.

Heare also what saint John sayeth.

If any man sinne, we haue an aduocate with the father, Jesus Christ the righteous, and he is the propiciacion for our sinnes.

Then shall the Priest turnyng him to gods boord knele down, and say in the name of all of them, that shall receyue the Communion, this prayer folowing.

WE do not presume to come to this thy table (o mercifull lord) trusting in our owne righteousnes, but in thy manifold & great mercies: we be not woorthie so much as to gather up the cromes under thy table, but thou art the same lorde whose propertie is alwayes to haue mercie: Graunt us therefore (gracious lorde) so to eate the fleshe of thy dere sonne Jesus Christ, and to drynke his bloud in these holy Misteries, that we may continuallye dwell in hym, and he in us, that oure synfull bodyes may bee made cleane by his body, and our soules washed through hys most precious bloud. Amen.

Then shall the Prieste firste receiue the Communion in both kindes himselfe, and next deliuer it to other Ministers, if any be there presente (that they may bee ready to helpe the chiefe Minister) and after to the people.
And when he deliuereth the Sacramente of the body of Christe, he shall say to euery one these woordes.

The body of our Lorde Jesus Christe whiche was geuen for thee, preserue thy bodye and soule unto euerlasting lyfe.

And the Minister deliuering the Sacramēt of the bloud, and geuing euery one to drinke once and no more, shall say.

The bloud of our Lorde Jesus Christe which was shed for thee, preserue thy bodye and soule unto euerlasting lyfe.

If there be a Deacon or other Priest, then shal he folow with the Chalice: and as the priest ministreth the Sacramēt of the body, so shal he (for more expediciō) minister the Sacrament of the bloude, in fourme before written.
In the Communion tyme the Clarkes shall syng.

ii. O lambe of god that takeste away the sinnes of the worlde: haue mercie upon us.

O lambe of god that takeste away the synnes of the worlde: graunt us thy peace.

Beginning so soone as the Prieste doeth receyue the holy Communion: and when the Communion is ended, then shall the Clarkes syng the post Communion.

Sentences of holy scripture, to be sayd or song euery day one, after the holy Communion, called the post Communion.

If any man will folowe me, let him forsake hymselfe, and take up his crosse and folowe me. (Math. xvi.)

Whosoeuer shall indure unto thende, he shalbe saued. (Mar. xiii.)

Praysed be the Lorde god of Israell, for he hath visited and redemed hys people: therefore let us serue hym all the days of our lyfe, in holines and righteousnes accepted before hym. (Luc. i.)

Happie are those seruauntes, whome the Lord (when he cummeth) shall fynde waking. (Luc. xii.)

Be ye readye, for the sonne of manne will come, at an hower when ye thinke not. (Luc. xii.)

The seruaunte that knoweth hys maisters will, and hath not prepared himself, neither hath doen according to his will, shalbe beaten with many stripes. (Luc. xii.)

The howre cummeth and now it is, when true woorshippers shall wurship the father in spirite and trueth. (John. iiii.)

Beholde, thou art made whole, sinne no more, lest any wurse thing happen unto thee. (John. v.)

If ye shall continue in my woorde, then are ye my very disciples, and ye shall knowe the truth, and the truth shall make you free. (John. viii.)

While ye haue lighte, beleue on the lyght, that ye may be the children of light. (John. xii.)

He that hath my commaundemētes, and kepeth them, the same is he that loueth me. (John. xiiii.)

If any man loue me, he will kepe my woorde, and my father will loue hym, and wee will come unto hym and dwell with hym. (Jhon. xiiii.)

If ye shall byde in me, and my woorde shall abyde in you, ye shall aske what ye will, and it shall bee doen to you. (John. Xv.)

Herein is my father gloryfyed, that ye beare muche fruite, and become my disciples. (John. xv.)

This is my commaundement, that you loue together as I haue loued you. (John. xv.)

If God be on our syde, who can be agaynst us? which did not spare his owne sonne, but gaue him for us all. (Roma. viii.)

Who shall lay any thing to the charge of Goddes chosen? it is GOD that iustifyeth, who is he that can condemne? (Rom. viii.)

The nyght is passed, and the day is at hande, let us therfore cast away the dedes of darkenes, and put on the armour of light. (Rom. xiii.)

Christe Jesus is made of GOD, unto us wisedome, and righteousnes, and sanctifying, and redemption, that (according as it is written) he whiche reioyceth shoulde reioyce in the Lorde. (i. Corin. i.)

Knowe ye not that ye are the temple of GOD, and that the spirite of GOD dwelleth in you? if any manne defile the temple of GOD, him shall God destroy. (i. Corin. iii.)

Ye are derely brought, therfore glorifye God in your bodies, and in your spirites, for they belong to God. (i. Corin. vi.)

Be you folowers of God as deare children, and walke in loue, euen as Christe loued us, and gaue hymselfe for us an offeryng and a Sacrifyce of a sweete sauoure to God. (Ephes. v.)

Then the Priest shall geue thankes to God, in the name of all them that haue communicated, turning him first to the people, and saying.

The Lorde be with you.

The aunswere.

And with thy spirite.

The priest.

Let us pray.

ALmightye and euerlyuyng GOD, we moste hartely thanke thee, for that thou hast vouchsafed to feede us in these holy Misteries, with the spirituall foode of the most precious body and bloud of thy sonne, our saviour Jesus Christ, and hast assured us (duely receiuing the same) of thy fauour and goodnes toward us, and that we be very membres incorporate in thy Misticall bodye, whiche is the blessed companye of all faythfull people: and heyres through hope of thy euerlasting kingdome, by the merites of the most precious death and passion, of thy deare sonne. We therfore most humbly beseche thee, O heauenly father, so to assist us with thy grace, that we may continue in that holy felowship, and doe all suche good woorkes, as thou hast prepared for us to walke in, through Jesus Christe our Lorde, to whome with thee, and the holy goste, bee all honour and glory, world without ende.

Then the Priest turning hym to the people, shall let them depart with this blessing.

The peace of GOD (whiche passeth all understandyng) kepe your heartes and mindes in the knowledge and loue of GOD, and of hys sonne Jesus Christe our lorde. And the blessing of God almightie, the father, the sonne and the holy gost, be emonges you, and remayne with you alway.

Then the people shall aunswere.

Amen.

Where there are no clerkes, there the Priest shall say al thinges appoynted here for them to sing.

When the holy Communion is celebrate on the workeday or in priuate howses: Then may be omitted, the Gloria in excelsis, the Crede, the Homily, and the exhortacion, beginning.

Dearely beloued. &c.

¶ *Collectes to bee sayed after the Offertory, when there is no Communion, euery such day one.*

ASsist us mercifully, O Lord, in these our supplicacions & praiers, and dispose the way of thy seruauntes, toward the attainement of euerlasting saluacyon, that emong all the chaunges and chaunces of thys mortall lyfe, they maye euer bee defended by thy moste gracious and readye helpe: through Christe our Lorde. Amen.

O Almightie Lorde and euerlyuyng GOD, vouchesafe, we beseche thee, to direct, sanctifye and gouerne, both our heartes and bodies, in the wayes of thy lawes, and in the workes of thy cōmaundementes: that through thy most mightie proteccion, both here and euer, we may be preserued in body and soule: Through our Lorde and sauiour Jesus Christ. Amen.

GRaunt we beseche thee almightie god, that the wordes whiche we haue hearde this day with our outwarde eares, may throughe thy grace, bee so grafted inwardly in our heartes, that they may bring foorth in us, the fruite of good liuing, to the honour and prayse of thy name: Through Jesus Christe our Lorde. Amen.

PReuent us, O lorde, in all our doinges, with thy most gracious fauour, and further us with thy continuall helpe, that in al our woorkes begonne, continued and ended in thee: we may glorifye thy holy name, and finally by thy mercy obteine euerlasting life. Through. &c.

ALmightie God, the fountayn of all wisdome, which knowest our necessities beefore we aske, and our ignoraunce in asking: we beseche thee to haue compassion upon our infirmities, and those thynges which for our unwoorthines we dare not, and for our blindnes we can not aske, vouchsaue to geue us for the woorthines of thy sonne Jesu Christ our Lorde. Amen.

ALmightie god, which hast promised to heare the peticions of them that aske in thy sonnes name, we beseche thee mercifully to inclyne thyne eares to us that haue made nowe our prayers and supplicacions unto thee, and graunte that those thynges whiche we haue faythfullye asked accordyng to thy will, maye effectually bee obteyned to the reliefe of oure necessitye, and to the settyng foorth of thy glorye: Through Jesus Christ our Lorde.

For rayne.

O God heauenly father, which by thy sonne Jesu Christ, hast promised to al thē that seke thy kingdom, & the righteousnes therof, al thinges necessary to the bodely sustenaunce: send us (we beseche thee) in this our necessitie, such moderate rayne and showers, that we may receiue the fruites of the earth, to our comfort and to thy honor: Through Jesus Christ our Lord.

For fayre wether.

O Lorde God, which for the sinne of manne, didst once drowne all the worlde, except eight persons, and afterwarde of thy great mercye, didste promise neuer to destroy it so agayn: We hūbly beseche thee, that although we for oure iniquities haue woorthelye deserued this plague of rayne and waters, yet upon our true repentaunce, thou wilt sende us suche wether whereby we may receiue the fruites of the earth in due season, and learne both by thy punishment to amende our liues, and by the graunting of our peticion, to geue thee prayse and glory: Through Jesu Christ our Lorde.

¶ *Upon wednesdaies & frydaies, the English Letany shalbe said or song in all places, after suche forme as is appoynted by the kynges maiesties Iniunccions: Or as is or shal bee other wyse appoynted by his highnes. And thoughe there be none to cōmunicate with the Prieste, yet these dayes (after the Letany ended) the Priest shall put upon him a playn Albe or surplesse, with a cope, and say al thinges at the Altar (appoynted to bee sayde at the celebracyon of the lordes supper) untill after the offertory. And then shall adde one or two of the Collectes afore written, as occasion shall serue by his discrecion. And then turning him to the people shall let them depart, with the accustomed blessing. And the same order shall be used all other dayes, whensoeuer the people be customably assembled to pray in the churche, and none disposed to communicate with the Priest.*

Lykewyse in Chapelles annexed, and all other places, there shalbe no celebracion of the Lordes supper, except there be some to communicate with the Priest. And in suche Chapelles annexed where ye people hath not bene accustomed to pay any holy bread, there they must either make some charitable prouision for the bering of the charges of the Communion, or elles (for receyuyng of the same) resort to theyr Parish Churche.

For aduoyding of all matters and occasyon of dyscencyon, it is mete that the breade prepared for the Communion, bee made through all thys realme, after one sort and fashion: that is to say, unleauened, and rounde, as it was afore, but without all maner of printe, and somethyng more larger and thicker then it was, so that it may be aptly deuided in diuers pieces: and euery one shall be deuided in two pieces, at the leaste, or more, by the discrecion of the minister, and so distributed. And menne muste not thynke lesse to be receyued in parte, then in the whole, but in eache of them the whole body of our sauiour Jesu Christ.

And forsomuche as the Pastours and Curates within thys realme, shal continually fynd at theyr costes and charges in theyr cures, sufficient Breade and Wyne for the holy Communion (as oft as theyr Parishioners shalbe disposed, for theyr spiritual comfort to receyue the same) it is therefore ordered, that in recompence of suche costes and charges, the Parishioners of euerye

Parishe shall offer euery Sonday, at the tyme of the Offertory, the iuste valour and price of the holy lofe (with all suche money, and other thinges as were wont to be offered with the same) to the use of theyr Pastours and Curates, and that in suche ordre and course, as they were woont to fynde and pay the sayd holy lofe.

Also, that the receiuing of the Sacrament of the blessed body and bloud of Christ, may be most agreable to the institucion therof, and to the usage of the primatiue Churche: In all Cathedrall and Collegiate Churches, there shal alwaies some Communicate with the Prieste that ministreth. And that the same may bee also obserued euery where abrode in the countrey: Some one at the least of that house in euery Parishe, to whome by course after the ordinaunce herein made, it apperteyneth to offer for the charges of the Communiō, or some other whom they shall prouide to offer for them, shall receiue the holye Communion with the Prieste: the whiche may be the better doen, for that they knowe before, when their course commeth, and maie therfore dispose thēselues to the worthie receiuyng of the Sacramente. And with hym or them who doeth so offre the charges of the Communion: all other, who be then Godly disposed thereunto, shall lykewyse receiue the Communion. And by this meanes the Minister hauyng alwaies some to communicate with him, maie accordyngly solempnise so high and holy misteries, with all the suffrages and due ordre appoynted for the same. And the Priest on the weke daie, shall forbeare to celebrate the Communion, excepte he haue some that will communicate with hym.

Furthermore, euery man and womā to be bound to heare and be at the diuine seruice, in the Parishe churche where they be resident, and there with deuout prayer, or Godlye silence and meditacion, to occupie themselues. There to paie their dueties, to communicate once in the yeare at the least, and there to receyue, and take all other Sacramentes and rites, in this booke appoynted. And whosoeuer willyngly upon no iust cause, doeth absent themselues, or doeth ungodly in the Parishe church occupie thēselues: upon proffe therof, by the Ecclesiasticall lawes of the Realme to bee excomunicate, or suffre other punishement, as shall to the Ecclesiastical iudge (accordyng to his discrecion) seme conuenient.

And although it bee redde in aunciente writers, that the people many yeares past, receiued at the priestes hādes, the Sacrament of the body of Christ in theyr owne handes, and no commaundemēt of Christ to the contrary: Yet forasmuche as they many tymes conueyghed the same secretelye awaye, kept it with them, and diuersly abused it to supersticion and wickednes: lest any suche thyng hereafter should be attempted, and that an uniformitie might be used, throughoute the whole Realme: it is thought conuenient the people commōly receiue the Sacramēt of Christes body, in their mouthes, at the Priestes hande.

NOTES

1. Transcribed verbatim from a microfilm copy of the original text, obtained from the Huntingdon Library. In some places the marginal notes have had to be reconstructed (due, apparently, to faulty trimming of the margins); in such cases the additional letters or figures are set off in brackets.

The book of[1]
common prayer, and ad=
ministracion of the
Sacramentes,
and other
rites
and ceremonies of
the Churche of
Englande.

Londini, in officina
Edovardi Whytchurche.
Anno. 1552.

The order for the
administracion of the Lordes
Supper or holye
Communion.

SO many as entende . . . [1549 b]
  And yf any of those . . . [1549 b]

  ¶ *The same ordre shall the Curate use* . . . [1549 a]

  ¶ *The Table hauyng at the Communion tyme a fayre white
  lynnen clothe upon it, shall stande in the body of the
  Churche, or in the chauncell, where Morninge prayer,
  and Eueninge prayer be appoynted to bee sayde. And
  the Priest standing at the northsyde of the Table, shal
  saye the Lordes prayer with thys Collecte folowinge.*

ALmightie God, unto whom al heartes be open . . .
[1549 a]

  ¶ *Then shal the Priest rehearse distinctly all the .x. Commaundementes: and the people knelyng, shal after
  euerye Commaundement aske Gods mercy for theyr
  transgression of thesame, after thys sorte.*

b = changes in spelling and minor changes in the text.
a = changes in spelling.

269

Ministre.

God spake these wordes, and sayd: I am the Lorde thy God. Thou shalt haue none other Goddes but me.

People.

Lorde haue mercye upon us, and encline oure heartes to kepe thys lawe.

Ministre.

Thou shalte not make to thy selfe any grauen ymage, nor the lykenes of any thyng that is in heauen aboue, or in the earth beneath, nor in the water under the earth. Thou shalte not bowe downe to them, nor worshyppe them: for I the Lorde thy God am a gelous God, and visite the sinne of the fathers upon the childrē, unto the thyrde and fourth generacion of them that hate me, and shewe mercy unto thousandes in them that loue me and kepe my commaundementes.

People.

Lorde haue mercy upon us, and encline our heartes to kepe thys lawe.

Ministre.

Thou shalt not take the name of the Lord thy God in vayne: for the lorde wil not holde him gilteles that taketh hys name in vayne.

People.

Lorde haue mercy upon us, and encline our. &c.

Ministre.

Remembre that thou kepe holy the Sabboth daye. vi. dayes shalt thou laboure and doe all that thou haste to doe, but the seuenth daye is the sabboth of the lorde thy God. In it thou shalt doe no maner of worke, thou and thy sonne and thy daughter, thy man seruaunt, and thy maide seruaunte, thy Catel, & the straunger that is within thy gates: for in .iv. dayes the lord made heauen and earth, the Sea, and all that in them is, and rested the seuenth day. Wherefore the Lord blessed the seuenth day, and halowed it.

People.

Lorde haue mercy upon us, and encline our. &c.

Ministre.

Honour thy father and thy mother, that thy dayes may be long in the land which the lord thy God geueth thee.

People.

Lord haue mercy upon us, and encline our. &c.

Ministre.

Thou shalt doe no murther.

People.

Lorde haue mercy upon us, and encline our. &c.

Ministre.

Thou shalt not commit adulterie.

People.

Lorde haue mercy upon us, and encline our. &c.

Ministre.

Thou shalt not steale.

People.

Lorde haue mercy upon us, and encline our. &c.

Ministre.

Thou shalt not beare false witnesse against thy neighboure.

People.

Lorde haue mercy upon us and encline our heartes to kepe thys lawe.

Ministre.

Thou shalt not couet thy neyghbours house. Thou shalte not couet thy neighbours wife, nor hys seruaunt, nor hys mayde, nor hys oxe, nor hys asse, nor any thyng that is hys.

People.

Lord haue marcy upon us, and wryte al these thy lawes in our heartes we beseche thee.

¶ *Then shall folowe the Collecte of the daye, with one of these two Collectes folowyng for the king: the Priest standing up and saying.*

¶ Let us praye.   *Priest.*

ALmightie God, whose kyngdome is euerlastyng . . . [1549 ª]

ALmightie and euerlasting god, we be taught . . . [1549 ª]

¶ *Immediatly after the Collectes, the priest shal reade the Epistle, begynnyng thus.*

¶ The Epistle written in the.   Chapter of.

And the Epistle ended, he shal saye the Gospel, beginninge thus.

The Gospell, wrytten in the.   Chapter of.

And the Epistle and Gospel beyng ended, shalbe sayed the Crede.

I Beleue in one god, the father almightie . . . [1549 ᵇ]

After the Crede, yf there be no sermon, shall folowe one of the homelies already set forth, or hereafter to be set forth by commune auctoritie.
After suche sermon, homelie, or exhortacion, the Curate shall declare unto the people whether there be any holye dayes or fasting daies the weke folowing: and earnestly exhorte them to remembre the poore, saying one or moē of these sentēces folowing, as he thinketh most cōuenient by his discrecion.

Let your lyght so shine . . . [1549 ª]
    Laye not up for yourselves . . . [1549 ª]
    Whatsoeuer you woulde that men . . . [1549 ᵇ]
    Not euery one that sayth unto me . . . [1549 ª]
    Zache stode forth, and said . . . [1549 ª]
    Who goeth a warrefare at any time . . . [1549 ᵇ]
    If we have sowen unto you spiritual thynges . . . [1549 ª]
    Doe ye not knowe, that they which minister . . . [1549 ª]
    He which soweth little, shal reape little . . . [1549 ª]
    Let him that is taught in the word . . . [1549 ª]
    Whyle we haue time, let us doe good . . . [1549 ª]
    Godlynes is great ryches, if a mā be contented . . . [1549 ª]

272

Charge them which are tiche . . . [1549 ^a]

Charge them which are tiche . . . [1549 ᵃ]
God is not unrighteous . . . [1549 ᵇ]
To doe good, and to distribute [1549 ᵃ]
Whoso hath this worldes good . . . [1549 ᵃ]
Geue almose of thy goodes . . . [1549 ᵃ]
Be merciful after thy power . . . [1549 ᵃ]
He that hath pietie . . . [1549 ᵃ]
Blessed be the man that prouideth . . . [1549 ᵇ]

¶ *Then shal the Churche wardens, or some other by*
them appointed, gather the deuocion of the people, and
put the same into the pore mens boxe: and upon the
offering daies appointed, euery man and woman shall
paye to the curate the due and accustomed offeringes:
after whiche done, the priest shal saye.

Let us pray for the whole state of Christes Churche militant
here in earth.

Yf there be
none almose
geuen unto
the poore,
than shall
ye wordes of
acceptyng our
almes be
lefte out
unsayed.

ALmightie and euerliuing God, which by
thy holy Apostle haste taughte us to make
prayers and supplicacions, and to geue
thankes for all menne: we humbly beseche
thee moste mercifully to accepte our almose,
and to receiue these our prayers whiche we
offre unto thy diuine Maiestie: beseching
thee to inspire continuallye, the uniuersal
churche with the spirite of trueth, unitie and
concorde: and graunte that al they that doe confesse thy holy
name, maye agree in the trueth of thy holy word, and lyue
in unitie and Godly loue. We beeseche thee also to saue and
defende all Christian kynges, Princes, and gouernours, and
speciallye thy seruaunte, Edwarde our Kyng, that under hym
we maye be Godlye and quietly gouerned: and graunte unto
hys whole counsayle, and to al that be put in auctoritie under
hym, that they may truely and indifferentlye minister iustice,
to the punishmente of wickednesse and vice, and to the
mayntenaunce of Gods true religion and vertue. Geue grace
(O heauenly father) to all Bisshops, pastoures and Curates,
that they may both by theyr lyfe and doctryne set foorth thy
true and lyuely worde, and rightly and duely administer thy
holy Sacramentes: and to al thy people geue thy heauenly
grace, and especially to thys congregaciō here present, that
with meke hearte & due reuerence, they maye heare and receiue thy holy worde, truely seruynge thee in holynes and

righteousnesse al the dayes of their lyfe. And we most humbly beseche thee of thy goodnesse (O Lord) to coumforte and succoure al them whiche in thys transitorye life be in trouble, sorowe, nede, sickenes, or any other aduersitie: Graunt this O father, for Jesus Christes sake our onely mediatour and aduocate. Amē.

> *Then shal folowe this exhortacion, at certaine times when the Curate shal see the people negligent to come to the holy Communion.*

WE bee come together at this time derely beloued brethren, to fede at the lordes supper, unto the whiche in Goddes behalfe I bydde you all that be here presente, and beseche you for the Lorde Jesus Christes sake, that ye wyll not refuse to come thereto, being so louingly called and bydden of god hymselfe. Ye knowe howe greuouse and unkynde a thynge it is, when a man hath prepared a ryche feaste, decked his table with al kinde of prouision, so that there lacketh nothyng but the geastes to sit downe: & yet they which be called, without any cause most unthankefully refuse to come. Which of you in such a case would not be moued? Who would not thynke a great iniury & wrong done unto him? Wherefore most derely beloued in Christ, take ye good hede, leste ye with drawynge youre selues frō this holy supper, prouoke gods indignaciō againste you. It is an easye matter for a man to saye, I wyll not Communicate, because I am otherwyse letted with worldly busynes: but such excuses be not so easely accepted and allowed beefore God. If any man saye, I am a greuouse sinner, and therfore am afraied to come: wherfore then doe you not repent and amend. When god calleth you, be you not ashamed to saye you wil not come? When you shoulde returne to God, will you excuse youre selfe and saye that you be not ready? Consydre earnestly with your selues how little suche feyned excuses shall auayle beefore God. They that refused the feaste in the gospell, because they had boughte a farme, or would trie theyr yokes of oxen, or beecause they were maried, were not so excused, but counted unworthy of the heauenlye feast: I for my part am here present, and according unto mine office, I bidde you in the name of God, I cal you in Christes behalfe, I exhorte you, as you loue youre owne saluacion, that ye wilbe partakers of thys holy Communion. And as the sōne of god did vouchesafe to yelde up his soule by death upon the Crosse for your

274

healthe: euen so it is youre duetie to receyue the Communion together in the remembraunce of hys death, as he himselfe commaunded. Nowe if you wyll in nowyse thus dooe, considre with your selues howe greate iniurye you doe unto God, and howe sore punishmente hangeth ouer your heades for the same. And wheras you offend god so sore in refusinge thys holy Banquet, I admonyshe, exhort, and beseche you, that unto this unkindnes ye wyll not adde any more. Which thyng ye shall doe, if ye stand by as gasers and lokers on thē that doe communicate, and be ño partakers of the same your selues. For what thing can this be accoumpted els, thē a further cōtempt and unkindnes unto god? Truly it is a great unthankfulnes to saye naye when ye be called: but the faulte is muche greater when men stande by, and yet wil neither eate nor drynke thys holy Communion with other. I pray you what can this be els, but euen to haue the misteries of Christ in derision? It is said unto al: Take ye and eate. Take and drynke ye all of thys: doe this in remembraunce of me. With what face then, or with what coūtenaunce shal ye heare these wordes? What wil this be els but a neglectyng, a despysing, and mocking of the Testament of Christ? Wherfore, rather then you should so doe, depart you hence and geue place to them that be Godly disposed. But when you departe, I beseche you, pondre with your selues from whom you depart: ye depart from the lordes table, ye depart from your brethrē, and from the banquete of moste heauenly foode. These thynges if ye earnestly considre, ye shall by Gods grace re-turne to a better mynd, for the obteyning whereof, we shall make our humble peticions while we shal receyue the holy Communion.

¶ *And some tyme shalbe sayed this also, at the discrecion of the Curate.*

DErely beloued, forasmuche as oure duetye is to rendre to Almightie God our heauēly father moste hartye thankes, for that he hath geuen his sonne our sauioure Jesus Christe, not onely to die for us, but also to be our spiritual fode & sus-tenaūce, as it is declared unto us, as wel by Gods worde, as by the holy Sacramentes of his blessed body, and bloud, the which being so comfortable a thyng to them whiche receiue it worthely, and so daungerous to them that wyl presume to receiue it unworthely: My duetie is to exhort you to con-sidre the dignitie of the holy mistery, and the greate perel of the unworthy receiuing therof, and so to search and examine your own consciences, as you should come holy and cleane to a moste Godly and heauenly feaste: so that in no wise you come but in the mariage garmēt, required of god in holy scripture: and so come and be receiued, as worthy partakers of suche a heauenly table. The way and meanes therto is: First to examine youre liues and conuersacion by the rule of Goddes commaūdementes, and wherinsoeuer ye shal perceiue your selues to haue offended, eyther by wyl, worde, or dede, there beewaile your own sinfull liues, confesse your selues to almightie God with full purpose of amendmente of lyfe. And if ye shal perceiue your offences to be suche, as bee not only against god, but also against your neighbours: then ye shall reconcile youre selues unto them, ready to make restitucion & satisfaccion accordynge to the uttermost of your powers, for al iniuries & wronges done by you to any other: & like wise beeyng readye to forgeue other that haue offended you, as you would haue forgeuenes of your offences at Gods hand: for otherwise the receiuing of the holy Communion, doth nothyng els but encreace youre damnacion. And beecause it is requisite that no man shoulde come to the holy Communyon but with a ful trust in gods mercy, & with a quiet conscience: therfore if there be any of you which by the meanes afore said, cannot quiet his own conscience, but requireth further confort or counsel: then let him come to me, or some other discrete and learned ministre of Gods worde, and open his griefe, that he may receiue such gostly counsail, aduise, and coumfort, as his conscience may be relieued: & that by the ministery of Gods worde, he maye receyue comforte & the benefite of absolucion, to the quietinge of his cōscience, & aduoiding of al Scruple & doubtfulnes.

Then shal the priest say thys exhortacion.

DErely beloued in the lorde: ye that mynde to come to the holy Communion of the body & bloud of our sauioure Christe, must consider what S. Paul writeth to ye Corinthiās, how he exhorteth all persons diligentlye to trye and examine themselues, before they presume to eate of that bread, and drynke of that cup: for as the benefite is great if with a truly penitent heart and liuely faith, we receiue that holy Sacrament, (for then we spirituallye eate the fleshe of Christ, and drynke his bloude, then we dwel in Christ and Christ in us, we be one

276

with Christ, & Christ with us:) so is the daunger great, if we receyue the same unworthely. For then we be giltie of the body and bloud of Christ our sauiour. We eate and drinke our own damnacion, not considering the Lordes body. We kindle Goddes wrath agaynste us, we prouoke hym to plague us with diuerse diseases, and sundrye kyndes of death. Therfore, yf any of you be a blasphemer of God, an hynderer or slaunderer of hys worde, an adulterer, or be in malice or enuie, or in any other greuous cryme, beewayle your synnes, and cone not to thys holy Table, lest after the takyng of that holy Sacrament, the Deuil entre into you, as he entred into Judas, and fil you full of al iniquities, and bryng you to destruccio, both of bodye and soule. Judge therfore youre selues (brethren) that ye be not iudged of the Lorde. Repente you truely for youre synnes paste, haue a lyuely and stedfast fayth in Christ our Sauiour. Amende your lyues, and bee in perfecte charitie with al men, so shall ye be meete partakers of those holy misteries. And aboue all thynges, ye must geue moste humble and hartie thankes to god the father, the sonne, and the holy gost, for the redempcyon of the worlde, by the death and passion of our Sauioure Chryste both God, and man: who did humble hymselfe, euen to the death upon the Crosse, for us miserable synners, whiche laye in darkenes, and shadowe of death, that he might make us the children of God, and exalte us to euerlastynge lyfe. And to thende that we shoulde alway remembre the excedyng great loue of our maister and onely Sauioure Jesu Christ, thus dying for us, and the innumerable benefites (whiche by hys precyous bloudsheding) he hath obteined to us, he hath instituted and ordayned holy misteries, as pledges of his loue, and continual remembraunce of his death, to our great and endles comforte. To hym therfore with the father and the holy gost, let us geue (as we are most bounden) continuall thankes: submitting oure selues wholy to hys holy wil and pleasure, and studying to serue him in true holynesse and ryghteousnesse all the dayes of oure lyfe. Amen.

¶ *Then shal the Priest saye to them that come to receiue the holy Communion.*

YOu that doe truely and earnestly repent you of youre synnes, and bee in loue and charitie with your neighbours, and entende to leade a newe lyfe, folowyng the commaundementes of God, and walking frō henceforth in his holy wayes: Drawe

277

nere, and take this holy Sacramente to youre comfort: make your humble confession to almightie god before this congregacion here gathered together in hys holy name, mekely knelyng upon your knees.

¶ *Then shal this general confession be made, in the name of al those that are mynded to receyue the holy Communion, eyther by one of them, or els by one of the ministers, or by the Priest hymself, al kneling humbly upō theyr knees.*

↧Lmightie God, father of oure Lorde Jesus Christe, maker of ↧ll thynges, Judge of all men, we knowledge and bewayle oure manyfolde synnes and wyckednes, whiche we from tyme to tyme most greuously haue committed, by thoughte, worde and dede, agaynst thy deuine Maiestie: prouoking most iustely thy wrath and indignacion againste us: we doe earnestlye repente, and be hartely sory for these oure misdoynges: the remembraunce of them is grieuouse unto us, the burthen of them is intollerable: haue mercy upon us, haue mercye upon us moste mercyfull father, for thy sonne oure LORDE Jesus Chrystes sake: forgeue us all that is past, & graunt that we maye euer hereafter, serue and please thee, in newnesse of lyfe, to the honour & glory of thy name: Through Jesus Christ our lord. Amen.

Then shall the Priest or the Bisshop (being present) stand up, and turning himselfe to the people, saye thus.

ALmightie God our heauenly father, who of his great mercy, hath promised forgeuenesse of synnes to al them, which with heartie repentaunce and true fayth turne unto hym: haue mercy upon you, pardō and deliuer you from all your synnes, confirme and strength you in all goodnesse, and bryng you to euerlasting life: through Jesus Christ our Lord. Amen.

Then shall the Priest also saye.

Heare what comfortable wordes our sauioure Christe sayth, to al that truly turne to hym.

Come unto me all that trauaile and be heauy laden, and I shal refreshe you. So God loued the worlde, that he gaue hys only begotten sonne, to thende that al that beleue in him, shoulde not perishe, but haue lyfe euerlastynge.

Heare also what sainct Paul sayeth.

278

This is a true saying, and worthy of al men to be receiued, that Jesus Christe came into the worlde to saue synners.

Heare also what Sainct John sayeth.

If any man synne, we haue an aduocate with the father, Jesus Christ the righteous, and he is the propiciacion for our synnes.

¶ *After the whiche, the priest shal procede, saying.*

Lyfte up your heartes.

Aunswere.

We lyfte them up unto the Lorde.

Priest.

Let us geue thankes unto our Lorde God.

Aunswere.

It is mete and ryghte so to doe.

Priest.

It is very mete, righte, and oure bounden duetie, that we should at al times, & in al places, geue thankes unto thee, O Lord holy father, almightie euerlastynge God.

¶ *Here shall folowe the proper Preface, accordinge to the tyme, yf there be any specially appointed: or els immediatly shall folowe. Therefore with Angelles. &c.*

PROPRE PREFACES.

¶ *Upon Christmas daye, and seuen dayes after.*

BEcause thou diddest geue . . . [1549 a]

¶ *Upon Easter daye, and seuen dayes after.*

BUt chieflye are we bounde to prayse thee . . . [1549 a]

¶ *Upon the Ascencion daye, and seuen dayes after.*

THrough thy most dere beloued sōne . . . [1549 b]

¶ *Upon Whitsundaye, and sixe dayes after.*

THrough Jesus Christ our Lorde . . . [1549 a]

¶ *Upon the feast of Trinitie onely.*

IT is very mete, right and our bounden duetie . . . [1549 b]

After whiche preface, shal folowe immediatly.

¶ Therefore with Angelles, and Archangelles, and with al the company of heauen, we laude and magnify thy gloryous neme, euermore praisyng thee, and saying.

Holy, holy, holy, Lorde God of hostes: heauen and earth are full of thy glory: glorye be to thee, O Lorde most hygh.

Then shal the priest, kneling down at Goddes borde, say in the name of all them that shal receiue the Communion, this praier folowynge.

WE doe not presume to come to this thy table (O mercyfull Lorde) trustinge in our owne righteousnesse, but in thy manifolde and greate mercies: we bee not worthye so muche as to gather up the crommes under thy table, but thou art the same Lorde, whose propertie is alwayes to haue mercy: graūt us therfore (gracious lord) so to eate the fleshe of thy dere sonne Jesus Christe, & to drinke his bloud, that our synfull bodyes maye be made cleane by his body, and our soules wasshed through his most precious bloud, and that we may euermore dwel in him, and he in us. Amen.

Then the priest standing up, shal saye as foloweth.

ALmighty God oure heauenly father, whiche of thy tender mercye dyddest geue thine onely sonne Jesus Christ, to suffre death upon the crosse for our redempcion, who made there (by hys one oblacion of hymselfe once offered, a full, perfecte and sufficiente sacrifice, oblacion, and satisfaccion for the synnes of the whole worlde: and dyd institute, and in hys holye Gospell commaunde us, to continue a perpetuall memorye of that his precious death, untyll hys comynge agayn. Heare us O mercyfull father wee beeseche thee: and graunte that wee receyuing these thy creatures of bread and wyne, accordynge to thy sonne our Sauioure Jesu Christes holy institucion, in remembraunce of his death and passion, may be partakers of his most blessed body & bloud: who in the same night that he was betrayed, toke bread, and when he had geuen thankes, he brake it, and gaue it to his Disciples, saying: Take, eate, this is my body which is geuen for you. Doe this in remembraunce of me. Likewise after supper he tooke the cup, and when he had geuen thankes, he gaue it to them, saying: drinke ye all of this, for this is my bloud of the new Testament, whiche is shed for you and for many, for remission of synnes: doe this as ofte as ye shal drinke it in remembraunce of me.

¶ *Then shal the minister first receyue the Communion in*
bothe kyndes him selfe, and next deliuer it to other
ministers, yf any be there present (that they may help
the chief minister) and after to the people in their
handes kneling. And when he delyuereth the bread, he
shall saye.

Take and eate this, in remembraūce that Christ dyed for
thee, and feede on him in thy hearte by faythe, with thankes
geuinge.

¶ *And the minister that delyuereth the cup, shall saye.*

Drinke this in remembraunce that Christes bloude was shed
for thee, and be thankefull.

¶ *Then shall the priest saye the Lordes prayer, the people*
repeating after him euery peticion.

¶ *After shalbe sayde as foloweth.*

O Lorde and heauenly father, we thy humble seruauntes,
entierly desyre thy fatherly goodnes, mercifully to accepte this
our Sacrifice of prayse and thankes geuing: most humbly besechyng thee to graunt that by the merites & death of thy
sonne Jesus Christ, and through faith in his bloud, we and al
thy whole church, may obtaine remission of our synnes, & al
other benefites of his Passion. And here we offre and present
unto thee, O lord, our selfes, our soules & bodies, to be a
reasonable, holy, & liuely Sacrifice unto thee: humbly beseching thee, that all we which be partakers of this holy
Communion, may be fulfilled with thy grace & heauenly
benediccion. And althoughe we bee unworthy, throughe our
manifolde sinnes, to offre unto thee any sacrifice: yet we
beseche thee to accept this our bounden duetie and seruice,
not weighing oure merites, but pardoninge oure offences,
through Jesus Christe oure Lord: by whom and with whom,
in the unitie of the holy gost, al honour and glory be unto thee
O father almightie, worlde withoute ende. Amen.

Or thys.

ALmightie and euerliuinge God, we most hartely thāke thee,
for that thou dooeste vouchsafe to fede us, whiche haue duely
receiued these holy misteries, with the spirituall foode of the
most precious body and bloud of thy sonne our sauiour Jesus
Chryst: and doest assure us thereby of thy fauoure and dood-

nesse towarde us, and that we bee very membres incorporate
in thy mistical body, whiche is the blessed companie of al
faithful people, and be also heyres throughe hope, of thy
euerlastyng kingdome, by the merites of the moste precious
death and Passion of thy deare sonne: we now most humbly
beseche thee, O heauenly father, so to assist us with thy grace,
that we maye continue in that holy felowship, and doe all
suche good workes as thou hast prepared for us to walke in,
throughe Jesus Christ our Lorde: to whom with thee and the
holy goste, be al honour and glory, world without ende.
Amen.

Then shalbe sayd or song.

GLorye bee to God on hyghe. And in earth peace, good wyll
towardes men. We prayse thee, we blesse thee, we worshippe
thee, we glorifie thee, we geue thankes to thee, for thy greate
glorye. O Lorde God heauenlye kyng, god the father almightie. O lord, the only begotten sonne Jesu Christ: O lord
god, Lambe of god, sonne of the father, that takest away the
sinnes of the worlde, haue mercy upō us: Thou that takest
away the sinnes of the worlde, haue mercy upon us. Thou that
takest away the synnes of the world: receiue our prayer. Thou
that sittest at the ryghte hande of God the father, haue mercy
upon us: For thou only art holy: Thou only art the Lord:
Thou only (O Christ) with the holy gost, art most high, in
the glory of god the father. Amen.

*Then the Priest or the Bisshoppe, if he be present, shal
let them depart with this blessyng.*

THe peace of god which passeth all understanding, kepe
youre heartes and myndes in the knowledge and loue of god,
and of hys sonne Jesu Christ our lorde: and the blessing of
god almightie, the father, the sonne, and the holy gost, be
amongest you, and remaine with you alwayes. Amen.

> *Collectes to be saied after the Offertorie, when there
> is no Communyon, euery suche daye one. And the same
> maye be sayed also as often as occasion shall serue, after
> the Collectes, eyther of Mornyng and Euenyng prayer,
> Communion, or Letany, by the discreciō of the minister.*

ASsist us mercifully, O Lorde . . . [1549 a]
O Almightie Lord and euerliuing god . . . [1549 a]
GRaunte we beseche thee . . . [1549 a]

PReuent us O lord . . . [1549 ^b]

ALmightie god, the fountayne of al wisedome . . . [1549 ^a]

ALmightie God, whiche haste promysed . . . [1549 ^a]

¶ *Upō the holy dayes, yf there be no Communion, shalbe sayde all that is appoynted at the Communion, untyl the ende of the Homelie, concluding with the general prayer, for the whole state of Christes churche militante here in earth: and one or moe of these Collectes before rehearsed, as occasyon shal serue.*

¶ *And there shalbe no celebracion of the lordes Supper, excepte there bee a good noumbre to communicate wyth the priest, accordynge to hys discrecion.*

And yf there be not aboue twentie persons in the Parishe, of discrecion to receyue the Communion: yet there shalbe no Communion, excepte foure, or three at the least communicate wyth the prieste. And in Cathedrall & Collegiate churches, where be many Priestes and Deacons, they shall all receyue the Communion wyth the minister euery Sundaye at the least, excepte they haue a reasonable cause to the contrary.

And to take awaye the supersticion, whiche any person hathe, or myghte haue in the bread and wyne: it shall suffyse that the bread bee suche, as is usuall to bee eaten at the Table wyth other meates, but the beste and pureste wheate bread, that conueniently maye be gotten. And yf any of the bread or wine remayne, the Curate shal haue it to hys owne use.

¶ *The bread and wyne for the Communion shall be prouyded by the Curate & the churchwardēs, at the charges of the Parishe, and the Parishe shalbe discharged of such summes of moneye, or other dueties, which hetherto they haue payde for the same, by order of theyr houses euerye Sundaye.*

¶ *And note, that euery Parishioner shall communicate, at the least thre tymes in the yere: of which, Easter to be one: And shal also receyue the Sacramentes, and other rytes, according to the order in this boke appointed. And yerely at Easter, euery Parishioner shal reken with his Person, Vicare, or Curate, or his, or their deputie or deputies, & paye to them or hym, all Ecclesiasticall dueties, accustomably due, then and at that tyme to be payde.*

ALthough no ordre can be so perfectlye deuysed, but it may be of some, eyther for theyr ignoraunce and infirmitie, or els of malice and obstinacie, mysconstrued, depraued, and interpreted in a wrong parte. And yet because brotherly charitie willeth, that so muche as conueniently may be, offences should be taken away: therfore we willing to dooe the same. Wheras it is ordeyned in the booke of common prayer, in the administracion of the Lordes Supper, that the Communicantes kneelynge shoulde receiue the holye Communion: whiche thyng beynge well mente, for a sygnificacyon of the humble and gratefull acknowledgeynge of the benefites of Chriſte, geuen unto the woorthye receyuer, and to auoyde the prophanacion and dysordre whiche about the holye communion myghte elles ensue. Lest yet the same kneelynge myght be thought or taken otherwyse, we dooe declare that it is not mente thereby, that any adoracion is doone, or oughte to bee doone, eyther unto the Sacramentall bread or wyne there bodelye receyued, or unto anye reall and essenciall presence there beeyng of Chrystes naturall fleshe and bloude. For as concernynge the Sacramentall bread and wyne, they remayne styll in theyr verye naturall substaunces, and therfore may not bee adored, for that were Idolatrye to be abhorred of all faythfull christians. And as concernynge the naturall bodye and bloud of our sauiour Christ, they are in heauen and not here: for it is agaynst the trueth of Christes true naturall bodye, to be in moe places then in one at one tyme.

NOTES

1. Transcribed (with deletions as noted) from a microfilm copy of the original text, obtained from the Huntingdon Library.

IX

JOHN KNOX

The Forme of Prayers
Geneva, 1556

KNOX

On the death of Edward VI, in 1553, Mary Tudor brought back the Roman religion to England, and a number of influential Protestants found it expedient to flee the realm. In June, 1554, some two hundred of the exiles took refuge in the hospitable city of Frankfort-am-Main.• They were, however, a divided people. Some were called "Anglicans" because they held, as part and parcel of their evangelical religion, a deep attachment to *The Book of Common Prayer* (1552), which had been framed by godly Englishmen and was soon to be hallowed by their blood. If a revision of the liturgy was needed, they wanted it to be along Anglican lines, and no mere translation of Calvin. Opposed to them stood the "Calvinists," who were intent upon following the Reformer of Geneva in worship as in doctrine. From this

• A congregation of Walloon weavers, lately of Glastonbury, had already arrived. Their leader was Valerand Pullain who had been a presbyter in the French church at Strassburg soon after Calvin's tenure. Given oversight of the Walloons at Glastonbury *ca.* 1550, he established a French church after the manner of that in Strassburg. Moreover, he translated Calvin's Strassburg liturgy into Latin and dedicated it to Edward VI, that perchance it would contribute to the proposed revision of the English Prayer Book, for which reason also he supplied extensive rubrics so that even an outsider could understand the exact nature of the rite. Forsaking Marian England, Pullain led his people to Frankfort; and there, in 1554, he published a further edition of *Liturgia sacra* ("the holy liturgy"), which may have been used by the compilers of *The Forme of Prayers*. The English and Walloon congregations shared the Weissfrauenkirche in Frankfort.

cleavage arose the notorious "troubles at Frankfort," of which William Whittingham kept record in his *Brieff discours*. John Knox was called to minister to this divided people in September, 1554. Although he had formerly spoken favorably of the Prayer Book, he was convinced that it contained "things superstitious, impure, unclean and unperfect."

At first the exiles used an interim liturgy modeled after the Genevan rite. In December, however, they decided to introduce a permanent form of worship; and the suggestion was offered that William Huycke's (1550) English translation of Calvin's order should be used, since it was deemed "moste godly and fardeste off from superstition." That idea did not win swift approval; and when Knox stoutly refused to employ the 1552 Prayer Book because it was partially based on human warrant, affairs at Frankfort reached an impasse. In January, 1555, a committee consisting of Knox, Whittingham, Gilby, Fox, and Cole attempted to settle the dispute by putting aside both the Prayer Book and the Genevan order and arriving at an independent liturgy that would be acceptable to all. But that committee—strange to say—was made up of "Calvinists" to the man, and was quite unable to quit the Genevan liturgy or Huycke's translation of the same. Out of their labors came the first version of *The Forme of Prayers*. Inasmuch as it savored of Geneva, the manuscript was not well received and apparently never used. The "troubles" grew daily more vexing.

Finally, Knox and Whittingham ("Calvinists") and Parry and Lever ("Anglicans") succeeded in bringing out a liturgy of compromise, based on the 1552 Prayer Book. It was accepted in February; and peace endured for a short season. In March, however, Richard Cox arrived with a fresh contingent of Anglicans; and within twelve days they accomplished the fall of John Knox.

Knox repaired to Geneva. In October he was joined there by certain of his collaborators from Frankfort. That little group, augmented by some twenty of their countrymen already in the city, organized an English congregation at the church of Marie la Nove. They drew their liturgy from the unused manuscript prepared at Frankfort, to which they added a collection of metrical psalms and a translation of Calvin's catechism. On February 10, 1556, *The Forme of Prayers* appeared from John Crespin's press.

The English congregation at Geneva existed four years,

enrolled one hundred eighty souls, and provided Knox with
the happiest days of his ministry. But Mary Tudor suc-
cumbed, and, as early as 1559, the exiles began to return to
Elizabethan England. They carried back their liturgy, which
was soon taken up by Englishmen of "Puritan" leanings.
Knox was unwelcome there, on account of his ill-timed tract,
*First Blast of the Trumpet Against the Monstrous Regiment
of Women,* which was aimed at Mary but smote Elizabeth.
So he returned instead to Scotland, full of zeal to reform the
Kirk according to the measure of Geneva, which he pronounced "the maist perfyt schoole of Chryst that ever was in
the erth since the dayis of the Apostillis."

We must remember, however, that the Scottish reformation
was well advanced by 1559. Heretofore the Scots had been
accustomed to use the Anglican Prayer Book (1552), which
was the only such book readily available in English and
which furnished a desirable bond with the English Protestants. In earlier times Knox himself could "think well of" that
Prayer Book which his own stormy preachments had helped
to modify in 1552. Thus, when the Lords of the Congregation
(i.e., the Protestant nobles) entered into their first covenant
in December, 1557, they resolved to adopt "the common
prayers" of the Church of England.

We must also remember that the Scots suffered none of
the restraints of Elizabeth's religious settlement, but were
free to carry forth the reformation of worship as they saw fit.
Knox, having been smitten by the "Anglicans" at Frankfort
and being newly out of favor in Elizabethan England, returned to Scotland with a decided prejudice in favor of
things Genevan. Now he noted certain "diabolicall inven-
tiouns" in the Prayer Book and pronounced Anglican worship
a "mingle-mangle." Thus a preference was given to the Knox
Liturgy, although the Prayer Book was neither suppressed nor
wholly superseded. *The Book of Common Order,* as it came
to be called, was required for the administration of the sacraments in 1562 and for all liturgical purposes in 1564. It
served the Kirk for some eighty years, till the appearance of
the Westminster *Directory,* in 1645.

By structure and text, *The Forme of Prayers* belonged to
the liturgical tradition of Strassburg and Geneva, although
some few parts of the book came immediately from the
English rite, notably the first section of the Communion
Exhortation and portions of the Marriage service. The spirit

of the liturgy was likewise Reformed. The minister enjoyed a large measure of freedom, that, at the inspiration of the Spirit, he might now and then frame his own prayers. Yet he was expected to honor the liturgy, which belonged, after all, to the whole people and was the instrument of "common" worship. Indeed, every means was taken to make worship a corporate action, in which the New Testament Gospel could be expressed with clarity and simplicity. The vernacular was used and loudly spoken, that everyone could participate by the direct medium of speech. As the people were no longer dependent upon ceremonial to follow the service, only the simplest and most useful forms were retained. Even those symbols that were hallowed by time and usage were cast out of the churches if they were apt to mislead the people: It was wrong to proclaim one thing and symbolize another; it was right to say plainly what was meant. The ministers diminished the distinction between clergy and laity by discarding priestly vestments and wearing none but the preaching habit. The Scriptures were translated for the benefit of everyman; and every parish was admonished to have "a Bibill in Inglische," which was to be expounded regularly so that even those who did not read could profit. Psalms were cast into metrical forms and set to common tunes, in order to give the people themselves a voice in worship. A complete Psalter appeared in *The Book of Common Order* of 1564.

It is unlikely, however, that the minister conducted worship from the Communion table, as the custom was at Strassburg and probably at Geneva. According to the third Communion rubric, the greater part of the Sunday service was read from the pulpit, perhaps for acoustical reasons. Yet the symbolism remained strong at two salient points. First, the pulpit and table, together, were the most powerful signs in Scottish worship, being symbols of the Word that goes forth to the people, and of the sustenance of Holy Communion. Both meant that God comes to men, that he *speaks* and *gives* to his people, and invites them, before all else, to hear his Word of judgment and reconciliation and to receive his gifts of forgiveness and sonship. True worship occurs when the Word of God is given and received in the church by audible and visible means, and the church makes its response of praise and prayer, trust and obedience. Second, the Sunday service was based upon the Eucharist, for its origins can be traced, through Calvin and Bucer, to the German Mass of Diobald

Schwarz. Thus, on those Sundays when the Eucharistic portions were necessarily omitted the liturgy took the form of Ante-Communion. But we must admit that in Scotland, where the Supper was celebrated infrequently, the union of Word and Sacrament was not as palpably experienced as elsewhere in the Reformed tradition; and the use of the pulpit, instead of the table, as the locus of worship may reflect this separation.

The word "Sermon," as it was used in these rubrics, meant both lesson and proclamation—one inseparable element, which was delivered according to the method called *lectio continua*. Said the first *Book of Discipline* (1560):

> We think it most expedient that the Scripturis be red in ordour, that is, that some one buke of the Auld and the New Testament be begun and ordourlie red to the end. And the same we judge of preching. . . . For this skipping and divagatioun frome place to place of the Scripture, be it in reiding or be it in precheing, we judge not so proffitabill to edifie the Churche as the continewall following of ane text.

Scarcely anything was less appropriate of a minister than he presume to control or obscure God's way among men by parceling out the Scriptures in bits and snatches. On the contrary, the Scriptures should be expounded book by book, chapter by chapter, in a continuous and orderly fashion. This procedure also implied that the sermon was not precisely the preacher's device to warm hearts, win souls, inculcate piety for the oncoming week. It was the Word of God, made real, alive, and effective in the hearts of men through the action of the Holy Spirit.

The first Communion rubric suggested a monthly celebration of the Lord's Supper in the English congregation of Geneva. That rubric, though repeated in the Scottish editions, was soon overcome by the first *Book of Discipline,* which declared that "foure tymes in the yeare" was "sufficient" for the Eucharist. And since care was to be taken to avoid "the superstitioun of tymes" (i.e., the Church Year), the first Sundays in March, June, September, and December were arbitrarily appointed. The drift toward occasional Communion, which became exaggerated in actual practice, was caused perhaps by a shortage of ministers and by popular reluctance to communicate so often. At least it did not derive from a

Zwinglian view of the Supper. "We utterly damn," said the first *Scots Confession,* "the vanity of those who affirm sacraments to be nothing else but naked and bare signs." The approved doctrine was set forth in that confession and somewhat more simply in the Communion Exhortation of the liturgy: "We spiritually eate the fleshe of Christ, and drinke his bloude; then we dwell in Christ, and Christ in vs; we be one with Christ, and Christ with vs."

In an appendix ("To the Reader") of the Communion liturgy, the compilers gave a full rationale of "this holy action," in which nothing was to be attempted without Christ's "woorde and warrante." First came the *Words of Institution,* which were not rehearsed to effect a Consecration, but rather to set forth the warrant and true manner of the sacrament ("to teache vs how to behaue our selues in this action") and perhaps also to fulfill the Augustinian requirement that the Word must be joined to the sacrament to make it valid. There followed an *Exhortation* to self-examination "according to saint Pauls rule," in the course of which the unworthy were fenced from the table. Then came the *fourfold action* of the liturgy: "Takyng bread, wee geue thankes, breake, and distribute it, as Christe our sauior hath taught vs."

The Forme of Prayers made no provision for a consecration of the elements. The Word, which supplied validity and reality to the sacrament, was not addressed to the bread and wine, as if to change them; it was addressed to the people, so (said the appendix) that "Christe might witnes vnto owr faithe, as it were, with his owne mowthe," promising us the communion of his body and blood. Thus, the essential point was the lively preaching of the promises of Christ, which underlay the Lord's Supper; and such preaching, whether it be the sermon or the Words of Institution, was addressed to those who proposed to communicate. Moreover, the relationship between the sacramental action and the Word that had been spoken was never to be taken lightly. At St. Andrews, for instance, the church doors were locked after the sermon, so that only those who had "heard the preaching should communicate." And the elements were purposely withheld from the table until the time of the second psalm, that is, immediately after the sermon, immediately before the Words of Institution.

The Communion Exhortation commenced with self-examination and the excommunication of the unworthy; it proceeded to invite to the table all those who sought their "life and perfection in Iesu Christ"; and it closed with the typical Reformed admonition not to cleave to "the earthlie and corruptible" signs, as if Christ were "inclosed in the breade or wyne," but "to lift vp our mindes by fayth . . . into heauen, that we may finde and receiue Christ where he dwelleth." Though its initial paragraphs were drawn from the 1552 Prayer Book, the Exhortation gave full expression to the Reformed concern for discipline, upon which the integrity of the church was thought to depend. The Lord's Supper was reserved for those who were distinguished by sincerity of faith and holiness of life, and who were therefore fit to engage in this Holy Communion with Christ and with one another as members of his Body. The unfaithful, who were strangers to Christ, and the callous sinners, whose conduct made it plain that they did not belong to him either, were denied a place at his table, lest the sacrament be profaned and they be guilty of the Lord's body and blood. The Scots maintained a disciplinary system, which included, besides the fencing of the table, a greater and a lesser excommunication, and the use of Communion tokens that could be withheld for deficiencies in conduct, charity, or Christian knowledge.

At the end of the Exhortation, the minister left the pulpit and took his place at "the holy table." The communicants likewise came forward and sat down at the table, which was ample in size and usually arranged in a U or T shape in the chancel or on the floor of the nave. Such was the setting for the fourfold action. The minister *took bread.* He *gave thanks,* using an original prayer that was truly Eucharistic in its scope; it included adoration, thanksgiving for creation and redemption, a brief anamnesis, and a doxology. Some ministers, who found the liturgy deficient in the matter of Consecration, supplied an epiclesis at this time. Then the minister *broke the bread,* taking care to make the Fraction a distinct feature of the action. Finally, having partaken himself, he *delivered the bread* to the people, who "divided" the same among themselves. This manner of delivery, which had been practiced in the 1550's in the Strangers' Church of London, was conceived to be at Christ's command; and it obviated kneeling at the reception, which was so abhorrent to Knox. It also implied that the Lord's table was appointed for the whole family of God. By sitting down together and by serving the elements to one another, the people were able to realize their fellowship and mutual priesthood in the Body of Christ. Pew Communion was the way of the English Nonconformists; and the Scots did not hesitate to brand it a "mangling of the sacrament"—until, alas, a Glasgow divine introduced it to the Scottish Kirk in the first quarter of the nineteenth century.

FOR FURTHER READING

A brieff discours off the troubles begonne at Franckford in Germany. Presumably the work of William Whittingham. Edited by Edward Arber. London, 1908.

George B. Burnet, *The Holy Communion in the Reformed Church of Scotland.* Edinburgh, 1960.

Gordon Donaldson, *The Making of the Scottish Prayer Book of 1637.* Edinburgh, 1954.

William McMillan, *The Worship of the Scottish Reformed Church, 1550-1638.* London, 1931.

W. D. Maxwell, *A History of Worship in the Church of Scotland.* London, 1955.

W. D. Maxwell, *John Knox's Genevan Service Book, 1556.* Edinburgh, 1931.

294

THE FORME OF PRAYERS[1]
AND MINISTRATION OF THE SACRAMENTS,
&c. VSED IN THE
ENGLISHE CONGREGATION AT GENEUA:
AND APPROUED, BY THE
FAMOUS AND GODLY LEARNED MAN,
IOHN CALUYN.

GENEVA M.D.LVI.

THE PROPHECIE [2]
INTERPRETATION OF THE SCRIPTURES.

Everie weeke once, the congregation assemble to heare some place of the scriptures orderly expounded. At which tyme, it is lawfull for euery man to speake or enquire as God shall moue his harte, and the text minister occasiō, so it be without pertinacitee or disdayne, as one that rather seketh to proffit then to contend. And if so be any contencion rise, then suche as are appointed moderatours, either satisfie the partie, or els if he seme to cauill, exhorte hym to kepe silence, referring the iudgement therof to the ministers, and elders, to be determined in their assemblie or consistorie before mencioned.

THE PRAYERS.[3]

When the cōgregation is assembled, at the houre appointed, the minister vseth one of these two confessions, or lyke in effect: exhorting the people diligētly, to examine thēselues, following in their hartes the tenor of his wordes.

A CONFESSION OF OVR SYNNES, FRAMED
to our tyme, out of the 9. chap. of Daniel.[4]

O lord God which arte mightie, and dreadeful, thou that kepest couenant, and shewest mercie to theym that loue thee, and do thy commaundementes: we haue synned, we haue offended, we haue wickedly, and stubburnely gone backe, frome thy lawes, and preceptes. We wolde neuer obey thy seruantes the Prophetes that spake in thy name, to our kinges and princes, to our forfathers, and to all the people of our lande. O lord rightuousnes belongeth vnto thee, vnto vs,

295

perteyneth nothing but open shame, as it ys come to passe this day, vnto our miserable contry of Englande, yea vnto all our nation whether they be farre, or nere, through all landes, wherein they are scattered for the offences that they and we haue committed against thee: so that the curses and ponishmentes which are wryten in thy lawe, are nowe powred vpon vs, and thou hast perfourmed those wordes wherwith thou didest menace vs and our rulers, that gouerned vs, in bringinge the same plagues vpon vs which before were threatened. And yet notwithstandinge bothe they, and we procede in our iniquitie and sease not to heape synne vpon synne. For they which once were well instructed in the doctrine of thy gospel, are nowe gone backe frome the obedience of thy trueth, and are turned agayne to that moste abhominable Idolatrie, from the which they were once called by the lyuely preachinge of thy worde. And we alas, to this day do not earnestly repent vs of our former wickednes, neither do we rightly consider, the heauynes of thy displeasure. Suche is thy iuste iudgementes (ò lord) that thou ponishes synne by synne, and man by his owne inuentions, so that there can be no ende of iniquitie, except thou preuent[5] vs with thy vndeserued grace. Therfore conuert vs (ò lord) and we shalbe conuerted: for we do not offer vp our prayers trustinge in our owne rightuousnes, but in thy manifolde mercies. And althoghe thou haste once of thy especial grace deliuered vs frõm the miserable thraldome of error and blindnes, and called vs many tymes, to the swet libertie of thy gospell which we notwithstãdīge haue moste shamefully abused, in obeinge rather our owne lustes, and affections, then the admonitions of thy prophetes: yet we beseche thee once agayne for thy nams sake, to powre some comfortable droppe of thy accustomed mercies vpon vs: incline thyne eares, and open thyne eyes, to beholde the greuous plagues of our contrie, the continuall sorrowes of our afflicted bretherne, and our wofull banishment. And let our afflictions and iuste ponishemente be an admonition and warninge to other nations, emongest whome we are skattered that with all reuerence they may obey thy holy gospell: lest for like contempte, in the ende, like, or wourse plagues fall vpon theym. Wherfore ò lord heare vs, ò lord forgiue vs, ò lord consider and tary not ouer longe, but for thy deare sonne Iesus Christe sake, be mercifull vnto vs, and delyuer vs. So shall it be knowen to all the worlde, that thou onely

296

arte the selfe same God, that euer sheweth mercie, to all
suche, as call vpon thy holy name.

AN OTHER CONFESSION
for all states and tymes.

O Eternall God and moste mercifull father, we confesse,
and acknowlage, here before thy diuine maiestie, that we
are miserable synners, conceyued and borne in synne and
iniquitie, so that in vs there is no goodnes. For the fleshe
euermore rebelleth against the spirite, wherby we con-
tynually transgresse thy holy preceptes, and commaundementes, and so purchase to our selues, through thy iuste
iudgement, death and damnation. Notwithstandinge (ò
heauenly father) forasmoche as we are displeased with our
selues for the synnes, that we haue committed against thee,
and do vnfeynedly repent vs of the same: we moste humbly
beseche thee, for Iesus Christes sake, to shewe thy mercie
vpon vs, to forgiue vs all our synnes, and to increase thy holy
spirite in vs: that we acknowlaginge, from the botome of our
hartes, our owne vnrightuousnes, may from hensforth, not
onely mortifie our sinfull lustes and affections, but also bringe
forth suche fruites, as may be agreable to thy moste blessed
wyll,[6] not for the worthynes thereof, but for the merites of
thy dearely beloued sonne Iesus Christe our onely sauyour,
whom thou hast already giuen an oblation and offeringe for
our synnes: and for whose sake, we are certainly persuaded,
that thou wylt denye vs nothinge, that we shall aske in his
name, accordinge to thy wyl. For thy spirite doth assure
our consciences, that thou arte our mercifull father, and so
louest vs thy childrene through hym, that nothinge is able
to remoue thy heauenlye grace, and fauor, from vs: to thee
therfore ò father, with the sonne and the holy ghoste, be all
honor, and glorye, worlde with owt ende. So beit.

*This done, the people singe a Psalme all together, in a
playne tune, which ended, the minister prayeth for thassist-
ance of Gods holy spirite as the same shall moue his harte,
and so procedeth to the sermon,[7] Vsinge after the sermon
this prayer followinge or suche lyke.*

A PRAYER FOR THE WHOLE ESTATE
OF CHRISTES CHURCHE[8]

297

Almightie God, and moste mercifull father we humbly submit our selues and fall downe before thy maiestie, besechinge thee frome the botome of our hartes, that this seede of thy worde, nowe sowen emongest vs, may take suche depe roote, that neither the burninge heate of persecution, cause it to wither, nether the thorny cares of this lyfe, do choke it, but that as seede sowen in good grownde, it may bringe forth thirtie, sixtie, ād an hundreth folde, as thy heauenly wisdome, hathe appointed. And becawse we haue nede continuallie, to craue many thinges at thy handes, we humbly beseche thee (ò heauēly father) to graunt vs thy holy spirite, to directe our peticions, that they may procede, frome suche a feruēt mynde, as may be agreable to thy moste blessed wyll. And seinge that our infirmitie is hable to do nothinge, without thy helpe: and that thou arte not ignorant with how many, and greate temptations, we poore wretches, are on euery side inclosed, and compassed: let thy strenghe (ò lord) susteyne our weaknes, that we beinge defended, with the force of thy grace, may be sauely preserued, against all assaultes of Satan: who goeth abowte cōtinually, like a roaringe lyō sekinge to deuoure vs. Encrease our faith (ò mercifull father) that we do not swarue at any tyme, frome thy heauēly worde, but augment in vs, hope, and loue, with a carefull kepinge of all thy commaundementes: that no hardnes of harte, no hypocrisie, no concupiscence of the eys, nor intysementes of the worlde, do drawe vs away, frome thy obedience. And, seinge we lyue nowe in these moste perillous tymes, let thy fatherly prouidēce defende vs, against the violence of all our enemies, which do euery where pursue vs: but chiefely againste the wicked rage, and furious vproares of that Romyshe idoll, ennemie to thy Christe. Fordermore forasmoche as by thy holy Aposile we be taught, to make our prayers, and supplications for all men, we praye not onely for our selues here present, but beseche the also, to reduce all suche as be yet ignorant, from the miserable captiuitie of blindnes and error, to the pure vnderstandinge, and knowlage, of thy heauenly trueth: that we all, with one consent and vnitie of myndes, may wourshippe thee our onely God and sauiour. And that all Pastors, shepherds, and ministers, to whome thou hast committed the dispensation of thy holy woord, and charge of thy chosen people, may bothe in their lyfe and doctrine, be fownde faithfull: settinge onely before their eyes, thy glorie: and that by theim all poore shepe which wander and go astray, may be gathered, ād broght home to thy foulde. More-ouer, becawse the hartes of rulers are in thy hands, we beseche thee to direct, and gouerne, the hartes of all kinges, Princes, and Magistrates, to whome thou haste cōmitted the sworde, especially (ò lord) accordinge to ourbondendutie, we beseche thee to mainteyne ād increase, the honorable estate of this Citie, into whose defense we are receyued: the Magistrates, the counsell, and all the whole bodye of this commō weale. Let thy fatherlye fauor so preserue theym, and thy holy spirite so gouerne their hartes, that they may in suche sorte execute their office that thy religion may be purely mainteyned, māners refourmed, ād synne ponished accordinge to the precise rule of thy holy woord. And for that we be all mēbres of the mysticall body of Christ Iesu, we make our requestes vnto the (ò heauenly father) for all suche as are afflicted with any kinde of crosse, or tribulation, as warre, plague, famine, sickenes, pouertie, imprisonement, persecution, banishemēt, or any other kinde of thy roddes: whether it be calamitie of bodie, or vexation of mynde, that it wold please thee, to gyue them pacience, and constancie, tyll thou send them full deliuerance, of all their troubles. And as we be bownde to loue, and honor our parentes, kins-folkes, friendes, and contrye: so we moste humbly beseche thee, to shewe thy pitie, vpon our miserable contrie of Eng-land, which once through thy mercie, was called to libertie, and now for their and our synnes, is broght vnto moste vile slauery, and Babylonicall bondage. Roote owte from thence (ò lord) all raueninge wolues which to fyll their bellies, destroie thy flocke. And shewe thy great mercies vpon those our bretherne, which are persecuted, cast in prison, and dayly condemned to deathe, for the testimonie of thy trueth. And thogh they be vtterly destitute of all mans ayde, yet let thy swete comfort neuer departe frome them: but so inflame their hartes, with thy holy spirite, that thei may boldely and chearefully abide suche tryall, as thy godly wisdome shall appoint. So that at lenght• aswell by their deathe, as by their life, the kingdome of thy sonne Iesus Christ, may increase, and shyne through all the worlde. In whose name, we make our humble peticions vnto thee, as he hath taught vs.

Our father Which arte in heauen. etc.

• Misprint: length.

Almightie and euer lyuinge God, vouchsaue we beseche thee, to grant vs perfite contynuance in thy liuely faith, augmentinge the same in vs dayly, tyll we growe to the full measure of our perfection in Christ, wherof we make our confession, sayinge.

I beleue in God. &c.[9]

Then the people singe a Psalme, which ended, the minister pronounceth one of these blessinges, and so the congregation departeth.

The lord blesse you, and saue you, the lord make his face shyne vpon you, and be mercifull vnto you, the lord turne his countenance towardes you, and graunt you his peace.

The grace of our lord Iesus Christ, the loue of God, and communion of the holie ghoste, be with you all: so be it.

It shall not be necessarie for the minister dayly to repete all these thinges before mentioned, but beginnynge with some maner of confession, to procede to the sermon. which ended, he either vseth the prayer, for all estates before mentioned, or els prayeth, as the spirite of God shall moue his harte: framinge the same, according to the tyme and matter which he hath intreated of. And yf there shalbe at any tyme, any present plague, famine, pestilence, warre, or such like, which be euident tokens of Gods wrath: as it is our parte to acknowlage our synnes to be the occasion therof, so are we appointed by the scriptures to giue our selues to mournynge, fastinge, and prayer, as the meanes to turne awaye Gods heauie displeasure. Therfore, it shalbe conuenient, that the minister at suche tyme, do not onely admonyshe the people therof, but also vse some forme of prayer, accordinge as the present necessitie requireth, to the which he may appoint, by a common consent, some seuerall daye after the sermon wekely to be obserued.[10]

THE MANER OF THE LORDES SVPPER [11]

The day when the lordes supper is ministred which commōlye is vsed once a monthe,[12] or so oft as the Congregation shall thinke expedient, the minister vseth to saye as followeth.

Let vs marke deare bretherne, and cōsider how Iesus Christ did ordayne vnto vs his holy supper according as S. Paule

maketh rehearsall in the 11. chap. of the first Epistle to the
Cor. I haue (saith he) receyued of the lorde that which I
haue deliuered vnto you, to witt, that the lorde Iesus the same
night he was betrayed toke breade, and when he had geuen
thankes, he brake it sayinge. Take ye, eate ye, this is my
bodie, which is broken for you: doo you this in remēbrance of
me. Likewise after supper, he toke the cuppe, sayīge. This
cuppe is the newe testamēt or couenāt in my bloude; doo ye
this so ofte as ye shall drinke therof, in remēbrance of me. For
so ofte as you shal eate this bread, and drinke of this cuppe,
ye shall declare the lordes deathe vntill his cōminge. Therfore
whosoeuer shall eate this bread, and drinke the cuppe of the
lorde vnworthely, he shalbe giltie of the bodye and bloud of
the lord. Then see that euerymā proue ād trye hym selfe,
ād so let hym eate of this bread ād drīke of this cuppe, for
whosoeuer eateth or drinketh vnworthelye, he eateth and
drinketh his owne damnation, for not hauinge due regarde
and consideration of the lordes bodye.

This done, the minister proceadith to the exhortation.

Dearely beloued in the lorde, forasmoch as we be nowe
assembled, to celebrate the holy communion of the body and
bloud of our sauiour Christ, let vs consider these woordes of
S. Paule, how he exhorteth all persons diligently to trye and
examine thē selues, before they presume to eate of that bread,
ād drinke of that cuppe. For as the benefite ys great, if with a
truly penitent hart, and liuely faith, we receyue that holy
sacrament (for then we spiritually eate the fleshe of Christ,
and drinke his bloude, thē we dwell in Christ, ād Christ in
vs, we be one with Christ, and Christ with vs) so is the
daūger great, if we receyue the same vnworthely, for then we
be giltie of the bodye, and bloud of Christ our sauiour, we
eate ād drīke our own dānation, not considering the lordes
bodye: we kīdle godes wrath agaīst vs, ād prouoke him to
plague vs with diuerse diseases and sundry kindes of death.
Therfore if any of you be a blasphemer of God, an hinderer
or slaunderer of his worde, an adulterer, or be in malice or
enuie, or in any other greuous cryme, bewaylle your synnes,
and come not to this holy table: lest after the takynge of
this holy sacramēt, the diuell entre into you as he entred into
Iudas, and fill you full of all iniquities, and bring you, to
destruction, bothe of bodye and soule. Iudge therfore your
selues bretherne, that ye be not iudged of the lorde: repent

301

you truly for your synnes paste, and haue a lyuely and stedfast fayth, in Christ our sauiour,[13] sekinge onely your saluation in the merites of his death, and passion, from hensforth
refusinge, and forgettinge all malice and debate, with full
purpose to liue in brotherly amytie, and godlye conuersation,
all the dais of your lyfe. And albeit we fele in ourselues muche
frailtie and wretchednes, as that we haue not our faith so
perfite, and constant, as we ought, being many tymes readye
to distruste Godes goodnes through our corrupt nature,
and also that we are not so throughlye geuen to serue
God, neyther haue so feruent a zeale to set forth his glory,
as our duetye requireth, felinge still such rebellion in our
selues, that we haue nede dayly to fight against the lustes
of our fleshe, yet neuertheles seinge that our lorde hath dealed
thus mercifully with vs, that he hath printed his gospell in
our hartes, so that, we are preserued from falling into des-
peratiō and misbeliefe: and seing also he hath indued vs with
a will, and desire to renownce and withstand our own affections, with a longing for his righteousenes and the keping of
his commaundementes, we may be now right well assured,
that those defautes and manifolde imperfections in vs, shalbe
no hinderance at all against vs, to cause him not to accept
and impute vs as worthie to come to his spirituall table, For
the ende of our comming thyther, is not to make protestation,
that we are vpright or iuste in our liues, but contrariwise, we
come to seke our life and perfectiō, in Iesu Christ, acknowledging in the meane tyme, that we of our selues, be the
children of wrath, and damnation. Let vs consider then, that
this sacrament is a singuler medicine for all poore sicke
creatures, a comfortable helpe to weake soules, and that our
lord requireth no other worthines on our parte, but that we
vnfaynedly acknowlege our noghtines, and imperfection. Then
to the end that we may be worthy partakers of his merites, ād
moste comfortable benefits (which ys the true eatinge of
his fleshe, and drinkinge of his bloud) let vs not suffer our
mindes to wander aboute the consideration of these earthlie,
ād corruptible thynges (which we see present to our eies and
fele with our hādes) to seeke Christ bodely presente in thē,
as if he were inclosed in the breade or wyne, or as yf these
elementes were tourned and chaunged into the substaunce, of
his fleshe and blood.・ For the only waye to dispose our soules

・ Transsubstantiation, Transelemētatiō, Transmutation and Transformation as the papistes vse them are the doctrine of diuells.

to receiue norishment, reliefe, and quikening of his substance, is to lift vp our mindes by fayth aboue all thinges wordlye• and sensible, and therby to entre into heauen, that we may finde, and receiue Christ,•• where he dwelleth vndoutedlye verie God, and verie man, in the incomprehensible glorie of his father, to whome be all praise, honor and glorye now and euer. Amen.

The exhortation ended, the minister commeth doune from the pulpet,[14] and sitteth at the Table, euery man and woman in likewise takinge their place as occasion best serueth, then he taketh bread and geueth thankes, either in these woordes followinge, or like in effect.

O Father of mercye and God of all consolation, seinge all creatures do knowlege and confesse thee, as gouerner, and lorde, it becommeth vs the workemanship of thyne own handes, at all tymes to reuerence and magnifie thy godli maiestie, first for that thou haste created vs to thyne own Image and similitude: but chieflye that thou haste deliuered vs, from that euerlasting death and damnation into the which Satā drewe mankinde by the meane of synne: from the bondage wherof (neither man nor angell was able to make vs free) but thou (ò lord) riche in mercie and infinite in goodnes, haste prouided our redemption to stande in thy onely and welbeloued sone: whom of verie loue thou didest giue to be made man, lyke vnto vs in all thynges, (synne except) that in his bodye he myght receiue the ponishmentes of our transgression, by his death to make satisfaction to thy iustice, and by his resurrection to destroye hym that was auctor of death, and so to reduce and bring agayne life to the world, frome which the whole ofspringe of Adame moste iustly was exiled. O lord we acknowlege that no creature ys able to comprehende the length and breadthe, the depenes and height, of that thy most excellent loue which moued thee to shewe mercie, where none was deserued: to promise and giue life, where death had gotten victorie: to receue vs into thy grace, when we could do nothyng but rebell against thy iustice. O lord the blynde dulnes of our corrupt nature will not suffer vs sufficiently to waye these thy moste ample benefites: yet neuertheles at the commaundement of Iesus Christ our lorde, we present our selues to this his table (which

• Misprint: worldlye.
•• The true eatyng of Christ in the sacrament.

303

he hath left to be vsed in remembrance of his death vntyll hys comming agayne) to declare and witnes before the world, that by him alone we haue receued libertie, and life: that by hym alone, thou doest acknowledge vs thy chyldren and heires: that by hym alone, we haue entrance to the throne of thy grace: that by hym alone we are possessed in our spirituall kingedome, to eate and drinke at his table: with whome we haue our conuersation presently in heauen, and by whome, our bodies shalbe reysed vp agayne frome the dust, and shalbe placed with him in that endles ioye, which thow (ò father of mercye) hast prepared for thyne elect, before the foundation of the worlde was layde. And these moste inestimable benefites, we acknowlege and cõfesse to haue receaued of thy free mercie and grace, by thy on'ely beloued sonne Iesus Christ, for the which therfore we thy congregation moued by thy holy sprite render thee all thankes, prayse, and glorie for euer and euer.

This done, the minister breaketh the breade and delyuereth it to the people, who distribute and deuide thesame amongst theim selues, accordinge to our sauiour Christes cõmande-ment, and in likewise geueth the cuppe. Duringe the which tyme, some place of the scriptures is read, which doth lyuely set forth the death of Christ, to theintene that our eyes and senses may not onely be occupiede in these outwarde signes of bread and wyne, which are called the visible woorde: but that our hartes and myndes also may be fully fixed in the contemplation of the lordes death, which is by this holy sacrament representede. And after the action is done, he geueth thanckes, saing.[15]

Moste mercifull father,[16] we render to the all prayse thankes and glorie, for that thou hast vouchsafed to graunt vnto vs miserable synners so excellent a gifte and threasor, as to receaue vs into the felowship and company of thy deare sonne Iesus Christ our lorde, whome thou deliueredst to deathe for vs, and haste giuē hym vnto us, as a necessarie foode and norishment vnto euerlastynge life. And now we beseche the also (ò heauenly father) to graunt vs this request, that thou neuer suffer vs to become so vnkinde as to forget so worthy benefittes: but rather imprint and fasten them sure in our hartes, that we may growe and increase dayly more and more in true faithe, which continually ys excersised in all maner of goode workes, and so moche the rather ò lord,

304

cōfirme vs, in these perelous daies and rages of satan, that we may constanly· stande and continewe in the confession of the same to the aduancement of thy glorye, which art God ouer all things blessed for euer. So be it.

The action thus ended, the people singe the 103 psal. My soule giue laud &c. or some other of thancks giuynge, which ended, one of the blessings before mencionede is recitede, and so they ryse from the table and departe.

To the reader.

If parchaunce any wolde maruell why we followe rather this order, then any other in the administration of this sacrament, let him diligently consider, that first of all we vtterly renownce the error of the papistes: secondly we restore vnto the sacramētes theyr owne substaunce: and to Christe his proper place. And as for the wordes of the lordes supper we rehearce theym not bicawse they shuld chaunge the substaunce of the bread or wyne, or that the repeticion therof with the intent of the sacrificer should make the sacrament as the papistes falselie beleue: but they are read and pronownced to teache vs how to behaue our selues in this actiō ād that Christe might witnes vnto owr faithe as it were with his owne mowthe, that he hath ordayned these signes for our spirituall vse and comforte. wee do firste therefore examyne owr selues, accordyng to saint Pauls rule, and prepare our myndes that we may be worthie partakers of so high mysteries. Then takyng bread, wee geue thankes, breake, and distribute it, as Christe our sauior hath taught vs. Fynally the ministration ended, we gyue thankes agayne accordyng to his example. So that without his woorde, and warrante, there is nothyng in this holy action attempted.

NOTES

1. The text has been reproduced exactly—spelling, punctuation, and paragraphing—from a microfilm of the original volume obtained from the National Library, Edinburgh. Marginal references to Scripture have been omitted, and the rubrics italicized.
2. Original edition, pp. 50f. For the type of prophecy practiced by Zwingli, cf. the Zurich church-order of 1535, *CR* 4: 701.

· Misprint: constantly.

The Scottish prophecy corresponds somewhat more to the version of John à Lasco, published in *Forma ac Ratio* and used in the Strangers' Church of London; cf. Kuyper, *Joannis à Lasco Opera*, II, 101-4.

3. Original edition, pp. 52-63. In both Scottish and Puritan practice, a "Reader's Service" was prefixed to the Sunday Morning Service. That office, conducted by a lay reader whom the elders appointed, preceded the main service by an hour or so, while the full congregation assembled; its purpose was to read through the Scriptures and engage the people in the singing of psalms. Readers were appointed in Scotland beginning in 1560; cf. Laing, *Works of John Knox*, II, 195-6, 238. W. D. Maxwell suggests that the origin of the office lies in Matins: *John Knox's Genevan Service Book*, App. A, pp. 177-9. For the Puritan practice, cf. the initial rubric in the Middleburg Liturgy (below).

4. An original composition, found in neither Calvin nor Pullain, but framed (as the title suggests) to express the sense of national calamity that had overtaken Marian England. Omitted in *BCO*, 1562ff.; omitted also in the Middleburg Liturgy.

5. In the sense of *praevenire:* to precede, to go before.

6. To this point: Calvin's Prayer of Confession. For its origin, cf. Bucer's second Confiteor, which he himself composed. Calvin adapted it; Huycke and Pullain reproduced it. The remainder is a Petition for Pardon, added by the compilers to replace an Absolution.

7. "Sermon" included both lesson and proclamation, as one inseparable element. The lesson was read "in course." Bucer permitted only the Gospels to be expounded on Sunday morning (cf. his rubric). Calvin followed the same practice (*Calv. opera* VI, 194-6), while Pullain allowed the entire New Testament to be used (*Liturgia sacra*, 1554 edition, pp. 61f.). In accord with à Lasco (*Opera*, II, 82), Knox opened both Testaments to Sunday morning preaching, probably in Geneva (*Works*, IV, 138f.) and certainly in Scotland according to the first *Book of Discipline* (*Works*, II, 240-1).

On Communion Sunday, attendance at the sermon was virtually a prerequisite for participation in the sacrament. In 1598 the Session of St. Andrews ordered the doors to be locked at "the end of the Psalm" so that only those who "heard the preaching should communicate." W. D. Maxwell, *John Knox's Genevan Service Book*, p. 143, n. 16.

8. An original composition, with some verbal resemblance to Calvin's Great Prayer.

9. A prose version of the Creed, recited by the minister alone. In the Reformed Communion service, a metrical Creed was often sung by the people while the elements were brought to the table. Cf. *Calv. opera*, VI, 197; Pullain's *Liturgia sacra*,

1551 edition, p. 7. In the English congregation of Geneva, which apparently lacked a metrical version of the Creed, the elements were brought forward during the psalm that followed.

10. In Pullain's congregation, a service of Repentance was conducted on Thursday; cf. *Liturgia sacra*, 1554 edition, p. 25.

11. Original edition, pp. 71-80.

12. Thus monthly Communion was the practice of the English congregation in Geneva. The rubric remained unchanged in the Scottish editions; but it was overcome by the first *Book of Discipline*, which declared that "four tymes a yeare" was "sufficient" for the Eucharist. Permission was given "to minister ofter," granted there were "reasonable causses." Laing, *Works of John Knox*, II, 239f.

13. To this point, the Exhortation corresponds to that of the BCP, 1552, which was composed by Cranmer; cf. F. E. Brightman, *The English Rite*, II, 650-2, 677-9. The remainder was taken directly from Calvin's Exhortation, or, more likely, from Huycke's translation of the same. The *Sursum corda*, at the end, can be traced ultimately to Farel's *La Maniere et fasson* (ed. Baum), pp. 64, 65.

14. Does this not indicate that the greater part of Knox's liturgy was conducted from the pulpit?

15. The Fraction, conceived as a separate and distinct part of the action, was typical of Reformed practice at this time and has continued so in the Scottish church; cf. W. D. Maxwell, *John Knox's Genevan Service Book*, p. 136, n. 6. An order of receiving was not specified, although it was the Reformed custom, except in Strassburg and in the Danish Calvinist church, to have the ministers' Communion precede that of the people; cf. W. D. Maxwell, *John Knox's Genevan Service Book*, App. F, pp. 206-9. The method of Delivery, with the people seated at the table, resembles à Lasco's practice in *Forma ac Ratio;* cf. Kuyper, *Joannis à Lasco Opera*, II, 162ff. For Calderwood's complete description of the Scottish method of Delivery, ca. 1623, cf. G. W. Sprott, *The Book of Common Order*, pp. xxxviii-ix. Words of Delivery, though not specified, were used in Scottish and Puritan practice; cf. the Communion rubric in the Middleburg Liturgy (below), the relevant passage in the Westminster *Directory* (below), and W. D. Maxwell, *John Knox's Genevan Service Book*, pp. 138-9, n. 9. Silence was not kept during the Reformed Communion. Zwingli, Knox, and à Lasco prescribed the reading of Scripture; Calvin at Geneva, Pullain at Frankfort, and the Palatinate Liturgy permitted either the singing of psalms or the reading of Scripture. At Strassburg, singing was the custom in the congregations of both Bucer and Calvin.

16. Adapted from Calvin, who in turn drew it from Bucer's second form of the Post-Communion thanksgiving.

X

THE MIDDLEBURG LITURGY
OF THE ENGLISH PURITANS

1586

THE PURITANS

Around 1570, there arose a new generation of Puritans, who were not content to inveigh against Anglican vestments, but proposed in earnest to presbyterianize the Church of England in polity, discipline, and worship. Chief of them was Thomas Cartwright, who used his Cambridge professorship to inculcate presbyterian ideas and succeeded thereby in revitalizing the Puritan movement. Soon removed from his post, he repaired to Geneva to observe firsthand the shape of the Reformed system.

The Parliament of 1571 contained several bold spirits who seem to have been influenced by Cartwright. Peter Wentworth asserted the right of Parliament, over that of the bishops, to determine religious affairs; and Walter Strickland, a Puritan protagonist in Commons, proposed alterations in the Prayer Book, for which deed he was forbidden to attend the House. When Parliament met again, in 1572, the Puritan ranks had begun to re-form; and Cartwright was called home to help press the opportunity. Serious consideration was given to a bill that promised to legalize Puritan nonconformity.·

· The authors of the bill confessed that "a grate number of lerned pastors" had ceased to use the Prayer Book at every point, but were apt to use services that represented "the best reformed churches in Europe." The Knox Liturgy was current in 1567. In that year a Puritan spokesman, John Smith, informed the Ecclesiastical Commission that "we now hold" the Genevan book, and "will stand to it by the grace of God." Cf. *The Remains of Grindal* (Cambridge, 1843), pp. 203f.

311

Its authors proposed that the Act of Uniformity should be enforced only against papists, while Puritans were to be allowed, by their bishops' leave, to alter the Prayer Book on occasion or to take up the liturgies of the Dutch and French Reformed churches. The bill had passed three readings when Elizabeth quashed it.

Having scored no decisive victory by parliamentary tactics, the Puritans turned next to the power of the pamphlet. In June, 1572, there appeared the first *Admonition to Parliament,* for which John Field and Thomas Wilcox were deemed the culprits and sent to Newgate. It set forth a "true platforme of a church reformed" according to Cartwrightian principles. The clergy of the Establishment were assailed for their ignorance, covetousness, popish attire, and abject dependence upon the Prayer Book; the bishops for their pomp, idleness, and rich livings. The Anglican liturgy, with its dregs of antichrist, was shamefully compared to the simple, sufficient worship of the Apostolic Church. Finally, the Admonitioners proposed to divest the lordly hierarchy of the government of the church, which properly belonged to the joint rule of "ministers, seniors, and deacons." Attached to the pamphlet was a truculent piece entitled "A View of Popishe Abuses Yet Remaining in the Englishe Church." In the course of twenty-one numbered sections, it directed voluminous criticism against the Anglican liturgy, which had been "culled & picked out of that popishe dunghil, the Masse booke full of all abhominations."

Thus began an era of pamphleteering called the Admonition Controversy, in the course of which Cartwright affirmed the Scriptural warrant for presbyterianism against the published rebuttals of John Whitgift, who was the very model of a good Elizabethan cleric. The Puritan contagion spread in the highest circles at Court, and ran its course in London and the East Midlands. But toward the close of 1573 the Crown took drastic measures to undo the dangerous doctrine, prodding the bishops to enforce the Act of Uniformity. Prominent Puritans were silenced; and Cartwright fled to the Continent before a warrant for his arrest.

A sore point, which the Puritans did not cease to probe, was the lack of capable ministers in the Elizabethan church. According to the Admonitioners the Anglican clerics were "dumb dogs" and "bare readers," who read a homily and thought it a proper sermon and whose only gift of prayer was the meager ability to intone a collect from the liturgy. To repair this defect and to exercise the laity in Holy Scripture, the Puritans introduced a custom called "prophesying" from the Reformed churches abroad. Zwingli created *Prophezei,* in 1525, primarily to train the clergy of Zurich in Scripture. In the Genevan congregation of Knox and in the Strangers' Church of London, over which John à Lasco presided, prophesying became a congregational meeting for biblical discussion. Features of both systems were incorporated in the Puritan practice. The weekly "exercise," attended by ministers and qualified laymen, was devoted to a detailed exposition of an assigned passage of Scripture by learned clergy, one after the other. The moderator, who was "one of the gravest and best learned among them," gave judgment on the true sense of the text, after which questions were posed by the audience.

The resemblance of these exercises to certain features of the presbyterian system did not escape notice. ("Embryonic presbyteries," one scholar has called them.) They were, moreover, a forum for the dissemination of presbyterian ideas and the chief instrument of presbyterian life within the Establishment. Therefore Elizabeth determined to suppress them. The assignment fell to Edmund Grindal, who became Archbishop of Canterbury in 1576. Having spent the Marian Exile in Strassburg, which supplied him with Puritan sympathies, Grindal was willing to control the exercises but certainly not suppress them. In reply to Elizabeth, he wrote: "Bear with me , . . Madam, if I choose rather to offend your earthly majesty, than to offend the heavenly majesty of God." But the "earthly majesty" sequestered him; and, proving obdurate, he remained sequestered until death, in 1583.

The See of Canterbury then fell to Whitgift, Cartwright's stout opponent, who lost no time in giving battle to the Puritans. At once he demanded their subscription to three articles, the second of which declared that "the Book of Common Prayer . . . containeth nothing in‐ it contrary to the Word of God." They would rather have believed that black is white. Thus a new phase of the struggle began, as John Field dispatched exhortations to the faithful, urging resistance against subscription.

In 1584 the Puritans began a concerted effort to introduce the presbyterian system on the basis of two standards: (1) the Knox Liturgy and (2) a formal Discipline that was then being prepared The first of these was presented to the Parliament of 1584-5 by Peter Turner in the form of "a bill and a book." The "bill" was a proposal to make the Genevan liturgy authoritative in public worship. In his *Dangerous Positions and Proceedings* (III. x), Richard Bancroft reported the text of the petition:

> May it therefore please your Majesty, &c. that it may be enacted, &c. that the Book hereunto annexed, &c. intitled, A Booke of the Forme of Common Prayers, Administration of the Sacraments, &c. and everything therein contained, may be from henceforth authorized, put in use, and practiced throughout all your Majesty's dominions.

The "book" was not precisely the Knox Liturgy but an adaptation of it published in London during this era by the Puritan printer, Robert Waldegrave; hence it is called the Waldegrave Liturgy. In his *Laws of Ecclesiastical Polity* (V. xxvii), Richard Hooker suggested that the liturgy had been edited by "Admonitioners" • —perhaps Cartwright, Walter Travers, or Dudley Fenner. At any rate, it was based upon Knox's service-book, to which the Puritan editors made minor alterations, taking care to supply Scriptural marginalia as the warrant for each liturgical usage. It is therefore clear that the Cartwrightian Puritans did not favor free services of worship, but a liturgy that was drawn upon the Genevan model. Moreover, they meant to impose that liturgy upon England in the name of liberty to worship God according to his Word—a presumption that vexed both Bancroft and Hooker. But the House resolved not to entertain the bill and book, while the astute Archbishop obstructed a further Puritan program of sixteen reforms, one of which would have allowed ministers to alter the Anglican services.

In the course of their struggle with Whitgift, the Puritans attempted to erect a system of presbyterian government within the Established church. By extensive correspondence, Field encouraged the prophesyings to conceive of themselves as "classes" in a national organization, consisting of provincial synods and a general assembly. Closely related to this activity was the preparation of a formal Discipline. A decade earlier

---

• The suggestion becomes credible when one compares the Sunday Service in the Waldegrave Liturgy with that outlined in *A Directory of Church Government,* which was found among Cartwright's papers after his decease. Cf. Davies, pp. 124f.

(1574), Walter Travers had written a lengthy exposition of presbyterian principles, which Cartwright translated as *A Full and Plain Declaration of Ecclesiastical Discipline*. By 1586, a brief new manual, for which Travers was apparently responsible, was being circulated in manuscript drafts for discussion and criticism. It made provision for the government of the local church by a consistory, and prescribed the functions of the other graded assemblies: the classis (twelve churches), the provincial synod (twenty-four classes), and the national assembly. In pursuing these activities the Puritans did not wish to exceed the law of the land or the peace of the church. But until their aims were served by Parliament, they intended by these means to illustrate their keen desire that the Discipline and Genevan liturgy would soon be established.

When the Star Chamber restricted Puritan printing (June, 1586), the Waldegrave Liturgy was taken to Middleburg, an English trading community in the Low Countries where Travers, Cartwright, and Fenner served successive pastorates; and there it was republished by the Puritan printer, Richard Schilders, in 1586. The Middleburg Liturgy (reproduced below) was faithful to *The Forme of Prayers*, with a few notable exceptions. In the initial rubric of the Sunday Service, the Middleburg editors prescribed a "Reader's Service," which was not mentioned in the Knox Liturgy (but nevertheless became current in Scotland after 1560). That service was to be conducted prior to the liturgy proper, by a lay reader who was appointed by "the Eldership." For an hour or so, while the full congregation assembled, he read the Scriptures "in course" and directed the singing of psalms. The intent of this practice was to exercise the people in Holy Scripture and, apparently, to relieve the ministers who were often in short supply. Presently the "pastor" arrived and commenced the liturgy itself. In Middleburg usage he began with the solemn declaration of man's helplessness ("Our helpe be in thee name of the Lorde . . ."), which was used by Calvin invariably but omitted by Knox. The Middleburg editors also rejected the first form of Confession in the Knox Liturgy, retaining the second, which was the notable prayer of Bucer and Calvin. They added still a third alternative version of the Great Prayer—a ponderous and penitential piece, with parts of Calvin's Great Prayer as an appendage. In the Eucharistic liturgy, the editors were content to augment the list of offenders to be fenced from the table, and to add Words of Delivery where the Knox Liturgy specified none. Communion continued to be delivered to the people as they sat about the long table.

Again, in 1587, the Puritans pressed their desires in Parliament. Anthony Cope, a member of Commons, introduced "a bill and a book" in which he proposed to abolish all the laws touching ecclesiastical government, and to appoint in their place "The Form of Prayer" as the exclusive instrument of discipline and worship. Elizabeth promptly sent for the bill and book; and when Peter Wentworth took the occasion to deliver another oration against such infringements of the liberties of the House, he and Cope and three kindred spirits were sent to the Tower.

The death of Field, in 1588, cost the classis movement its chief organizer. Already internal divisions had begun to occur over the Discipline, which was being circulated for adoption by 1587. Whether it was agreeable to Scripture, whether it jeopardized the peace of the church, whether it should be installed, law or no—these were the questions that divided the presbyterians. The Marprelate tracts (1588), with their scurrilous attacks upon prelacy, cast a pall of disfavor over the whole Puritan movement; and in vain did Cartwright protest his "mislike and sorrow for such kind of disordered proceeding." Upon the defeat of the Spanish Armada in 1588, England was also delivered from the imminent danger of a resurgent Catholicism—a peril that the Puritans had hitherto used to advantage. With increasing severity did Whitgift apply the machinery of the church against the Puritans. In the production of anti-Puritan propaganda, his chief agent was Bancroft, who laid bare the whole presbyterian scheme as a vast effort at sedition. The persons implicated, Cartwright among them, were taken into custody in 1590 and were subsequently released only to prevent them from attaining the blessedness of martyrdom. Thus the presbyterian organization was overcome by patriotism and by the administrative persistence of Crown and Canterbury.

The Middleburg Liturgy purported to be "agreeable to Gods worde and the vse of the reformed Churches." In that subtitle lie two of the chief characteristics of Puritan worship.

First, it was based entirely upon "the pure Word of God." The Puritans held that the Scriptures were authoritative not only for doctrine, but every aspect of Christian life. William Bradshaw (1571-1618) labored the "absolute perfection" of the Word, which was given to the church "as the sole Canon and rule of all matters of Religion, and the worship and service of God whatsoever." The Anglican reformation was therefore unfinished, the Elizabethan church only a temporary expedient. The Puritans anticipated yet another stage of reformation in which the warrant of Holy Writ would be applied against the Prayer Book, which was full of the relics of Catholicism, a patched-up thing about which no Puritan was of two minds.

The Puritan ideal was to revive the simplicity and vitality of the Apostolic Church, or, as John Owen (1616-83) put it, "the old glorious beautiful face of Christianity." This could only be accomplished by scrupulous attention to the will of God, which meant that each liturgical usage, to be acceptable, must have a warrant in Scripture. Acts 2:41-2 was the high text of Christian worship; but other passages supplied directions for its several parts. The manner of prayer was set forth in I Tim. 2:1f., while Neh. 8:6 and I Cor. 14:14-16 prompted the pastor to pray audibly and the people to follow silently, adding their "Amen" at the end. Directions for praise came from the Psalms and from such texts as Eph. 5:19. The sermon, to which the whole of Scripture gave importance, was conceived to be the veritable message of God, made lively in the heart by the Holy Spirit, and without which no man came to faith or salvation. The two Dominical sacraments, being fully laid out in the New Testament, obliged the church to adhere exactly to the Lord's institution, both in word and in action. Catechizing was "proved" by II Tim. 1:3: "Hold fast the form of sound words. . . ." And discipline, which the Puritans, as Calvin before him, considered one of the marks of the true church, had no dearth of Scriptural examples. These six were the major ordinances of worship.·

In view of the Puritan stance, a concerted attack on *The Book of Common Prayer* was inevitable. It came clearly into

· Davies adds (pp. 55f.) that while the Puritans sometimes scrutinized a text beyond reason (one must be seated to communicate because the Lord said to the heavy laden, "I will give you rest."), they did not lose sight of the spirit of Scripture in their zeal for the letter; and this is apparent in their fight with the Anglicans over vestments and such, when they, rather than their opponents, pursued theological arguments, instead of those drawn from isolated texts.

light with the first *Admonition to Parliament*. And it was conducted by militant men who knew not the art of group discussion, but believed true Christians must renounce the things of Rome as well as the vain pomp and glory of the world.

The contest over vestments was renewed in 1559 when Elizabeth reinstated the 1549 apparel and other scenic apparatus. The Puritans, who deemed this an intolerable retrogression, complained that vestments were imposed against their Christian liberty, and involved them anew with Romish superstition. These were the garments of "popish priestes" who offered the sacrifice of the Mass. They were, therefore, a frightful burden upon the conscience; they restored pomp to the ministry, offended the weak, encouraged the obstinate, and defeated the edification of men in the Gospel.

By much the same reasoning, Puritans objected to certain ceremonies in the Prayer Book, especially kneeling to communicate, the ring in Marriage, and the sign of the cross in Baptism. While all of these might be deemed "indifferent" matters, they were associated with Roman superstition and therefore ceased to be indifferent. Symbolism was never to be taken lightly. One could ill afford to profess one thing and symbolize another. If kneeling at Communion was the device of papists, "who thereby adore their breaden God," then it must be abolished as an instrument of confusion and error.

Criticism was also levied at the "bare readers" of Anglicanism, who were bound to the use of homilies, being unprepared to preach. "Reading is not feeding," warned the Admonitioners; and those clerics who must rely on homilies are "emptie feeders . . . Prophets who cannot declare the wil of the Lorde . . . blinde guides, sleepie watchmen, untrustie dispensers of Gods secretes." The Puritan was persuaded that the Word of judgment and reconciliation was not likely to move the worshiper unless it were vigorously applied from the pulpit to the several needs of the congregation. Cartwright put it exactly: "As the fire stirred giveth more heat, so the Word, as it were, blown by preaching, flameth more in the hearers than when it is read."

Additional criticism was directed to the brevity of the collects and the "vain repetitions" of the litanies. Some prayers were deemed indecently interested in material goods, while others were found wanting in evangelical confidence. The order of service itself was considered a "confusion," with psalms being tossed in "like tennice balles." A host of faults were found in the Eucharistic liturgy, the chief of them being that, for the lack of discipline, the unworthy were allowed to receive. Finally, disapproval was given to the entire Church Year, save for the weekly observance of the Lord's Day.

This partial account will indicate the nature and strength of the Puritan polemic against the Prayer Book. Blunt, sometimes narrowly conceived, dreadful in its condemnation of human inventions, it was yet a most serious appeal away from tradition to the sufficiency of Scripture and the purity and simplicity of the Apostolic Church.

Second, the Puritans illustrated in a number of ways that they intended to frame their worship according to the Reformed churches. The Waldegrave and Middleburg texts were drawn almost verbatim from the Genevan tradition of Calvin and Knox; the Westminster *Directory* and the Savoy Liturgy belonged to the same lineage. Puritan apologetics were filled with citations to the liturgical ideas of the Reformed divines. And the service-books themselves gave testimony, in title or preface, that a fellowship of worship ought to exist between "the Godly at home" and "the Reformed Churches abroad."

From Calvin, moreover, the Puritans inherited those doctrines that controlled the very nature of worship. Calvin found in Scripture "the holy Law and Word of God," which was confirmed to the conscience by the Holy Spirit. As such, Scripture was meant to govern the whole realm of human life and every detail of ecclesiastical practice; it was "the perpetual rule to which true religion ought to be conformed." Worship itself must adhere precisely to the will of God— the more so since human contrivances were inevitably vitiated by the sinfulness of man, and therefore "fruitless" if not utterly blasphemous. While Calvin himself admitted a principle of accommodation in certain nonessential matters; the Puritans brooked no compromise, holding firmly to the sufficiency of Scripture as a directory of worship.

Yet the Puritans had no intention of canonizing Reformed practice. Their criterion was the Word of God, by which Geneva and Zurich were also to be judged. Many, but not all, of them• eventually exceeded the Reformed tradition by

• The Waldegrave and Middleburg books were *liturgies,* while the Westminster *Directory* (1644) made provisions for both form and freedom. The Savoy Liturgy proves that as late as 1661 the con-

their hostility toward prescribed forms of worship. The Barrowists, Brownists, and some Independents even refused to repeat the Lord's Prayer in assembly, while the early Baptists dispensed as quickly as possible with the Bible—a form of words—so that the rest of worship could be genuinely pneumatic. In support of this policy, the Puritans contended that read prayers "quenched" the Holy Spirit who "helps us in our weakness, for we do not know how to pray as we ought" (Rom. 8:26). A prayer book seemed to them a product of human pride and sufficiency, which was imposed upon the church in lieu of God's own Spirit. Moreover, the "stinted" forms deprived clergy and people of the gift of prayer; failed to express the real necessities of every time and occasion; paid lip service to thoughts that were often unfelt; persuaded people to believe that such forms were the canons of God who could not be reached in any other way; and brought with them the "fire and faggot" of persecution.

While Calvin did not scruple at certain ceremonies—so long as they were "manifestly useful and very few in number" —the Puritans inveighed against all unscriptural customs, and especially against those "badges of Antichrist" that were associated with Romish error (e.g., kneeling at Communion). Moreover, they abolished the entire Christian Year, keeping but one festival, the Lord's Day, in which all the saving acts of God were drawn together for weekly commemoration. Thus the other festivals were superfluous and deprived the Lord's Day of its uniqueness, while saints' days were intolerable because they confounded the sole mediation of Jesus Christ and diverted man from the true end of worship, which was *soli Deo gloria*. They were somewhat more faithful to Calvin, however, in relating Holy Communion to the Lord's Day. The dictum of the great Genevan, that the Eucharist was meant to be celebrated every Sunday, did not die as quickly among the Puritans as elsewhere.· And the manner of their celebra-

---

ception of liturgical worship had not been rejected by all manner of Puritans. In controversy with the Anglicans, however, the Puritans as a whole were driven further away from the Reformed position on this issue. Davies argues (pp. 112ff.) that Puritan opinion was consolidated in the days of the Commonwealth by the preponderant influence of the Independents, who insisted (to quote John Owen) "that all liturgies, as such, are false worship."
· The Middleburg text suggested a monthly Communion, while the Westminster *Directory* reiterated Calvin's desire that it be celebrated "frequently," but did not specify the times. According to

tion, with preached Word and discipline, was quite in accord with Calvin's practice.

Although the Puritans professed fraternal ties with the Reformed churches abroad, they in fact exceeded that tradition in those matters we have indicated (and there were others), and sought a cultus still more uncorrupted. Davies believes that in this instance they were influenced far more than they knew by the Separatists (Barrowists, Brownists, Baptists) who insisted upon "reformation without tarying for anie." Having excluded themselves from the Established church, the Separatists could no longer afford simply to assail the Prayer Book, hoping for alterations eventually, but were forced to provide specific illustrations of worship drawn within the compass of God's Word. In making such a contribution, they shaped the character of Puritan worship in a number of ways, most of all by their opposition to the "stinted" forms.

FOR FURTHER READING

Horton Davies, *The Worship of the English Puritans*. Westminster, 1948.
W. H. Frere and C. E. Douglas (eds.), *Puritan Manifestoes*. London, 1907.
Peter Hall (ed.), *Reliquiae Liturgicae*, Vol. I. Bath, 1847.
M. M. Knappen, *Tudor Puritanism*. Chicago, 1939.
A. G. Matthews, "The Puritans" in *Christian Worship*, edited by Nathaniel Micklem. Oxford, 1936.

Davies (pp. 43f.), a weekly Eucharist was common in the first half of the seventeenth century; but monthly Communion eventually became the rule for most Puritans, and the Presbyterians communicated only four times a year.

A BOOKE
OF THE FORME OF COMMON PRAYERS, ADMINISTRATION OF THE SACRAMENTS, &C. AGREABLE TO GODS WORDE, AND THE VSE OF THE REFORMED CHURCHES. MIDDELBVRGH, 1586[1]

PUBLIKE EXERCISES IN THE ASSEMBLIES

¶ *Vpon[2] the dayes appointed for the preaching of the Worde, when a conuenient number of the Congregation are come togither, that they maye make fruite of their presence, till the Assemblie be full, one appointed by the Eldership, shall reade some Chapters of the Canonicall bookes of Scripture, singing Psalmes betweene at his discretion: and this reading to bee in order as the bookes and Chapters followe, that so from time to time the holy Scriptures maye bee readde throughout. But vppon speciall occasion, speciall Chapters may bee appointed. When the houre, appointed for the Sermon is come, beginning with these wordes: Our helpe be in thee name of the Lorde, who hath made both Heauen and Earth: vsed after the Confession following, or the like in effecte, sayinge to the people: Lette vs fall downe before the Maiestie of Almightie God, humblye confessinge our sinnes, and followe in your hartes the tenor of my wordes.[3]*

THE CONFESSION OF OVR SINNES VSED BEFORE SERMON [4]

O Eternall God, and most mercifull Father, we confesse and acknoweledge here before thy divine Maiestie, that wee are miserable sinners, conceiued and borne in sinne and iniquitie, so that in vs there is no goodnesse. For the fleshe euermore rebelleth against the spirit, wherby vve continuallie transgresse thine holy precepts and commaundementes, and so purchase to our selues thorough thy iuste iudgement death and damnation. Notwithstanding, o Heauenlye Father, forasmuch as thou hast vouchsafed to offer pardon to all that repent, and seeke it in the Name of thy beloued Sonne Christ Iesus, & that by thy grace we are displeased with our selues for the sinnes that we haue committed against thee, and do vnfaynedly repent vs of the same, we most humblye beseech thee for Iesus Christes sake, to shew thy mercie vppon vs, to forgiue vs all our sinnes, and to increase thine holy Spirit in vs, that we acknowledging frō the bottome of our harts our owne vnrighteousnesse, maye from hencefoorth not only mortifie our sinnfull lustes and affections, but also bring foorth such fruites, as maye please thee: not for any worthinesse thereof, but for the merites of thy dearely beloued Sonne Iesus Christ our onely Sauiour, whom thou hast alreadie giuen an oblation and sacrifice for our sinnes, and for whose sake we are certainlie persuaded, that thou wilt denie vs nothing, that we shal aske in his name, according to thy will. For thy Spirit doth assure our consciences, that thou art our mercifull Father, and so louest vs thy children through him, that nothing is able to remooue thine heauenlie grace and fauour from vs. To thee therefore, o Father, with the Sonne and the holy Ghost, be all honor and glorie, world without ende, So be it.

¶ *This cōfession made, the people are to sing a Psalme as the Minister appointeth: which ended,*[5] *the Pastor prayeth for the assistance of Gods holy Spirite, that the Worde may be expounded faithfullie, to the honor of his Name, and the edification of the Church, and that it may be re- ceiued with such humilitie and obedience, as thervnto be- longeth: concluding with the Lords prayer. Then he is to reade the texte: alwayes to bee taken out of some part of the Canonicall Scriptures, and so to proceede to the ser- mon. The sermon ended, the Pastor is to vse one of these prayers following.*

A PRAYER FOR THE WHOLE STATE OF CHRISTES CHVRCH [6]

Almighty God, and most merciful Father, we humbly sub- mit our selues, and fall downe before thy Maiesty, beseech- ing thee from the bottome of our harts, that this seede of thy worde, now sowen amongst vs, may take such deepe roote, that neither the burning heate of persecution cause it to wither, neither the thorny cares of this life do choake it: but that as seede sovven in good grounde, it may bring foorth thirty, sixty, or an hundred fold, as thine heauenly wisdom hath appointed. And because wee haue neede cōtinually to craue many things at thine handes, we humbly beseech thee, o Heauenlie Father, to graunt vs thine holy Spirite, to direct our petitions, that they may procede from such a feruent minde, as may be agreeable to thy moste blessed will.

And seeing that our infirmitie is able to do nothing without thine help, & that thou art not ignorant with how manie & how great tentations wee poore wretches are on euerie side inclosed and compassed, let thy strength, o Lorde, sustaine our weakenesse, that we, being defended with the force of thy grace, may be safelie preserued against al assaults of Satan, who goeth about continuallie like a roaring Lion, seeking to deuoure vs. Increase our Faith, o mercifull Father, that we do not swarue at anie time from thine heauenly Worde, but augment in vs hope and loue, with a care to keepe al thy commandements, that no hardenesse of heart, no hypocrisie, no concupiscence of the eyes, nor intisementes of the worlde, doe drawe vs awaye from thine obediēce: And seeing we liue now in these most perillous times, lett thy fatherlie prouidence defende vs against the violence of all our enimies, whiche do euery where pursue vs, but chieflie against the wicked rage and furious vprores of the Antichrist of Rome.

Furthermore, forasmuch as by thine holy Apostle we be taught to make our prayers & supplications for all men, we praye not onelie for our selues here present, but beseeche thee also to reduce all such as be yet ignorant, from the miserable captiuitie of blindnesse & error, to the pure vnderstanding of thine Heauenlie trueth, that wee all with one consent and vnitie of mindes, may worshippe thee our only God and Sauiour: and that all Pastors, Shepheardes, & Ministers, to whom thou hast committed the dispensation of thine holy worde, and charge of thy chosen people, maye both in their life and doctrine, be found faithfull, setting onely before their eyes thy glorie, and that by them all poore sheepe which vvander and goe astraye, may be gathered and brought home to thy folde.

Moreouer, because the hartes of rulers are in thine handes, we beseech thee to directe and gouerne the hartes of all Kinges, Princes and Magistrates, to whō thou hast cōmitted the sword: especiallie, o Lorde, according to our bounded duetie, wee beseeche thee to maintaine and increase the prosperous estate of our moste noble Queene ELIZABETH: Whō as thou hast placed ouer vs in thy great mercie, & preserued her by thy mightie power: so wee beseeche thee, o Lorde, by the same mercie, to multiplie on her the excellent giftes of the holy Spirite: And by the same power as thou hast alvvayes preserued her, so to preserue her still. And as thou hast discouered the vnnaturall treasons, and vvicked practises, so to discouer them still: that as for all other thy singular graces, so also for this great mercy, both Prince and people may reioyce & magnifie thy great Name. Also we pray thee for her Maiesties right Honorable Coūcell, that thy good Spirite may furnishe euerie one of them with wisedome and strength, and other excellent giftes, fitte for their callinge. Furthermore, we pray thee for all other Mgistrates,• and for the whole Realme, that all men in their calling may be founde faithfull in seeking to set foorth thy glorie, & to procure the godlie peace and prosperitie of all the lande: And lette thy fatherlie fauour so preserue them, and thine holie Spirit so gouerne their hartes, that they may in such sorte execute their office, that thy Religion may be purelie maintained, manners reformed, and sinne punished, according to the precise rule of thine Holie Worde.

And for that we be all members of the mysticall body of Christ Iesus, vve make our requestes vnto thee, o Heauenlie Father, for all such as are afflicted with any kinde of crosse or tribulation, as warre, plague, famine, sicknesse, pouertie, imprisonment, persecution, banishement, or anie other kinde of thy roddes: whether it be griefe of bodie, or vnquietnes of minde, that it would please thee to giue them patiēce and constancie, till thou sende them ful deliuerance of all their troubles. Finallie, O Lorde, we most humblie beseeche thee, to shewe thy great mercies vppon our brethren, which are persecuted, cast in prison, and dailie condemned to death for the testimonie of thy trueth. And though they be vtterlie destitute of al mans ayde, yet let thy sweete cōfort neuer depart from them: but so inflame their hartes with thine holy Spirite, that they may boldlie & chearefullie abyde such triall, as thy godlie wisedome shall appoint, so that at length as well by their death as by their life, the kingdome of thy Sonne Iesus Christ may increase and shine throughout all the worlde.

AN OTHER PRAYER
that may sometimes be vsed after the Sermon.

Almightie God and Heauenlie Father, since thou hast promised to graunt our requestes, whiche wee shall make

• Misprint: Magistrates.

vnto thee in the Name of our Lord Iesus Christ thy welbeloued Sōne, and that we are also taught by him and his
Apostles, to assemble our selues in his Name, promising that
he will bee among vs, and make intercession for vs vnto thee,
for the obtaining of all suche thinges, as we shall agree vppon
here in Earth: we therefore (hauinge firste thy cōmande-
ment to pray for such as thou hast appointed rulers and
gouuernours ouer vs, and also for all things needfull both
for thy people, and for all sortes of men, forasmuch as our
faith is groūded on thine holy Word & promises, & that wee
are here gathered togither before thy face, and in thy· Name
of thy Sonne our Lord Iesus) we, I say, make our earnest
supplication vnto thee, our moste mercifull God and bountifull Father, that for Iesus Christes sake our onely Sauior &
Mediator, it may please thee of thine infinit mercie freelie to
pardon our offences, & in such sorte to draw & lift vp our
hartes & affections towardes thee, that our requestes may both
proceede of a feruent minde, and also be agreeable vnto thy
most blessed will and pleasure, which is only to be accepted.

(.) Wee beseeche thee therefore, O Heauenlie Father, for
all Princes & Rulers, vnto whom thou hast committed the administration of thy iustice, and namelie, for the excellent
estate of the Queenes Maiestie, and all her Honorable Counsell, with the rest of her Magistrates and Commons of the
Realme, that it would please thee to graunt her thine holy
Spirit, and increase the same from time to time in her, that
shee may with a pure faith acknowledge IESVS Christ thine
onelie Sonne our Lorde, to be King of all Kings, and gouuernour of all gouuernours, euen as thou hast giuen all power
vnto him both in Heauen and in Earth: and so giue her selfe
wholie to serue him, and to aduaunce his kingdome in her
Dominions, rulinge according to thy worde, her subiectes,
which are thy creatures, and the sheepe of thy pasture, that
wee being mainteyned in peace & tranquillitie, may serue thee
in all holinesse and vertue: and finallie, being deliuered from
all feare of enimies, may render thankes vnto thee all the
dayes of our life.

We beseeche thee also most deare Father, for all such as
thou hast appointed Ministers vnto thy faithfull people, and
vnto whome thou hast committed the charge of soules, and

· Misprint: the.

the ministerie of thine holie Gospell, that it would please thee
so to guide them with thine holie Spirite, that they may bee
founde wise, faithfull and zealous of thy glorie, directing
alwayes their whole studies vnto this ende, that the poore
sheepe whiche are gone astraye out of thy flocke, maye be
sought out and brought againe vnto the Lorde IESVS, who
is the chiefe Shephearde and prince of Pastors, to the intent
they may from day to day growe and increase in him to al
righteousnesse and holinesse: And on the other parte, that it
would please thee to deliuer all the Churches from the
daunger of rauening Wolues, and from hyrelinges, who seeke
their owne ambition and profite, and not the setting foorth of
thy glorie onelie, and the safegarde of thy flocke.

Moreouer, we make our prayers vnto thee, o Lord God,
moste mercifull Father for all men, that as thou wouldest
haue all sortes of men saued, and come to the knowledge
of the trueth: so it may please thee, that such as haue bene
hitherto holden captiue in darkenesse and ignorance, for lacke
of the knoweledge of thy Gospell, may thorough the preaching thereof, and the cleare light of thine Holie Spirite, bee
brought into the right way of saluation, which is, to knowe
thee the onely true God, and Iesus Christ, whom thou hast
sent. Likevvise that they vvhom thou hast alreadie endued
with thy grace, & illuminated their hartes with the knowledge
of thy Worde, may continuallie increase in godlinesse, and be
plenteously enriched with spirituall benefites: So that wee
maye altogither worshippe thee, both with harte and mouth,
and render due honor & seruice vnto Christ our Lord.

In like maner, o Lord of al true comfort, wee commende
vnto thee in oure prayers all such persons as thou hast visited
and chastised with anie crosse and tribulation: all such people
as thou hast punished with pestilence, warre, or famine: & all
other persons afflicted with pouertie, imprisonment, sicke-
nesse, banishment, or any like bodily aduersitie, or hast otherwise afflictect in spirit: that it may please thee to make them
feele thy fatherlie affection towardes them, and to know that
these crosses are chastisements for their amendement, to the
ende that they may vnfainedlie turne vnto thee, and so receyue
full comforte and be deliuered from their euils. But especiallie
wee commende vnto thy diuine protection, all suche as are
vnder the tyrannie of Antichriste, and both lacke the preachinge of the Worde, the foode of life, and haue not libertie

327

to call vppon thy Name in open Assemblie: chieflie our poore
brethren whiche are imprisoned and persecuted by the enimies of thy Gospell, that it may please thee, O Father of
consolations, to strengthen them by the power of thine holy
Spirite, in suche sorte, as they neuer shrinke backe, but may
constantlie perseuere in their holy faith, and so to succour
and assiste them as thou knowest to bee moste expedient,
comfortinge them in their afflictions, maintayninge them in
thy safegarde against the rage of the enemies, and increasinge
in them the gifts of thy holy Spirite, that they maye glorifie
thee their Lorde God, both in their life & in their death.

Finallie, o Lorde God most deare Father, we beseeche thee
to grant vnto vs also, which are here gathered togither in the
Name of thy Sonne Iesus Christ, to heare his Word preached,·
that we may acknowledge truelie and without hypocrisie in
howe miserable a state of damnation we are by nature, and
howe worthilie we procure vnto our selues euerlasting death,
prouoking from time to time thy grieuous punishementes
against vs, through our wicked and sinfull life, to the end,
that seeing there remaineth no sparke of goodnes in our nature, and that there is nothing in vs, as touching our first
birth, meete to enioye the heritage of thy kingdome, wee may
whollie render vpp our selues with all our hartes, and with an
assured confidence vnto thy dearely beloued Sonne Iesus
Christ our Lorde, our onely Sauiour and Redeemer, that he
dwelling in vs, may mortifie our olde man and sinfull affections, that we may be renewed into a more godlie life,
Hallowed   whereby thine Holie Name may be aduanced &
bee thy   magnified in vs: likewise, that thou mayest haue
Name.   the tuition and gouuernance ouer vs, and that wee
may learne dailie more and more to humble and submitte
our selues vnto thy Maiestie, in such sorte that thou mayest
be counted King and gouernour ouer all, guyding thy people
Thy king-   with the scepter of thy Worde, & by the vertue
dome come.   of thine holy Spirit, to the confusion of all thine
enimies, thorough the might of thy trueth and righteousnesse,
so that by this meanes all power and height whiche with-
standeth thy glorie, may be continuallie throwne downe &
abolished, vntill such time as the ful and perfect face of thy
kingdome shall appeare, when thou shalt shewe thy selfe in
iudgement in the person of thy Sonne: wherby also we with

· If the lords Supper bee ministred, then is here added this clause.
And to celebrate his holy Supper.

328

Thy will bee don in earth as it is in heauen. the rest of thy children, may render vnto thee perfect and true obedience, euen as thine Heauenlic· Angels doe applie them selues onelie to the performing of thy commaunde-ments: so that thine onelie will may be fulfilled without any contradiction, & that euerie man may bende him selfe to serue and please thee, renouncing their owne willes, with all the affections and desires of the fleshe. Graunt vs also, good Lord, that we thus walking in the loue and dread of thine Holie Name, may be nourished thorough thy goodnesse, Giue vs this day our dai-ly breade. and that wee may receiue at thy handes all thinges expedient and necessarie for vs, and so vse thy giftes peaceablie & quietlie, to this ende, that when we see that thou hast care of vs, we maye the more effectuallie acknowledge thee to be our Father, look-inge for all good giftes at thine hande, and by withdrawinge and pulling backe all our vaine confidence from creatures, may set it wholly vppon thee, and so rest only in thy most bountifull mercie. And for so much as whilest we continue here in this transitorie life, we are so miserable, so fraile, and so much enclined vnto sinne, that wee fall continuallie and swarue from the right way of thy commaundements, wee beseeche thee pardon vs our innumerable offences, whereby And for-giue vs our trespasses. we deserue thy iuste iudgement & condemnation, and forgiue vs so freelie, that death and sinne may hereafter haue nothing against vs, neither laye vnto our charge that wicked roote of sinne, whiche doeth euermore remaine in vs: graunt that by thy commaundement we may forgette the wronges which other doe vnto vs, & in steede of seeking vengeance, may procure the wealth of our enimies. And for as much as of our selues we are weake, And lead vs not into ten-tation. vtterlie vnable to stand, & assalted euermore with such multitude of most dangerous eni-mies, the Deuill, the World, sinne, and oure owne concupiscences which do neuer leaue of to fight against vs, let it be thy good pleasure, to strengthen vs with thy holie Spirit, & to arme vs with thy grace, that thereby we maye be able constantlie to withstande all tentations, and to perseuere in this spirituall battell against sinne, vntill such time as we shall obtaine the full victorie, and so at length may trium-phantlie raigne in thy kingdome, with our Captaine & gouuer-

• Misprint: Heauenlie.

nour Iesus Christ our Lorde, in whose name we further pray as he hath taught vs.

¶ *This prayer following may be also vsed to bee saide after the sermon, on the day whiche is appointed for common prayer: and it is very proper for our state and time, to mooue vs to true repentance, and to turne backe Gods sharpe roddes which yet threaten vs.*

O God almightie and Heauenlie Father, we acknowledge in our consciences & confesse, as the trueth is, that we are not worthie to lift vp our eyes to Heauen, much lesse meete to come into thy presence, & to be so bold as to think that thou wilt heare our prayers, if thou haue respecte to that which is in vs: for our consciences accuse vs, and our own sinnes do beare witnesse against vs: yea, and we know that thou art a righteous iudge, which punished the faults of such as transgresse thy commaundements: Therefore, O Lord, when wee consider our whole life, we haue cause to be confounded in our owne hartes, and to be swalowed vp in the depe gulfe of death. Notwithstanding, most mercifull Lorde, since it hath pleased thee of thine infinite mercie to commaund vs to cal vppon thee for helpe, euen from the deepe bottome of hell: and that the more lack and defaulte vve feele in our selues, so much the rather we shuld haue recourse vnto thy gratious bountie: since also thou hast promised to heare and accept our requestes and supplications; without hauing anie respecte to our vnworthines, for the merites of our Lorde Iesus Christe, whome alone thou hast appointed to be our Intercessour and Aduocate, wee humble our selues before thee, renouncing al vaine confidence in mans helpe, & cleaue onelie to thy mercie, callinge vppon thy Holie Name; to obteine pardon for our sinnes.

First, O Lorde, besides the innumerable benefites whiche thou doest vniuersallie bestowe vppon all men, thou hast giuen vs such speciall graces, that it is not possible for vs to rehearse them, no nor sufficientlie to conceiue them in our mindes. It hath pleased thee to call vs to the knowledge of thy holy Gospel, drawing vs out of the miserable bondage of the deuil, whose slaues we were, and deliuering vs from most cursed idolatrie and wicked superstition, wherin we were plunged, to bringe vs into the meruailous light of thy trueth. Notvvithstanding such is our vnthankefulnesse, that not onely we forget those thy benefites, vvhiche we haue receyued at

thy bountifull hande, but haue gone astray from thee, & haue
turned our selues from thy Lavve, to go after our own concupiscences and lustes, and neyther haue giuen worthie
honour and due obedince of thine Holy Worde, neyther
haue aduaunced thy Glorie, as our dueties required. And
although thou hast not ceassed continuallie to admonishe vs
most faithfullie by thy Worde, yet we haue not giuen eare to
thy Fatherlie admonition.

Wherefore, o Lorde, we haue sinned and haue grieuouslie
offended agaynst thee, so that shame and confusion apper-
tayneth to vs: and vvee acknovveledge that vve are altogither
guiltie before thy iudgement, and that if thou vvouldest
deale with vs according our demerites, we could looke for
no other then euerlasting death and damnation. For although
vvee vvould excuse our selues, yet our owne consciences
would accuse vs, and our wickednesse would appeare before
thee to condemne vs. And in verie deede, o Lorde, we see
by the corrections which thou hast alreadie layde vpon vs,
that wee haue giuen thee great occasion to bee displeased
with vs: for seeing thou art a iust & vpright Iudge, it cannot
be without cause, that thou punishest thy people. Wherefore,
for as much as we haue felt thy stripes, vve acknovvledge
that we haue iustlie stirred vp thy displeasure against vs:
yea, & yet we see thine hande lifted vp to strike vs againe:
for the roddes and vveapons, vvherevvith thou art accustomed
to execute thy vēgeance, are alreadie in thine hande, and in
ful readinesse. Whervvith though thou shouldest punish vs
much more grieuously then thou hast hitherto done, and
that, vvhereas vve haue receyued one stroke, thou vvouldest
giue vs a thousande: yea, if thou vvouldest bring vppon vs
all the curses vvritten in thy Lavve, and pursue vs vvith the
grieuous punishementes, vvherevvith thou diddest punishe
thy people Israel, vvee confesse that thou shouldest do therein
most righteouslie, and wee can not denie, but wee haue fullie
deserued the same.

Notwithstanding, o Lorde, our heauenlie Father, seeing
thou art our maker, and we the workmanship of thine handes,
seeing thou art our Pastor, and we thy flocke, seeing also that
thou art our Redeemer, & we the people whom thou hast
bought: finallie, because thou art our God, & we thy chosen
Heritage, suffer not thine anger so to kindle against vs, that
thou shouldest punish vs in thy wrath, neither remember our

331

wickednesse so, as to take vengeance therof, but rather chastise vs accordinge to they mercie.

We confesse, O Lorde, that our misdedes haue enflamed thy wrath against vs, yet, considering that by thy grace we call vpon thy Name, & make profession of thy trueth: mainteine, wee beseeche thee, the worke that thou hast begon in vs, to the ende that all the worlde maye know that thou art our God & Sauior. Thou knowest that suche as thou hast destroied and brought to confusion, do not set forth thy praises, but the heauie soules, the humble hartes, the consciences oppressed and loaden with the grieuous burden of their sinnes, & therefore thirste after thy grace, they shall set forth thy prayse and glorie.

Thy people of Israell oftentimes prouoked thee to anger through their wickednesse, wherevpon thou diddest iustlie punishe them: but so soone as they acknowledged their offences, & returned to thee, thou diddest receyue them alwayes to mercie: and were their enormities and sinnes neuer so grieuous, yet for thy Couenantes sake, whiche thou haddest made with thy seruantes, Abraham, Isaac, and Iacob, thou diddest alwayes withdraw from them thy roddes and curses, whiche were prepared for them, in such sorte, that thou dided neuer refuse to heare their prayers.

We haue obtained by thy goodnesse in a farre more excellēt maner, the same Couenaunt, stablished by the meanes of Iesus Christ our Sauior, written with his bloud, and sealed with his death and passion.

Therefore, O Lorde, we renouncing our selues, and all vaine confidence in mannes helpe, haue our onelye refuge to this thy moste blessed Couenaunt, whereby our Lorde IESVS, thorough the offering vp of his bodie in sacrifice, hath reconciled vs vnto thee. Beholde vs therefore, O Lorde, in the face of Christ thine annoynted, that by his intercession thy wrath and indignation may be appeased, and that the grieuous plagues & iudgementes which we haue deserued, may be remooued from vs, & that the bright beames of thy countenance may shine vppon vs, to our great comfort & assured saluation: and from this time forward, vouchsafe to receiue vs vnder thine holie tuition, and gouuerne vs with thy holie Spirite, whereby we may be regenerate a newe vnto a far better life.

And albeit wee be most vnworthie in our owne selues, to open our mouthes, and to intreate thee in our necessities, yet for so muche as it hath pleased thee to commaunde vs to praye one for another, wee make also our humble prayers vnto thee, for our poore brethren, whome thou dooest visite and chastise with thy roddes and corrections, moste instantlie desiringe thee, to turne away thine anger from them. Remember, o Lord, that they are thy children, as we are: and though they haue offended thy Maiestie, yet wee beseeche thee that it may please thee not to cease to proceede in thine accustomed bountie and mercie, which thou hast promised, should euermore continue towards thine elect. Vouchsafe therfore, o Lord, to extende thy pitie vpon all thy Churches, & towardes all thy people, whom thou dost now chastise, either with pestilence or warre, or such like thine accustomed roddes, as sicknesse, prison, pouertie, or any other affliction of body or minde, that it would please thee to comfort them as thou knowest to be moste expedient for them, so that thy roddes may be instructions for them, to assure them of thy fauour, and for their amendement, when thou shalt giue them cōstancie and patience, and also asswage & stay thy corrections: and so at length by deliuering them from al their troubles, giue them iust occasion to rejoice in thy mercie, and to praise thine Holy Name. Especiallie, o Lord, haue compassion on those that employe them selues for the maintenance of thy Trueth: strengthen them with an inuincible constancie: defende and assiste them: ouerthrowe the craftie practices & conspiracies of their enimies: bridle their rage, and lett their bold enterprises, which they vndertake against thee & the members of thy Son, turne to their owne confusion: and suffer not thy kingdome to be vtterlie desolate, neither suffer the remēbrance of thine holy Name to be cleane abolished, nor that they, among whom it hath pleased thee to haue thy praise set forth, bee destroied, and that the Turkes, Paganes and other infidels, the church of Rome, or other heretikes by suche occasion boast them selues thereby, & blaspheme thy Name. (.)·

¶ *Then the people are to singe a Psalme, as the Pastor appointeth: which ended, he is to prononce one of these blessinges, and so the Congregation departeth.*

The Lorde blesse vs and saue vs: the Lorde make his face to shine vppon vs, and be mercifull vnto vs: the Lorde turne his countenance towardes vs, and graunt vs his peace.

· To this the Minister addeth that part whiche is in the former prayer marked thus (.).

The grace of our Lorde Iesus Christ, the loue of God, & communion of the holy Ghost be with vs all. So be it.

¶ *It shall not be necessarie for the Pastor dayly to repeate all these thinges before mentioned, but beginning with some like confession, to proceede to the Sermon, which ended, he eyther is to vse the prayer for all estates, before mencioned, or else to pray, as the Spirit of god shall moue his harte, framing the same according to the time and matter whiche hee hath intreated of. And if there shalbe at any time any present plague, famine, pestilence, warre, or such like, which be euident tokens of gods wrath, as it is our parte, to acknowledge oure sinnes to be the occasion thereof, so are we appointed by the scriptures, to giue our selues to mourning, fasting and prayer, as the meanes to turne away Gods heauie displeasure. Therfore it shall be conuenient, that the Minister, during such time, doo not onelye admonishe the people thereof, but also vse some forme of prayer, accordinge as the present necessitie requireth, to the which he may appoint by consent of the Eldership, some seuerall day after the Sermon, weekelie to bee obserued, where it may be done conuenientlie.*

THE MANNER OF ADMINISTRING
THE LORDS SVPPER

¶ *The day when the Lordes Supper is to be ministred, which shalbe cōmonly once a moneth, or so ofte as the Congregation shal thinke expedient, the Minister shal vse to say as followeth.*

Let vs marke, deare brethren, and consider howe Iesus Christ did ordaine vnto vs his Holie Supper, according as S. Paule maketh rehearshall in the 11.Chap. of the firste Epistle to the Corint. saying:

I haue receyued of the Lorde, that whiche I haue deliuered vnto you, to witte, that the Lorde IESVS the same night he was betrayed, tooke bread, and when he had giuen thankes, he brake it saying: Take yee, eate ye, this is my bobie,• which is broken for you: doo you this in remembrance of mee. Likewise after Supper, he tooke the Cuppe, saying: This Cuppe is the newe Testament or Couenant in my bloud: doo ye this so ofte as yee shall drinke thereof, in remembrance

• Misprint: bodie.

of mee. For so ofte as you sall · eate this bread, and drinke of this Cuppe, ye shall declare the Lords death vntill his comming. Therefore whosoeuer shall eate this breade, and drinke the Cuppe of the Lorde vnworthely, he shall be guiltie of the body and bloud of the Lorde. Then see that euery man prooue and trie him selfe, & so let him eate of this breade, and drinke of this Cuppe: for whosoeuer eateth or drinketh vnworthily, he eateth & drinketh his owne damnation, for not hauing due regarde and consideration of the Lords bodie.

¶ *This done, the Pastor is to proceede to the exhortation,*[7] *saying:*

Dearely beloued in the Lorde, forasmuch as we be now assembled to celebrate the holy communion of the bodie and bloud of our Sauiour Christ, let vs consider these wordes of Saint Paule, howe he exhorteth all persons diligently to trie and examine them selues, before they presume to eate of that bread, and drinke of that Cuppe. For as the benefite is great, if with a truelie penitent heart, and liuelie faith wee receyue that holie Sacrament (for then we spirituallie eate the fleshe of Christ, & drinke his bloude: then wee dwell in Christe, and Christ in vs, we be one with Christ, and Christe with vs) so is the daunger exceeding great, if we receyue this holie Sacramente vnworthilie: for then wee be guiltie of the bodie and bloud of Christ our Sauiour: we eate and drink our owne damnation, not consideringe the Lorde his bodie, which is offered in this Sacramente to the worthie receyuer: wee kindle Gods heauie wrath against vs, and prouoke him to plague or chastise vs, with diuerse diseases, and sundrie kindes of death.

Therefore, if anie of you bee ignoraunt of GOD, a denier of the faith, an hereticke or scismatike an Idolatour, a worshipper of Angells, Saintes, or anie other creatures, a vvitch, sorcerour, southsayer, or suche as haue anie truste or confidence in them, a mainteyner of Images or mannes inuentions in the seruice of GOD, a neglecter, contemner, hinderer or slaunderer of God, his holye Worde, Sacramentes, and Discipline, a periured person, a prophaner of the Lords Sabboth: disobedient to parents, Magistrates, Ministers, and other Superiours, or bee a murderer, or in malice and enuie, or bee mercylesse and cruell, or an oppressour, Vsurer, or fornica-

· Misprint: shall.

tour, adulterour, an incestuous person, buggerer, or bee a theefe, a false dealer in bargayninge, or anie the like matter: a slaunderour, backebyter, or false witnesse bearer, or in anie other grieuous crime, lament & bewayle your sinnes and iniquities, and presume not to come to this holie Table, least the Deuill enter into you, as hee entred into Iudas, and fill you full of all iniquities, and bringe you to destruction, both of bodie and soule.

Iudge therefore your selues, examine and trie your heartes (Brethren) that ye bee not iudged of the Lorde: Repente you truelie for your sinnes past, and haue a liuelie and stedfast fayth in Christe oure Sauiour, seekinge onelie your saluation in the merites of his death and passion, of his righteousnesse and obedience: from hence foorth refusinge and forgettinge all enuie and malice, with full purpose and deliberation, to liue in Brotherlie amitie, and all godlie and honest conuersation, all the dayes of your life.

And albeit we feele in our selues much fraieltie and wretchednesse, as that wee haue not our faith so perfect, and constant, as we ought, being manye times readie to distrust Gods goodnesse thorough our corrupt nature, and also that we are not so thoroughlie giuen to serue GOD, neither haue so feruent a zeale to set forth his glorie, as our duetie requireth, feeling still such rebellion in our selues, that we haue neede dailie to fight against the lustes of our flesh, yet neuerthelesse, seeing that our Lorde hath dealt thus mercifullie with vs, that he hath printed his Gospell in oure heartes, so that we are preserued from falling into desperation and misbeliefe: and seeing also he hath indued vs with a will, and desire to renounce and withstande our owne affections, with a longing for his righteousnes & the keeping of his commaundementes, we may be nowe right well assured, that those defaultes and manifolde imperfections in vs shal be no hinderance at all against vs, to cause him not to accepte and impute vs as worthie to come to his spirituall Table. For the ende of our comming thither is not to make protestation that we are vpright or iust in our liues, but cōtrariwise, we come to seeke our life and perfection in Iesus Christe, acknowledging in the meane time, that vve of our selues be the children of vvrath and damnation.

Let vs consider then, that the Sacrament is an excellent medicine for all poore sicke creatures, a cōfortable helpe to weake soules, and that our Lorde requireth no other worthi-

nesse on oure parte, but that vve vnfainedlie acknowledge
our wickednesse, and imperfection. Then to the ende that we
may bee worthie partakers of his merites, and most comfortable benefites, by the true and spirituall eating of his
fleshe, & drinking of his bloude, let vs not suffer our mindes
to wander about the consideration of these earthlie and corruptible things, (which we see present to our eies, and feele
with our handes) to seeke Christe bodily present in them,·
as if hee were inclosed in the bread or wine, or as if these Elementes vvere turned & chaūged into the substance of his
fleshe and bloude. For the only way to dispose our soules to
receiue nourishement, releefe and quickening of his sub-
staunce·· is to lift vppe our mindes by faith aboue all thinges
worldlie and sensible, and therby to enter into Heauen, that
wee maye finde and receiue Christe, where he dwelleth vn-
doubtedlie verie God, and verie man, in the incomprehensible
glorie of his Father, to whom be all prayse, honour and
glorie, nowe and euer, Amen.

¶ *The exhortation ended,*[8] *the Minister is to giue thankes,
either in these wordes following or like in effect.*[9]

O Father of mercie and God of all consolation, seeing all
creatures doe acknowledge and confesse thee as Gouuernour
and Lorde, it becommeth vs the workemanshippe of thine
owne handes, at all times to reuerence and magnifie thy godlie Maiestie: first, for that thou hast created vs to thine owne
image and similitude, but chieflie because thou hast deliuered
vs from that euerlasting death and damnation, into the v·hich
Satan drewe mankinde by the meane of sinne: from the
bondage whereof, neither man nor Angell vvas able to make
vs free, but thou, o lord, rich in mercie, & infinite in goodnesse, hast prouided our redemtion to stand in thy onely &
welbeloued Sōne, whom of very loue thou didest giue to
be made man like vnto vs in all things, sinne excepte, that in
his body he might receiue the punishment of our transgression, by his death to make satisfaction to thy iustice, and by
his resurrection to destroye him that was the authour of
death, and so to bring againe life to the worlde, from whiche
the whole ofspring of Adam most iustly was exiled.

O Lorde, wee acknowledge that no creature is able to

· Transubstantiation, Transelemētatiō, Transmutation & Transformation, as the papistes vse them, ar the doctrine of Deuilles.
·· The true eatinge of christ in the Sacrament.

337

comprehende the length and breadth, the deepnesse and height of that thy moste excellent loue vvhich mooued thee to shewe mercie where none was deserued: to promise and giue life, where death had gotten victorie: to receiue vs into thy grace, when we could do nothing but rebell against thy iustice. O Lorde, the biinde· dulnesse of our corrupt nature, will not suffer vs sufficiently to vveighe these thy moste ample benefites: yet neuerthelesse, at the commandement of IESVS Christ our Lorde, we present our selues to this his Table (whiche hee hath lefte to bee vsed in remembrounce of his death vntill his comming againe) to declare & witnesse before the vvorld, that by him alone we haue receiued libertie, and life: that by him alone thou doest acknowledge vs thy children and heyres: that by him alone wee haue entrance to the throne of thy grace: that by him alone we are possessed in our spiritual kingdome, to eate and drink at his Table, vvith whom we haue our conuersation presentlie in heauen, and by vvhome our bodies shalbe raised vp againe from the dust, and shal be placed with him in that endlesse ioye, which thou, o Father of mercie, hast prepared for thine electe before the foundation of the worlde was laide. And these moste inestimable benefites we acknowledge and confesse to haue receiued of thy free mercie and grace, by thine only beloued Sōne Iesus Christ: for the which therefore we thy Congregation mooned·· by thine holye Spirite, render thee all thankes, praise and glorie, for euer and euer.

¶ *This done, the Minister comming to the Table, and the Table being furnished, is to break the breade and deliuer it to the people, saying:*[10] *Take & eate, this bread is the body of Christ that was broken for vs, Doo this in remembrance of him: who distribute and diuide the same among them selues, according to our Sauiour Christes commaundement. Likewise he shall giue the Cuppe, saying: Drinke ye all of this: This Cuppe is the newe Testament in the bloud of Christ, which was shedde for the sinnes of manie: Doo this in the remembrance of him. During the which time, some place of the Scriptures is to bee read, whiche doeth liuely set forth the death of Christe, to the intent that our eyes and senses maye not onely be occupied in these outwarde signes of bread and wine, whiche are called the*

• Misprint: blinde.
•• Misprint: mooued.

338

visible worde, but that our heartes and mindes also may be fullie fixed in the contemplation of the Lordes death, which is by this holy Sacrament represented. And after the actiō is done, he is to giue thankes, saying:[11]

Most mercifull Father, we render to thee all prayse, thankes and glorie, for that it hath pleased thee of thy great mercies, to graunt vnto vs miserable sinners so excellent a gift and treasure, as to receyue vs into the felowship and companie of thy deare Sonne IESVS Christ our Lorde, whom thou haste deliuered to death for vs, and hast giuen him vnto vs, as a necessarie foode & nourishement vnto euerlastinge life. And nowe we beseech thee also, O heauenlie Father, to graunt vs this request, that thou neuer suffer vs to become so vnkinde, as to forgette so worthie benefites, but rather imprint and fasten them sure in our hearts, that we may grow and increase daylye more and more in true faith, which continuallie is exercised in all manner of good workes, and so much the rather, O Lorde, confirme vs in these perillous dayes, and rages of Satan, that we may constantlie stande and continue in the confession of the same, to the aduancement of thy glorie, which art God ouer all things blessed for euer. So be it.

¶ *The action thus ended, the people are to sing the 103 Psalme, My soule giue laude, &c. or some other of thankes giuing: which ended, one of the blessings before mentioned, is to be recited, and so they rise from the Table and departe.*

¶ If so be that any would maruell why we followe rather this order, then any other in the administration of this Sacrament, let him diligentlie consider, that first of all wee vtterlie renounce the errour of the Papistes: secondlie, we restore vnto the Sacrament his owne substance, and to Christ his proper place. And as for the wordes of the Lordes Supper, we rehearse thē not bicause they shuld change the substance of the breade or wine, or that the repetition thereof with the intent of the sacrificer, should make the Sacrament (as the Papistes falslie beleeue) but they are redde and pronounced to teache vs howe to behaue our selues in that action,• and that Christe might witnesse vnto our fayth, as it were with his owne mouth, that he hath

• Why this order is to bee obserued rather than anie other.

339

ordeined these signes for our spirituall vse and comfort. We doo firste therefore examine our selues, according to Saint Paules rule, and prepare our mindes that we may be worthie partakers of so high mysteries. Then takinge breade, we giue thankes, breake and distribute it, as Christe our Sauiour hath taught vs. Finallie, the ministration ended, wee giue thankes againe, accordinge to his example: so that without his worde and warrant, there is nothinge in this holy action attempied.·

NOTES

1. "Middlebvrgh. By Richard Schilders, Printer to the States of Zealande, 1586." Reproduced verbatim—spelling, punctuation, and paragraphing—from a microfilm of the original volume, obtained from the British Museum. Marginal references to Scripture have been omitted, and the rubrics italicized.
2. There follows a description of the Reader's Service, which also came into practice in Scotland after 1560; cf. W. D. Maxwell, *John Knox's Genevan Service Book,* App. A, pp. 177-9.
3. There is an obvious defect of meaning here. The liturgies of Calvin, Pullain, and Knox enable us to see the proper order of events. When the minister arrived, he commenced the Sunday Service by saying, "Our helpe be in thee name of the Lorde. . . ." Then he invited the people to confession, saying, "Lette vs fall downe before the Maiestie of Almightie God. . . ." Directly he recited the Prayer of Confession on behalf of the congregation. Notice that the initial sentence of Scripture, found in Calvin but omitted in *The Forme of Prayers* (1556), has been replaced.
4. The editors of the Middleburg Liturgy omitted the first order of Confession in *The Forme of Prayers* (1556) and retained the second, namely, Calvin's prayer, to which Knox and his associates had added a petition for pardon.
5. Here is the traditional Calvinistic order of proclamation: the prayer for illumination, followed by the lesson and the sermon. For details, cf. the notes on the corresponding rubric in *The Forme of Prayers.*
6. Three forms of the Great Prayer are here provided. The first is the original composition of *The Forme of Prayers* (1556). The second is Calvin's Great Prayer, including the lengthy paraphrase of the Lord's Prayer. The editors of the Middleburg Liturgy likely supplied the third—a heavy, penitential

· Misprint: attempted.

piece, to which a substantial part of Calvin's prayer was to be appended.

7. The Middleburg editors reproduced, for the most part, the Exhortation of *The Forme of Prayers* (1556). The only major change the editors made was to augment the list of offenders to be fenced from the table. The new list resembles more or less that of Calvin. The first three paragraphs of the Exhortation came originally from *The Book of Common Prayer,* the last two from Calvin.

8. At this point in *The Forme of Prayers,* the minister left the pulpit and took his place at the table, where he was joined by the people. The Middleburg editors did not change the method of Delivery, however, for in the final rubric the people are summoned to "rise from the Table and departe."

9. The Eucharistic prayer of thanksgiving was taken verbatim from *The Forme of Prayers.*

10. Notice the inclusion of Words of Delivery, which may also indicate that a similar practice was followed in Knox's congregation at Geneva. For details of the Delivery, cf. the introduction and the notes to *The Forme of Prayers.*

11. The remainder of the text was taken almost verbatim from *The Forme of Prayers.* The Post-Communion prayer of thanksgiving came originally from Bucer and Calvin.

XI

THE WESTMINSTER DIRECTORY
FOR THE PUBLIQUE WORSHIP OF GOD

1644

THE WESTMINSTER DIRECTORY

The history of the liturgy now coincides with the effort of the early Stuart kings to impose the Anglican rite upon the Kirk of Scotland. At the Hampton Court Conference in 1604, James I vented his wrath against "Scottish presbytery, which as well agreeth with a monarchy as God with the devil." Royal absolutism could ill afford the challenge of presbyterian polity, which allowed every "Tom, Will, and Dick" to censure the king. That view of the matter prompted James to harry the Puritans in England and to bring the Church of Scotland into conformity with Anglican polity and worship. In 1612, he succeeded in introducing an episcopal regime in Scotland, which provided him a useful instrument for his liturgical designs.

In August, 1616, at the king's instruction, the Scottish General Assembly "ordained that a uniform order of liturgy . . . be set down to be read in all the kirks," and it named a committee of four to make the revision. This language was prejudicial; it implied that *The Book of Common Order* had been eroded by Puritan ideas and divers prejudices, till it was no more a liturgy, but a "sampler" to be used (and abused) by the clergy. Archbishop Spottiswoode of St. Andrews had intimated as much to the king in the previous year: "There is lacking in our Church a form of divine service; and . . . every minister is left to the framing of public prayer by himself."

Led by Peter Hewat (Howat), an Edinburgh minister of moderate views, the committee prepared a Sunday Morning

Service on the broad lines of Knox's liturgy. In Hewat's draft, permissive rubrics disappeared, and the service acquired a distinctly liturgical character, with the addition of fixed prose psalms, lessons from the Epistles and Gospels, and prayers for special occasions. Evidently there was no resistance to liturgical revision, even among men who intended to honor the ways of John Knox.

Meanwhile James pursued his purposes in another way, by seeking the restoration of the Church Year and other observances which would more nearly consolidate the religions of England and Scotland. At the General Assembly, which met at Perth in 1618, and which was packed to do the royal will, James put upon the Kirk the five Articles of Perth. They enjoined kneeling to communicate, private administration of the two sacraments, the rite of Confirmation, and the observation of Christmas, Good Friday, Easter, Ascension, and Whitsunday. The first of the Articles aroused bitter hostility among the laity, who could scarcely forget the dreadful admonitions of Knox against the Mass, nor his specific injunction against kneeling at Communion.

Amidst the tumult raised against the king's machinations, the revision of the liturgy had proceeded without interruption; and at the same Perth Assembly, or shortly after, Bishop Cowper of Galloway produced the text of a complete prayer book, which exceeded Hewat's draft in conformity to the English rite, but did not obliterate the structure of the Knox Liturgy.• The king deemed, however, to shelve this latest revision, realizing how sorely he had tried the Scots' patience by the Articles of Perth. William Laud admonished him to persevere; but James warned that leader of the younger Anglicans that "he knew not the stomach" of the Scottish people. Parliament ratified the five Articles (1621) on the understanding that James would desist in the matter of liturgi-

---

• The structure of Holy Communion was as follows: Collect for Purity (BCP); Words of Institution; Exhortation with excommunication (BCO); Invitation (BCP); a long prayer of five parts: (1) Confession (BCP), (2) Humble Access (BCP, modified), (3) Invocation ("Send down, O Lord, thy blessing upon this Sacrament. . . ."), (4) Commemoration & Thanksgiving, and (5) the Lord's Prayer; the Words of Institution (repeated "for consecrating the elements"); the Reformed *Sursum corda* (but without any disparagement of the bread and wine); Words of Delivery (BCP, modified); Communion (kneeling); etc. See the text in Sprott, pp. 25ff.

cal reform. And so the issue remained until his death, in 1625.

Laud became bishop of London in 1628 and the primate of England five years hence. It was his policy—in which Charles I concurred—that the Anglican rite should be established in all His Majesty's dominions. Such an overarching sense of uniformity might even bring the Puritans to submission. In 1629, John Maxwell of Edinburgh delivered Cowper's draft to the king, with the observation that the Scots would prefer to frame a native liturgy than "to have the English liturgy put upon them." He was told in reply that "the English service without any alterations" was meet for the Kirk. In time, however, Charles yielded to the representations of the Scots, and in 1634 gave them leave to prepare their own services. It was, at that, a small concession, for he instructed the Scottish bishops to "draw up a liturgy as near that of England as might be." Moreover, when Maxwell (then bishop of Ross) went south later in the year to hear the king's advice, he was sent away with a copy of the English Prayer Book, signed by Charles, in which certain trivial alterations were proposed.• The Scots could scarcely miss the point that their liturgy was to be a replica of the English book. Upon receipt of this intelligence, the bishops set to work; and, being not overly taxed by the job, they completed a draft in six months and sent it south with Maxwell. Charles corrected it, signed the text, and ordered it printed.

Publication commenced in September, 1635, but was soon interrupted. At this juncture, apparently, the younger bishops overruled their cautious colleagues, to urge a further revision of the text, insisting that the liturgy must now be "perfected," else it could never be. James Wedderburn, who attained a bishopric in 1636, sent suggestions to Laud that caused substantial changes to be made in the Communion service. (1) Three prayers were removed to a position between the Consecration and the Administration—namely, the Oblation, the Lord's Prayer, and the Humble Access, in that order. (2) In accord with Scottish custom, the Manual Acts were in-

---

• The Authorised Version of Scripture was permitted, and some freedom was granted in the observance of the Church Year. On the other hand, "minister" was changed to "priest," "congregation" to "church," and the word "saint" (or "S.") was supplied at appropriate points. In the 1637 edition, however, "presbyter" prevailed over "priest."

cluded with the Consecration. (3) The second sentence in the Words of Delivery was stricken because it seemed "to relish somewhat of the Zwinglian tenet." Weighing *all* of Wedderburn's proposals, it is fairly clear that he and his associates meant to "perfect" the liturgy by making it conform, not to the current Anglican usage, but to the more catholic usage of the 1549 Prayer Book. At any rate, these changes came exclusively from the Scottish bishops; and Laud admitted as much (*Works* 3: 356). It is therefore somewhat beside the truth to refer to the Scottish Prayer Book of 1637 as "Laud's Liturgy."

Unfortunately, Laud inscribed these alterations into a copy of the English Prayer Book *in his own hand.* On April 19, 1636, Charles· signed that book and issued a warrant, saying, "I gave the Archbp. of Canterbury command to make the alteracions expressed in this booke, and *to fitt a liturgy for the Church of Scotland.*" Taken together, these innocent but untoward circumstances aroused the fury of the Scots, who were already brimful of discontent over the policies of Charles. In December, at the behest of the Crown, the Scottish Privy Council enjoined the nation to conform to the new book, which neither Parliament nor the Generai Assembly nor the rank and file of the clergy had seen or approved.

The Book of Common Prayer . . . for the Use of the Church of Scotland · came from the press in the spring of 1537. When it was introduced at St. Giles on July 23, hired rascals provoked a furious, if premeditated, riot against that "black, popish, and superstitious book." As resistance spread on cries of "Antichrist," the liturgy was doomed. In February of 1638, representatives of all estates swelled Greyfriars Church in Edinburgh to sign the National Covenant. Led by Alexander Henderson, the Covenanters renewed the "King's Confession" (1581), which was fiercely anti-Roman, and pledged their mutual support for the preservation of "the true worship of God." Later that year the Glasgow Assembly struck down the episcopate and prayer book.

Scottish resistance to the royal policy invigorated the Puritans in England. Since the accession of James I their lot had not been easy. Conformity had been meted out to them with a heavy hand. Their Sabbatarianism had been mocked by the *Book of Sports.* They had been politically disaffected by arbitrary taxation without the consent of Parliament, or, in

· For text and commentary, see Donaldson, pp. 60-247.

the case of Charles, by royal rule without any Parliament at all (1629-40). Meanwhile the acquiescence of the Anglicans in the policies of the Crown and in the narrow designs of Laud brought the English bishops into mounting disfavor. Thus, with the advent of the Long Parliament (1640), in which presbyterian Puritanism gained ascendancy, there occurred a series of decisive strokes against the religious structure. Laud was sent to the Tower; his ecclesiastical machinery was demolished. And following the outbreak of civil war, the episcopal hierarchy and the established liturgy were abolished.

The Westminster Assembly, a creature of Parliament, convened on July 1, 1643, to reform the standards of the church in a manner "most agreeable to God's holy word." Of the "learned, godly, and judicious Divines" who gathered at Westminster Abbey, the presbyterian Puritans were in the majority, while the Independents constituted a vigorous minority dedicated to the principles of congregational polity and opposed to liturgical prayer. Presently the Long Parliament and the Westminster Assembly adopted the Solemn League and Covenant, recently drawn between the Scottish General Assembly and an English delegation sent north to Edinburgh. Designed to enlist the effectual aid of the Scots in the English crisis, the Covenant bound the parties to "the preservation of the reformed religion in the Church of Scotland" and "the reformation of religion in the kingdoms of England and Ireland." By virtue of this instrument, five Scots commissioners joined the Assembly without vote.

The preparation of a service-book was given over to a subcommittee that included presbyterians, the Scots commissioners, and one articulate Independent named Thomas Goodwin. When their chairman, Stephen Marshall, laid the first draft of the work before the full Assembly (May, 1644), he reported that "many serious and sad debates" had taken place over the crucial issue of form and freedom. To satisfy the desires and scruples of all the parties the subcommittee had found it expedient to produce a *directory*, as opposed to a liturgy, which outlined the main headings of worship, and described the substance of each element in such a way that "by altering here and there a word, a man may mould it into a prayer." Where disagreement could not be overcome, the committee made compensation by allowing variety in practice or by using rubrics of lesser compulsion. Apparently

Goodwin supplied much of this resistance to prescribed forms, while the Scots were chiefly responsible for the affinity of the manual to *The Book of Common Order*.

Completed in 1644, the manuscript was entitled *A Directory for the Publique Worship of God* (below). The Preface commenced with a typical Puritan thesis: the Anglican reformation remains to be finished. *The Book of Common Prayer*, while commendable in its day, had become a burden upon the conscience of "sundry good Christians," causing ministers to be deprived and laity to be kept from the Lord's table. It produced prayer-book idolatry to the depreciation of preach-ing. It confirmed the papists in their own superstition, rendered the clergy "idle and unedifying," and brought untold contention upon the church. Therefore, after earnest consultation with the Word of God, the divines resolved "to lay aside the former Leiturgie" and to install the new *Directory*, which had three notable virtues. (1) It contained ordinances that were "of Divine Institution" as well as other matters that were "agreeable to the generall Rules of the VVord of God." (2) It promised to achieve uniformity by setting forth the principal headings of worship and the sense and scope of prayers. (3) As a directory, it provided ministers "some help and furniture" without depriving them of the gift of prayer.

When the congregation had assembled on the Lord's Day,• the minister issued a solemn call to worship and proceeded to frame an opening prayer according to the italicized directions. Thus his prayer normally included the adoration of God and a corresponding confession of the "vilenesse and unworthinesse" of man; it closed with a plea for God's blessing upon that "portion of his Word then to bee read." Thereupon a chapter from each of the testaments was read "in course," after which the people engaged in singing a psalm. The minister was forbidden to use the Apocrypha. He was also admonished against "lecturing"—a practice, current among certain Puritans and Scots, of giving a running commentary to the lessons, sometimes in lieu of reading them. If the minister insisted upon such commentary, let him refrain until the whole passage had been read. There followed a rubric sup-

---

• Of Sunday, the *Directory* said: "There is no Day commanded in Scripture to be kept holy . . . but the Lords day, which is the Christian Sabbath. Festivall daies, vulgarly called Holy daies, having no warrant in the word of God, are not to be continued." On the question of the Reader's Service, see Leishman, pp. 87ff.

350

plied by the House of Commons: those who could read were exhorted to purchase a Bible and use it; those who could not read were urged to learn. In such a way the *Directory* renewed the mandate of Luther and Calvin, that believers were obliged to be lifelong disciples of the Word of God.

The Prayer of Confession, which followed, rehearsed in stern detail the Original and actual sins of men (wherein the Puritans found the Anglican rite deficient); then it proceeded to sundry petitions for pardon, reconciliation, and sanctification, and closed with a long season of Intercessions. This catchal-prayer was the ultimate Puritan answer to the brevity of Anglican collects; and the Independents in particular found virtue in such comprehensiveness. In deference to Scottish practice, however, allowance was made in a concluding rubric for those who wished to defer the Intercessions until the prayer after the sermon.

The directions for preaching belie the assumption that Puritan clergy were a mean lot. "The Minister of Christ" was expected to know Greek and Hebrew, the arts and sciences, and the whole body of theology, and to be experienced in Scripture "above the common sort of Beleevers." The preparation of sermons was outlined in great detail, according to the current threefold method of Doctrine, Reason, and Use.

Having preached the Word, the minister offered thanksgiving to God, in the course of which he rehearsed the saving benefits of the Gospel, ("as namely, Election, Vocation, Adoption, Justification, Sanctification, and the hope of Glory"), and prayed over the chief points of the sermon—all of which illustrates (as Davies said) that Puritan prayer was "excessively edifying." In a succeeding rubric, the Lord's Prayer was "recommended" as a "Pattern of Prayer" (the Independent view), but also as a "comprehensive Prayer" and thus appropriate to be used here or elsewhere in worship. The service closed with a psalm and the blessing. No liturgical provision was made for the *Gloria patri*, the Creed, or the Ten Commandments. Baillie, a Scot who could not abide the Independents, accused them of casting out the Creed "as an old Patchery of evil stuff."

The Communion liturgy began with a declaration that the Lord's Supper ought to be celebrated "frequently"; but, there being no unanimity over the precise schedule, the matter was left to the local congregations. Where it was held infrequently, the Super was to be attended by solemn preparation, either on the Sunday or a weekday preceding, so that "all may come better prepared to that heavenly Feast." On the day itself, an Exhortation was given at the start of the liturgy which re-emphasized the peril of unworthy reception and fenced the table against obdurate offenders, but which also invited those to participate who sighed under the burden of their sins.

The minister proceeded to "set apart" the elements from all common use, and to "sanctify" and "bless" them for "holy use" by "Word and Prayer." (These terms were most carefully chosen.) First he read the Words of Institution from one of the Gospels or from Paul, which he could also "explaine and apply" if it seemed appropriate. Then he offered the short Eucharistic Prayer which included: Humble Access; Thanksgiving for creation, redemption, and the means of grace; and the Epiclesis. In this notable prayer, the divines laid stress upon the positive features of Calvin's liturgy, leaving out the Reformed *Sursum corda* with its depreciation of "the earthly and corruptible elements" and its suggestion that the Lord was exalted far off in heaven. The emphasis fell rather upon the reception of Christ's body and blood, that "he may be one with us and we with him."

The elements having been "sanctified by the Word and Prayer," the minister performed the Fraction, spoke the Dominical Words, and delivered bread and cup to the people who sat "about" the table or "at" it. Great vexation was hidden in those two prepositions. The Puritans preferred to receive the elements from the hands of the minister as they sat "about" the table—in their "pews" as we would say. But the Scots insisted upon their custom of sitting "at" the table, and of handing the elements to one another. Thus, the *Directory* made provision for both methods of Administration. Moreover, it contained no mention of successive tables, because the Independents preferred to communicate together, at one time, in token of their unity in Christ. In Scottish practice, however, the minister communicated first, apart from the people; and in light of this additional disparity, the rubric that dealt with the minister's Communion was made ambiguous.

The Westminster *Directory* was received by Parliament on January 3, 1645, at which time *The Book of Common Prayer* was officially abrogated. The Church of Scotland adopted it by the Act of Assembly, February 3, 1645, but

352

The Westminster Directory

with the proviso that it should "be no prejudice to the order and practice of this Kirk." Its reception in England was by no means hearty. The Anglicans, who understandably found it odious, heaped ridicule upon it, while the Independents considered it excessively precise. Though it was not the first such "directory"—Farel had tried his hand at one in the sixteenth century—it was nonetheless a monumental effort to comprehend the virtues of form and freedom. Drawn agreeably to the use of the Reformed churches, the *Directory* was yet an authentic creation of the Puritan spirit and the truest exemplar of Puritan worship.

FOR FURTHER READING

George B. Burnet, *The Holy Communion in the Reformed Church of Scotland*. Edinburgh, 1960.
Horton Davies, *The Worship of the English Puritans*. Westminster, 1948.
Gordon Donaldson, *The Making of the Scottish Prayer Book of 1637*. Edinburgh, 1954.
T. Leishman, *The Westminster Directory*. Edinburgh, 1901.
William McMillan, *The Worship of the Scottish Reformed Church, 1550-1638*. London, 1931.
W. D. Maxwell, *A History of Worship in the Church of Scotland*. London, 1955.
G. W. Sprott, *Scottish Liturgies of James VI*. Edinburgh, 1901.

A DIRECTORY FOR THE
PUBLIQUE VVORSHIP OF GOD
THROUGHOUT THE THREE KINGDOMS
OF ENGLAND, SCOTLAND, AND IRELAND.
LONDON, 1644 [1]

The Preface

In the beginning of the blessed Reformation, our wise and pious Ancestors took care to set forth an Order for Redresse of many things, which they, then, by the VVord discovered to be Vain, Erroneous, Superstitious and Idolatrous in the Publique VVorship of God. This occasioned many Godly and Learned men to rejoyce much in the Book of Common-Prayer at that time set forth; Because the Masse, and the rest of the Latine-Service being removed, the Publique VVorship was celebrated in our own Tongue; many of the common People also received benefit by hearing the Scriptures read in their own Language, which formerly were unto them as a Book that is sealed.

Howbeit, long and sad Experience hath made it manifest, That the Leiturgie used in the Church of *England,* (notwithstanding all the pains and Religious intentions of the Compilers of it) hath proved an offence, not only to many of the Godly at home; but also to the Reformed Churches abroad. For, not to speak of urging the Reading of all the Prayers, which very greatly increased the burden of it; the many unprofitable and burdensome Ceremonies, contained in it, have occasioned much mischief, as well by disquieting the Consciences of many godly Ministers and people who could not yeeld unto them, as by depriving them of the Ordinances of God, which they might not enjoy without conforming or Subscribing to those Ceremonies. Sundry good Christians have been, by means thereof, kept from the Lords Table; and divers able and faithfull Ministers debarred from the exercise of their Ministery (to the endangering of many Thousand Souls, in a time of such scarcity of faithfull Pastors) and spoiled of their livelyhood, to the undoing of them and their Families. Prelates and their Faction have laboured to raise the Estimation of it to such an height, as if there were no other VVorship, or way of VVorship amongst us, but onely the

Service-Book; to the great hinderance of the Preaching of the VVord, and (in some places, especially of late) to the justling of it out, as unnecessary; or (at best) as far inferiour to the Reading of Common-Prayer; which was made no better then² an Idol by many Ignorant and Superstitious People, vvho pleasing themselves in their presence at that Service, and their Lip-labour in bearing a part in it, have thereby hardened themselves in their ignorance and carelesnesse of saving knowledge and true piety.

In the mean time Papists boasted, that the Book was a compliance with them in a great part of their Service, and so were not a little confirmed in their Superstition and Idolatry, expecting rather our return to them, then² endeavouring the Reformation of themselves: In which expectation they were of late very much incouraged, when, upon the pretended warrantablenesse of imposing of the former Ceremonies, new ones were dayly obtruded upon the Church.

Adde hereunto (which was not foreseen, but since hath come to passe) that the Leiturgie hath been a great means, as on the one hand to make and increase an idle and unedifying Ministery, which contented itself with set Forms made to their hands by others, without putting forth themselves to exercise the gift of Prayer, with which our Lord *Jesus Christ* pleaseth to furnish all his Servants whom he calls to that office: So on the other side it hath been (and ever would be, if continued) a matter of endlesse strife and contention in the Church, and a snare both to many godly and faithfull Ministers, who have been persecuted and silenced upon that occasion, and to others of hopefull parts, many of which have been, and more still would be, diverted from all thoughts of the Ministery to other studies; especially in these latter times, wherein God vouchsafeth to his people more and better means for the discovery of Error and Superstition, and for attaining of knowledge in the mysteries of godliness, and gifts in Preaching and Prayer.

Upon these, and many the like weighty considerations, in reference to the whole Book in generall, and because of divers particulars contained in it; not from any love to Novelty, or intention to disparage our first Reformers (of whom we are perswaded, that, were they now alive, they would joyn with us in this work, and whom we acknowledge as Excellent Instruments raised by God to begin the purging and building of his House, and desire they may be had of us and Posterity in everlasting Remembrance, with thankfulnesse and honour;) but that we may in some measure answer the gracious Providence of God, which at this time calleth upon us for further Reformation, and may satisfy our own Consciences, and answer the expectation of other Reformed Churches, and the desires of many of the godly among our selves, and withall give some publique Testimony of our endeavors for Uniformity in Divine Worship, which we have promised in our Solemn League and Covenant: VVe have, after earnest and frequent calling upon the Name of God, and after much Consultation, not with flesh and blood, but with his holy VVord, resolved to lay aside the former Leiturgie, with the many Rites and Ceremonies formerly used in the VVorship of God: And have agreed upon this following Directory for all the parts of Publique VVorship, at ordinary and extraordinary times.

Wherein our care hath been to hold forth such things as are of Divine Institution in every Ordinance; and other things we have endeavored to set forth according to the Rules of Christian Prudence, agreeable to the generall Rules of the VVord of God. Our meaning therein being onely that the generall heads, the sense and scope of the Prayers and other parts of Publique VVorship being known to all, there may be a consent of all the Churches, in those things that contain the substance of the Service and VVorship of God; And the Ministers may be hereby directed in their Administrations to keep like soundnesse in Doctrine and Prayer; and may, if need be, have some help and furniture: And yet so, as they become not hereby slothfull and negligent in stirring up the gifts of Christ in them: But, that each one, by meditation, by taking heed to himself and the Flock of God committed to him, and by wise observing the wayes of Divine Providence, may be carefull to furnish his heart and tongue with further, or other materials of Prayer and Exhortation, as shall be needfull upon all occasions.

OF THE ASSEMBLING OF THE CONGREGATION, AND THEIR BEHAVIOUR IN THE PUBLIQUE WORSHIP OF GOD

When the Congregation is to meete for Publique Worship, the people (having before prepared their hearts thereunto) ought all to come, and joyne therein: not absenting them-selves from the Publique Ordinances, through negligence, or upon pretence of Private meetings.

Let all enter the Assembly, not irreverently, but in a grave and seemly manner, taking their seates or places without Adoration, or Bowing themselves towards one place or other.

The Congregation being assembled; the Minister, after solemne calling on them to the worshiping of the great name of God,[3] is to begin with Prayer;

In all Reverence and Humility acknowledging the incom-prehensible Greatnesse and Majesty of the Lord, (in whose presence they doe then in a speciall manner appeare) and their own vilenesse and unworthinesse to approach so neare him; with their utter inability of themselves, to so great a Work: And humbly beseeching him for Pardon, Assistance, and Acceptance in the whole Service then to bee performed; and for a Blessing on that particular portion of his Word then to bee read: and all, in the Name and Mediation of the Lord Jesus Christ.

The Publique Worship being begun, the people are wholly to attend upon it; forbearing to Reade any thing, except what the Minister is then reading or citing; and abstaining much more from all private whisperings, conferences, saluta-tions, or doing reverence to any persons present, or coming in; as also from all gazing, sleeping, and other undecent be-haviour, which may disturbe the Minister or people, or hinder themselves or others in the service of God.

If any through necessity be hindred from being present at the beginning, they ought not, when they come into the Congregation, to betake themselves to their private Devo-tions, but reverently to compose themselves to joyne with the Assembly, in that Ordinance of God which is then in hand.

OF PUBLIQUE READING OF THE HOLY SCRIPTURES

Reading of the Word in the Congregation, being part of the publique Worship of God, (wherin we acknowledge our dependence upon him, and subjection to him) and one Means sanctified by him for the edifying of his People, is to bee performed by the Pastors and Teachers.

Howbeit, such as intend the Ministery, may occasionally

both reade the Word, and exercise their gift in Preaching in Congregation, if allowed by the Presbytery thereunto.

All the Canonicall Books of the Old and New Testament, (but none of those which are commonly called Apocrypha) shall be publiquely read in the vulgar Tongue, out of the best allowed Translation, distinctly, that all may heare and understand.

How large a portion shall be read at once, is left to the wisdome of the Minister: But it is convenient that ordinarily one Chapter of each Testament bee read at every meeting; and sometimes more, where the Chapters be short, or the coherence of matter requireth it.

It is requisite that all the Canonical books bee read over in order, that the people may be better acquainted with the whole Body of the Scriptures: And ordinarily, where the Reading in either Testament endeth on one Lords day, it is to begin the next.[4]

Wee commend also the more frequent reading of such Scriptures, as hee that readest shall thinke best for edification of his Hearers; as the Book of Psalmes, and such like.

When the Minister, who readeth, shall judge it necessary to expound any part of what is read, let it not bee done untill the whole Chapter, or Psalme bee ended:[5] and regard is alwayes to be had unto the time, that neither Preaching or other Ordinance bee straitned,[6] or rendred tedious. Which Rule is to be observed in all other publique performances.

Beside Publique Reading of the Holy Scriptures, every person that can reade, is to be exhorted to reade the Scriptures privately (and all others that cannot reade, if not disabled by age, or otherwise, are likewise to bee exhorted to learne to reade) and to have a Bible.

OF PUBLIKE PRAYER BEFORE THE SERMON

After Reading of the Word (and singing of the Psalme) the Minister who is to Preach, is to endeavour to get his own, and his Hearers hearts to be rightly affected with their Sinnes, that they may all mourn in sense[7] thereof before the Lord, and hunger and thirst after the grace of God in Iesus Christ, by proceeding to a more full Confession of Sinne with shame and holy confusion of face; and to Call upon the Lord to this effect;

To acknowledge our great sinfulnesse; First, by reason of *Originall* sin, which (beside the guilt that makes us liable to everlasting *Damnation*) is the seed of all other sinnes, hath depraved and poysoned all the faculties and powers of *Soule* and *Body*, doth defile our best actions, and (were it not restrained, or our hearts renewed by *Grace*) would breake forth into innumerable transgressions, and greatest rebellions against the *Lord*, that ever were committed by the vilest of the sons of *Men*. And, next, by reason of *Actuall* sins, our own sins, the sins of *Magistrates*, of *Ministers*, and of the whole *Nation*, unto which wee are many wayes accessory. Which sins of ours receive many fearefull aggravations, wee having broken all the *Commandements* of the holy, just, and good *Law* of God, doing that which is forbidden, and leaving undone what is enjoyned; and that not onely out of *Ignorance*, and *Infirmity*, but also more presumptuously against the light of our *Minds*, checks of our *Consciences*, and motions of his own *Holy Spirit* to the contrary, so that we have no cloak for our sins; *Yea*, not onely despising the riches of *Gods* goodnesse, forbearance and long-suffering, but standing out against many invitations and offers of grace in the *Gospel*, not endeavouring as wee ought to receive *Christ* into our hearts by *Faith*, or to walke worthy of him in our lives.

To bewaile our blindnesse of minde, hardnesse of heart, unbelief, impenitency, security, lukewarmnesse, barrennesse, our not endeavouring after mortification and newness of life; not after the exercise of godlinesse in the power thereof; and that the best of us have not so stedfastly walked with *God*, kept our garments so unspotted, nor been so zealous of his glory, and the good of others, as wee ought: And to mourn over such other sins as the *Congregation* is particularly guilty of; notwithstanding the manifold and great *Mercies* of our *God*, the *Love* of *Christ*, the *Light* of the *Gospel*, and the *Reformation* of *Religion*, our own purposes, promises, vows, solemn *Covenant*, and other speciall obligations to the contrary.

To acknowledge and confesse, that, as wee are convinced of our guilt, so, out of a deep sense thereof, wee judge our selves unworthy of the smallest benefits, most worthy of *Gods* fiercest wrath, and of all the *Curses* of the *Law* and heaviest *Judgements* inflicted upon the most rebellious *Sinners*; and that hee might most justly take his *Kingdome* and *Gospel* from us, plague us with all sorts of spirituall and *temporall judgements in this life, and after cast us into utter Darknesse, in the Lake that burneth with fire and brimestone, where is weeping and gnashing of teeth for evermore.*

Notwithstanding all which, To draw neare to the Throne of Grace, encouraging our selves with hope of a gracious Answer of our Prayers, in the riches and all-sufficiency of that onely one oblation, the satisfaction and intercession of the Lord Jesus Christ at the right hand of his Father, and our Father; and, in confidence of the exceeding great and precious promises of mercy and grace in the new Covenant, through the same Mediator thereof, to deprecate the heavy wrath and curse of God, which wee are not able to avoid, or beare; and humbly, and earnestly to supplicate for mercy in the free and full remission of all our sins, and that onely for the bitter sufferings and pretious merits of that our onely Saviour Jesus Christ.

That the Lord would vouchsafe to shed abroad his love in our hearts by the Holy Ghost; seale unto us by the same Spirit of Adoption, the full assurance of our Pardon and Reconciliation; comfort all that mourn in Zion, speak peace to the wounded and troubled spirit, and bind up the broken hearted: And as for secure and presumptuous sinners, that he would open their eyes, convince their Consciences, and turn them from darknesse unto light, and from the power of Satan unto God, that they also may receive forgivenesse of sin, and an inheritance among them that are sanctified by faith in Christ Jesus.

With remission of sins through the blood of Christ, To pray for sanctification by his Spirit; the Mortification of sinne dwelling in, and many times tyrannizing over us, the quickening of our dead spirits with the life of God in Christ, grace to fit and inable us for all duties of conversation and callings towards God and Men, strength against temptations, the sanctified use of blessings and crosses, and perseverance in Faith, and obedience unto the end.

To pray for the Propagation of the Gospell and Kingdome of Christ to all Nations, for the conversion of the Jewes, the fulnesse of the Gentiles, the fall of Antichrist, and the hastening of the second comming of our Lord; For the deliverance of the distressed Churches abroad, from the tyranny of the Antichristian faction, and from the cruell oppressions and blasphemies of the Turke: For the blessing of God upon all the Reformed Churches, especially upon the Churches and

Kingdomes of ENGLAND, SCOTLAND, *and* IRELAND, *now more strictly and religiously united in the solemne Nationall League and Covenant; and for our Plantations in the remote parts of the World: more particularly for that Church and Kingdome whereof we are Members, that therein God would establish Peace and Truth, the purity of all his Ordinances, and the power of Godlinesse; prevent and remove heresie, schisme, prophanenesse, superstition, security, and unfruitfulnesse under the meanes of Grace, heale all our rents and divisions, and preserve us from breach of our solemne Covenant.*

To pray for all in Authority, especially for the Kings Majesty, that God would make him rich in blessings, both in his Person and Government; establish his Throne in Religion and Righteousnesse, save him from evill Counsell, and make him a blessed and glorious Instrument for the conservation and propagation of the Gospell, for the encouragement and protection of them that doe well, the terrour of all that doe evill, and the great good of the whole Church, and of all his Kingdomes; for the conversion of the Queen, the religious education of the Prince, and the rest of the Royall seed; For the comforting of the afflicted Queen of Bohemia, sister to our Soveraign, and for the restitution and establishment of the illustrious Prince Charles, Elector Palatine of the Rhene, to all his Dominions and Dignities; For a blessing upon the High Court of Parliament, (when sitting in any of these Kingdomes respectively) the Nobility, the subordinate Iudges and Magistrates, the Gentry, and all the Commonalty; For all Pastors and Teachers, that God would fill them with his Spirit, make them exemplarily holy, sober, just, peaceable, and gratious in their lives; sound, faithfull, and powerfull in their Ministery and follow all their labours with abundance of successe and blessing; and give unto all his people Pastors according to his owne heart; For the Universities, and all Schooles and Religious seminaries of Church and Commonwealth, that they may flourish more and more in Learning and piety; For the particular City or Congregation, that God would powre out a blessing upon the Ministery of the Word, Sacraments and Discipline, upon the Civill Government, and all the severall Families and persons therein; For mercy to the afflicted under any inward or outward distresse; For seasonable weather and fruitfull seasons as the time may require; For averting the Judgements, that wee either feele or

361

feare, or are liable unto, as famine, pestilence, the sword, and such like.

And, with confidence of his mercy to his whole Church, and the acceptance of our persons, through the merits and mediation of our great High Priest the Lord Jesus, To professe that it is the desire of our soules to have fellowship with God in the reverent and conscionable use of his holy Ordinances; and, to that purpose to pray earnestly for his grace and effectuall assistance to the sanctification of his holy Sabbath, the Lords day, in all the duties thereof, publike and private, both to our selves, and to all other Congregations of his people, according to the riches and excellency of the Gospel this day celebrated and enjoyed.

And, because wee have been unprofitable hearers in times past, and now cannot of our selves receive as we should, the deep things of God, the mysteries of Jesus Christ, which require a spirituall discerning, To pray that the Lord who teacheth to profit, would graciously please to poure out the Spirit of Grace, together with the outward means thereof, causing us to attain such a measure of the excellency of the knowledge of Christ Jesus our Lord, and in him, of the things which belong to our peace, that wee may account all things but as drosse in comparison of him: And that wee, tasting the first fruits of the glory that is to be revealed, may long for a more full and perfect communion with him, that where he is, we may be also, and enjoy the fulnesse of those joyes and pleasures which are at his right hand for evermore.

More particularly, that God would in speciall manner furnish his Servant (now called to dispense the bread of life unto his household) with wisdome, fidelity, zeale, and utterance, that hee may divide the Word of God aright, to every one his portion, in evidence and demonstration of the Spirit and power; and that the Lord would circumcise the cares and hearts of the Hearers, to heare, love, and receive with meeknesse the ingrafted Word, which is able to save their soules, make them as good ground to receive in the good seed of the Word, and strengthen them against the temptations of Satan, the cares of the World, the hardnesse of their owne hearts, and whatsoever else may hinder their profitable and saving hearing; that so Christ may be so formed in them, and live in them, that all their thoughts may bee brought into captivity to the obedience of Christ, and their hearts established in every good word and work for ever.

362

We judge this to be a convenient Order, in the ordinary Publique Prayers; yet so, as the Minister may deferre (as in prudence he shall think meet) same part of these Petitions, till after his Sermon, or offer up to God some of the Thanksgivings, hereafter appointed, in his Prayer before his Sermon.

OF THE PREACHING OF THE WORD

Preaching of the Word, being the power of God unto Salvation, and one of the greatest and most excellent Works belonging to the Ministry of the Gospell, should bee so performed, that the Workman need not bee ashamed, but may save himself, and those that heare him.

It is presupposed (according to the Rules for Ordination) that the Minister of Christ is in some good measure gifted for so weighty a service, by his skill in the Originall Languages, and in such Arts and Sciences as are handmaids unto Divinity, by his knowledge in the whole Body of Theology, but most of all in the holy Scriptures, having his senses and heart exercised in them above the common sort of Beleevers; and by the illumination of Gods Spirit, and other gifts of edification, which (together with reading and studying of the Word) hee ought still to seek by Prayer, and an humble heart, resolving to admit and receive any truth not yet attained, when ever God shall make it known unto him. All which hee is to make use of, and improve, in his private preparations, before hee deliver in publike what he hath provided.

Ordinarily, the subject of his Sermon is to be some Text of Scripture, holding forth some principle or head of Religion; or suitable to some speciall occasion emergent; or hee may goe on in some Chapter, Psalme, or Booke of the holy Scripture, as hee shall see fit.

Let the Introduction to his Text be brief and perspicuous, drawn from the Text it self, or context, or some parallel place, or generall sentence of Scripture.

If the Text be long (as in Histories and Parables it sometimes must be) let him give a briefe summe of it; if short, a Paraphrase thereof, if need be: In both, looking diligently to the scope of the Text, and pointing at the chief heads and grounds of Doctrine, which he is to raise from it.

In Analysing and dividing his Text, hee is to regard more the order of matter, then of words; and neither to burden the memory of the hearers in the beginning, with too many members of Division, nor to trouble their minds with obscure termes of Art.

In raising Doctrines from the Text, his care ought to bee, First, that the matter be the truth of God. Secondly, that it be a truth contained in, or grounded on that Text, that the hearers may discern how God teacheth it from thence. Thirdly, that he chiefly insist upon those Doctrines which are principally intended, and make most for the edification of the hearers.

The Doctrine is to be expressed in plaine termes; or if any thing in it need explication, is to bee opened, and the consequence also from the Text cleared. The parallel places of Scripture confirming the Doctrine are rather to bee plaine and pertinent, then many, and (if need bee) somewhat insisted upon, and applyed to the purpose in hand.

The Arguments or Reasons are to be solid; and, as much as may bee, convincing. The illustrations of what kind soever, ought to bee full of light, and such as may convey the truth into the Hearers heart with spirituall delight.

If any Doubt, obvious from Scripture, Reason, or Prejudice of the Hearers, seem to arise, it is very requisite to remove it, by reconciling the seeming differences, answering the reasons, and discovering and taking away the causes of prejudice and mistake. Otherwise, it is not fit to detain the hearers with propounding or answering vaine or wicked Cavils, which as they are endlesse, so the propounding and answering of them doth more hinder then promote edification.

Hee is not to rest in generall Doctrine, although never so much cleared and confirmed, but to bring it home to speciall Use, by application to his hearers: Which albeit it prove a worke of great difficulty to himselfe, requiring much prudence, zeale, and meditation, and to the naturall and corrupt man will bee very unpleasant; yet hee is to endeavour to perform it in such a manner that his Auditors may feele the Word of God to bee quick and powerfull, and a discerner of the thoughts and intents of the heart; and that if any un beleever or ignorant person bee present, hee may have the secrets of his heart made manifest, and give glory to God

In the Use of Instruction or information in the knowledge of some truth, which is a consequence from his Doctrine, he may (when convenient) confirm it by a few firm Argument from the Text in hand, and other places of Scripture, or from the nature of that Common place in Divinity, whereof that truth is a branch.

In Confutation of false Doctrines, he is neither to raise an old Heresie from the grave, nor to mention a blasphemous opinion unnecessarily: but if the people be in danger of an Errour, he is to confute it soundly, and endeavour to satisfie their judgements and consciences against all objections.

In Exhorting to Duties, he is, as he seeth cause, to teach also the meanes that helpe to the performance of them.

In Dehortation, Reprehension, and publique Admonition (which require speciall wisedome) let him, as there shall be cause, not only discover the nature and greatnesse of the sin, with the misery attending it, but also shew the danger his hearers are in to be overtaken and surprized by it, together with the Remedies and best way to avoyd it.

In applying Comfort, whether generall against all tentations, or particular against some speciall troubles or terrours, he is carefully to answer such objections, as a troubled heart and afflicted spirit may suggest to the contrary.

It is also sometimes requisite to give some Notes of tryall (which is very profitable, especially when performed by able and experienced Ministers, with circumspection and prudence, and the Signes cleerely grounded on the holy Scripture) whereby the Hearers may be able to examine themselves, whether they have attained those Graces, and performed those duties to which he Exhorteth, or be guilty of the sin, Reprehended, and in danger of the Judgements Threatned, or are such to whom the Consolations propounded doe belong; that accordingly they may be quickned and excited to Duty, humbled for their Wants and Sins, affected with their Danger, and strengthned with Comfort, as their condition upon examination shall require.

And, as he needeth not alwayes to prosecute every Doctrine which lies in his Text, so is he wisely to make choice of such Vses, as, by his residence and conversing with his flock, he findeth most needfull and seasonable: and, amongst these, such as may most draw their soules to Christ, the fountaine of light, holinesse and comfort.

This Method is not prescribed as necessary for every man, or upon every Text; but only recommended, as being found by experience to be very much blessed of God, and very helpfull for the peoples understandings and memories.

But the Servant of Christ, what ever his Method be, is to performe his whole Ministery;

1. Painfully, not doing the work of the Lord negligently.

2. Plainly, that the meanest may understand, delivering the truth, not in the entising words of mans wisdome, but in demonstration of the Spirit and of power, least the Crosse of Christ should be made of none effect: abstaining also from an unprofitable use of unknowne Tongues,[8] strange phrases, and cadences of sounds and words, sparingly citing sentences of Ecclesiasticall, or other humane Writers, ancient or moderne, be they never so elegant.

3. Faithfully, looking at the honour of Christ, the conversion, edification and salvation of the people, not at his own gaine or glory: keeping nothing back which may promote those holy ends, giving to every one his own portion, and bearing indifferent respect unto all, without neglecting the meanest, or sparing the greatest in their sins.

4. Wisely, framing all his Doctrines, Exhortations, and especially his Reproofs, in such a manner as may be most likely to prevaile, shewing all due respect to each mans person and place, and not mixing his own passion or bitternesse.

5. Gravely, as becometh the Word of God, shunning all such gesture, voice and expressions as may occasion the corruptions of men to despise him and his Ministry.

6. With loving affection, that the people may see all coming from his godly zeale, and hearty desire to doe them good. And

7. As taught of God, and perswaded in his own heart, that all that he teacheth, is the truth of Christ; and walking before his flock as an example of them in it; earnestly, both in private and publique, recommending his labours to the blessing of God, and watchfully looking to himselfe and the flock whereof the Lord hath made him overseer, So shall the Doctrine of truth be preserved uncorrupt, many soules converted and built up, and himselfe receive manifold comforts of his labours, even in this life, and afterward the Crown of Glory laid up for him in the world to come.

Where there are more Ministers in a Congregation than one, and they of different guifts, each may more especially apply himselfe to Doctrine or Exhortation, according to the guift wherein he most excelleth, and as they shall agree between themselves.

OF PRAYER AFTER THE SERMON

The Sermon being ended, the Minister is;

To give thanks for the great Love of God in sending his Sonne Jesus Christ unto us; For the communication of his Holy Spirit; For the light and liberty of the glorious Gospell, and the rich and heavenly Blessings revealed therein; as namely, Election, Vocation, Adoption, Justification, Sanctification, and hope of Glory; For the admirable goodnesse of God in freeing the Land from Antichristian Darknesse and Tyranny, and for all other Nationall Deliverances; For the Reformation of Religion; For the Covenant; and for many temporal blessings.

To pray for the continuance of the Gospell, and all Ordinances thereof, in their purity, power and liberty. To turne the chiefe and most usefull heads of the Sermon into some few Petitions; and to pray that it may abide in the heart and bring forth fruit.

To pray for preparation for Death, and Judgement, and a watching for the coming of our Lord Jesus Christ. To intreat of God the forgivenesse of the iniquities of our holy things,[9] and the acceptation of our spirituall sacrifice, through the merit and mediation of our great High-Priest and Saviour the Lord Jesus Christ.

And because the Prayer which Christ taught his Disciples, is not only a Pattern of Prayer, but it selfe a most comprehensive Prayer, we recommend it also to be used in the Prayers of the Church.[10]

And whereas, at the Administration of the Sacraments, the holding Publique Fasts and dayes of Thanksgiving, and other speciall occasions, which may afford matter of speciall Petitions and Thanksgivings; It is requisite to expresse somewhat in our publike Prayers (as at this time, it is our duty to pray for a blessing upon the Assembly of Divines, the Armies by Sea and Land, for the defence of the King, Parliament and Kingdome,) Every Minister is herein to apply himselfe in his Prayer before, or after his Sermon to those occasions; but for the manner, he is left to his liberty as God shall direct and inable him, in piety and wisdome to discharge his duty.

The Prayer ended, let a Psalme be sung, if with conveniency it may be done. After which (unlesse some other

Ordinance of Christ that concerneth the Congregation at that time be to follow) let the Minister dismisse the Congregation with a solemne Blessing.

OF THE CELEBRATION OF THE COMMUNION, OR SACRAMENT OF THE LORDS SUPPER

The Communion, or Supper of the Lord is frequently to be celebrated: but how often, may be considered and determined by the Ministers and other Church-Governours of each Congregation, as they shall finde most convenient for the comfort and edification of the people committed to their charge. And when it shall be administred, we judge it convenient to be done after the morning Sermon.

The Ignorant and the Scandalous are not fit to receive this Sacrament of the Lords Supper.

Where this Sacrament cannot with conveniency be frequently administred, it is requisite that publike warning be given the Sabbath day before the administration thereof: and that either then, or on some day of that weeke, something concerning that Ordinance, and the due preparation thereunto, and participation thereof be taught, that by the diligent use of all meanes sanctified of God to that end, both in publique and private, all may come better prepared to that heavenly Feast.

When the day is come for administration, the Minister having ended his Sermon and Prayer, shall make a short Exhortation,

Expressing the inestimable benefit we have by this Sacrament; together with the ends and use thereof: setting forth the great necessity of having our comforts and strength renewed thereby in this our pilgrimage and warfare: How necessary it is that we come unto it with Knowledge, Faith, Repentance, Love, and with hungring and thirsting souls after Christ and his benefits: How great the danger, to eat and drink unworthily.

Next, he is, in the Name of Christ, on the one part, to warn all such as are Ignorant, Scandalous, Profane, or that live in any sin or offence against their knowledge or conscience, that they presume not to come to that holy Table, shewing them, That he that eateth and drinketh unworthily, eateth and drinketh judgement unto himself: And on the other part, he is in especiall manner to invite and encourage all that labour under the sense of the burden of their sins, and fear of wrath, and desire to reach out unto a greater progresse in Grace then yet they can attain unto, to come to the Lords Table; assuring them, in the same Name, of ease, refreshing and strength to their weak and wearied souls.

After this Exhortation, Warning, and Invitation, the Table being before decently covered, and so conveniently placed, that the Communicants may orderly sit about it, or at it,[11] The Minister is to begin the action with sanctifying and blessing the elements of Bread and Wine set before him (the Bread in comely and convenient vessels, so prepared, that being broken by him, and given, it may be distributed amongst the Communicants: The Wine also in large Cups;) having first in a few words shewed, That those elements, otherwise common, are now set apart and sanctified to this holy use, by the word of Institution and Prayer.

Let the words of Institution be read out of the Evangelists, or out of the first Epistle of the Apostle *Paul* to the Corinthians. Chap. 11. verse 23. *I have received of the Lord, &c.* to the 27. verse, which the Minister may, when he seeth requisite, explaine and apply.

Let the Prayer, Thanksgiving, or Blessing of the Bread and Wine, be to this effect;

With humble and hearty acknowledgement of the greatnesse of our misery, from which neither man nor Angel was able to deliver us, and of our great unworthinesse of the least of all Gods mercies; To give thanks to God for all his benefits, and especially for that great benefit of our Redemption, the love of God the Father, the sufferings and merits of the Lord Jesus Christ the Son of God, by which we are delivered; and for all means of Grace, the Word and Sacraments, and for this Sacrament in particular, by which Christ and all his benefits are applied and sealed up unto us, which, notwithstanding the deniall of them unto others, are in great mercy continued unto us, after so much and long abuse of them all.

To professe that there is no other name under Heaven, by which we can be saved, but the Name of Jesus Christ, by whom alone we receive liberty and life, have accesse to the throne of Grace, are admitted to eat and drink at his own

369

Table, and are sealed up by his Spirit to an assurance of happinesse and everlasting life.

Earnestly to pray to God, the Father of all mercies, and God of all consolation, to vouchsafe his gracious presence, and the effectuall working of his Spirit in us, and so to sanctifie these Elements both of Bread and Wine, and to blesse his own Ordinance, that we may receive by Faith the Body and Blood of Jesus Christ crucified for us, and so to feed upon him, that he may be one with us, and we with him, that he may live in us, and we in him, and to him, who hath loved us, and given himself for us.

All which he is to endeavour to performe with suitable affections answerable to such an holy Action, and to stir up the like in the people.

The Elements being now sanctified by the Word and Prayer, The Minister, being at the Table, is to take the Bread in his hand, and say, in these expressions (or other the like, used by Christ, or his Apostle upon this occasion:)

According to the holy Institution, command, and example of our blessed Saviour Jesus Christ, I take this Bread, and having given thanks, I break it, and give it unto you (There the Minister, who is also himselfe to communicate, is to breake the Bread, and give it to the Communicants:) *Take yee, eat yee; This is the Body of Christ which is broken for you, Do this in remembrance of him.*

In like manner the Minister is to take the Cup, and say, in these expressions (or other the like, used by Christ, or the Apostle upon the same occasion;)

According to the Institution, command, and example of our Lord Jesus Christ, I take this Cup, and give it unto you (Here he giveth it to the Communicants,) *This cup is the new Testament in the Blood of Christ, which is shed for the remission of the sins of many; Drink ye all of it.*

After all have communicated, the Minister may, in a few words, put them in mind

Of the grace of God, in Jesus Christ held forth in this Sacrament, and exhort them to walk worthy of it.

The Minister is to give solemn thanks to God,

For his rich mercy, and invaluable goodness vouchsafed to them in that Sacrament, and to entreat for pardon for the

370

defects of the whole service, and for the gracious assistance of his good Spirit, whereby they may be enabled to walk in the strength of that Grace, as becometh those who have received so great pledges of salvation.

The Collection for the poore is so to be ordered, that no part of the publique worship be thereby hindred.

NOTES

1. Transcribed verbatim from a microfilm copy of the original, obtained from the Library of Congress, Washington, D. C. The Preface, pp. 1-8; the Sunday Morning Service, pp. 9-39; the Lord's Supper, pp. 48-56. For a complete text of the *Directory* in modern spelling, cf. Thomas Leishman, *The Westminster Directory* (London: Blackwood, 1901).
2. than. This usage is current throughout.
3. This practice, called "prefacing," was current in Scotland and to some extent in England. The *Directory* did not specify the posture at prayer.
4. Hence, the Puritans retained the Reformed practice of reading the Scriptures "in course." On this point, cf. W. D. Maxwell, *John Knox's Genevan Service Book* (Edinburgh: Oliver and Boyd, 1931), pp. 180-7.
5. Thus a limitation was placed upon "lecturing," i.e., a running exposition of the lessons. On this matter, cf. Horton Davies, *The Worship of the English Puritans* (Westminster: Dacre, 1948), pp. 95, 131.
6. That is, extended.
7. That is, in the realization thereof.
8. This refers to the use of Hebrew and Greek in the course of the sermon.
9. Obscure. The sentence intends to contrast our "iniquitous" dependence upon "holy things" to "our spiritual sacrifice."
10. The Barrowists, Brownists, and some Independents believed that, while the Lord's Prayer was the "pattern" of all prayer, it should not itself be recited in worship. Cf. Davies, *op. cit.*, pp. 99ff. The Westminster divines overruled this objection.
11. The expression, "sit about it, or at it," is explained in the introduction. Notice the permissive "may," which appears also to allow kneeling.

XII
RICHARD BAXTER

The Savoy Liturgy
1661

THE SAVOY LITURGY

In England the official tenure of the Westminster *Directory* was brought to an end by the restoration of the monarchy in 1660. The Anglican bishops shortly regained their places of pre-eminence; and there was every expectation that the Prayer Book would be reinstated by a new Act of Uniformity. Yet Charles II furnished hope that the Church of England would become sufficiently comprehensive to include some of the Puritans. On April 14, 1660, at Breda, he issued a declaration of "liberty to tender consciences," in which he promised to sanction an act of Parliament that would give "indulgence" to nonconformists. While an opportunity to negotiate was thereby given, the English Presbyterians were singularly able to seize it. They did not doubt "the lawfulness of a liturgy," nor close their minds against episcopacy, nor scruple at state interference in ecclesiastical affairs. But if those were to be the conditions of "comprehension," the Independents could only demur; for they were displeased at such Erastianism and insisted that Scripture gave no warrant to prescribed forms of prayer.

Following his return to England, Charles II received certain "Proposals of the Ministers." In this text, the Presbyterians declared their approval of a liturgy, so long as it was agreeable to God's Word and consonant with Reformed worship, and provided that it was not a collection of clipped prayers and "unmeet repetitions," nor so rigorously imposed that it deprived ministers of their spiritual gifts. Judging that the Anglican liturgy did not meet these specifications, they suggested that "some learned, godly, and moderate divines of both persuasions" be commissioned to prepare a Scriptural liturgy (one in which the language of Holy Writ would be used "as much as may be") or at least some alternative forms "in Scripture phrase" to be used at the minister's choice. Inasmuch as they professed God's Word to be "the perfect rule of faith and worship," they declared themselves unalterably opposed to human ceremonies, among which they listed: kneeling at Communion, the use of the surplice, the erection of altars, the sign of the cross in Baptism, and holy days humanly contrived.

In reply, the nine surviving bishops chided the ministers for their adulation of the Reformed churches and surmised that a more profitable norm would be "the liturgy of the ancient Greek and Latin Churches." They argued that ceremonies served to edify the people, while collects relieved their infirmities better than longer prayers. Free prayer was a "sufferance" that ought to be used with "the greatest inoffensiveness and moderation." All told, the episcopal rejoinder posed the stability of tradition and the value of uniformity against the whims of "private persons."

To resolve these issues, Charles issued a *Declaration concerning Ecclesiastical Affairs* (October 25, 1660), in which he promised the appointment of "an equal number of learned divines of both persuasions" to review and revise the Prayer Book, and to supply alternative forms in Scriptural phrase so that the minister might use "one or the other at his discretion." In the interim, the king gave the Puritans leave to dispense with those parts of the Book to which they took exception.· In March, he proceeded to appoint twelve bishops and twelve Puritan divines (one of the latter, Edward Reynolds, having just been consecrated bishop of Norwich), who were to meet in the Savoy and deliberate upon the liturgy.

When the Savoy Conference convened in April, the bishops nagged the ministers to set forth all their reservations in

· Charles also expressed pleasure to find that the "principal asserters of the presbyterian opinions" were "neither enemies . . . to episcopacy or liturgy"; and he proposed to nominate some of them for bishoprics. Baxter, Calamy, and Reynolds were so honored. Reynolds accepted and received the See of Norwich. Baxter and others hoped to resolve the issue of polity on the basis of Archbishop Ussher's *Reduction of Episcopacy* (1641).

writing. This was a serious tactical error on the part of the Puritans who were thus induced to submit a mass of objections, in which the essential ones became lost, thereby creating the impression that they quibbled at nearly everything in the Prayer Book. While his colleagues drew up the catalogue of objections, Richard Baxter labored in haste to prepare the alternative forms in biblical phrase. On May 4, the ministers produced their "Exceptions against the Book of Common Prayer"; and soon afterward Baxter submitted his *Reformation of the Liturgy,* which was in fact a complete service-book and thereafter acquired the name, "the Savoy Liturgy."

The "Exceptions" were given in two divisions: (1) general objections to principles and characteristics of the Book; (2) specific criticisms of details in the Book.

Of the general objections, some touched the nature of worship. The Puritans asked for a comprehensive, Scriptural liturgy, which would not alienate any who held "the substantials of the protestant religion." They opposed any type of uniformity that would stifle extempore prayer or deprive the minister of all discretion in the conduct of worship. They found the collect an objectionable form, and averred that "an orderly connection" of petitions into one longer prayer served the edification of the people and commanded their reverence. They deemed the Book defective because it lacked a preparatory prayer for God's assistance, failed to express Original sin or enumerate actual sins, and employed too much generalized speech. Finally, in a reversal of classical Reformed usage, they insisted that no minister be required to read the liturgy at the table, save for those parts that pertained to the Lord's Supper. The rest of the objections were the stock in trade of the Puritan position. They took exception to repetitions, the Litany, Lent, saints' days, the Apocrypha, and human ceremonies, and preferred the word "minister" to "priest" and the term "Lord's Day" to "Sunday."

Of the specific criticisms, some were designed to achieve a greater correspondence between Scripture and liturgy, others to serve the clarity of the biblical message. Thus, the doxology should be restored to the Lord's Prayer, the apocryphal *Benedicite* replaced by a psalm or hymn, and the Decalogue introduced by its full Scriptural preface.

377

The lessons should be read, not sung, and preaching more strictly enjoined. The Puritans insisted that Holy Communion should no longer be given to any persons except those who were prepared to receive it; and they proposed several measures to insure a more stringent administration of discipline. Communion should be celebrated thrice yearly in every parish, given enough people who were both qualified and disposed to receive it. On those occasions, the minister should resort to the Lord's own words and manual acts; but he should not be required to deliver the elements into the hands of every communicant. While the divines did not approve or disapprove of kneeling at reception, they thought it well to restore the Black Rubric of the 1552 Prayer Book, with its discourse against adoring the elements.

To this painstaking effort, the bishops gave a frosty reply. They declared that the liturgy could not be circumscribed by Scripture, but rightfully included those matters which were "generally received in the Catholic Church." Adherence to the Word and "the catholic consent of antiquity" were both valid criteria. Thus they appealed to ancient usage in order to justify the observance of saints' days, the keeping of Lent, and the minister's position at the holy table. It was their considered opinion that any compromise in uniformity simply "makes the liturgy void"; and they judged that extempore prayers were apt to be filled with "idle, impertinent, ridiculous, sometimes seditious, impious, and blasphemous expressions." The notion that the Prayer Book was defective because it dealt in generalizations brought the crisp response that such expressions were "the perfection of the liturgy." Particularities, with which the Lord's Prayer itself did not deal, would only destroy the character of the "common and general services." Finally, those brittle people who could not see that ceremonies served the order and comeliness of worship were deemed to be excessively scrupulous.

Nevertheless the bishops deigned to offer seventeen Concessions:

(1) Epistles and Gospels shall follow the version of 1611. (2) When the first lesson is not actually an Epistle, but, say, a passage from Acts, it shall be announced by the phrase, "For the Epistle." (3) The psalms shall be corrected by the Great Bible. (4) The words "this day," shall

378

be used in the collects and prefaces only on the day itself; on the following days shall be substituted: "as about this time." (5) A rubrical change shall be made requiring those who would receive the Lord's Supper to give notice "at least some time the day before." (6) The power to exclude scandalous persons from Communion shall be expressed in the rubric according to canons 26 and 27. (7) The whole Scriptural preface shall be prefixed to the Ten Commandments. (8) The second Exhortation of the Communion service shall be read some Sunday or Holy Day beforehand. (9) The Confession at Communion shall be said by one of the ministers, the people to say it after him, all kneeling. (10) The manual acts shall be made explicit in the Prayer of Consecration. The remainder of the Concessions had reference to other offices.

In their "Rejoinder" to the bishops, the Presbyterians expressed keen disappointment over "the paucity of the concessions and the inconsiderableness of them." They surmised that the intransigence of their opponents lay in the very prayers of the Anglican liturgy, which were evidently incapable of warming the episcopal hearts: "Cold prayers are like to have a cold return." By keeping the liturgy pure of all extempore expression, the bishops seemed determined to "help the tongue" even if it hurt the heart. With that, the Puritans took leave of the whole matter, noting that the Anglicans aimed to do no more than unite them in a dead religion. On July 24, 1661, without the slightest reconciliation having been achieved, the Savoy Conference came to a close.

Meanwhile the 1662 Prayer Book was in preparation. During the summer and autumn of 1661, the bishops were unofficially engaged in making alterations to the liturgy. They incorporated most of the amendments written out by Bishop Wren in 1660, many of the corrections noted in Bishop Cosin's *Particulars*, some of the significant changes in the Scottish Prayer Book of 1637, and fourteen of the Concessions made at the Savoy Conference, as well as certain other matters that the Puritans had listed in their "Exceptions." When Convocation reassembled in November, royal letters were read, directing a revision of the Common Prayer. The eight bishops, who were commissioned to prepare the text, shortly brought into shape the work that had been done during the summer and autumn; and, by December 20, the whole Book had been completed and adopted by the Convocations of Canterbury and York. The bishops supplied a humorless preface, in which they described the "vain attempts and impetuous assaults" recently made against the "publick Liturgie," and claimed that the Puritans had done "their vtmost . . . to hinder the restitution thereof" by mustering up their old objections, some of which were "of dangerous consequence" while others were "vtterly frivolous." No amount of repairs to the liturgy would ever please such "men of factious, peevish, and perverse spirits." •

On May 19, 1662, Charles gave assent to a Bill for Uniformity, which required the Book to be used by St. Bartholomew's next (August 24) and affixed penalties for nonconformity. The appointed day brought the Great Ejection, at which time some eighteen hundred ministers were deprived of their livings because they would not conform to the requirements of Prayer Book and Ordinal. The Presbyterians were thus put out of the Church of England and willy-nilly became dissenters. With Baptists and Independents they shared a common lot and a mounting hostility toward the Anglican rite.

The Savoy Liturgy (below) was the work of a fortnight. "I could not have time," wrote Baxter, "to make use of any book save the Bible and my Concordance, comparing all with the Assembly's Directory and the Book of Common Prayer." If written in haste, at the prodding of the bishops, his liturgy was nonetheless a product of long reflection. Baxter now committed to paper the ideas that had come to him during his pastorate at Kidderminster, when he used, and improvised upon, the Westminster *Directory*. Moreover, in his *Five Disputations of Church Government and Worship* (1659) he had already defended the view that a godly and comprehensive liturgy could be drawn out of the matter of Scripture and cast in Scriptural phrase. Contrary to long-standing prejudice, Baxter's work was not thrown together on the spur of the moment.

In the same preface the bishops also discussed the nature of the alterations they themselves had made, saying that some were made for clarity, some for a more faithful rendering of Scripture, while certain new prayers and offices had been added for the sake of convenience. It is understood that this description does not really comprehend the nature of the 1662 Prayer Book. For an extensive interpretation, see Brightman, I, cciv-xxv.

380

In a Preface "to the Right Reverend Bishops," he explained that his book was the positive counterpart of the Puritan "Exceptions": "We here tender you some of the said alterations, which in our former paper we shewed to be needful, and some additional forms in Scripture phrase." He had no thought of undoing the Prayer Book; his "alterations" and "additions" were rather designed to "be inserted into the several respective places of the [Anglican] Liturgy to which they do belong, and left to the Minister's choice to use the one or the other."

To a quite considerable extent, the Savoy Liturgy was constructed of biblical speech. It was a realization of the Puritan desire to have an exact correspondence between worship and the Word of God. Baxter was persuaded that such a liturgy would comprehend all manner of Christians: all would be satisfied by the infallible truths and apt phrases drawn out of God's own Word; and all would be free to interpret this liturgy "according to the sense they have in Scripture."

The Sunday Service commenced with a Preparatory Prayer that craved God's assistance, that worship might be effectual. Directly, the minister recalled the people to their Christian faith and obedience by reading "one of the Creeds" and the Ten Commandments. For their failures therein, he incited them, by sentences of Scripture, to make confession of their faults. The "vile and miserable sinners" rehearsed their offenses and begged to be forgiven and sanctified through the merits and intercession of Jesus Christ, "in whose comprehensive words" they summed up their requests, saying the Lord's Prayer. Then the minister "raised the penitents" by the comforting words of Scripture and proceeded to exhort them to holiness of life, using other appropriate sentences. To all of this, the church made response by using a psalm of praise. After the lessons had been read, the minister offered a prayer for the King and magistrates, and another for the necessities of the church; then he preached the sermon upon "some text of Holy Scripture," summoning to this task his own "faith and holy experience," but "waiting on God for the success." In response to the love of God made manifest in his Word, the church prayed Intercessions for all sorts and conditions of men, and at last received the Benediction. This description, though partial, is enough to suggest the aptness of Baxter's transitions and the completeness of his

381

service, which gathered up all the expressions of Christian worship and all the spiritual needs of man.

Holy Communion began with a discourse on "the nature, use, and benefits" of this sacrament, in which the Redeemed "signify and solemnize the renewal of their covenant with [Christ] and their holy communion with him and with one another." The qualifications necessary for participation in the Lord's Supper were enumerated in seven points; and an invitation was addressed to those alone who "truly repent and believe, and unfeignedly consent to the terms of the covenant." The Exhortation, which now followed, made no further reference to self-examination or excommunication,· but straightway began to "re-present" the saving work of Christ, renewing it for faith's participation, that it might be immediately operative in the lives of the communicants:

> See here Christ dying in this holy representation! Behold the sacrificed Lamb of God, that taketh away the sins of the world! It is his will to be thus frequently crucified before your eyes . . . Come near, observe, believe, and wonder at the riches of his love and grace.

There followed a prayer of Humble Access, with overtones of penitence and confession. After that, the bread and wine were brought to the table; and the minister proceeded to "bless" them by a brief prayer of Consecration. The Words of Institution were to be read either at this time or immediately prior to the foregoing prayer. It is therefore apparent that Baxter conceived of Consecration by *both* Word and Prayer, according to the practice of the Westminster *Directory;* and this is confirmed by the minister's statement just *after* the Words of Institution, to the effect that the bread and wine had now been "set apart and consecrated."

Then a prayer was addressed to the "merciful Saviour," beseeching his intercession with the Father for the forgiveness of sins, and his nourishment unto everlasting life. With deliberation, the minister performed the Fraction and the Libation "in the sight of the congregation." Then the church called upon the Holy Spirit, saying: "Sanctify and quicken us, that we may relish the spiritual food and feed on it to our nourishment and growth in grace." The minister was first to

· But see the office "Of Pastoral Discipline, Public Confession, Absolution, and Exclusion from the Holy Communion of the Church." In Hall, pp. 117-41.

communicate; and he in turn delivered the elements to the people, using the Words of the Westminster *Directory*. When all had partaken, he offered a prayer of thanksgiving, which presently drifted off into a series of urgent petitions that God would confirm these communicants in holiness of life. If there were time, the minister added an Exhortation that dwelt entirely on that same theme.

The excellence of the Savoy Liturgy consisted of several things. The mood of adoration, which was sometimes subdued in the Reformed rite by the somber note of human sinfulness, pervaded all of Baxter's services and acquired intense feeling:

> Let us magnify thee with thanksgiving, and triumph in thy praise. Let us rejoice in thy salvation, and glory in thy holy name.

Moreover, Baxter's use of Scripture to declare the forgiveness of sins, instead of the meager Petition for Pardon in the Knoxian liturgies, brought him closer to Calvin's view of Absolution. And while he did not use the Law as Calvin preferred—to incite the penitent to true piety—he achieved the same great emphasis upon holiness of life by certain other devices, namely, by the Scriptural sentences that evoked sanctity, by the Exhortation at the close of Communion, by the exercise of Discipline. His creative use of Reformed liturgical ideas was most apparent in the Communion service. There he transformed the Genevan Exhortation from an instrument of introspection and exclusion to an effective *anamnesis* or re-presentation of Christ's saving work. In place of the Reformed *Sursum corda*, he introduced a prayer that dwelt upon the effectual action of the Spirit in Holy Communion. In accordance with the Westminster *Directory*, he provided a means of consecrating the elements by both Word and Prayer. And he brought the whole celebration to a proper close on the note of moral earnestness. While he may have lacked Cranmer's consummate skill at liturgical composition, Baxter was remarkably successful at the difficult task of building divers phrases of Scripture into sustained orders of worship. But the events of 1662 brought it all to nought.

FOR FURTHER READING

R. S. Bosher, *The Making of the Restoration Settlement*. New York, 1951.

F. E. Brightman (ed.), *The English Rite*. 2 vols. London, 1921.

Horton Davies, *The Worship of the English Puritans*. Westminster, 1948.

Peter Hall (ed.), *Reliquiae Liturgicae*. Vol. IV. Bath, 1847.

F. J. Powicke, *A Life of the Reverend Richard Baxter*. 1924.

Francis Procter and W. H. Frere, *A History of the Book of Common Prayer*. London, 1949.

THE REFORMATION OF THE LITURGY

As it was Presented to the
Right Reverend BISHOPS by the DIVINES
Appointed by His Majesties *Commission*
to treat with them about the alteration of it.
LONDON,
Printed, *Anno Dom.* M D C L X I.[1]

The Ordinary Public Worship on the Lord's Day.

The Congregation being reverently composed, let the Minister first crave God's assistance, and acceptance of the Worship to be performed, in these or the like words.

Eternal, incomprehensible, and invisible God, infinite in power, wisdom and goodness; dwelling in the light which no man can approach, where thousand thousands minister unto thee, and ten thousand times ten thousand stand before thee, yet dwelling with the humble and contrite, and taking pleasure in thy people: thou hast consecrated for us a new and living way, that with boldness we may enter into the holiest, by the blood of Jesus; and hast bid us seek thee while thou mayest be found. We come to thee at thy call, and worship at thy footstool. Behold us in thy tender mercies. Despise us not, though unworthy. Thou art greatly to be feared in the assembly of the saints, and to be had in reverence of all that are about thee. Put thy fear into our hearts, that with reverence we may serve thee: sanctify us, that thou mayest be sanctified of us, when we draw nigh thee. Give us the Spirit of grace and supplication to help our infirmities, that our prayers may be faithful, fervent, and effectual. Let the desire of our souls be to thee: let us draw near thee with our hearts, and not only with our lips; and worship thee, who art a spirit, in spirit and truth. Let thy word be spoken and heard by us as the word of God. Give us attentive, hearing ears; and opened, believing, understanding hearts: that we may no more refuse thy calls, nor disregard thy merciful, outstretched hand, nor slight thy counsels and reproofs; but be more ready to hear, than to give the sacrifice of fools. Put thy laws into our hearts, and write them in our minds, and let us be all taught of God. Let thy word be unto us quick and powerful; a discerner of

385

the thoughts and intents of the heart; mighty to pull down strongholds; casting down imaginations and reasonings, and every high thing that advanceth itself against the knowledge of God; and bringing into captivity every thought to the obedience of Christ. Let us magnify thee with thanksgiving, and triumph in thy praise. Let us rejoice in thy salvation, and glory in thy holy name. Open thou our lips, O Lord, and let our mouths shew forth thy praise. And let the words of our mouths, and the meditation of our hearts, be acceptable in thy sight, through Jesus Christ our Lord and only Saviour. *Amen.*

Or thus, when Brevity is necessary.

O Eternal, almighty, and most gracious God: heaven is thy throne, and earth is thy footstool; holy and reverend is thy name. Thou art praised by the heavenly hosts, and in the congregation of thy saints on earth, and wilt be sanctified in all that come nigh unto thee. We are sinful and unworthy dust; but, being invited by thee, are bold, through our blessed Mediator, to present ourselves and our supplications before thee. Receive us graciously; help us by thy Spirit: let thy fear be upon us; let thy word come unto us in power, and be received in love, with attentive, reverent, and obedient minds. Make it to us the savour of life unto life. Cause us to be fervent in prayer, and joyful in thy praises, and to serve thee this day without distraction; that we may find that a day in thy courts is better than a thousand, and that it is good for us to draw near to God; through Jesus Christ our Lord and Saviour. *Amen.*

Next, let one of the Creeds be read by the Minister, saying,

In the profession of this holy Christian Faith we are here assembled.

I believe in God the Father, &c.

I believe in one God, &c.

And sometimes Athanasius' Creed.

The Ten Commandments.

God spake these words, and said, &c.

For the right informing and affecting the People, and moving them to a penitent believing Confession, some of these sentences may be read.[2] [Gen. i. 27; Rom. v. 12; Rom. iii.

386

Richard Baxter, The Savoy Liturgy

23; John iii. 16, 18, 19, 20; Gal. iii. 13; John iii. 5, 6; Matt. xviii. 3; Ezek. xxxiii. 11; Luke xv. 10, 18, 19.]

The Confession of Sin, and Prayer for Pardon and Sanctification.

O Most holy, righteous, and gracious God, who hatest all the workers of iniquity, and hast appointed death to be the wages of sin; but yet for the glory of thy mercy hast sent thy Son to be the Saviour of the world, and hast promised forgiveness of sin through his blood, to all that believe in him, and by true repentance turn unto thee, and that whosoever confesseth and forsaketh his sin, shall have mercy: we confess that we are vile and miserable sinners, being conceived in sin; by nature children of wrath, and transgressors from the womb. All we like sheep have gone astray, and turned every one to his own way. Thou madest us, and not we ourselves. Thou boughtest us with a price, and we are not our own; and therefore we should have wholly given up ourselves unto thee, and have glorified thee with our souls and bodies, as being thine. Whatever we did, should have been done to thy glory, and to please thee, in the obeying of thy will. But we have displeased and dishonoured thee, and turned from thee, exalting, seeking, and pleasing ourselves. Thou art the King of all the world, and thy laws are holy, just, and good. But we have denied thee our due subjection and obedience, being unruly and selfwilled, minding the things of the flesh, and making provision for its lusts: we have staggered at thy word through unbelief, and have not fully placed our trust and hope in thee. We have rather feared man that is dust, and can but kill the body, than thee, that canst destroy both soul and body in hell. Thou art infinitely good, and love itself: yet have we not fully taken thee for our portion, nor loved thee with all our heart, and soul, and might, nor made thee our full desire and delight. But we have inordinately loved ourselves, and the world, and the things of the world, and lived by sense when we should have lived by faith, and cared and laboured for the food that perisheth, when we should have laboured for the one thing needful, and that which endureth to everlasting life. We have been slothful servants, yielding to temptations, ashamed of our duty, losing our precious time; when we should have been fervent in spirit, serving the Lord, cleaving to thee with full resolution, redeeming the time, and with diligence making sure our calling and election. We have not with due holiness and reverence drawn near thee, and used thy holy name, thy worship and thy day: we have dishonoured and disobeyed our superiors, and neglected our inferiors. We have been guilty of not loving our neighbours as ourselves, and not doing to others as we would they should do to us: but have sought our own against their welfare, not forbearing and forgiving, not loving our enemies, as we ought; not following peace, nor studying to do good to all according to our power. We have sinned secretly and openly; in thought, word, and deed; ignorantly and presumptuously; in passion, and upon deliberation; against thy precepts, promises, and threats; against thy mercies and thy judgments; under thy patience, and in thy sight; against our consciences, our purposes, and our covenants; when we were hastening to death and judgment, for which through all our lives we should have prepared. Thou hast commended thy wonderful love towards us in giving thy Son to die for sinners, to reconcile us to thee while we were enemies: and all things being made ready, thou hast sent thy messengers to invite us to come in, preaching to us the glad tidings of salvation, and freely offering us pardon and life in Jesus Christ. But we have made light of it, and neglected this great salvation, and made excuses, or too long delays; undervaluing our Redeemer, his blood and merits, his offered grace and endless glory; rejecting his holy doctrine and example, resisting his Spirit, ministers and word. We have sinned, O Lord, against thee, and against our own souls, and are not worthy to be called thy children. We have deserved everlasting wrath. To us belongeth confusion, but mercy and forgiveness to thee. Have mercy upon us, O God, according to the multitude of thy mercies. Heal our souls that have sinned against thee, and enter not into judgment with thy servants. Hide thy face from our sins, and blot out all our iniquities. Cast us not away from thy presence, and avenge not upon us the quarrel of thy covenant. Wash us in the blood of the Lamb of God, who taketh away the sins of the world. Accept us in thy beloved Son, who was made a curse for us, and was wounded for our transgressions, that we might be healed by his stripes. Turn us, O God of our salvation, and cause thy face to shine upon us. Give us repentance unto life; cause us to loathe ourselves for all the evils that we have committed. Give us that broken contrite spirit, which thou wilt not despise. Create in us a clean heart, O God, and renew a right spirit within us. Take out of us the old and strong· heart, and give us a new and tender heart. Give us the Spirit of thy Son, and be our God, and let us be thy people. Enlighten our understandings to know the wonderful things of thy law, the dimensions of thy love in Christ, the mysteries of thy kingdom, and the riches of the glory of thy inheritance in the saints; and that we may approve the things that are excellent, and may escape the snares of the devil, and may hate every false way. Shed abroad thy love in our hearts by thy Holy Spirit; and cause us so to love thee, that nothing may separate us from thy love. Put thy fear into our hearts, that we may never depart from thee. Cause us to seek first thy kingdom, and its righteousness, and (as those that are risen with Christ) to seek the things that are above, and to lay up a treasure in heaven; and let our hearts and conversations be there. Mortify our earthly inclinations and desires. Crucify the world to us, and us unto the world by the cross of Christ. Cause us to live by faith, and look at the things that are unseen; and use the world, as not over-using it, seeing the fashion of it passeth away: striving to enter in at the strait gate, and running so as to obtain. Let us no longer live the rest of our time to the lusts of men, but to the will of God; studying in all things to please thee, and to be accepted of thee. Let us not seek our own wills, but the will of him that called us; yea, let us delight to do thy will, O God. Let our delight be in thy law, and let us meditate therein day and night. Cause us to deny ungodliness and worldly lusts, and to live soberly, and righteously, and godly in this present world; as obedient children, not fashioning ourselves to the former lusts of our ignorance: but as he that hath called us is holy, let us be holy in all manner of conversation. Cause us to love one another with a pure heart fervently, forbearing and forgiving one another, if any have a quarrel against another, even as Christ forgave us. Give us the wisdom which is first pure, and then peaceable. In our eyes let a vile person be contemned, but let us honour them that fear the Lord. Cause us to walk circumspectly without offence, and to be zealous of good works; to love our enemies, and not to give place to wrath; and in patience to possess our souls. Help us to deny

· Probably an error of the press. Calamy's edition reads "stony heart."

ourselves, and take up our cross, and follow Christ; esteeming his reproach to be greater riches than the treasures of the world: that, having suffered with him, we may also be glorified with him. Though we must be tempted, help us to overcome, and be faithful unto the death; and then let us receive that crown of life, through the merits and intercession of Christ Jesus our Lord and only Saviour, in whose comprehensive words we sum up our requests; saying as he hath taught us:

Our Father which art in heaven, hallowed be thy name: thy kingdom come, &c.

Or thus, when brevity is necessary.

O most great, most just and gracious God, thou art of purer eyes than to behold iniquity. Thou condemnest the ungodly, impenitent, and unbelievers; but hast promised mercy through Jesus Christ to all that repent and believe in him. We confess that we were conceived in sin, and are by nature children of wrath; and have all sinned, and come short of the glory of God. In our baptism thou tookest us into the bond of the holy covenant; but we remembered not our Creator in the days of our youth, with the fear, and love, and obedience which we owed thee: not pleasing and glorifying thee in all things, nor walking with thee by faith in an heavenly conversation, nor serving thee fervently with all our might: but fulfilled the desires of the flesh, and of the carnal mind. We have neglected and abused thy holy worship, thy holy name, and thy holy day. We have dishonoured our superiors, and neglected our inferiors: we have dealt unjustly and uncharitably with our neighbours, not loving them as ourselves, nor doing to others as we would they should do to us. We have not sought first thy kingdom and righteousness, and been contented with our daily bread; but have been careful and troubled about many things, neglecting the one thing necessary. Thou hast revealed thy wonderful love to us in Christ, and offered us pardon and salvation in him: but we made light of it, and neglected so great salvation, and resisted thy Spirit, word, and ministers, and turned not at thy reproof. We have run into temptations; and the sin which we should have hated, we have committed in thy sight, both secretly and openly, ignorantly and carelessly, rashly and presumptuously, against thy precepts, thy promises, and threats, thy mercies and thy judgments. Our trans-

gressions are multiplied before thee, and our sins testify
against us; if thou deal with us as we deserve, thou wilt cast
us away from thy presence into hell, where the worm never
dieth, and the fire is not quenched. But in thy mercy, thy
Son, and thy promises is our hope. Have mercy upon us,
most merciful Father. Be reconciled to us, and let the blood
of Jesus Christ cleanse us from all our sins. Take us for thy
children, and give us the Spirit of thy Son. Sanctify us wholly,
shed abroad thy love in our hearts, and cause us to love thee
with all our hearts. O make thy face to shine upon thy
servants; save us from our sins, and from the wrath to come;
make us a peculiar people to thee, zealous of good works,
that we may please thee, and show forth thy praise. Help us
to redeem the time, and give all diligence to make our calling
and election sure. Give us things necessary for thy service,
and keep us from sinful discontent and cares. And seeing
all these things must be dissolved, let us consider what manner of person we ought to be, in all holy conversation and
godliness. Help us to watch against temptations, and resist
and overcome the flesh, the devil, and the world; and being
delivered out of the hand of all our enemies, let us serve
thee without fear, in holiness and righteousness before thee
all the days of our life. Guide us by thy counsel, and after
receive us into thy glory, through Jesus Christ our only
Saviour. *Amen.*

Here use the Lord's Prayer as before.

*For the strengthening of faith, and raising the penitent, some
of these sentences of the Gospel may be here read.*

Hear what the Lord saith to the absolution and comfort of
penitent believers.[2]

[2 Chron. xxx. 9; I John ii. 2; Acts xiii. 38, 39; Rom. v. 20,
21; I John i. 7, 8, 9; Matt. xi. 28, 29, 30; Rev. xxii. 17; John
vi. 27; Heb. viii. 12.]

Hear also what you must be, and do, for the time to come, if
you would be saved.[2]

[Rom. viii. 9; 2 Cor. v. 17; Rom. viii. 1, 5, 6, 7; Rom. viii. 8,
13; Gal. v. 19, 20, 21, 22, 23, 24; Rom. xiii. 13; Rom. xiii.
14; I John ii. 15, 16; Matt. vii. 13, 14; Tit. ii. 11, 12, 13, 14;
Psal. i. 1, 2, 5; Heb. xii. 28, 29; 2 Pet. iii. 11, 12; I Cor. xv. 58.]

*Then may be said the 95th, or the 100th Psalm; or the 84th.
And next the Psalms in order for the day: and next shall be*

read a chapter of the Old Testament, such as the Minister findeth most seasonable; or with the liberty expressed in the Admonition before the Second Book of Homilies.

After which may be sung a Psalm, or the Te Deum said: then shall be read a chapter of the New Testament, and then the Prayer for the King and Magistrates.[3] And after that, the 67th, or 98th, or some other Psalm, may be sung or said; or the Benedictus, or Magnificat. And the same order to be observed at the Evening worship, if time allow it.

Next after the Psalm, the Minister shall (in the pulpit) first reverently, prudently, and fervently pray, according to the state and necessities of the Church, and those especially that are present, and according to the subject that he is to preach on. And after prayer, he shall preach upon some text of Holy Scripture, suiting his matter to the necessities of the hearers, and the manner of delivery to their quality and benefit: always speaking from faith and holy experience in himself, with plainness and perspicuity, with reverence and gravity, with convincing evidence and authority, with prudence, caution, faithfulness, and impartiality, with tender love and melting compassion, with fervent zeal and persuading importunity, and with frequency and unwearied patience; waiting on God for the success. After Sermon, he shall pray[4] for a blessing on the word of instruction and exhortation, which was delivered: and in his prayers (before or after Sermon) ordinarily he shall pray for the conversion of Heathens, Jews, and other infidels; the subversion of idolatry, infidelity, Mahometanism, heresy, Papal tyranny and superstition, schism and profaneness; and for the free progress of the Gospel, and the increase of faith and godliness, the honouring of God's name, the enlargement of the kingdom of Christ, and the obedience of his saints through the nations of the earth. And in special for these nations: for the King's Majesty, and the rest of the Royal Family; for the Lords of his Majesty's Council; for the Judges and other Magistrates of the land; for the Pastors of the Church, and all Congregations committed to their care and government: always taking heed that no mixtures of imprudent, disorderly expressions, of private discontent and passion, of unreverent, disobedient, seditious, or factious intimations, tending to corrupt, and not to edify the people's minds, do turn either prayer or preaching into sin. And ordinarily in Church-communion, especially on the Lord's-day (which is purposely separated for the joyful commemoration of the blessed work of man's redemption) a considerable proportion of the public worship must consist of thanksgiving and praises to God, especially for Jesus Christ, and his benefits; still leaving it to the minister's discretion to abbreviate some parts of worship, when he seeth it needful to be longer on some other.

The Sermon and Prayer being ended, let the Minister dismiss the Congregation with a Benediction, in these or the like words.

Blessed are they that hear the word of God, and keep it.

The Lord bless you, and keep you; the Lord make his face to shine on you, and be gracious unto you; the Lord lift up his countenance upon you, and give you peace.

The grace of our Lord Jesus Christ, and the love of God the Father, and the communion of the Holy Ghost, be with you all. *Amen.*

The Order of Celebrating the Sacrament of the Body and Blood of Christ

This, or the like explication of the nature, use, and benefits of this Sacrament, may be used at the discretion of the minister, when he seeth it needful to the instruction of the communicants.

That you may discern the Lord's body, and understand the nature, use, and benefits of this Sacrament, you must know that God created man in his own image, to know, and love, and serve his Maker. That man fell under the guilt of sin, and condemnation, and left his holy fitness for the work for which he was created. That hereupon the wonderful love and wisdom of God provided us a remedy in our Redeemer, to the end he might not lose the glory of his creation: that he might pardon and save us upon terms securing the honour of his justice, and attaining the ends of his law and government; and recover us to his love and service, by appearing to the world in the greatest demonstrations of goodness, love, and mercy. By the greatest miracle of condescension, he first promised, and then gave, his only Son, the eternal Word, to take man's nature into personal union with his Godhead; that, being God and man, he might be a fit Mediator between God and man, to restore us and reconcile us to himself. Thus Jesus Christ, conceived by the Holy Ghost, and born of the Virgin Mary, became the second Adam, the Physician and Saviour of undone sinners, the Captain of our salvation, to be the glorious King and Head of all that are sanctified and saved. He revealed the holiness, the goodness, and the love of God, by the perfect holiness, the goodness and love, of his blessed person, doctrine, and conversation and by suffering for us all the afflictions of this life, and at last the cursed death of the cross, as a sacrifice and ransom for us. That all this might be effectual to our recovery, he made for us a new and better covenant, and preached it himself, undertaking the pardon, justification, and sanctification of all that by unfeigned faith do take him for their Saviour, repenting of their sins, and consenting to be sanctified by his word and Spirit; (by which also he inviteth and draweth men to himself, and giveth them to believe.) Into this blessed, pardoning, saving covenant we are first solemnly entered by baptism. And when Christ was ready to leave the world, and to give up himself a sacrifice for us, and intercede and exercise the fulness of his kingly power, as the Church's Head, and by his grace to draw men to himself, and prepare them for his glory; he did himself institute this Sacrament of his body and blood at his last supper, to be a continued representation and remembrance of his death, and therein of his own and his Father's love, until his coming: appointing his ministers, by the preaching of the Gospel, and administration of these sacraments, to be his agents without, and his Spirit within effectually to communicate his grace.

[The Lord's Supper, then, is an holy Sacrament, instituted by Christ: wherein bread and wine, being first by consecration made sacramentally, or representatively, the body and blood of Christ, are used by breaking and pouring out to represent and commemorate the sacrifice of Christ's body and blood upon the cross once offered up to God for sin; and are given in the name of Christ unto the Church, to signify and solemnize the renewal of his holy covenant with them, and the giving of himself unto them, to expiate their sins by his sacrifice, and sanctify them further by his Spirit, and confirm their right to everlasting life. And they are received, eaten, and drunk by the Church, to profess that they willingly receive Christ himself to the ends aforesaid, (their justification, sanctification, and glorification,) and to signify and

solemnize the renewal of their covenant with him, and their
holy communion with him and with one another.]

It being the renewing of a mutual covenant that is here
solemnized, as we commemorate Christ's sacrifice, and receive him and his saving benefits; so we offer and deliver to
him ourselves, as his redeemed, sanctified people, to be a
living acceptable sacrifice, thankfully and obediently to
live unto his praise.

Before the receiving of this holy Sacrament, we must examine ourselves, and come preparedly: in the receiving of it,
we must exercise holy affections suited to the work: and
after the receiving of it, we must, by consideration of it,
endeavour to revive the same affections, and perform our
covenant there renewed.

The holy qualifications, to be before provided, and in receiving exercised, and after receiving, are these:—1. A true
belief of the articles of the Christian faith concerning Father,
Son, and Holy Ghost; the person, offices, works and sufferings, and benefits of Christ. 2. The sense of our sinful and
undone condition, as in ourselves, and of our need of Christ;
so as humbly to loathe ourselves for our transgressions: with
the sense of our present weaknesses to be strengthened, and
sins to be forgiven. 3. A true desire after Christ for pardon,
and spiritual nourishment, and salvation. 4. A thankful sense
of the wonderful love of God, declared in our redemption,
and in the present offers of Christ, and life. 5. The exercise
of holy love and joy in the sense of this unspeakable love: if
these two be not felt before we come, yet in and after the
Sacrament we must strive to exercise them. 6. A love to one
another, and forgiving wrongs to one another, with a desire
after the communion of saints. 7. The giving up ourselves
in covenant to God, with resolution of renewed obedience. 8.
A patient hope for the coming of Christ himself, and of the
everlasting kingdom, where we shall be perfectly united in
him, and glorified with him.

Those only are to be invited to the Lord's table, and to
come, that truly repent and believe, and unfeignedly consent
to the terms of the covenant; (though all are not to be invited thus to believe and repent, and so [to] come). But
those are to be admitted by the pastors, if they come, who,
having the use of reason to understand what they do, and
examine themselves, have made a personal profession of faith,
repentance, and obedience; and are members of the Church,

and not justly for heresy, or scandalous sin, removed from its present communion.

The benefit of the Sacrament is not to be judged of only by present experience and feeling, but by faith. God having appointed us to use it, and promised his blessing, we may and must believe that he will make good his promise; and whatever we feel at present, that we sincerely wait not on him in vain.

THE EXHORTATION

You are invited hither, dear brethren, to be guests at this holy Table, by the Lord's command, to receive the greatest mercy, and to perform the greatest duty. On Christ's part all things are made ready. The feast is prepared for you, even for you that by sin have deserved to be cast out of the presence of the Lord; for you that have so oft neglected and abused mercy: a feast of the body and blood of Christ, free to you, but dear to him. You were lost, and in the way to be lost for ever, when, by the greatest miracle of condescending love, he sought and saved you. You were dead in sin, condemned by the law, the slaves of Satan; there wanted nothing but the executing stroke of justice to have sent you into endless misery; when our Redeemer pitied you in your blood,• and shed his own to wash and heal you. He suffered that was offended, that the offender might not suffer. He cried out on the cross, "My God, my God, why hast thou forsaken me?" that we, who had deserved it, might not be everlastingly forsaken. He died, that we might live. O, how would the mercy of redemption have affected you, if you had first lien one year, or month, or day in hell! Had you but seen your dying Lord, or seen the damned in their misery, how do you think you should have valued the salvation that is now revealed and tendered to you? See here Christ dying in this holy representation! Behold the sacrificed Lamb of God, that taketh away the sins of the world! It is his will to be thus frequently crucified before our eyes. O, how should we be covered with shame, and loathe ourselves, that have (both) procured the death of Christ by sin, and sinned against it! And how should we all be filled with joy, that have such mysteries of mercy opened, and so great salvation freely offered to us! O, hate sin! O, love this Saviour! See that you

• The original reads, evidently by mistake, "in his blood."

come not hither without a desire to be more holy, nor with a purpose to go on in wilful sin. Be not deceived, God is not mocked: but if you heartily repent, and consent to the covenant, come and welcome. We have commission from Christ to tell you that you are welcome. Let no trembling, contrite soul draw back, that is willing to be Christ's upon his covenant terms; but believe that Christ is much more willing to be yours. He was first willing, and therefore died for you, and made the covenant of grace, and sent to invite and importune you to consent, and stayed for you so long, and gave you your repentance, your willingness and desire. Question not then his willingness, if you are willing: it is Satan and unbelief that would have you question it, to the injury both of Christ and you. Come near, observe, believe, and wonder at the riches of his love and grace; for he hath himself invited you to see and taste, that you may wonder. You are sinners, but he inviteth you to receive a renewed, sealed pardon of your sins, and to give you more of his Spirit to overcome them. See here his broken body and his blood, the testimonies of his willingness. Thus hath he sealed the covenant, which pardoneth all your sins, and secureth you of your reconciliation with God, and your adoption, and your right to everlasting blessedness. Deny not your consent, but heartily give up yourselves to Christ; and then doubt not but your scarlet, crimson sins shall be made as white as wool or snow. Object not the number of greatness of them against his grace: there is none too great for him to pardon to penitent believers. Great sins shall bring great glory to his blood and grace. But strive you then for great loathing of your sins, and greater love to such a God, and greater thanks to such a Saviour. Unfeignedly say, I am willing, Lord, to be wholly thine; and then believingly take Christ, and pardon, and life, as given you by his own appointment in the sealed covenant. And remember that he is coming. He is coming with thousands of his mighty angels, to execute judgment on the ungodly; but to be glorified in his saints, and admired in all that do believe. And then we shall have greater things than these. Then shall you see all the promises fulfilled, which now are sealed to you, on which he causeth you to trust. Revive now your love to one another, and forgive those that have wronged you, and delight in the communion of the saints: and then you shall be admitted into the Church triumphant, where, with perfect saints, you shall perfectly rejoice, and love and praise the Lord for ever. Receive now a crucified Christ here represented, and be contented to take up your cross, and follow him. And then you shall reign with a glorified Christ, in the blessed vision and fruition of that God, to whom by Christ you are now reconciled. Let faith and love be working upon these things, while you are at this holy table.

Then shall the Minister use this, or the like Prayer.

Most holy God, we are as stubble before thee, the consuming fire. How shall we stand before thy holiness? For we are a sinful people, laden with iniquity, that have gone backward and provoked the Holy One of Israel. When we were lost, thy Son did seek and save us; when we were dead in sin, thou madest us alive. Thou sawest us polluted in our blood, and saidst unto us, Live! In that time of love thou coveredst our nakedness, and enteredst into a covenant with us, and we became thine own. Thou didst deliver us from the power of darkness, and translate us into the kingdom of thy dear Son; and gavest us remission of sin, through his blood. But we are grievous revolters; we have forgotten the covenant of the Lord our God. We were engaged to love thee with all our hearts, and to hate iniquity, and serve thee diligently, and thankfully to set forth thy praise. But we have departed from thee, and corrupted ourselves by self-love, and by loving the world, and the things that are in the world; and have fulfilled the desires of the flesh, which we should have crucified. We have neglected our duty to thee, and to our neighbour, and the necessary care of our own salvation. We have been unprofitable servants, and have hid thy talents; and have dishonoured thee, whom in all things we should have pleased and glorified. We have been negligent in hearing and reading thy holy word, and in meditating and conferring of it; in public and private prayer and thanksgiving, and in our preparation to this holy Sacrament; in the examining of ourselves, and repenting of our sins; and stirring up our hearts to a believing and thankful receiving of thy grace, and to love and joyfulness in our communion with thee and with one another. We have not duly discerned the Lord's body, but have profaned thy holy name and ordinance, as if the table of the Lord had been contemptible. And when thou hast spoken peace to us, we returned again to folly. We have deserved, O Lord, to be cast out of thy presence, and to be for-

398

saken, as we have forsaken thee, and to hear to our confusion, Depart from me, I know you not, ye workers of iniquity. Thou mayest justly tell us thou hast no pleasure in us, nor wilt receive an offering at our hand. But with thee there is abundant mercy; and our Advocate, Jesus Christ the righteous, is the propitiation for our sins: who bare them in his body on the cross, and made himself an offering for them, that he might put them away by the sacrifice of himself. Have mercy upon us, and wash us in his blood; clothe us with his righteousness: take away our iniquities, and let them not be our ruin; forgive them, and remember them no more. O thou that delightest not in the death of sinners, heal our backslidings, love us freely, and say unto our souls, that thou art our salvation. Thou wilt in no wise cast out them that come unto thee; receive us graciously to tne feast thou hast prepared for us. Cause us to hunger and thirst after Christ and his righteousness, that we may be satisfied. Let his flesh and blood be to us meat and drink indeed; and his Spirit be in us a well of living water, springing up to everlasting life. Give us to know thy love in Christ, which passeth knowledge. Though we have not seen him, let us love him; and though now we see him not, yet believing let us rejoice with joy unspeakable and full of glory. Though we are unworthy of the crumbs that fall from thy table, yet feed us with the bread of life, and speak and seal up peace to our sinful, wounded souls. Soften our hearts, that are hardened by the deceitfulness of sin: mortify the flesh, and strengthen us with might in the inward man: that we may live, and glorify thy grace, through Jesus Christ our only Saviour. *Amen.*

Here let the Bread be brought to the Minister, and received by him, and set upon the Table; and then the Wine in like manner: or if they be set there before, however let him bless them, praying in these or the like words.

Almighty God, thou art the Creator and the Lord of all things. Thou art the Sovereign Majesty whom we have offended. Thou art our most loving and merciful Father, who hast given thy Son to reconcile us to thyself: who hath ratified the new testament and covenant of grace with his most precious blood; and hath instituted this holy Sacrament to be celebrated in remembrance of him till his coming. Sanctify these thy creatures of bread and wine, which, according to thy institution and command, we set apart to this holy use, that they may be sacramentally the body and blood of thy Son Jesus Christ. *Amen.*

Then (or immediately before this Prayer) let the Minister read the words of the institution, saying:

HEAR what the apostle Paul saith: For I have received of the Lord that which also I deliver unto you; that the Lord Jesus, the same night in which he was betrayed, took bread, and when he had given thanks, he brake it, and said, Take, eat, this is my body which is broken for you: this do in remembrance of me. After the same manner also he took the cup, when he had supped, saying, This cup is the new testament in my blood; this do ye, as oft as ye drink it in remembrance of me: for as often as ye eat this bread, and drink this cup, ye do shew the Lord's death till he come.

Then let the Minister say:

This bread and wine, being set apart, and consecrated to this holy use by God's appointment, are now no common bread and wine, but sacramentally the body and blood of Christ.

Then let him thus pray:

Most merciful Saviour, as thou hast loved us to the death, and suffered for our sins, the just for the unjust, and hast instituted this holy Sacrament to be used in remembrance of thee till thy coming; we beseech thee, by thine intercession with the Father, through the sacrifice of thy body and blood, give us the pardon of our sins, and thy quickening Spirit, without which the flesh will profit us nothing. Reconcile us to the Father: nourish us as thy members to everlasting life. *Amen.*

Then let the Minister take the Bread, and break it in the sight of the people, saying:

The body of Christ was broken for us, and offered once for all to sanctify us: behold the sacrificed Lamb of God, that taketh away the sins of the world.

In like manner let him take the Cup, and pour out the Wine in the sight of the congregation, saying:

We were redeemed with the precious blood of Christ, as of a Lamb without blemish and without spot.

400

Then let him thus pray:

Most Holy Spirit, proceeding from the Father and the Son: by whom Christ was conceived; by whom the prophets and apostles were inspired, and the ministers of Christ are qualified and called: that dwellest and workest in all the members of Christ, whom thou sanctifiest to the image and for the service of their Head, and comfortest them that they may shew forth his praise: illuminate us, that by faith we may see him that is here represented to us. Soften our hearts, and humble us for our sins. Sanctify and quicken us, that we may relish the spiritual food, and feed on it to our nourishment and growth in grace. Shed abroad the love of God upon our hearts, and draw them out in love to him. Fill us with thankfulness and holy joy, and with love to one another. Comfort us by witnessing that we are the children of God. Confirm us for new obedience. Be the earnest of our inheritance, and seal us up to everlasting life. *Amen.*

Then let the Minister deliver the Bread, thus consecrated and broken, to the Communicants, first taking and eating it himself as one of them, when he hath said:

Take ye, eat ye; this is the body of Christ, which is broken for you. Do this, in remembrance of him.

In like manner he shall deliver them the Cup, first drinking of it himself, when he hath said:

This cup is the New Testament in Christ's blood, [*or,* Christ's blood of the New Testament,] which is shed for you for the remission of sins. Drink ye all of it, in remembrance of him.

Let it be left to the Minister's choice, whether he will consecrate the bread and wine together, and break the bread, and pour out the wine immediately; or whether he will consecrate and pour out the wine, when the communicants have eaten the bread. If he do the latter, he must use the foregoing prayers and expressions twice accordingly. And let it be left to his discretion, whether he will use any words at the breaking of the bread and pouring out the wine, or not. And if the Minister choose to pray but once at the consecration, commemoration, and delivery, let him pray as followeth, or to this sense.

Almighty God, thou art the Creator and the Lord of all. Thou art the Sovereign Majesty whom we have offended.

Thou art our merciful Father, who hast given us thy Son
to reconcile us to thyself; who hath ratified the new testament
and covenant of grace with his most precious blood, and hath
instituted this holy Sacrament to be celebrated in memorial
of him till his coming. Sanctify these thy creatures of bread
and wine, which, according to thy will, we set apart to this
holy use, that they may be sacramentally the body and
blood of thy Son Jesus Christ. And, through his sacrifice and
intercession, give us the pardon of all our sins, and be reconciled to us, and nourish us by the body and blood of Christ
to everlasting life. And, to that end, give us thy quickening
Spirit to shew Christ to our believing souls, that is here
represented to our senses. Let him soften our hearts, and
humble us for our sins, and cause us to feed on Christ by
faith. Let him shed abroad thy love upon our hearts, and
draw them on in love to thee, and fill us with holy joy and
thankfulness, and fervent love to one another. Let him comfort us by witnessing that we are thy· children, and confirm
us for new obedience, and be the earnest of our inheritance,
and seal us up to life everlasting, through Jesus Christ, our
Lord and Saviour. *Amen.*

*Let it be left to the Minister's discretion, whether to deliver
the bread and wine to the people, at the table, only in
general, each one taking it and applying it to themselves;
or to deliver it in general to so many as are in each particular form; or to put it into every person's hand: as
also at what season to take the contribution for the poor.
And let none of the people be forced to sit, stand, or kneel
in the act of receiving, whose judgment is against it.*

*The participation being ended, let the Minister pray thus,
or to this sense.*

Most glorious God, how wonderful is thy power and wisdom, thy holiness and justice, thy love and mercy, in this work
of our redemption, by the incarnation, life, death, resurrection, intercession, and dominion of thy Son! No power or wisdom in heaven or earth could have delivered us, but thine.
The angels desire to pry into this mystery: the heavenly host
do celebrate it with praises, saying, Glory be to God in the
highest; on earth peace, good-will towards men. The whole
creation shall proclaim thy praises: Blessing, honour, glory,
and power, be unto him that sitteth upon the throne, and

· The original reads: "*his* children," which is corrected in Calamy.

unto the Lamb for ever and ever. Worthy is the Lamb that was slain, to receive power, and honour, and glory: for he hath redeemed us to God by his blood, and made us kings and priests unto our God. Where sin abounded, grace hath abounded much more. And hast thou, indeed, forgiven us so great a debt, by so precious a ransom? Wilt thou, indeed, give us to reign with Christ in glory, and see thy face, and love thee, and be beloved of thee for ever? Yea, Lord, thou hast forgiven us, and thou wilt glorify us; for thou art faithful that hast promised. With the blood of thy Son, with the Sacrament, and with thy Spirit, thou hast sealed up to us these precious promises. And shall we not love thee, that hast thus loved us? Shall we not love thy servants, and forgive our neighbours their little debt? After all this, shall we again forsake thee, and deal falsely in thy covenant? God forbid! O set our affections on the things above, where Christ sitteth at thy right hand. Let us no more mind earthly things; but let our conversation be in heaven, from whence we expect our Saviour to come and change us into the likeness of his glory. Teach us to do thy will, O God, and to follow him who is the author of eternal salvation to all them that do obey him. Order our steps by thy word, and let not any iniquity have dominion over us. Let us not henceforth live unto ourselves, but unto him who died for us and rose again. Let us have no fellowship with the unfruitful works of darkness, but reprove them. And let our light so shine before men, that they may glorify thee. In simplicity and godly• sincerity, and not in fleshly wisdom, let us have our conversation in the world. O that our ways were so directed, that we might keep thy statutes! Though Satan will be desirous again to sift us, and seek as a roaring lion to devour, strengthen us to stand against his wiles, and shortly bruise him under our feet. Accept us, O Lord, who resign ourselves unto thee as thine own; and with our thanks and praise, present ourselves a living sacrifice to be acceptable through Christ, useful for thine honour. Being made free from sin, and become thy servants, let us have our fruit unto holiness, and the end everlasting life, through Jesus Christ our Lord and Saviour. *Amen.*

Next add this, or some such exhortation, if there be time.

Dear brethren, we have been here feasted with the Son of God at his table, upon his flesh and blood, in preparation

• The word "godly" is supplied from Calamy.

for the feast of endless glory. You have seen here represented what sin deserveth, what Christ suffered, what wonderful love the God of infinite goodness hath expressed to us. You have had communion with the saints; you have renewed your covenant of faith, and thankful obedience unto Christ; you have received his renewed covenant of pardon, grace and glory, unto you. O carry hence the lively sense of these great and excellent things upon your hearts. You came not (only) to receive the mercy of an hour only, but that which may spring up to endless joy: you came not only to do the duty of an hour, but to promise that which you must perform while you live on earth. Remember daily, especially when temptations to unbelief and sinful heaviness assault you, what pledges of love you here received; remember daily, especially when the flesh, the devil, or the world, would draw your hearts again from God, and temptations to sin are laid before you, what bonds God and your own consent have laid upon you. If you are penitent believers, you are now forgiven, and washed in the blood of Christ. O go your way, and sin no more; no more through wilfulness: and strive against your sins of weakness. Wallow no more in the mire, and return not to your vomit. Let the exceeding love of Christ constrain you, having such promises, to cleanse yourselves from all filthiness of flesh and spirit, perfecting holiness in the fear of God; and as a chosen generation, a royal priesthood, an holy nation, a peculiar people, to be zealous of good works, and shew forth the praises of him that hath called you.

Next sing part of the Hymn in metre, or some other fit Psalm of praise, (as the 23rd, 116th, 103rd, or 100th, &c.) and conclude with this, or the like, blessing:

Now the God of peace, which brought again from the dead our Lord Jesus Christ, that great Shepherd of the sheep, through the blood of the everlasting covenant, make you perfect in every good work to do his will, working in you that which is well-pleasing in his sight, through Jesus Christ; to whom be glory for ever and ever. *Amen.*

NOTES

1. This text has been reproduced from Peter Hall (ed.), *Reliquiae Liturgicae: Documents Connected with the Liturgy of the*

Richard Baxter, The Savoy Liturgy

Church of England, Vol. IV (Bath: Binns and Goodwin, 1847),
pp. 9-33; 55-79. To conserve space all Scriptural marginalia
have been omitted.
2. In the original, these sentences were printed in full.
3. Cf. *A Prayer for the King, the Royal Family, and Magistrates*;
Hall, *op. cit.*, pp. 34-6.
4. Cf. *The General Prayer*; Hall, *op. cit.*, pp. 36-44.

XIII
JOHN WESLEY

The Sunday Service
of the Methodists in North America
London, 1784

WESLEY

It was the way of John Wesley to espouse extempore prayer, yet esteem the prayer book; to give free expression to evangelical power, yet prize the structures of the church; to provide Methodist meetings for preaching, yet encourage his followers to participate fully in the ministries of the Anglican parishes. Therefore, at the conclusion of the American Revolution, when he beheld his "poor sheep in the wilderness," estranged from the Anglicans in America, often without benefit of the holy sacraments, Wesley determined to provide them with an ecclesiastical constitution, the main lines of which are set out in his letter from Bristol, September 10, 1784 (below).

That constitution was delivered in *The Sunday Service of the Methodists in North America* (London, 1784), which contained: (1) a revision of *The Book of Common Prayer*, (2) a revision of the Thirty-nine Articles, and (3) an Ordinal that established episcopal oversight and presbyteral orders in the new church. Companion to this volume was *A Collection of Psalms and Hymns for the Lord's Day*, prepared by the Wesleys and published in London, 1784. Those two books were intrusted to Thomas Coke, whom Wesley "set apart" as Superintendent for the American Methodists on September 2, 1784, and to Richard Whatcoat and Thomas Vasey, who were ordained "elders" on the same day. The three of them arrived in New York on November 5 of that year.

Francis Asbury, whom Wesley had appointed Superintendent alongside Coke, spoke the mind of the American preachers when he insisted that the conference, rather than Wesley's personal arbitration, was the proper means to reach final decisions on all these matters. At the Christmas Conference, which convened at Baltimore in 1784, Asbury was duly elected and ordained Superintendent, and Coke was received in the same office. The *Sunday Service* with its Ordinal and Articles of Religion, the Wesleyan hymnal, and the Form of Discipline, recently drawn from the Wesleyan Large Minutes, were all adopted in the course of ten days; and thus the organization of the new church was finished.

But its liturgical character, provided by Wesley and established at Baltimore, did not persist for long. The second edition of the *Sunday Service* (London, 1786) was also the last; and in 1792 the sacramental rites, occasional offices, and Articles of Religion were incorporated into the Discipline, while the rest of the book disappeared. The demise of "Mr. Wesley's liturgy" came not by official abrogation, but by disuse, and (as Jesse Lee suggested) by outright unpopularity:

At this time the prayer book, as revised by Mr. Wesley, was introduced among us; and in the large towns, and in some country places, our preachers read prayers on the Lord's day: and in some cases the preachers read part of the morning service on Wednesdays and Fridays. But some of the preachers who had been long accustomed to pray extempore, were unwilling to adopt this new plan. Being fully satisfied that they could pray better, and with more devotion while their eyes were shut, than they could with their eyes open. After a few years the prayer book was laid aside, and has never been used since in public worship.

Paul Sanders offers several main reasons for the failure of the *Sunday Service* among American Methodists. First, "they held the dominant evangelical conviction, nourished in a pietistic and sectarian environment, that salvation is solely a matter of personal relationship between God and the individual." Many who had experienced the grace of God apart from liturgical worship, apart even from the sacraments, felt no need of the *Sunday Service;* "and there were doubtless as many, more strongly motivated by principles of radical sectarianism, who felt prayer book worship inconsistent with

410

sincere faith and therefore harmful and wrong." Second, neither the Methodist preachers nor their constituents were apt to be well educated or accustomed to elegant literary forms. "Living remote from centers of education, culture and refinement, and worshipping in open fields, in brush arbors . . . , in their cabins around their hearthsides, or at best, in plain, rustic meeting-houses, how little in keeping must the staid beauty of the English liturgy have seemed to these folk." And if that liturgy neither incited their devotion nor expressed their religious ardor, how useless and wrong was this "praying from a book." In any case, the bond between Anglicans and Methodists in the colonies was slight; and many of the latter, if they understood Anglicanism at all, found little appeal in its characteristic life and worship.

Wesley's esteem for the Anglican Prayer Book, though qualified, was great indeed; and he expressed it at conferences and in sermons and correspondence (*Letters* 3: 143, 152). But nowhere did he declare himself so favorably disposed toward the Common Prayer than in his letter from Bristol, September 9, 1784 (below), which was prefixed to certain editions of the *Sunday Service*. Here he listed the four alterations he had made: (1) he omitted holy days, Lent, and the season of Epiphany, referring instead to "Sundays after Christmas"; (2) in Morning and Evening Prayer he left out the Venite, the alternate canticles, and the suffrages preceding the collects; (3) he made substantial changes in the Baptismal Office and omitted the Committal in the Burial of the Dead; (4) he excised whole psalms and parts of others "as being highly improper" for Christian use. Besides these were other changes that he did not mention. He omitted Confirmation and the Visitation of the Sick; he deleted nearly all of the material from the Apocrypha and removed the Athanasian and Nicene Creeds. "Priest" became "elder" or "Minister"; and "bishops," "priests," and "curates" became "ministers of the Gospel."

In appraising this revision, Wesley scholars do not agree. Cooke and Harmon believe that it was a Puritan revision, not that Wesley was self-consciously a Puritan or the chief agitator of liturgical reform, but because he was the great exponent of evangelical religion on the English scene. Others argue that Wesley's revision corresponded to the changes desired by the Presbyterian party at the Savoy Conference in 1661. Rattenbury and Sanders take exception to both of these positions. Rattenbury cites some practical considerations that must have motivated Wesley: his habitual passion for abridgment, his desire to have the liturgy acceptable in America where the Puritan tradition was strong and the bitterness toward the Church of England was scarcely forgotten. Sanders, who does not minimize Wesley's participation in the Anglican tradition, doubts that the revision was made under Puritan persuasion or motivated primarily by pragmatic considerations; he is content to say that "the *Sunday Service* was produced in conformity with Wesley's own deepest evangelical convictions."

Wesley's Eucharistic liturgy—"The Order for the Administration of the Lord's Supper"—was a conservative revision of the Anglican office. It was supplied with Collects, Epistles and Gospels for each Sunday of the year, in keeping with Wesley's recommendation that Communion ought to be celebrated every Lord's Day, and ought to be received as often as one had the opportunity. His own precept and practice proved difficult to follow in America, where there were few established pastorates and a dearth of elders who alone could administer the sacrament.

Throughout the liturgy, "elder" was substituted for "priest." But lest we be misled by this evidence, we must also note that, according to the early Disciplines, only the elders were allowed to celebrate; deacons could assist, but unordained preachers had no sacramental ministry at all. Not only did this preclude lay celebration, but it suggested that the sacramental ministry was different in kind from the preaching ministry, as indeed Wesley frequently asserted. Moreover, he believed in a Eucharistic sacrifice, namely, the self-offering of the whole Church in union with Christ's re-presented offering of Himself. Sacrifice implies a priesthood; in this case it is the priesthood of the whole Church, of which the elder stands as surrogate. Thus, Wesley must have had no theological objection to the word "priest," but dropped it for its popular connotations.

Calvin's doctrine of the spiritual real presence was the one to which Wesley subscribed; but it was mediated to him through a century and a half of Anglican discussion on the subject. By the operation of the Holy Spirit, Christ is present in a personal, dynamic fashion, bestowing His power (*virtus*) upon true believers. While His presence does not depend upon the subjective faith of the worshiper, but rather upon

412

the Lord's own promises and upon the work of the Holy Spirit, only those of faith do actually receive Him and participate in His benefits. Yet, unlike many in the Reformed and Puritan traditions, Wesley did not require whole faith for Communion. He taught, indeed he knew by experience, that the sacrament was a converting ordinance, meant also for "the honest seeker," who, though not yet possessed of justifying faith, was already responsive to the Gospel. Such a view was consistent with Wesley's whole theological stance: salvation is always moment by moment; and he is "safe" who is answering as fully as he can to the grace of which he is aware at the time.

Though he did not define it precisely, Wesley believed that a connection existed between the Eucharistic elements and the grace of the sacrament. In one instance he referred to "the mystical relation which the bread, by consecration, has to Christ's body." More than symbols, the elements were actual instruments by which the promised benefits of the Supper were communicated. Apparently the Anglican prayer of consecration expressed these ideas to his satisfaction, for he made no critical alterations to it. But for some unknown reason, two versions of that prayer were given in separate issues of the 1784 *Sunday Service:* one with, and one without, the Manual Acts. Which was prior, which was Wesley's or Coke's, which was "higher" are all vexing questions. We have simply printed both versions, one after the other.·

At the time of Delivery, the elder placed both bread and wine into the hands of the communicant, using the Words from the 1662 Prayer Book. Wesley preferred to have the people kneel, but not at the expense of their conscience. The early Disciplines allowed them to stand or sit when receiving, and Wesley omitted the direction, "all meekly kneeling" from the Communion rubric. It was the practice, though unsaid in the liturgy, to sing hymns during the Communion; and many of the Wesleyan Eucharistic hymns succeeded in encompassing both the virtue of Christ's passion and the joy of His resurrection, renewing them for the participation of faith, and giving reality to the sense of union with the living Lord. Wesley omitted the second Post-Communion prayer of thanksgiving, leaving the first, which was the Oblation from

· It is important to notice that the *Puritans* insisted upon the observance of the Manual Acts in deference to the Lord's own institution. See Ch. XII.

the 1549 Prayer Book. Thus the liturgy closed with emphasis upon the remission of sins and upon the "bounden duty" of the communicants to offer themselves as a "lively sacrifice." After the Gloria in excelsis, which was said instead of sung, occasion was given for extempore prayer.

Whatever be the fine points of interpretation, one can scarcely doubt that the *Sunday Service* was cast in the tradition of the English Prayer Book and its Eucharistic doctrine, with certain new provisions for evangelical expression. In his entire view of worship, Wesley drew the balance between the stability of tradition and the dynamism of the Spirit; and he knew no conflict between the evangelical reality and the sacramental reality of Christian experience.

FOR FURTHER READING

John Bishop, *Methodist Worship in Relation to Free Church Worship*. London, 1950.

J. C. Bowmer, *The Sacrament of the Lord's Supper in Early Methodism*. Westminster, 1951.

R. J. Cooke, *History of the Ritual of the Methodist Episcopal Church*. New York, 1900.

Horton Davies, *Worship and Theology in England: From Watts and Wesley to Maurice, 1690-1850*. Princeton, 1961.

Nolan B. Harmon, *The Rites and Ritual of Episcopal Methodism*. Nashville, 1926.

J. F. Rattenbury, *The Eucharistic Hymns of John and Charles Wesley*. London, 1948.

Paul S. Sanders, *An Appraisal of John Wesley's Sacramentalism in the Evolution of Early American Methodism*. Th.D. dissertation. New York: Union Theological Seminary, 1954.

THE SUNDAY SERVICE
OF THE METHODISTS IN NORTH AMERICA
With other Occasional Services.
LONDON:
Printed in the Year MDCCLXXXIV.[1]

BRISTOL, Sept. 10, 1784.[2]
To Dr. COKE, Mr. ASBURY, and our Brethren in NORTH-
AMERICA.

1. By a very uncommon train of providences, many of
the provinces of *North-America* are totally disjoined from
their mother-country, and erected into Independent States.
The English government has no authority over them either
civil or ecclesiastical, any more than over the States of *Hol-
land*. A civil authority is exercised over them, partly by the
Congress, partly by the provincial Assemblies. But no one
either exercises or claims any ecclesiastical authority at all.
In this peculiar situation some thousands of the inhabitants
of these States desire my advice; and in compliance with their
desire, I have drawn up a little sketch.

2. Lord King's account of the primitive church convinced
me many years ago, that Bishops and Presbyters are the
same order, and consequently have the same right to ordain.
For many years I have been importuned from time to time,
to exercise this right, by ordaining part of our travelling
preachers. But I have still refused, not only for peace' sake:
but because I was determined, as little as possible to violate
the established order of the national church to which I
belonged.

3. But the case is widely different between England and
North-America. Here there are Bishops who have a legal
jurisdiction. In America there are none, neither any parish ministers. So that for some hundred miles together there is none
either to baptize or to administer the Lord's supper. Here
therefore my scruples are at an end: and I conceive myself
at full liberty, as I violate no order and invade no man's
right, by appointing and sending labourers into the harvest.

4. I have accordingly appointed Dr. COKE and Mr. FRANCIS ASBURY, to be joint *Superintendents* over our brethren in North-America: As also RICHARD WHATCOAT and THOMAS VASEY, to act as *Elders* among them, by baptizing and administering the Lord's supper. And I have prepared a liturgy little differing from that of the church of England (I think, the best constituted national church in the world) which I advise all the travelling-preachers to use, on the Lord's day, in all their congregations, reading the litany only on Wednesdays and Fridays, and praying extempore on all other days. I also advise the elders to administer the supper of the Lord on every Lord's day.

5. If any one will point out a more rational and scriptural way, of feeding and guiding those poor sheep in the wilderness, I will gladly embrace it. At present I cannot see any better method than that I have taken.

6. It has indeed been proposed, to desire the English Bishops, to ordain part of our preachers for *America*. But to this I object, 1. I desired the Bishop of *London*, to ordain only one; but could not prevail: 2. If they consented, we know the slowness of their proceedings; but the matter admits of no delay. 3. If they would ordain them *now*, they would likewise expect to govern them. And how grievously would this intangle us? 4. As our *American* brethren are now totally disentangled both from the State, and from the English Hierarchy, we dare not intangle them again, either with the one or the other. They are now at full liberty, simply to follow the scriptures and the primitive church. And we judge it best that they should stand fast in that liberty, wherewith GOD has so strangely made them free.

JOHN WESLEY.

•

I BELIEVE [3] there is no LITURGY in the World, either in ancient or modern language, which breathes more of a solid, scriptural, rational Piety, than the COMMON PRAYER of the CHURCH of ENGLAND. And though the main of it was compiled considerably more than two hundred years ago, yet is the language of it, not only pure, but strong and elegant in the highest degree.

Little alteration is made in the following edition of it,

(which I recommend to our SOCIETIES in AMERICA) except in the following instances:

1. Most of the holy-days (so called) are omitted, as at present answering no valuable end.

2. The service of the LORD'S DAY, the length of which has been often complained of, is considerably shortened.

3. Some sentences in the offices of Baptism, and for the Burial of the Dead, are omitted.—And,

4. Many Psalms left out, and many parts of the others, as being highly improper for the mouths of a Christian Congregation.

JOHN WESLEY.

Bristol, September 9, 1784.

•

The ORDER for
MORNING PRAYER,

Every Lord's Day⁴

At the Beginning of Morning Prayer, the Minister shall read with a loud Voice some one or more of these Sentences of the Scriptures that follow: And then he shall say that which is written after the said Sentences.

When the wicked man turneth away from his wickedness that he hath committed, and doeth that which is lawful and right, he shall save his soul alive. *Ezek. xviii. 27.*

The sacrifices of God are a broken spirit: a broken and a contrite heart, O God, thou wilt not despise. *Psal. li. 17.*

To the Lord our God belong mercies and forgivenesses, though we have rebelled against him: neither have we obeyed the voice of the Lord our God, to walk in his laws which he set before us. *Dan. ix. 9, 10.*

I will arise, and go to my father, and will say unto him, Father, I have sinned against Heaven and before thee, and am no more worthy to be called thy son. *Luke, xv. 18, 19.*

Enter not into judgment with thy servant, O Lord; for in thy sight shall no man living be justified. *Psal. cxliii. 2.*

Dearly beloved brethren, the Scripture moveth us, in sundry places, to acknowledge and confess our manifold sins and wickedness, and that we should not dissemble or cloke them before the face of Almighty God, our heavenly Father; but confess them with an humble, lowly, penitent, and obedient heart; to the end that we may obtain forgiveness of the same, by his infinite goodness and mercy. Wherefore I pray and beseech you, as many as are here present, to accompany me with a pure heart and humble voice, unto the throne of the heavenly grace, saying after me.

A general Confession, to be said by the whole Congregation, after the Minister, all kneeling.

Almighty and most merciful Father, We have erred and strayed from thy ways like lost sheep. We have followed too much the devices and desires of our own hearts. We have offended against thy holy laws. We have left undone those things which we ought to have done; And we have done those things which we ought not to have done; And there is no health in us. But thou, O Lord, have mercy upon us, miserable offenders. Spare thou them, O God, which confess their faults. Restore thou them that are penitent; According to thy promises declared unto mankind in Christ Jesus our Lord. And grant, O most merciful Father, for his sake, That we may hereafter live a godly, righteous, and sober life; To the glory of thy holy Name. Amen.

Then the Minister shall say,

O Lord, we beseech thee, absolve thy people from their offences; that, through thy bountiful goodness, we may be delivered from the bands of those sins, which by our frailty we have committed. Grant this, O heavenly Father, for Jesus Christ's sake, our blessed Lord and Saviour.

The People shall answer here, and at the End of all other Prayers. Amen.

Then the Minister shall say the Lord's Prayer; the People also repeating it with him, both here, and wheresoever else it is used in Divine Service.

Our Father who art in Heaven, Hallowed be thy Name; Thy kingdom come; Thy Will be done on Earth, As it is in Heaven: Give us this day our daily bread; And forgive us our trespasses, As we forgive them that trespass against us;

418

And lead us not into temptation; But deliver us from evil: For thine is the Kingdom, and the Power, and the Glory, For ever and ever. Amen.

Then likewise he shall say,

O Lord, open thou our lips.
Answ. And our mouth shall shew forth thy praise.
Minist. O God, make speed to save us;
Answ. O Lord, make haste to help us.

Here all standing up, the Minister shall say,

Glory be to the Father, and to the Son, and to the Holy Ghost;
Answ. As it was in the beginning, is now, and ever shall be, world without end. Amen.
Minist. Praise ye the Lord.
Answ. The Lord's Name be praised.

Then shall follow the Psalms, in order as they are appointed. And at the End of every Psalm, shall be repeated,

Glory be to the Father, and to the Son, and to the Holy Ghost;
As it was in the beginning, is now, and ever shall be, world without end. Amen.

Then shall be read distinctly, the First Lesson taken out of the Old Testament, as is appointed in the Table of proper Lessons: He that readeth, so standing, and turning himself as he may be best heard of all. And after that, shall be said the following Hymn:

We praise thee, O God: we acknowledge thee to be the Lord.
All the earth doth worship thee, the Father everlasting.
To thee all Angels cry aloud: the Heavens, and all the powers therein.
To thee Cherubin and Seraphin continually do cry,
Holy, holy, holy, Lord God of Sabaoth;
Heaven and Earth are full of the Majesty of thy Glory.
The glorious company of the Apostles praise thee.
The goodly fellowship of the Prophets praise thee.
The noble army of Martyrs praise thee.
The Holy Church throughout all the world doth acknowledge thee;
The Father of an infinite Majesty;

Thine honourable, true, and only Son;

Also the Holy Ghost, the Comforter.

Thou art the King of glory, O Christ;

Thou art the everlasting Son of the Father.

When thou tookest upon thee to deliver man, thou didst not abhor the Virgin's womb.

When thou hadst overcome the sharpness of death, thou didst open the kingdom of Heaven to all believers.

Thou sittest at the right hand of God, in the glory of the Father.

We believe that thou shalt come to be our Judge.

We therefore pray thee, help thy servants, whom thou hast redeemed with thy precious blood.

Make them to be numbered with thy Saints in glory everlasting.

O Lord, save thy people, and bless thine heritage.

Govern them, and lift them up for ever.

Day by day we magnify thee;

And we worship thy name ever, world without end.

Vouchsafe, O Lord, to keep us this day without sin.

O Lord, have mercy upon us: have mercy upon us.

O Lord, let thy mercy lighten upon us, as our trust is in thee.

O Lord, in thee have I trusted: let me never be confounded.

Then shall be read in like manner the Second Lesson, taken out of the New Testament: and after that, the following Psalm:

O Be joyful in the Lord, all ye lands: serve the Lord with gladness, and come before his presence with a song.

Be ye sure that the Lord he is God; it is he that hath made us, and not we ourselves: we are his people, and the sheep of his pasture.

O go your way into his gates with thanksgiving, and into his courts with praise: be thankful unto him, and speak good of his Name.

For the Lord is gracious, his mercy is everlasting: and his truth endureth from generation to generation.

Glory be to the Father, and to the Son, and to the Holy Ghost;

As it was in the beginning, is now, and ever shall be, world without end. Amen.

420

Then shall be said the Apostles' Creed by the Minister and the People, standing.

I Believe in God the Father Almighty, Maker of Heaven and Earth:

And in Jesus Christ his only Son our Lord; Who was conceived by the Holy Ghost; Born of the Virgin Mary; Suffered under Pontius Pilate; Was crucified, dead, and buried, He descended into hell: The third day he rose again from the dead: He ascended into Heaven, And sitteth on the right hand of God, the Father Almighty; From thence he shall come to judge the quick and the dead.

I believe in the Holy Ghost; The Holy Catholick Church; The Communion of Saints; The Forgiveness of Sins; The Resurrection of the Body, And the Life everlasting. Amen.

And after that, the Minister shall pronounce with a loud Voice,

The Lord be with you;
Answ. And with thy spirit.

Minister. Let us pray.

Lord, have mercy upon us.
Answ. Christ have mercy upon us.
Minist. Lord, have mercy upon us.

Then shall follow three Collects; the first of the Day, which shall be the same that is appointed at the Communion; the second for Peace; the third for Grace to live well; all devoutly kneeling.

The Second Collect, for Peace.

O God, who art the author of peace, and lover of concord, in knowledge of whom standeth our eternal life, whose service is perfect freedom; Defend us thy humble servants in all assaults of our enemies; that we, surely trusting in thy defence, may not fear the power of any adversaries, through the might of Jesus Christ our Lord. *Amen.*

The Third Collect, for Grace.

O Lord our heavenly Father, Almighty and everlasting God, who hast safely brought us to the beginning of this day; Defend us in the same with thy mighty power; and grant that this day we fall into no sin; neither run into any kind of danger; but that all our doings may be ordered by thy governance, to do always that is righteous in thy sight, through Jesus Christ our Lord. *Amen.*

Then these Prayers following are to be read.

A Prayer for the Supreme Rulers.

O Lord our heavenly Father, high and mighty, King of kings, Lord of lords, the only Ruler of princes, who dost from thy throne behold all the dwellers upon earth; Most heartily we beseech thee, with thy favour to behold the Supreme Rulers of these United States, and so replenish them with the grace of thy Holy Spirit, that they may alway incline to thy will, and walk in thy way; through Jesus Christ our Lord. *Amen.*

Almighty God, who hast given us grace at this time with one accord, to make our common supplications unto thee, and dost promise that when two or three are gathered together in thy Name, thou wilt grant their requests; Fulfil now, O Lord, the desires and petitions of thy servants, as may be most expedient for them: granting us in this world knowledge of thy truth, and in the world to come life everlasting. *Amen.*

2 Cor. xiii 14.

The grace of our Lord Jesus Christ, and the love of God, and the fellowship of the Holy Ghost, be with you all evermore. *Amen.*

Here endeth the Order of Morning Prayer.

The Order for the Administration of the Lord's Supper[5]

The Table at the Communion-time, having a fair white Linen Cloth upon it, shall stand where Morning and Evening Prayers are appointed to be said. And the Elder, standing at the Table, shall say the Lord's Prayer, with the Collect following, the People kneeling.

Our Father, who art in Heaven, Hallowed be thy Name; Thy Kingdom come; Thy will be done on earth, as it is in heaven; Give us this day our daily bread; And forgive us our trespasses, as we forgive them that trespass against us; And lead us not into Temptation, but deliver us from evil. *Amen.*

The Collect.

Almighty God, unto whom all hearts be open, all desires known, and from whom no secrets are hid; cleanse the thoughts of our hearts by the inspiration of thy Holy Spirit, that we may perfectly love thee, and worthily magnify thy holy Name, through Christ our Lord. *Amen.*

The shall the Elder, turning to the People, rehearse distinctly all the TEN COMMANDMENTS: and the People still kneeling shall, after every Commandment, ask God Mercy for their Transgression thereof for the Time past, and Grace to keep the same for the Time to come, as followeth:

Minister.

God spake these words, and said, I am the Lord thy God: Thou shalt have none other gods but me.

People. Lord, have mercy upon us, and incline our hearts to keep this law.

Minist. Thou shalt not make to thyself any graven image, nor the likeness of any thing that is in heaven above, or in the earth beneath, or in the water under the earth. Thou shalt not bow down to them, nor worship them: for I the Lord thy God am a jealous God, and visit the sins of the fathers upon the children, unto the third and fourth generation of them that hate me, and shew mercy unto thousands in them that love me, and keep my commandments.

People. Lord, have mercy upon us, and incline our hearts to keep this law.

Minist. Thou shalt not take the Name of the Lord thy God in vain: for the Lord will not hold him guiltless that taketh his Name in vain.

People. Lord, have mercy upon us, and incline our hearts to keep this law.

Minist. Remember that thou keep holy the Sabbath-day. Six days shalt thou labour, and do all that thou hast to do; but the seventh day is the Sabbath of the Lord thy God: in it thou shalt do no manner of work, thou, and thy son, and thy daughter, thy man-servant, and thy maid-servant, thy cattle, and the stranger that is within thy gates. For in six days the Lord made heaven and earth, the sea, and all that in them is, and rested the seventh day; wherefore the Lord blessed the seventh day, and hallowed it.

People. Lord, have mercy upon us, and incline our hearts to keep this law.

Minist. Honour thy father and thy mother, that thy days may be long in the land which the Lord thy God giveth thee.

People. Lord, have mercy upon us, and incline our hearts to keep this law.

Minist. Thou shalt do no murder.

People. Lord, have mercy upon us, and incline our hearts to keep this law.

Minist. Thou shalt not commit adultery.

People. Lord, have mercy upon us, and incline our hearts to keep this law.

Minist. Thou shalt not steal.

People. Lord, have mercy upon us, and incline our hearts to keep this law.

Minist. Thou shalt not bear false witness against thy neighbour.

People. Lord, have mercy upon us, and incline our hearts to keep this law.

Minist. Thou shalt not covet thy neighbour's house, thou shalt not covet thy neighbour's wife, nor his servant, nor his maid, nor his ox, nor his ass, nor any thing that is his.

People. Lord, have mercy upon us, and write all these thy laws in our hearts, we beseech thee.

Then shall follow this Collect.

Let us pray.

Almighty and everlasting God, we are taught by thy holy word, that the hearts of the Princes of the earth are in thy rule and governance, and that thou dost dispose and turn them as it seemeth best to thy godly wisdom; we humbly beseech thee so to dispose and govern the hearts of the Supreme Rulers of these United States, our Governors, that in all their thoughts, words, and works, they may ever seek thy honour and glory, and study to preserve thy people committed to their charge, in wealth, peace, and godliness. Grant this, O merciful Father, for thy dear Son's sake, Jesus Christ our Lord. *Amen.*

Then shall be said the Collect of the day. And immediately after the Collect, the Elder shall read the Epistle, saying, The Epistle [*or,* The Portion of Scripture appointed for

424

the Epistle] is written in the ——— Chapter of ———
beginning at the ——— Verse. *And the Epistle ended, he
shall say,* Here endeth the Epistle. *Then shall he read the
Gospel (the People all standing up), saying,* The holy
Gospel is written in the ——— Chapter of ——— beginning at the ——— Verse.

Then shall follow the Sermon.
Then shall the Elder say one or more of these Sentences.

Let your light so shine before men, that they may see your
good works, and glorify your Father who is in heaven. *Matth.
v. 16.*

Lay not up for yourselves treasures upon earth, where
moth and rust do corrupt, and where thieves break through
and steal: but lay up for yourselves treasures in heaven,
where neither moth nor rust doth corrupt, and where thieves
do not break through nor steal. *Matth. vi. 19, 20.*

Whatsoever ye would that men should do unto you, even
so do unto them; for this is the law and the prophets. *Matth.
vii. 12.*

Not every one that saith unto me, Lord, Lord, shall enter
into the kingdom of heaven; but he that doeth the will of my
Father who is in heaven. *Matth. vii. 21.*

Zaccheus stood forth, and said unto the Lord, Behold, Lord,
the half of my goods I give to the poor; and if I have done
any wrong to any man, I restore him four-fold. *Luke, xix. 8.*

Who goeth a warfare at any time of his own cost? who
planteth a vineyard, and eateth not of the fruit thereof? or
who feedeth a flock, and eateth not of the milk of the flock?
1 Cor. ix. 7.

If we have sown unto you spiritual things, is it a great
matter if we shall reap your worldly things? *1 Cor. ix. 11.*

Do ye not know, that they who minister about holy things,
live of the sacrifice? and they who wait at the altar, are
partakers with the altar? Even so hath the Lord also ordained,
that they who preach the Gospel, should live of the Gospel.
1 Cor. ix. 13, 14.

He that soweth little, shall reap little: and he that soweth
plenteously, shall reap plenteously. Let every man do according as he is disposed in his heart; not grudgingly, or of
necessity: for God loveth a chearful giver. *2 Cor. ix. 6, 7.*

Let him that is taught in the Word, minister unto him that

teacheth in all good things. Be not deceived, God is not mocked: for whatsoever a man soweth, that shall he reap. *Gal. vi. 6, 7.*

While we have time, let us do good unto all men, and especially unto them that are of the household of faith. *Gal. vi. 10.*

Godliness with contentment is great gain: for we brought nothing into the world, and it is certain we can carry nothing out. 1 *Tim. vi. 6, 7.*

Charge them who are rich in this world, that they be ready to give, and ·glad to distribute, laying up in store for themselves a good foundation against the time to come, that they may attain eternal life. 1 *Tim. vi. 17, 18, 19.*

God is not unrighteous, that he will forget your works and labour that proceedeth of love; which love ye have shewed for his Name's sake, who have ministered unto the saints, and yet do minister. *Heb. vi. 10.*

To do good, and to distribute, forget not; for with such sacrifices God is well pleased. *Hebr. xiii. 16.*

Whoso hath this world's good, and seeth his brother have need, and shutteth up his compassion from him, how dwelleth the love of God in him? 1 *John, iii. 17.*

Be merciful after thy power: If thou hast much, give plenteously: If thou hast little, do thy diligence gladly to give of that little: for so gatherest thou thyself a good reward in the day of necessity. *Tob. iv. 8, 9.*

He that hath pity upon the poor, lendeth unto the Lord; and look what he layeth out, it shall be paid him again. *Prov. xix. 17.*

Blessed is the man that provideth for the sick and needy: the Lord shall deliver him in the time of trouble. *Psal. xli. 1.*

While these Sentences are in reading, some fit person appointed for that purpose, shall receive the alms for the poor, and other devotions of the people, in a decent Bason, to be provided for that purpose; and then bring it to the Elder, who shall place it upon the Table.

After which done, the Elder shall say,

Let us pray for the whole state of Christ's Church militant here on earth.

Almighty and everliving God, who, by thy holy Apostle, hast taught us to make prayers and supplications, and to give

426

thanks for all men; We humbly beseech thee most mercifully [· *to accept our alms and oblations, and*] to receive these our prayers, which we offer unto thy Divine Majesty; beseeching thee to inspire continually the universal Church with the spirit of truth, unity, and ccncord: and grant that all they that do confess thy holy Name, may agree in the truth of thy holy word, and live in unity and godly love. We beseech thee also to save and defend all Christian Kings, Princes, and Governors; and especially thy Servants the Supreme Rulers of these United States; that under them we may be godly and quietly governed: and grant unto all that are put in authority under them, that they may truly and indifferently administer justice, to the punishment of wickedness and vice, and to the maintenance of thy true religion and virtue. Give grace, O heavenly Father, to all the Ministers of thy Gospel, that they may both by their life and doctrine set forth thy true and lively word, and rightly and duly administer thy holy Sacraments. And to all thy people give thy heavenly grace; and especially to this Congregation here present; that with meek heart and due reverence they may hear and receive thy holy word, truly serving thee in holiness and righteousness all the days of their life. And we most humbly beseech thee of thy goodness, O Lord, to comfort and succour all them, who in this transitory life are in trouble, sorrow, need, sickness, or any other adversity. And we also bless thy holy Name, for all thy servants departed this life in thy faith and fear; beseeching thee to give us grace so to follow their good examples, that with them we may be partakers of thy heavenly kingdom. Grant this, O Father, for Jesus Christ's sake, our only Mediator and Advocate. *Amen.*

Then shall the Elder say to them that come to receive the Holy Communion.

Ye that do truly and earnestly repent of your sins, and are in love and charity with your neighbours, and intend to lead a new life, following the commandments of God, and walking from henceforth in his holy ways; Draw near with faith, and take this holy Sacrament to your comfort; and make your humble confession to Almighty God, meekly kneeling upon your knees.

· *If there be no alms or oblations, then shall the words* [of accepting our alms and oblations] *be left unsaid.*

Then shall this general Confession be made by the Minister in the Name of all those that are minded to receive the Holy Communion, both he and all the people kneeling humbly upon their knees, and saying,

Almighty God, Father of our Lord Jesus Christ, Maker of all things, Judge of all men; We acknowledge and bewail our manifold sins and wickedness, Which we from time to time most grievously have committed, By thought, word, and deed, against thy Divine Majesty, provoking most justly thy wrath and indignation against us. We do earnestly repent, and are heartily sorry for these our misdoings; The remembrance of them is grievous unto us. Have mercy upon us, have mercy upon us, most merciful Father; For thy Son our Lord Jesus Christ's sake, forgive us all that is past; And grant, that we may ever hereafter serve and please thee in newness of life, To the honour and glory of thy Name, Through Jesus Christ our Lord. *Amen.*

Then shall the Elder say,

O Almighty God, our heavenly Father, who of thy great mercy hast promised forgiveness of sins to all them that with hearty repentance and true faith turn unto thee; Have mercy upon us; pardon and deliver us from all our sins, confirm and strengthen us in all goodness, and bring us to everlasting life, through Jesus Christ our Lord. *Amen.*

Then all standing, the Elder shall say.

Hear what comfortable words our Saviour Christ saith unto all that truly turn to him:

Come unto me, all ye that are burdened and heavy-laden, and I will refresh you. *Matth. xi. 28.*

So God loved the world, that he gave his only-begotten Son, to the end that all that believe in him, should not perish, but have everlasting life. *John, iii. 16.*

Hear also what St. Paul saith:

This is a true saying, and worthy of all men to be received, That Christ Jesus came into the world to save sinners. 1 *Tim. i. 15.*

Hear also what St. John saith:

If any man sin, we have an Advocate with the Father, Jesus Christ the righteous: and he is the propitiation for our sins. 1 *John, ii. 1, 2.*

428

After which the Elder shall proceed, saying,

Lift up your hearts.

Answ. We lift them up unto the Lord.

Elder. Let us give thanks unto our Lord God.

Answ. It is meet and right so to do.

Then shall the Elder say,

It is very meet, right, and our bounden duty, that we should at all times, and in all places, give thanks unto thee, O Lord, Holy Father,· Almighty, Everlasting God.

Here shall follow the proper Preface, according to the Time, if there be any especially appointed; or else immediately shall follow;

Therefore with Angels and Archangels and with all the company of heaven, we laud and magnify thy glorious Name, evermore praising thee, and saying, Holy, holy, holy, Lord God of hosts, heaven and earth are full of thy glory. Glory be to thee, O Lord most high. Amen.

Proper Prefaces.

Upon Christmas-day.

Because thou didst give Jesus Christ thine only Son to be born as at this time for us, who, by the operation of the Holy Ghost, was made very man, and that without spot of sin, to make us clean from all sin. Therefore with Angels, &c.

Upon Easter-day.

But chiefly we are bound to praise thee for the glorious Resurrection of thy Son Jesus Christ our Lord: for he is the very Paschal Lamb, which was offered for us, and hath taken away the sin of the world; who by his death hath destroyed death, and by his rising to life again, hath restored to us everlasting life. Therefore with Angels, &c.

Upon Ascension-day.

Through thy most dearly beloved Son, Jesus Christ our Lord; who, after his most glorious Resurrection, manifestly appeared to all his Apostles, and in their sight ascended up into heaven, to prepare a place for us; that where he is,

· *These Words [Holy Father] must be omitted on Trinity Sunday.*

thither we might also ascend, and reign with him in glory. Therefore with angels, &c.

Upon Whitsunday.

Through Jesus Christ our Lord; according to whose most true promise the Holy Ghost came down, as at this time, from heaven with a sudden great sound, as it had been a mighty wind, in the likeness of fiery tongues, lighting upon the Apostles, to teach them, and to lead them to all truth; giving them both the gift of divers languages, and also boldness, with fervent zeal, constantly to preach the Gospel unto all nations, whereby we have been brought out of darkness and error, into the clear light and true knowledge of thee, and of thy Son Jesus Christ. Therefore with Angels, &c.

Upon the Feast of Trinity.

Who are one God, one Lord: not one only person, but three persons in one substance. For that which we believe of the glory of the Father, the same we believe of the Son, and of the Holy Ghost, without any difference or inequality. Therefore with Angels, &c.

After each of which Prefaces shall immediately be said,

Therefore with Angels and Archangels, and with all the company of heaven, we laud and magnify thy glorious Name, evermore praising thee, and saying, Holy, holy, holy, Lord God of hosts, heaven and earth are full of thy glory. Glory be to thee, O Lord most high. Amen.

Then shall the Elder, kneeling down at the Table, say, in the Name of all them that shall receive the Communion, this Prayer following; the People also kneeling:

We do not presume to come to this thy Table, O merciful Lord, trusting in our own righteousness, but in thy manifold and great mercies. We are not worthy so much as to gather up the crumbs under thy table. But thou art the same Lord, whose property is always to have mercy: Grant us therefore, gracious Lord, so to eat the flesh of thy dear Son Jesus Christ, and to drink his blood, that our sinful bodies may be made clean by his body, and our souls washed through his most precious blood, and that we may evermore dwell in him, and he in us. *Amen.*

Then the Elder shall say the Prayer of Consecration, as followeth:

Almighty God, our heavenly Father, who, of thy tender mercy, didst give thine only Son Jesus Christ to suffer death upon the cross for our redemption; who made there (by his oblation of himself once offered) a full, perfect, and sufficient sacrifice, oblation, and satisfaction for the sins of the whole world; and did institute, and in his holy Gospel command us to continue a perpetual memory of that his precious death until his coming again; hear us, O merciful Father, we most humbly beseech thee, and grant that we, receiving these thy creatures of bread and wine, according to thy Son our Saviour Jesus Christ's holy institution, in remembrance of his death and passion, may be partakers of his most blessed Body and Blood: who, in the same night that he was betrayed, took bread; and when he had given thanks, he brake it, and gave it to his disciples, saying, Take, eat; this is my Body which is given for you: Do this in remembrance of me. Likewise, after supper, he took the cup; and when he had given thanks, he gave it to them, saying, Drink ye all of this; for this is my blood of the New Testament, which is shed for you, and for many, for the remission of sins: Do this, as oft as ye shall drink it, in remembrance of me. *Amen.*

---

who,[6] in the same night that he was betrayed· took bread; and when he had given thanks, he brake it··; and gave it to his disciples, saying, Take, eat;··· this is my Body which is given for you; do this in remembrance of me. Likewise after Supper···· he took the Cup; and when he had given thanks, he gave it to them, saying, Drink ye all of this; for this····· is my Blood of the New Testament, which is shed for you, and for many, for the remission of sins: Do this as oft as ye shall drink it, in remembrance of me. *Amen.*

· *Here the Elder is to take the Patten into his Hands:*
·· *And here to break the Bread:*
··· *And here to lay his Hand upon all the Bread.*
···· *Here he is to take the Cup into his Hand.*
····· *And here to lay his Hand upon every Vessel (be it Chalice or Flaggon) in which there is any Wine to be consecrated.*

Then shall the Minister first receive the Communion in both kinds himself, and then proceed to deliver the same to the other Ministers in like manner, (if any be present) and after that to the People also, in order, into their Hands. And when he delivereth the Bread to any one, he shall say,

The Body of our Lord Jesus Christ, which was given for thee, preserve thy body and soul unto everlasting life. Take and eat this in remembrance that Christ died for thee, and feed on him in thy heart by faith with thanksgiving.

And the Minister that delivereth the Cup to any one shall say,

The Blood of our Lord Jesus Christ, which was shed for thee, preserve thy body and soul unto everlasting life. Drink this in remembrance that Christ's Blood was shed for thee, and be thankful.

If the consecrated Bread or Wine be all spent before all have communicated, the Elder may consecrate more, by repeating the Prayer of Consecration.

When all have communicated, the Minister shall return to the Lord's Table, and place upon it what remaineth of the consecrated Elements, covering the same with a fair Linen Cloth.

Then shall the Elder say the Lord's prayer, the People repeating after him every Petition.

Our Father who art in Heaven, Hallowed be thy Name; Thy kingdom come; Thy will be done on Earth, As it is in Heaven: Give us this day our daily bread; And forgive us our trespasses, As we forgive them that trespass against us; And lead us not into temptation; But deliver us from evil: For thine is the Kingdom, and the Power, and the Glory, For ever and ever. *Amen.*

After which shall be said as followeth:

O Lord and heavenly Father, we thy humble servants desire thy Fatherly goodness mercifully to accept this our sacrifice of praise and thanksgiving; most humbly beseeching thee to grant that, by the merits and death of thy Son Jesus Christ, and through faith in his blood, we and all thy whole Church may obtain remission of our sins, and all other benefits of his passion. And here we offer and present unto thee, O Lord, ourselves, our souls and bodies, to be a reasonable, holy, and lively sacrifice unto thee; humbly beseeching thee that all we who are partakers of this holy Communion, may be filled with thy grace and heavenly benediction. And although we be unworthy, through our manifold sins, to offer unto thee any sacrifice, yet we beseech thee to accept this our bounden duty and service; not weighing our merits, but pardoning our offences, through Jesus Christ our Lord; by whom, and with whom, in the unity of the Holy Ghost, all honour and glory be unto thee, O Father Almighty, world without end. *Amen.*

Then shall be said,

Glory be to God on high, and on earth peace, good-will towards men, We praise thee, we bless thee, we worship thee, we glorify thee, we give thanks to thee for thy great glory, O Lord God, heavenly king, God the Father Almighty.

O Lord, the only-begotten Son Jesus Christ; O Lord God, Lamb of God, Son of the Father, that takest away the sins of the world, have mercy upon us. Thou that takest away the sins of the world, have mercy upon us. Thou that takest away the sins of the world, receive our prayer. Thou that sittest at the right hand of God the Father, have mercy upon us.

For thou only art holy, thou only art the Lord, thou only, O Christ, with the Holy Ghost, art most high in the glory of God the Father. *Amen.*

Then the Elder, if he see it expedient, may put up an Extempore Prayer; and afterwards shall let the People depart with this Blessing:

May the peace of God, which passeth all understanding, keep your hearts and minds in the knowledge and love of God, and of his Son Jesus Christ our Lord; and the blessing of God Almighty, the Father, the Son, and the Holy Ghost, be amongst you, and remain with you always. *Amen.*

NOTES

1. Reproduced from the first (1784) edition, obtained on microfilm from the library of Drew Theological Seminary, Madison, N.J.
2. Original edition, pp. i-iii.
3. Original edition, p. iv.
4. Original edition, pp. 7-14.
5. Original edition, pp. 125-39.
6. An alternative version of the first (1784) edition included the

Manual Acts. See introduction. The pertinent text, here inserted, has also been reproduced verbatim from a microfilm of the original, obtained from the library of Drew Theological Seminary.